WOOLWICH
EQUITABLE BUILDING SOCIETY

BOWLS
YEARBOOK 91

DONALD NEWBY
Foreword by John Price

𝕿𝖍𝖊 𝕯𝖆𝖎𝖑𝖞 𝕿𝖊𝖑𝖊𝖌𝖗𝖆𝖕𝖍

WOOLWICH
EQUITABLE BUILDING SOCIETY

BOWLS

YEARBOOK 91

DONALD NEWBY
Foreword by John Price

Pan

Editor: Donald Newby, Bowls Correspondent, *The Daily Telegraph*
Editorial Assistant: Margaret Housden
Other contributors:
Gordon Allan, *The Times;* Geoff Clare, Crown Green writer; Jimmy Davidson, bowls writer, secretary WIBC: Stuart Dorney-Kingdom, Welsh bowls writer; Jack Drummond-Henderson, county bowler; Gordon Dunwoodie, Scottish bowls writer; Hywell Griffiths; Ron Hails; Ronnie Harper, *Belfast Telegraph;* Doug Hughes; · Mal Hughes, England team manager; Don MacQuarrie; Chris Mills, editor *Bowls International;* Bill Meredith, *Daily Telegraph;* Mary Price, international bowler; David Rhys Jones, TV commentator, bowls writer; Ray Potten; Patrick Sullivan, editor *World Bowls.*
Drawings: Peter Davis.

Published 1990 by Pan Books Ltd
Cavaye Place, London SW10 9PC
in association with The Daily Telegraph

ISBN 0 330 31664 8

Typeset by Micropress Printers Ltd., Halesworth, Suffolk.
Printed in England by Clays Ltd, St Ives plc

Contents

Cover picture: Andy Thomson

Bowls with the Woolwich

During our past ten years involvement with the sport, we have made a great many friends amongst bowlers and the game's officials. It was particularly pleasing to note the success of two of these friends at events sponsored by the Woolwich over the past year.

The first achievement involved a new sponsorship for the Society, the Woolwich Scottish Masters at Aberdeen, where Lord Thomson, our deputy chairman, had the pleasure of presenting the trophy to fellow Scot, Willie Wood. Willie's win delighted the home crowd and, hopefully, went some way to compensate for his near-misses at several major championships over recent years.

Despite his many successes indoors and at world championships, it was surprising to realise that Tony Allcock had never won an English national outdoor title in 23 attempts over 17 years. He certainly made up for this at the 1990 Woolwich EBA National Championships at Worthing when he won the Triples and the Singles titles. Our congratulations to Tony and to all the other national winners.

This year we anticipate a greater involvement in the preparations for the 1992 Woolwich World Bowls. At the time of going to press, the number of nations taking part has not been finalised but one thing is certainly clear, this will be the biggest and best festival of bowls ever seen.

It is a great pleasure for the Woolwich to sponsor this fourth edition of The Daily Telegraph Bowls Year Book. It is established as the authoratative reference book on the game which is only to be expected of a publication from the newspaper whose coverage of the sport has always been of top quality. I hope you will enjoy referring to it and that it will enhance your pleasure in the game of bowls.

Donald Kirkham
Chief Executive
Woolwich Building Society

Foreword — John Price

I consider it a privilege to follow in the footsteps of a number of distinguished bowls personalities who have provided the foreword to this annual volume. The game has grown considerably in the last decade; sponsorship and television coverage has brought the game to the attention of many people who had never previously shown any interest in it and the numbers playing the sport continue to increase.

In my own country, Wales, we have seen considerable growth in recent years, reflected in the greater number of indoor stadia being built which enable more bowlers to participate in bowls all the year round. The large increase in England, with its large population, in Scotland, and indoor developments overseas, underline the grip the game is getting.

The Year Book is not just another bowls publication; it provides a great service, not only to the expert bowler but also to the newcomer. The information it contains covers all aspects of the level green game from club level to the international arena, and it embraces activities of different codes and various associations. It is useful as a reference book for results, and is also interesting with its many reports and the pen pictures provided by a number of fine journalists who write about the game.

During 1990 I achieved one of my greatest ambitions in winning the World Indoor Bowls Championship, and I shall always look back on that week in Preston as my finest since I first started playing bowls. My success crowned years of going near and was rewarding, too, for those who have had such an influence on my game — my father and Ray Hill, now the Welsh indoor secretary. The congratulations I received not only from my countrymen, but from opponents and lovers of the game everywhere, provided further proof, if any were needed, of the great fellowship and friendship which exists in this marvellous game. I hope, not only that the forthcoming year will be as successful and personally satisfying, but also that my success will encourage even greater interest within Wales, especially from the younger generation.

As for my own future ambitions, I hope that one day I may be fortunate to follow in the footsteps of David Bryant and Tony Allcock and concentrate on full time employment centred on the sport. I can think of no finer way of earning a living than playing the sport you enjoy.

This book illustrates how widespread the playing of bowls has become, and the great variety it offers both to competitive and social players. It also provides a service to bowlers at all levels of the game. I am pleased to pay tribute to its value, and on behalf of bowlers everywhere, may I applaud the Daily Telegraph and the Woolwich Building Society for their role in its production. Long may it continue to flourish along with our wonderful sport.

John Price.

Still fragmented

During 1990 wonderful bowling was seen in Britain, the indoor game flourished with an increasing number of stadia opening in Britain — one every two weeks — to bring more bowlers an opportunity to play throughout the winter months. Outdoor competitors and social bowlers alike revelled in a golden summer.

Yet in some quarters there was a degree of disquiet. What television had given the game in the 1980s it was taking away. Bowler's frustration at the loss was crystallised in these pages by David Rhys Jones, club colleague and Pairs winning partner of David Bryant, and a television commentator. Further comment is, perhaps, unnecessary except to pronounce that a game which persisted for centuries after being banned on the grounds that it interfered with the common herd's military training (namely archery) can survive the caprices of TV programme planners.

Those involved in securing televised bowls will simply have to get their version of the game up to date and project its entertainment value. The game as a whole at the moment, is too insular, too private, too secret. Despite the advantages derived from the Drake legend, there is no real bowls literature - for example no novels or thrillers about the game, no catchphrases, no bowls subjects in commercial television adverts. Much of the insularity of bowls stems from its fragmentation caused by too many difference authorities, too many administrative hangers-on, and too many different rules. Some in the game are aware that the communications of the game need streamlining. At the annual luncheon of the English Indoor Bowling Association, the 1990 President of the English Bowling Association John Hall referred to the need for closer co-operation between the indoor and outdoor games. His theme was to the effect that sponsors and others concerned in utilising projection of the game did not always know with whom they were dealing. It is a pity his plea has fallen, apparently, on deaf ears.

The game's fragmentation is evident, not merely reflected in the variations of the Association, Crown Green, Federation, and Short Mat laws, but also by the formation in Great Britain alone of more than 20 national associations and authorities.

This is borne out noticably in the Association game in England, split, as it is, into differing outdoor and indoor laws, and variable scoring systems. Recruits to the game and armchair followers must surely wonder why there are so many different ways of settling a game. The following analysis underlines the confusion:

English national and county championships: Outdoor: Singles: men 25 shots up; women 21 shots up. Pairs (four bowls each player): men and women 21 ends. Triples (three bowls each player): men and women 18 ends. Fours (two bowls each player): men and women 21 ends. Indoor: Singles: men and women 21 up. Pairs, Triples and Fours, same as outdoor.

British International Series: Same as English national outdoor championships for men and women (Men Singles 25 up).

Televised tournaments: Singles: best of three or five sets of seven up. Pairs (two bowls each player): Same scoring as for Singles — best of three or five sets. Weekend tournaments: Often played in Singles and Triples in round robins of 15 shots up or on time limit basis.

Outdoor summer tournaments: Singles: usually 21 up with team events a specified number of ends or on a time limit basis.

Crown Green Games: Singles 21 up. Federation games: 21 up. National team championship: 31 up. Short mat: as agreed.

These variations have a logical base and are related partly to the duration of games, especially in team play. For example, the time taken to play a game of Triples more or less equates with Fours, with respective totals of 324 and 336 bowls being delivered (without any dead ends).

The departure from 21 up to 25 up for Singles play as laid down by the International Bowling Board, was a compromise with the Australians where longer games of 31 up had been the domestic practice. Though the English Women's Bowling Association settles its Singles championships at 21 up, its titleholder and those of other home countries play 25 up the following year in the British Isles championships.

The sets game introduced with television programmes in the early 80s continues to be used for the World Indoor Singles and Pairs Championships to increase dramatic content for viewers and is used for the Scottish indoor Singles championship which is now played in sets and televised in Scotland. The winner then reverts to 21 up when he plays as Scottish qualifier for the British Isles Singles title.

The English indoor game has taken one step towards unity through the introduction of a joint working party with the object of setting up a joint headquarters when the respective secretaries of the EIBA, Bernard Telfer and EWIBA, Pam Allison, retire in 1992. That is a step in the right direction, but although all the same players and club members are involved, the feeling persists that the authorities controlling the outdoor and indoor games, not only in England, but throughout the UK are much too far apart.

EWBA Diamond Jubilee

The English Women's Bowling Association will celebrate their 60th anniversary in what is a customary style for such occasions. On April 20th, after a thanksgiving service in Coventry Cathedral with members dressed in their traditional white uniform, 700 will be attending a luncheon at Chesford Grange, Kenilworth. Tickets for this event (price £15.50) are available from county secretaries.

The association, the governing body for 1813 clubs from 35 English counties, will also recognise its Diamond Jubilee by raising funds for its special charity — Guide Dogs for the Blind, hold a balloon race, sell souvenir badges, umbrellas and tea cloths etc., and stage special matches. The Henselite firm is also making and donating a commemorative set of bowls. All this, however, is a far cry from what happened 60 years ago.

Women bowlers have been playing in England throughout this century. Flat or crown was played in the Midlands and Lancashire in 1902 — and by 1906 the London County Council had decided that one rink on each park green should be reserved for women's games. The Kingston Canbury Ladies BC, formed in 1910, appears to be the earliest and other organised clubs followed. A county association came into being in Somerset in 1928, Leicestershire followed suit in 1930, and Sussex in the following year. This paved the way for a meeting on October 7th 1931 of 200 women bowlers called to form an association, duly reported by a W.F. Sanderson. The representatives of the three county associations were present and it is clear that right from the start masterful ladies were keen to steer the ship. Mr Sanderson takes up the story...

‘After two hours of storm and argument there was not one women's association, there were two. And this is how it all happened, and when:

3pm More than 200 women decided that Mrs Greenwood of Leicester, be in the chair.

3.7. Proposal: That an English Women's Bowls Association be formed and that officers be elected from county associations.

3.9 Another proposal from Mrs Johns of Eastbourne: That an English Women's Bowls Association be formed but that officers be chosen from the meeting. (Loud cheers).

3.10 to 3.25 General and heated argument.

3.40 A proposal that an English Women's Bowls Association be formed. Carried.

3.45 Nominations for president. Proposals: Mrs Greenwood of Leicester, Mrs Percy Smith (I could not hear where from), and Mrs Johns of Eastbourne. Ballot papers round. One was given to me.

3.55 Mrs Greenwood announces that she has retired from election and leaves the chair. Proposal from somebody that Mrs Johns takes the chair. Counter proposal: 'That Mrs Johns does not take the chair'. Mrs Smith takes the chair and someone starts to discuss a Surrey Association.

4.5 Return of scrutineers. Mrs Johns wins over Mrs Smith by 50 odd votes. Cries from all over the room: 'But what about Mrs Greenwood's votes that do not count'.

4.6 to 4.15 Too much noise to know what happened.

4.20 Discussion on committee. Suggestion of nine members. (Carried). Another suggestion: three members from North, South, East and West section. (Carried). "What about the Midlands?" cry from the hall. Suggestion three members as above and from the Midlands, 15 in all. (Carried).

4.50 Suggestion that every club present have a member on the committee. Eventually decided to form committee later. In another room: the only three county associations in England — Essex, Leicester and Somerset — headed by Mrs Greenwood, decided that other meeting unconstitutional. Agreed that they would not join that association but form another one to be called 'The English Ladies Bowls Association'. So, when on Tuesday there was no association for women's bowls, there are now two.⁹

What happened to the 'English Ladies Bowls Association', however, we will never know. What we do know is that Mrs Johns had the capacity to survive, as has the English Women's Bowling Association. She became the first President and Chairman, stayed in those offices for four years, and donated the Johns Trophy for the county championship, which has been played for since 1934.

Her daughter, Mrs Vi Doyle, well into her eighties, who now lives at Bridport, Dorset, followed her mother as President in 1975, remains a trustee of the association's Benevolent Association, and is a familiar figure at the national championships at Leamington Spa.

Such stamina is typical of women bowlers (noted for their long stints on the green at these championships). The EWBA has had only six secretaries in its 60 year life, and only four since 1954, Mrs D. M. Davenport (1954-1970), Mrs D. Ellis OBE (1970-1978, after 15 years as assistant secretary), Mrs Chris Tyler (1978-1980, after eight years as assistant secretary) and Mrs Nancie Colling, now in her twelfth year as secretary. Assistant secretary during Mrs Colling's tenure is Miss Mavis Steele MBE. Mrs Colling and Miss Steele, incidentally, are the only bowlers to have won the national Singles three times — Mrs Colling in 1956, when Miss Whalley, in 1958 when Mrs Evans, and in 1970 when Mrs Colling. Miss Steele won the title in 1961, 1962, and 1969, and then had to wait 20 years for her next national Singles success when she won the indoor title in 1989.

South African hopes

Though barred from the World Championships since 1976 when its players won every event, the South African Bowling Association has remained a member of the International Bowling Board and looks forward to the day when, with the easing of apartheid, it will be able to resume international competition.

That day may not be too far distant for the pace of political charge in international affairs in 1990 indicates that what was quite unpredictable until recently, is now becoming commonplace.

One thing too, is certain: when the South Africans once more compete, British, Australian and New Zealand bowlers will need to be at their best. The standard of South African bowlers in the past has been such a world championship from the standpoint of sporting excellence, is incomplete without them.

To be fair this point was not made by Gerald Turner, immediate Past President of the South African Bowling Association, wearing his country's colours, who I found on the bank engrossed in the play at the Woolwich National Championships at Worthing in August, but he made others.

Emphasising that he was not present in an official capacity, he contended that now that sport is multi-racial in character, South Africa should be allowed back.

His argument has, of course, been heard before — namely that the South African Bowling Associations constitution since its outset has stated that its object was "to promote, advance and control the game of bowls for men in South Africa without practising discrimination on the grounds of race, religion or political association."

It followed, he claimed, that nothing was to be gained from isolating sportsmen who have overcome prejudice and competed together on a regular basis. Bowls was not particularly popular with blacks, but both they and coloured teams played in the South African National Championships and had done so for a number of years.

"With some 37,500 men and little over 30,000 women bowlers, we are anxious to compete again at international level and sincerely believe that now President de Klerk has opened the door politically, it is unfair that we are being kept out," he said. "We need encouragement rather than isolation and condemnation."

It is surprising to see a South African occupying the moral ground even if this is written context of the game. Unfortunately in our pragmatic world today holding the moral ground is not sufficient. Whatever justification there may be for dropping the ban on South African bowlers that, when it happens, will have to have the assent of anti-apartheid campaigners and be a consensus decision from members of the International Bowling Board and of their governments who in the past have refused visas. But the climate for possible participation of the South Africans at next year's World Bowls Championships was looking favourable when we went to press.

Improve your game

Bowlers intent on improvement can learn much from master bowlers David Bryant and Tony Allcock, though neither has a conventional style. Their maxim could well be that of high priests in other fields. 'Don't do as I do — do as I tell you!'

Points which may be commonplace to coaches may never get across to the punters, most of whom have never received expert instruction. Nor do many books on the same pass on the tips their authors could. 'Keep it simple' is the experts advice. But many simple points are not often imparted. In his latest book written with the aid of his friend and fluent playing partner David Rhys Jones, Bryant offers homely advice like this: 'Watch your little finger. Don't let it creep up the wood — it causes a wobble'. And this . . . "In fast greens like those in Australia, drop the back knee, shorten the swing and slow down all movement'.

These sages of the green also ask you to remember that the forehand point of delivery is further from the centre line than the backhand because of the width of the body and the use of the right hand. It follows, of course, that a right handed player should never follow the line of a left hander and vice versa.

The Bryant-Rhys Jones book 'The Game of Bowls' is published by the Partridge Press, price £9.99. It is replete with such information. But bowls books on coaching cannot hold their own with videos and Allcock's four are first class. Each costs £13.99. Allcock recruited four bowling friends to make them and his choice was ideal involving Brian Duncan, the crown green master with the silky touch, the charismatic Margaret Johnston, a young club colleague Andrew Wills and the always engaging Wynne Richards. Keeping it simple, is a constant Allcock theme. Simple points are emphasised — e.g. using weight on the backhand is preferable to the forehand for the arm is closer to the body when the strike is made.

Bowls books and videos however have one point in common. They stress the value of practice. But where can the average bowler get it?

More money in the kitty

Examination of accounts published in bowls year books indicate that all the English national championships have accumulated substantial funds compared with their respective positions a decade or so ago.

This is not to suggest that they have money to spare nor indeed that the fund raising efforts for events like the World Championships, the English Bowls Association are staging at Worthing in 1992 can be ignored. Accumulated funds earn interest which helps with day-to-day running costs.

The latest treasurer's report of the English Bowling Association published in its 1990 year book for the period ended September 30th, 1989, revealed accumulated funds of £810,163; of this £372,305 represented the World Championship account for 1992. The fixed assets including the net book value of the national headquarters at Worthing (£309,511) were listed as £427,644. These figures, since increased, suggest that the EBA has taken full advantage of the expansion of the game in the 80s by sensible administration and correct business management.

The published accumulated funds of the EBA at September 30th, 1980 were £47,969 and at that time, the association had no headquarters.

The English Indoor Bowling Association has also improved its financial position though the huge increase of indoor bowling centres, some of which cost up to a million pounds to create, is not reflected in their balance. The EIBA has no headquarters of its own though this is a situation which may well be resolved in the next year or two. Jimmy Davidson, now the EIBA's Deputy President and chairman of the Executive Committee, told the annual meeting at Bedworth that when a new secretary was appointed in 1992 it was hoped to complete ownership of a new headquarters. The association's assets reported at that meeting and printed in the 1990-91 EIBA year book were listed as £92,156 — a far cry from September 30th, 1978 when the total assets stood at a mere £8,418. Since the meeting plans have been announced which include setting up a joint working party of EIBA & EWIBA representatives to discuss shared accommodation and office facilities when their respective secretaries Bernard Telfer and Pam Allison retire in 1992.

The 1990 English Women's BA year book reported a general fund of £94,215 for the year ended August 31st, 1989, and the balances of the English Women's Indoor BA at March 31st, 1990 stood at £38,040. The balance sheet of the EWBA, incidentally, included a legacy of £5,000 from the estate of Jeannie Croot a former international, who died in February 1989.

These figures show that the English outdoor game has profited at the centre from the exposure the game has received in recent years and hardly suggests that in Britain, the indoor game will take over. This is unlikely ever to happen since the flat green association rinks game is international in character. Most of the bowling countries of the world enjoy more sunshine than the British and are, therefore, not so preoccupied with indoor bowls.

Indeed, the main problem facing outdoor bowling clubs in Britain is not the absence of television but the upkeep of greens and that can never become the responsibility of national or county associations or of sponsors but will always be a matter for clubs themselves.

No financial statements were to be found in the year books of bowling associations in the other home countries which is not to suggest that there is anything irregular about their accounts. No doubt all clubs who have a right to be represented in some shape or form at annual meetings of Scottish, Welsh and Irish associations are satisfied with the financial reports they receive.

These national assocations and bodies like the International Bowling Board, the World Indoor Bowls Council and British Isles Bowling Councils are not in the habit of circulating clubs or press with information and financial matters though usually willing enough to do so when asked and they could claim that as they are private associations administering the affairs of organisations affiliated to them, their business affairs are private.

But, since they provide disciplines and rules for the rank and file, solicit advertising from suppliers of bowls goods and services and benefit from exposure by the press and other forms of communication, they might follow the example of the English national bowling associations who provide such facts in their year books clearly and accurately.

The EIBA certainly tries to help clubs over financial matters. John Stevens, its Hon Treasurer, has circulated all its 280 affiliated clubs pointing out that providing certain conditions are met exemptions from VAT can be obtained. The associations auditors had approached Customes and Excise headquarters in London and asked them to confirm (1) that they agreed that rink fees be exempt income for VAT purposes; (2) that clubs could go back for a certain period of years and reclaim output VAT overpaid, subject to the necessary documentation being available.

Customs and Excise had not commented on restrospective exemption but the associations accountants had written: "When clubs have been using the appropriate documentation in the part, we see no reason why they should not approach their own VAT offices with a view to the restrospective application of the exemption as now agreed with Customs and Excise."

Mr Rodwell advises clubs intending to set exemption from rink fees to seek as much advice as possible from their accountants and auditors since rink fees at indoor clubs run into thousands of pounds every year, considerable sums can be at stake for clubs.

Another service to assist clubs with financial matters has been introduced by *Bowls International* magazine by announcing a regular feature on "Money Matters" relating to the Poll Tax on non-domestic properties like bowls clubs. The magazine advises that discretionary relief can be obtained under the General Rate Act of 1967 (Part III, section 40, sub section 5 C) which provides for relief for clubs not conducted for profit which are wholly or mainly used for recreational purposes.

It has also pointed out that Scottish clubs which have been paying three or four times as much as English clubs because of difference in the salary systems have been reclaiming thousands of pounds under a new system introduced by the Scottish Sports Minister, David Allan of Edinburgh. Scottish Sports Association representatives for the Scottish Indoor Bowling Association reported that his own club Bainfield gained relief of £25,000 a year for five years. Relief was also possible in the area of water and sewage. Over VAT concessions, other rink fees were exempt if ten or more league matches were played. Glasgow Indoor Bowls Club estimated it was saving between £4,500-£5,000 as a result of such a claim.

Bowlers of the Year

Previous winners of the Telegraph Bowler of the Year award Tony Allcock, David Bryant and Andy Thomson have been relatively easy to determine since their respective feats were not only outstanding but achieved by solid and consistent performance outdoors and indoors, over a twelve month period.

This yardstick has been applied again this year and leads the committee of bowls writers who decide the award to the conclusion that for sheer all round talent, application to the interests of clubs and colleagues, and ability at last to overcome the psychological barriers presented by the outdoor game, the Woolwich trophy should go once again to Tony Allcock.

His record in 1990 speaks for itself. Little could have given him more satisfaction than his first victory in the Woolwich national Singles championship at Worthing on Friday, August 24th when, after three final appearances he lifted the magnificent EBA, Singles trophy for the first time.

Six days earlier he had won the Triples championship — with a young bowler of 20 and a veteran of 79 — and only a few days before that had captured the Singles title at the Bournemouth Open, the most prestigious British summer tournament. In July he had outbowled British international colleagues in the City of Westminster Singles event.

Earlier in the year at the Commonwealth Games he and the English team returned from New Zealand empty handed but the loss of a medal there hinged on a single shot.

Back at Preston Guild Hall for the Embassy world indoor championships, Allcock garnered honours. He reached the semi finals of the Singles before going out to Welshman John Price in a magnificient best-of-five sets semi final and then skipped David Bryant to the Pairs title for the fourth time in five years.

A week later he was at Melton Mowbray for the English Indoor BA national championships where he reached two of the four finals.

Allcock's feat of qualifying for the final stages of five of the eight national championships (four indoor and four outdoor), winning two of them and finishing runner-up in two is testimony not only to his skill but also to his dedication to the game and to the club system.

In future there will be a second Telegraph Bowler of the Year award for English bowlers. The committee has decided that there could be no more fitting recipient of the 1990 award than Gill Fitzgerald, the Northamptonshire bowler who had such a magnificent run at the Engliswomen's national championship in August 1990.

She will receive the Henselite Trophy, a replica presented by Douglas-Kenn Ltd., the Henselite distributors, who have also announced that they will be sponsoring the EWBA's Champion of Champions event in 1991.

Mrs. Fitzgerald defeated the redoubtable Mavis Steele to win the Champion of Champions in 1990, also won the Two-Wood Singles, defeating experienced internationals Brenda Alterton and Jayne Roylance on the way and finished runner-up in the Fours in company with her Kettering Lodge colleagues. The awards were being presented at the Telegraph reception to launch this yearbook in London on December 1st.

The ladies are not happy ...

Throughout the 1980's there was much billing and cooing at London's Cafe Royal every November between officers of Warwickshire District Council and the Englishwomen's Bowling Association who hold their annual dinner there. However, at Leamington in August 1990 this love affair was wearing thin.

The Council has hosted the women's national championships at Victoria Park, Leamington every August since 1976, but at last their guests are losing patience. The facilities at Victoria Park are not adequate, to cope with the 800 competitors and their supporters many of whom spend their holidays and money in the town during the championship fortnight and the ladies have made their position clear.

The objective observer will tell you that the toilets and cloakrooms at Leamington are inadequate, for the womens championships, that facilities for competitors, sponsors and accommodation for officials and the press fall short and that whilst the local club battles bravely in the catering field, these like other amenities bear unfavourable comparison with Worthing where the men's parallel event is held. Nor in 1990 were the greens, subject admittedly to scorching from summer heat waves, up to the standard expected of national championships, the edges near the ditches clearly being in need of a fringe — as well as raising — to give competitors a sporting chance of drawing to the brink.

EWBA secretary Nancie Colling tempered her public criticism in measured terms at this year's championships but the shafts struck home. Leamington has always been a popular venue with bowlers since its central position in the country cuts down travel distances for many people and accommodation at varying levels has never been an outstanding problem. But it cannot be denied that the Victoria Park greens with public roads on two sides and the river Leam and bank on the other have insufficient room for the expansion which will be necessary if the women's world championships are to be staged there in 1996.

A few years ago plans were formulated which with the object of establishing a hotel and an indoor and outdoor bowling complex in another part of the town, but the project was finally abandoned after planning difficulties.

The Englishwomen's Bowling Association would clearly like to continue their national championships at Leamington and the council, aware of their value to the local economy in high summer, should be equally keen to keep them. The warning has been sounded if these annual championships are to stay at Leamington and quite probably Warwick District Council will heed it by taking action. But unless far reaching improvements are introduced it is difficult to see how the 1996 women's world championships can be presented there.

With continued expansion of the world game, more countries may be wanting to take part in five years time and new greens and the provision of more space for amenities and car parking in the park itself would appear to be necessary.

Obituary

The passing of Percy Blake, England's great bowler of the first half of this century at the age of 94, has brought a fitting tribute in this edition from Gordon Allan, *The Times* bowls correspondent. Others who have left a mark on the game have gone too. Among them was former international and team manager, Northamptonshire's Bob Stenhouse, a life member of the EBA. An England outdoor international from 1962-1972 and an indoor one from 1968-1972, Bob played for his country in the 1966 world championship and the 1970 Commonwealth Games, managed the England team from 1972 to 1984, and was in charge of world championship teams during that period.

After playing in Northumberland and Yorkshire, he moved to Wellingborough. During his playing career, Bob won nine county championships.

Three other life members have also died since our last issue went to press — Henry Backhouse, Gerald Scott and Jack Peters, all stalwarts in their respective counties of Leicestershire, Hertfordshire and Cambridgeshire. Gerald Scott served on the EBA Executive for many years, was one of the organising committee of the original Kodak Masters, and was chairman of the EBA's Competition and Laws of the Game Committee.

Henry Backhouse was a former chairman of the English Bowls Umpires Association and also served on the EBA's selection committee. He had been treasurer of Leicester County BA for 31 years. John Livingston, a valued correspondent of *World Bowls* in the years when the magazine was in my ownership, and a leading figure in the London and Southern Counties, has also died, and two counties, Somerset and Middlesex lost both their presidents and secretaries. In addition to the death of secretary Dick Cheshire, Somerset and Bath also lost their President Cliff Harrod. The Middlesex losses were those of Ernie Rochester who had taken on the Middlesex secretaryship and had been a strong supporter of the game when a White Horse whisky executive, and the county President Bill Murton. Surrey has lost Fred Mortimore, a pillar of that county and of London and Southern Counties BA.

Yet another old friend to pass on was Bill Allison of Oxford, a member of the EIBA Executive for some years and husband of Pam Allison, the energetic secretary of the English Women's Indoor BA.

Switch off for armchair bowls

By David Rhys Jones

Bowls is a sport for which colour televisions must have been invented, suggested Keith Elliot of *The Independent* after David Bryant's triumph in the CIS UK Singles championship. 'Bowls is like watching grass grow', proclaimed Grey Dyke, Programme Controller for London Weekend Television, and Chairman of the ITV Sports Committee.

Elliot was speaking for the millions of armchair viewers who enjoy the gentler sports like snooker and bowls. Dyke represents the all-action lobby, who appreciate sport only at its most macho, and who reject anything that lacks the smell of bood or burning tyres. Which of them is right does not count. It is the Dykes of this world who have the power. His was the decision to drop Granada's excellent Superbowl — despite the pure theatre of the 1988 final between David Corkill and Margaret Johnston, in which the Irishwoman almost pulled off an amazing victory.

If Mr Dyke had watched that final, as more than 5,000,000 viewers did, perhaps he might have swallowed his pride and eaten his words. Or perhaps he would simply have written off those five million viewers as belonging to the wrong bracket — not big-spending, fun-loving Yuppies.

The BBC, who kept faith with bowls longer than ITV, now appears to share Dyke's view — although, it seems, sport in general is having a bad time at the Beeb, especially on BBC2, No one could imagine ditching the Big Events, like Wimbledon, the Cup Final, the Grand National, etc., but disposable items like darts, bowls and, to some extent snooker, are suffering from a strong and influential anti-sport lobby.

At the time of writing, it appears that the CIS United Kingdom events has joined the Superbowl on the television scrap-heap, which leaves only the World indoor championships in the sport's shop window. Two years ago, there were five major events on the television calendar — World indoor Singles, World indoor Pairs, UK indoor Singles, the Superbowl, and the Jack High Masters from Worthing. Now, with singles and pairs run in tandem, there is just the one.

Colour and simplicity

What is it that bowls has to offer? And is there any way in which bowls and bowlers could have halted what can only be described as a major handicap to the future of the sport?

Bowls, as Elliot pointed out, offers 'A green carpet to play on, red-shirted player with red stickers on his woods, blue-garbed player with blue logos. If red or blue gets nearest the little yellow ball more times, he's the winner. Two men, eight woods, one jack, and a scoring system even my four-year-old daughter can understand.'

Colour and simplicity are two qualities that give bowls a head start. Add a dash of skill, which everyone can understand and marvel at, and the primaeval conflict between one player and another, and there is, despite the deceptively slow pace of the game, drama aplenty for the spectator.

Indeed, the sense of . . . is so strong, because of the pace of the game, rather than in spite of it. Because it takes around fifteen seconds for the bowl to arrive at the head after it is dispatched from the hand, the essential quality of each delivery is suspense.

'It's a good line . . . but what about the weight? . . . looks good . . . it's on target . . . no it isn't . . . could get a wick? . . . oooh, just missed! bad luck.'

Sometimes, of course, the top exponents make the game look too easy, drawing wood after wood to within inches of the required spot. But, when we are reminded that they are propelling of a 5 inch spheroid maybe forty yards to a jack 2½ inches in diameter, their success rate is phenomenal and enthralling.

There is something magnetic about watching a skilled artist or craftsman at work, whether he is throwing a pot, wielding a brush, kicking a ball or rolling a wood. We can, identify with his efforts — even though ours fall short of his — because usually we have tried it ourselves and experienced the difficulties for ourselves. But, although he clearly has not tried his hand at bowls, Mr Dyke, without meaning to, has identified in his offensive grass-growing comment another quality of bowls that makes it suitable for television. If we want to, we can shut our minds to the skill and ignore the drama, and watch the screen in a kind of stupor, because the gentility of the game does not make too many demands.

Exactly the same thing applies to snooker, and, I believe, has contributed significantly to the success of that other green baize game. For late night viewers, who may not wish to be 'challenged', the screen can became an electronic aquarium: soothing green background, and gently moving objects drifting now from left to right, now back again — the insomniac's dream.

There is nothing wrong with that. Falling asleep in front of the TV set is neither a rare occurence nor a punishable offence — especially if we acknowledge that there are deeper levels to the game, and interesting tactical challenges to exercise us if we choose to pay attention. Something for everyone, in fact.

The idea that bowls is slow, however, is a misguided one. Of course, it can be slow, and very boring, too. But what sport can claim otherwise?

Bowls at its direst is no worse than a cricket match being played out to a draw, or a nil-nil draw at soccer with no goal-mouth action. Bowls may have a slow fuse, but be sure it can ignite at the drop of a hat. Although it may take almost an hour for a match to reach, say, 4-4 in the first set, Player A may establish a three-shots lie on the ninth end, only to see Player B steal the jack away for three shots for himself and win the set at a stroke.

The initiative can change so quickly, both on an end or in the match. A good lie can be destroyed in an instant, sometimes, alas, with a cruel, wicked wick. And the turning point in a game can often be traced to a fleeting moment of good play or good fortune.

Neither, tell Mr Dyke, is aggression lacking from the game. Sometimes angst is disguised because a contestant may not wish to wear his heart on his sleeve. Sometimes, however, it is overt and obvious when, for example, a ferocious firing shot destroys the opponent's delicate drawing. But it is always there.

Television, with its big close-ups (BCU's), can probe into the player's mind, get into his brain, and make embarrassingly public those moments of disappointment and despair that galvanise him or her into action. Look at the eyes of Schuback, Belliss, Corkill or Parrella and you will see a burning commitment born of a combative spirit. These men are dedicated athletes — skilful, competitive and unashamedly aggressive.

The great 'sportsmanship' myth about bowls and bowlers is only partly true. Bowlers are, of course, for the most part, good sportsmen through and through. Their demeanour on the green and camaraderie in the clubhouse afterwards has often labelled them 'perfect ambassadors for their sport'. But perhaps the PR has been a bit too good. Namby pamby they are not.

Consider the case of the greatest bowler of all time: David Bryant, with his immaculate appearance, temperament as unruffled as his hairstyle, puffing phlegmatically at his pipe and applauding the skills of his opponents, even in a crisis. Is he soft or something? Don't you believe it! Despite his gentility, Bryant is a ruthless competitor, a hard man. His stength lies at least partly in the carefully cultivated impregnable image. Anyone who can be generous as to praise his opponent's best shots, is indicating that he is not going to be intimidated. His niceness is his greatest weapon and it hits hard. Ask those who have fallen for it.

Whiter than white image

But the myth persists. I have heard it said, bowls could do with a naughty boy in the style of a McEnroe, Higgins or Botham. Perhaps Achilles heel of bowls has been its whiter than white image. Perhaps Mr Dyke would have changed his mind if Corkill had spat at Margaret Johnston, if Allcock was into hard rock and motor-bikes rather than classical music and antiques, or if Bryant smoked something nefarious in his ever-present pipe.

One thing that separates bowls from snooker, whose development it has shadowed to some extent, is the public profile of the top competitors. Snooker players earn much more than bowlers, and prizes are on a much higher scale, but, at least until recently, bowls has been upwardly mobile, following dutifully in snooker's footsteps, albeit some ten years behind.

But, while the tabloids tell tales of what snooker's heroes are doing away from the table, no-one seems interested in what off-green activities the bowlers get up to. Thank heavens for that, most would say, but it is still an indication of the esteem in which bowls and bowlers are held at least by the so-called popular press.

Snooker players are liked or disliked for their personal habits, and this intimate knowledge helps the viewer respond to the men on screen. Whether we approve of the notion or not, the goodies-versus-baddies syndrome brings the contest on screen to life in a way that would be impossible without the scandal-mongering.

There has, of course, been virtually no effective management of the top bowls players. Their image has been left to form by accident, and there has been 'no marketing' of players as there has been in snooker. Again, most people would say that bowls has taken a more dignified route but there is little doubt that bowls has suffered in business terms as a result.

The alternative is that bowlers are less interesting, *per se,* than snooker players. My experience of both contradicts that theory. While bowlers may be thankful for the obscurity of being ignored by the popular press, the consequence, sadly, has been a low public profile and a dwindling response from the television companies.

Much has been done to make the game of bowls more attractive to television. The coloured shirts, for example, would have been considered sacrilege ten years ago, and the sets system has enabled games to be taken in smaller doses (very few bowlers will sit through a 21- or 25-up game!)

Players, I suppose, could have done more to enliven their performances on television. Some, like Wynne Richards, Gary Smith and John Evans have impressed with their expressive reactions and emotional responses, but most play a dour game. Singles, although it is classic head-to-head, is after all a lonely game, and does not lend itself to self-expression.

Recently, players, at the prompting of the tournament director, David Harrison, have begun to speed up the game. Too much time has been spent between bowls, with too many pointless visits to the head. This is a difficult area, because there are time when a bowler must see the position for himself — but even the players agree that something had to be done.

In the absence of tabloid revelations, television, I suppose, could have done more to 'introduce' the players to the public, who are given precious little to go on before deciding who they are going to support. More pre-match interviews might have done the trick.

The key to the future of televised bowls, however, lies not with the players, nor with the television companies, but with the general public. If the television companies continue to cover bowls, sponsors will continue to queue up to provide the money — and players, whose approach is becoming more professional, will continue to produce the goods.

Once upon a time, far more people played bowls than watched it. This is no longer true. Viewing figures have been consistently good — especially considering some of the anti-social time-slots that have been allocated. There were over half-a-million souls watching a semi final of a recent event at Preston, even though the recorded highlights did not start until 1.45am.

The UK singles final between the two Davids — Bryant and Corkill — referred to by Keith Elliott, was watched by many more non-bowlers than bowlers. 'The oddest sight of the weekend was my mother-in-law arguing with her husband about whether David Corkhill should run the jack' he wrote. 'What made this heated discussion extraordinary was that neither has ever picked up a wood, let alone stepped on a rink. But during the past week they had picked up the rules well enough to squabble over the finer points.'

What made the discussion relevant was that bowls is capable of inspiring and entertaining non-bowlers in great numbers. What made it sad was that people like Elliott's in-laws may soon have no bowls to watch on television at all.

Only an outcry from the general public will alert the powers-that-be to the popularity of the game. Complaints there certainly are, all around the country, but they are not getting through to the people who make the decisions because bowlers are not the most demonstrative of people.

Whatever decisions the television planners make however, bowls will survive and be the better for its ten-year flirtation with the cameras. It will, thank heavens, continue to be a thriving, therapeutic grass-roots sport, densely organised, and enthusiastically played, for a wide range of reasons, by people of all ages and abilities.

It will be a shame if the game loses its shop window. It will also be a pity that a wider audience may be denied the chance to experience the qualities of a vibrant, social, sociable, sporting, skilful game.

Forward to Worthing 1992

For most organisations, preparing for 1992 is all about the European Economic Community and the introduction of the Single European Market. But, for Worthing Borough Council, 1992 is something else, for Worthing will play host to the Woolwich World Championships. Here Hywell Griffiths, Community Services Officer Worthing Borough Council, unfolds what the council is doing to ensure success.

Hosting World Bowls is not new to Worthing. The greens at Beach House Park were the venue for the Championships in 1972 and in 1977 the Ladies World Championships were held there. Next year's event, however, will be exceptional for many reasons. Like most events with an international profile, World Bowls has grown enormously over the last twenty years, and it is now accompanied by all the razzamatazz of sponsorship, television, tented villages and publicity which major golf and cricketing occasions commonly enjoy, so the planning for the event has had to start early. As well as this, the game itself has grown in structure and popularity, both in the United Kingdom and internationally. In 1992 the championships will be attended by almost all the International Bowling Board's 30 members. This has meant that, for the first time at a major bowls event, five greens will be needed instead of the traditional four. Beach House Park in Worthing has five greens and, as the focal point of the championships, they have received particular attention.

Worthing was awarded the championships in 1986 and immediately a long term improvement programme for the greens and the general amenities of the Park was drawn up. The Sports Turf Research Institute at Bingley has been closely involved in helping the Council's head greenkeeper, Tony Patching, and his team to prepare the greens.

Improvements have been steady and, despite a problem caused by the drought in 1989, the greens are now coming to prime standard. The acquisition by the EBA of two 'turftrack' rollers from Australia, to give the greens a final 'polish', has proved a great success.

The EBA's World Bowls Executive Committee, under President, John Hall, regularly receives reports from its Greens committee chairman, Doug Partridge, and having the World Bowls secretary, Fred Inch, as a regular player at Beach House Park means that standards are closely monitored. As well as improving the levels and surface of the greens, new artificial grass banks and ditches have been built over the last two years. A completely new automatic watering and drainage system has also been installed.

£750,000 investment

To protect their investment in the greens and following some unfortunate incidents in the mid 1980's, Worthing has had to install security screening around all the Championship greens. A complex system of fences, infra red beams, lights and cameras, as well as human surveillance, protects the greens from the unwelcome attentions of vandals.

As well as spending money on the greens, the Council has also invested more than £750,000 in improving the amenities in and around Beach House Park. New roads, drains, paths and bases for stand seating have already been installed, and the tournament officials and the world bowling press will work in newly refurbished pavilions, while the EBA and IBB's guests will be entertained in the charming old world pavilion which featured for many years as the introductory shot in the BBC's 'Jack High' series, a regular event in the Park.

Also in the pipeline are contracts for providing seating for more than 4,500 spectators expected each day, accommodation for players and officials and facilities for the comfort of visitors to the event.

One of the unique aspects of World Bowls 1992 will be the tented village where visitors can see the latest in bowls products as well as catering and other services. The EBA's World Bowls Marketing Executive, David Harrison, is planning that visitors to the event will get the same quality of service and interest as visitors to the Open or Wimbledon.

Getting to the event has not been forgotten. Parking can be a major problem in seaside towns in the height of summer, and, when half of your catchment area is sea, finding a place to park can be a problem! The Council is looking to provide a 'park and ride' service for drivers from the outskirts of town to Beach House Park and courtesy buses will also run from the railway station and from the principal hotels.

The work of improving the Park's facilities has been underway since 1988 and the first three phases are completed. David Vine, the Council's Environmental Services Officer, has ensured that all the work has been done outside the bowling season, ensuring minimum disturbance to the four bowling clubs who regularly use the greens. The fourth and final phase, which is mainly made up of landscaping work, is being carried out over the 1990/91 close season so that everything is ready for the 1991 bowling season, giving the Council time to test out all the structures in readiness for 1992.

The Chairman of the Council's Bowls Sub-Committee, Councillor Stan Moore, is confident that everything will be ready for the visitors to enjoy the biggest and best World Bowls yet. "The EBA has shown its confidence in Worthing by designating Beach House Park the national centre for bowls, and we have set out to justify that trust", he says. "So far, everything is on target and the facilities will be ready. Given Worthing's traditional sunshine, we can look forward to a glorious two weeks of bowls from August 8th-23rd, 1992."

A game for all ages
By Jack Drummond-Henderson

One of the personalitis at the Woolwich/EBA national bowling championships at Worthing in August 1990 was Jack Drummond-Henderson, who was celebrating his 80th birthday later in the year on December 1st. Racing up and down the green, following his delivery, accurate in obeying his skip's instructions, enthusing his colleagues and displaying great tactical ability, he became England Triples champion in company with Andrew Wills and Tony Allcock. A qualified coach, Jack Drummond-Henderson passes on advice to those thinking of taking up the game . . .

I became involved in bowls quite by accident, 56 years ago, when visiting Cheltenham Bowling Club. At that time I was only a social member, being fully engaged in tennis, cricket and football.

It was a beautiful August Saturday afternoon in 1934 and the club team was playing away at Westlecot, Swindon, so both greens were free. On one, seven old gentlemen were playing for pennies on the jack. After a while one of them said to me "Come on Jack. Get some overshoes on and find some woods." I did just that. The bowls in those days were lignum vitae and I found ones of different sizes discarded by members who had changed to different sizes or makes. Having joined in the fun it was not long before I was winning pennies. In fact I won sufficient to pay for the tea and buns for all eight of us, provided by the club for the princely sum of six old pennies each.

It was a memorable afternoon, for during the course of it, international Jimmy Crankshaw, who played for England during the 1925-39 period, looked in after missing the coach to Westlecot. Noting my efforts with odd sized bowls, he offered to coach me. I accepted and from then on I was bitten with the bug. Older players encouraged me, for at that time bowls was considered an old man's game, and I was a mere stripling of 23! Soon I was a regular visitor to the green for practice. Jimmy obtained a second hand set of Thomas Taylor Lignums for me, size 5-1/16, and they cost me £5.

In 1935 I became a full bowling member and entered the Club Handicap Singles. Guess who my first round opponent was? Jimmy Crankshaw. He was on scratch, and I was seven plus. I managed to score one shot so the result was 21-8. After practising regularly I did much better the following year, so obviously the answer was more practice...

In 1949, after war service, I played my first game for Gloucestershire. Quite recently I have coached people of all ages, currently three young men in their early teens, and men of 75 and 79. All are coming along splendidly. My aim has always been to motivate players, whatever their ages, to make every effort. Even if a bowler is physically disabled he can play this game to the point of enjoying himself.

Bowls is indeed a marvellous game. It is specially so for those times when one has had a stressful spell, when tension has built up, caused by the various troubles which occur during the course of daily life. I know of no other game which assists so much to relieve such problems: go to your club, mix with the chaps, have a roll up. It will give you some respite.

It is amazing the changes which can be wrought in some people who take up bowls — particularly those in business. I can honestly state that many I have coached pass remarks like this after I have completed instruction in accordance with the EBA syllabus: "Why on earth did I not take this game up earlier? Thanks, Jack, for your help. I am really enjoying myself. Bowls is everything you said it is and more."

Among younger players, look what Andrew Wills has achieved. In 1986, when he was 16, his father convinced him it would be an ideal game for him. In 1990 he played three Middleton Cup games for Gloucestershire, won the Gloucestershire Under-21 championship, and was lead for Tony Allcock with myself at No.2 to win this year's Woolwich/EBA National Triples championship. If proof were needed here it is: bowls is for any age. He we are — Andrew 20, myself 80 on December 1st 1990, and Tony 35, all champions of England, all on cloud nine.

May I wish all who decide to take up this wonderful game all the luck and pleasure you wish yourselves. And here's a further tip from an 'old timer': Remember C.A.D. — concentration, application and determination, not necessarily in that order, plus the most important of all — ensure that you adopt the follow-through action when delivering the bowl. I strongly recommend every aspiring bowler to get in touch with a good coach. That is the short route, I am sure, to accomplishing a certain playing standard. I also suggest that all taking up the game should obtain the EBA booklet 'Guide for New Bowlers' and the EBA abridged version of the Laws of the Game. Each costs 35p and is available from the English Bowling Association.

Percy Baker . . . a great bowler
By Gordon Allan.

Percy Baker, England's greatest bowler before David Bryant, died last January at the age of 94, in hospital at Poole. He had been blind for some years. The end of his career — his era — and the beginning of Bryant's overlapped, with Bryant winning the first of his six EBA Singles Championships in 1960 and Baker losing the last of his five finals in the same event five years later.

Baker won the EBA Singles four times, in 1932, 1946, 1952 and 1955, a record that stood until Bryant surpassed it in 1973. He also won the EBA Pairs twice — with Len Piper in 1950 and Harry Shave in 1962 — the British Isles Pairs with Shave and the EBA Triples, with Ernie Milnthorpe and Shave, in 1960. The Triples success made Poole Park the first club to have won all four national championships, a record since equalled by Clevedon.

In the 1958 Empire Games at Cardiff, Baker took the Singles silver medal, the gold going to Pinkie Danilowitz of South Africa. His first match for England was in 1933, his last in 1959, and he was captain in 1950. He won the Dorset Singles 12 times, was one of ten Poole Park players in the Dorset team which won the Middleton Cup in 1938, and indoors he helped Bournemouth win the Denny Cup in 1954.

Like Bryant, Baker was born in Somerset, at Weston-Super-Mare, but his name will be associated with Dorset in general and Poole Park in particular. In the First World War he served with the artillery in France and Salonika, and after demobilization in 1919 he went to work for a photographic studio in Poole, remaining there for the rest of his life.

In his young days he was a cricketer who occasionally watched the other sort of bowlers on the adjacent green. Some of those bowlers played billiards with him and they badgered him to try their game, which eventually he did in 1921. He won a novices' competition in his first season, a foreshadowing of his 22 club championship Singles wins, the last in 1974. He presented one of his woods, mounted in a glass case, to Poole Park in 1981 to mark his completion of 60 year's membership; another is now on display in the EBA headquarters at Worthing.

Tall, slender and upright, Baker was an elegant stylist, a master of the draw and the yard-on trail, the shots that profoundly influence matches. The firing shot was rarely seen from him in Singles play "They're all mad", he said of those who fire a lot. Alone at practice, he would stay on the green until he had bowled an end that satisfied him all four woods tight round the jack; only then would he go home. His memory for bowls, like C B Fry's for cricket, was amazing, down to individual heads and shots in matches long ago.

After watching Baker win his fourth EBA Singles at Paddington in 1955, Roy Kivell, the England captain that year, said "Percy's deadly accuracy on the draw and his shrewd positioning make him outstanding. He can usually outdraw anyone and he seldom gives the other man the chance to gain anything by firing. Thus he has his matches tied up two ways."

Another international, Jack Bailey, said "Playing Percy is like running against Chataway. No matter what you try to do, Percy is always near. You know that sooner or later he is going to spring some phenomenal ends and therefore you do not play your best. If his opponents could only relax and forget they were playing against Percy Baker, they would do better".

I have been told that Baker never drove a car and often travelled to matches by bicycle, having to fit in bowls with full time work. He sometimes wondered how he managed it. To the end of his life he kept in touch, through calls and visits by friends, with the game he had adorned for so long.

In the souvenir programme produced for Poole Park's seventy-fifth anniversary in 1984, Harry Shave wrote of Baker "I had the good fortune to be closely acquainted with him both on and off the green. His standard in all things was very high. He was also a very modest individual and a perfect gentleman at all times, and I doubt if we shall ever see his like again."

Baker's EBA championships record: Singles finals — 1932 beat E W Fortune (St George's Bristol); 1946 beat E Newton (Windsor and Eton); 1952 beat A R Allen (Oxford City and County); 1955 beat J W Fletcher (York Co-op); 1965 lost to R E Lewis (Preston, Brighton). Pairs final: 1950 L H Pipler and Baker beat Edenside (Cumberland); 1962 H W Shave and Baker beat Atherley. Triples final: 1960 E E Milnthorpe, Shave and Baker beat Edenside.

I thought it was a stupid game...
By Mary Price

Mary Price, a former cricket, badminton, squash and hockey player, is now an outstanding international bowler. She became the first Englishwoman to win both outdoor and indoor national Singles titles, and has won a world championship team gold medal as well a bronze at the last two Commonwealth Games. Here she reflects on changes in the women's game.

Ladies' bowls is gently going through a transitional period — loudly applauded by most and still managing to retain its standards. Bowls today is a far cry from my first experiences of the hat and blazer brigade. A frightening Victorian atmosphere prevailed, so stereotyped it was unbelievable. It was enough to discourage the keenest. At the moment we have a nice blend of change and protocol. The old image of ladies being 'proper', standing to attention at the back of the rink, cursing the chains that bind them to being 'correct', is slowly vanishing. Team spirit, encouragement, and above all, enjoyment are creeping in to the ladies game. This has been achieved while retaining the old values and etiquette we all cherish.

The introduction of the junior international teams has done nothing but good for the game. Enthusiasm, team spirit and love of the game oozes out of them. The mother and daughter competition has added another dimension and is keenly and happily contested. The Under-25 Singles has produced some exciting new prospects — again all good for the future of the game.

One day, when I have time, I would like to do a survey on (1) What people get out of bowls (2) why they started (3) was there any change in their reasons for playing once they started? When we start to play bowls we do not know exactly what we are going to get out of the game. We do not know if we are going to spend our time rolling up, make the club side, get selected for a county team, or become an international. The great thing about it is that bowls can be played and enjoyed by all ages at various levels. You find your own level. To answer my own questions (1) I get terrific enjoyment out of bowls mixed with competitive excitement and personal challenges and self criticism. (2) I had no intention of playing bowls — I thought it was a stupid slow game that was very boring. One reason I started was I was quickly aware of the club atmosphere, of belonging almost to a large family. Another was the drug-like allure of it — one day you can bowl brilliantly, the next terribly, so you have to keep trying again to find out why one day you can perpetrate such brilliance, and the next rubbish. (3) The feeling of belonging to a club and taking part in club activities now plays a great part in my life, as does the constant challenge for improvement. The adrenalin coursing through the veins and camaraderie is second to none. None of this can possibly be forecast when you first embark on playing bowls. The old adage that you get out of the game what you put into it is worth following. Above all, do as I do — enjoy it!

The men who taught me a lot

By Mal Hughes
England team manager

England's long run of success in the British Isles international series continued at Methilhill, Fife, in July 1990. Managing the team for the sixth successive year was Mal Hughes, a former England captain and international, and long considered one of the game's outstanding personalities. Here he looks back on his international career, considers his role as England team manager and offers suggestions on the future of the game.

Bournemouth 1973 seems a long time ago now, for that is when I was pitched into the furnace of international competition, and if that was not an ordeal enough for a 'new boy', I was chosen as skip. There and then I received a most important lesson that I have tried to follow as an England skip, and as team manager.

My first three opponents were 'Big' Jock Thompson (Wales), Billy Tate (Ireland) and the Scottish legend Jock McAtee, and each in his own way, welcomed me to the international club and showed me that however much they wanted to beat me, I was one of them. I have never forgotten their kindness to one who had regarded them with awe. Indeed, I called Jock McAtee 'Mister' and received a gentle cuff round the ear with the advice "Jock will do son".

I am afraid that I repaid their friendship by winning two of my matches and tieing the other, but all three congratulated me warmly and I would like to think that I have been able to follow their example when I, with more experience, have faced newcomers to the international scene. To be chosen as skip in my first international series was the realisation of a dream that is surely in the mind of every bowler who starts playing this wonderful game. I had played in two trials at No.2 and was somewhat surprised on the next to be selected a skip. It was a great thrill when my opponent turned out to be David Bryant — the world's greatest bowler. I have to report that my rink won by nine shots on Rink 6 at the wonderful Watneys green at Mortlake. I was on my way to Bournemouth...

The influence of McAtee

Returning for a moment to my first meeting with 'Mr' McAtee, I learned, on reflection, that he had a great influence on my subsequent attitude to the game. I have always tried to emulate his bearing on the green, his etiquette, and his expertise in managing his rink. It is important that a skip should understand his players — as bowlers and as people. A rink should be a complete unit. It disappoints me to see leads and seconds deliver their bowls and stand back, as though the rest of the end had nothing to do with them. I want my front end to be involved, to offer encouragement, even advice, but not instruction. No skip can afford to ignore advice without weighing the advantages or otherwise. I have carried my 'skip's code' with me in my role as manager of the England team. I have tried to put the emphasis on the word team, where players (and reserves), manager and selectors, create a family atmosphere, living in the same hotel during the international series, talking out problems, discussing strengths and weaknesses, for the general good of the team. This is — thankfully — far cry from the 'them and us' days before England had a team manager. The captain was the feeder of information between players and selectors until the system changed for the better in 1976. The late Bob Stenhouse was then appointed team manager for the world championships in South Africa, and his influence on the England team has much to do with the success in recent years. Bob was the quiet man of bowls, a good listener, and a wise advocate who earned the total respect of his team. In my two years as team captain I had many beneficial 'consultations' with Bob and learned lessons which I have tried to apply as manager. I hope that in my six years of stewardship of England's fortunes I have never let down Bob Stenhouse or the EBA. There is a feeling amongst the bowling fraternity that the game lacks characters. There are certainly none to equal Scotland's Harry Reston who would pre-empt success with the cry "Well played Harry". Another Reston party piece was to drop flat behind his running bowl and demoralise the opposition by announcing "Harry's done it again boys". Welshman Gareth Humphreys was one you could not ignore as his exaggerated follow through as he stalked his bowl, or he asked for one more effort from his men in that lovely Welsh voice that could be heard on all rinks — if not back in the valleys.

Ireland's Wee Willie Murray — all 5′2″ of him — would race his bowl down the rink, giving advance warning to friend and foe alike that he "has a chance with this one".

I suppose I fall into the 'character' bracket. I chat on the green, and when I feel I have delivered a good one I find myself zig zagging down the green, sometimes arriving before the bowl, enabling me to coax it into the head.

Harmless fun really, but we do not seem to have much of it about these days. Do players take the game too seriously, or is it because they are afraid to express themselves in the way they want? When I played in the 1980 world championships in Australia, I was unable to change my style. The laws prevented you walking up the green more than nine yards, but whether from force of habit or nervous energy, my 'follow through' did not stop. The Aussie spectators did not object and they voted me Personality of the Games. Another gentle brush with tradition 'down under' came when I continued to wear my white cap instead of their conventional trilby. I noticed later that they changed the rule to allow the cap to be worn. One up to the Poms!

I had an earlier insight into Australian humour in 1979 when my good friend John Bell and I became the first non-Australians to win the prestigious International Masters Pairs held in Newcastle NSW. In those days my side-burns were long and bushy, sticking out when the wind blew. The Aussies, great ones for nicknames, promptly christened me 'Blinky Bill' after a cartoon character on their TV. I was still Blinky Bill to them nine years later when I returned to NSW as a member of the British Isles team to celebrate the bicentenary. I did not mind though, I played between Brian Middlemass and Jim Baker in the trio that won the gold medal, and my Aussie fan club honoured me again with the Personality of the Games award.

The Bicentenary tournament was held at the fabulous Tweed Heads bowling club, which boasts three first class greens, running at speeds between 17 and 20 seconds. To UK bowlers, playing on such fine surfaces was a great experience — and pleasure. Those memories bring me to earth with a bump when I compare those facilities with ours here in the UK. Even allowing for the benefits of the Australian climate, the greens in these islands do not begin to approach the humblest of club greens Down Under. I feel, and I am not alone, that over the years greens in the UK have deteriorated to an alarming degree, so much so in some areas, bowlers have called it a day outdoors and have moved indoors for the full twelve months.

So what is the problem? Obviously the quality of bowling greens will vary with the climate. Northern greens can never hope to match those in the South of England, particularly in the opening weeks of the season. I know from bitter experience that the early rounds of the Durham county championships are very much a lottery. But climatic conditions apart, I believe that the major problem is cash — or rather the lack of it. Nowadays there seems to be a dearth of good greenkeepers, and some we do have prepare greens as they would a lawn. Green, lush grass. Nice to look at? Yes, but hopeless for bowling.

Maybe the private clubs or councils cannot, or will not, pay enough to greenkeepers and for upkeep of greens and equipment. They get their priorities right in the Antipodes where greenkeepers are well paid and they work with top class equipment. The surface is maintained to a high standard, and although the club member has to put his hand in his pocket at subscription time, he reaps the benefit of playing on superb surfaces. I suppose what I am saying is that we, as players, do not contribute sufficiently to the upkeep of our club greens, and until we do, we will never have the luxury of first class surfaces. My own club fees are £34, which are pretty high compared with others in the North East, but compared with golf club membership, the cost of my membership is absurdly cheap, and on such a low income, even the best run club will have problems in these days of ever-increasing costs.

Yet the future of bowls, indoor and outdoor, looks reasonably rosy. The advent of sponsorship has made it possible to attract the interest of television, allowing our top performers to show the expertise of our wonderful game to the viewing millions. Sadly however, both BBC and ITV have recently cut coverage to a minimum; consequently sponsors are not so keen, and bowlers and the public suffer. Maybe the satellite stations will take up the challenge of showing some of our major tournaments, not only in the UK, but throughout the world.

One can foresee Test matches between all bowling nationals being shown without over exposing the sport, as tends to happen with cricket, snooker, golf and football. Both New Zealand and Australia play tests against each other, and each in turn play Fiji and Papua New Guinea. Let us widen the field a little. Hopefully BBC and ITV will see the light and give more exposure to the game. I have had many letters from non-bowlers about the two major tournaments that BBC present from Preston Guild Hall. This interest from non-participants shows the level of support for televised events, although I feel that many viewers are disappointed and frustrated when the major evening 'slot' is put back to the small hours, robbing many, particularly the elderly, of the opportunity to savour the skill, excitement, and tension that is generated in most matches.

Coaching now and in the future
By Jimmy Davidson

The 1980s was the decade in which bowls coaching was first accepted within the sport, and then became an established part of its framework; 1990 has seen new development in coaching in each of the major bowling countries.

New Zealand, where director of coaching John Murtagh spends half of each year touring his country on coaching duty, have just produced their first national coaching video.

Du.ing the year, Australia produced two big new volumes, appropriately one in green and one gold, containing the two levels of coaching promoted from national level. National coaching director Bob Williams is co-operating with Brian McLean, bio-mechanics lecturer at the Australian Institute of Sport, Canberra on a book on the bio-mechanics of lawn bowls.

I saw at first hand during the year that the Coaching Association of Canada has also done some pioneer work on bio-mechanics in bowls as part of their steady progress over the last decade in reaching Level 5 coaching. Their work reflects the academic background of National Coaching Committee Chairman Dan Milligan, who successfully marries that background to his international bowling experience. TV viewers will remember him representing Canada in the Masters at Worthing in the early 1980s.

The World Indoor Bowls Council have assisted for two years, using Embassy sponsorship money designated for the purpose, in the promotion of Schools of Excellence for young bowlers in each of its member countries, including Australia and New Zealand; (Canada will join the WIBC in February 1991 and President Bob Montgomery and I attended their excellent July 1990 Training Camp and World Indoor Singles Qualifier in Victoria, British Columbia, the venue for the 1996 Commonwealth Games).

In the United Kingdom, including Guernsey, the WIBC have similarly been involved in Schools of Excellence in each country for two years, but 1990 saw a new WIBC coaching venture. At the suggestion of the Welsh Indoor Bowling Association a seminar was staged in Guernsey in June 1990 for UK directors of coaching, giving the opportunity for the first time for a full exchange of information on coaching techniques adopted in each of the countries.

The English Bowls Coaching Scheme was represented by Gwyn John, the director of coaching and national development, and video operative Kelvin Carr.

Gwyn succeeded me as director a couple of years ago, and once described me as the 'midwife' of the infant English scheme. If that is true, or not, I have put on record that the baby could not have been passed on to safer hands. He brings his native Welsh fervour and passion to his post. Similar Welsh passion oozes out of Gareth Humphreys who represented Wales at the seminar. Early evidence of the Humphreys factor, I am sure, lies behind Welsh Under-25 victories in the first encounters again England in 1990 at that level at Perdiswell IBC indoor and Bristol outdoor. Again, like Gwyn John, Gareth brings long experience as a headmaster to his many roles in Welsh bowls, as well as many years international experience representing Wales on indoor and outdoor greens. Scotland were represented by their recently appointed director of coaching Bob Sutherland at the Guernsey seminar. Bob brought to that post several years coaching experience — being coached in football teams as centre-half for Glasgow Rangers, and some years practical experience as a bowls coach.

Bob won the World Indoor Singles Championship in 1983, the first year I was involved as WIBC Secretary in its presentation. It was during that first bond with Bob that I learned of his interest in bowls coaching, and he freely acknowledges that the Scottish coaching syllabus he has just produced owes much to the English scheme. Bob's forte in bowls coaching lies in his practical work on the green, and he has started to develop use of the video in ways other than the clinic in his coaching schools.

The Coaching and Umpire Associations in Ireland were represented at the seminar by Sandy Smith. We staged two Schools of Excellence, for ladies and young boys and girls as part of the seminar. Sandy quickly became known as Uncle Sandy to all taking part, for the quality and manner of his avuncular advice. Sandy shared a major role in Irish bowls coaching with association secretary David Corkill Snr. Many readers will have seen pictures of him receiving a national award from Sebastian Coe for his work on coaching wheelchair bowlers. How sad and ironic that David (to whom David Jnr attributes so much of his success) after winning an award covering all sports in the disabled section, should be unable to travel and attend the seminar because he himself now has to spend much of his time in a wheelchair.

Nothing happens in Guernsey without the involvement, hard work and expertise of WIBC Senior Vice President Henry Le Tissier and his wife Pam. They both learned from previous schools staged at the magnificent Guernsey indoor stadium, which now employs Henry on a full time basis, to the extent that they have added to their experience of representing Guernsey on and off the green, the ability to instruct the many bowls beginners attracted to our sport by the stadium.

In the UK the emphasis is on developing a natural delivery based on normal movement of the individual. The idiosyncratic styles of many of our top bowlers does not lend itself as support for a theoretical approach which suggests there is a single right and many wrong ways. The first English syllabus of 1980 suggested the first five minutes with a complete beginner, and no longer, should be devoted to covering the 'equipment used and the method of scoring' followed by a demonstration of different styles of delivery, one of which the beginner would be invited to adopt. In 1985 this was changed by the only amendment to the scheme in its first ten years. Without any preamble the beginner was now invited to stand on the mat and 'to roll a jack to the instructor positioned about seven yards in front'. From this beginning the instruction helps the pupil to adopt a style of delivery to match his first movement.

I wrote on the distributed card which introduced the change that the new method had been pioneered by the then National Development Officer Joe Burrows and that: 'This method has two prime advantages:- a) It builds on the natural movement of the beginner rather than on imitation of demonstrations; b) It avoids the possibility of imposing on the beginner stereotyped or uniform delivery actions'.

The major bowling countries of the southern hemisphere start from very different beginnings, which no doubt fit in with their playing beliefs and their very different playing conditions, e.g. speed of their greens. It is no doubt a reaction to their fast greens that the New Zealand scheme for beginners refers to the back foot as 'The Anchor Foot' (selling NZ butter?). Not only must it be kept in contact with the mat throughout delivery, beginners are instructed to point it carefully towards the exact intended line of delivery —

a wide swinging arc on their very fast greens.

David Bryant had the temerity to win in New Zealand and Australia, world championships and Commonwealth Games in the past, with his foot 'anchored' in mid air, (i.e. he adapted his grooved-in UK style to Anzac conditions).

The Australian syllabus carries 'right' and 'wrong' pictures on several pages. I did a double take at one 'wrong' picture. It looked just like a picture of the world class Irishwoman Margaret Johnston in her usual deep crouch before delivery. It suggested that the Margaret Johnston look-alike was 'wrong' to bend her knees so far, because she would need to straighten up and then go down again in the process of delivering the bowl. The fact is that since Margaret keeps her knees bent as she moves forward, so the fault does not occur.

I have written in praise of the South African Clinic style pioneered by Dr Julius Sergay. It is particularly suitable for those with poor co-ordination, for those who believe that if a delivery action has a minimum amount of movement it is to be commended. The less movement there is, the less there is to go wrong due to incorrect movement. I attended a clinic run by Dr. Sergay at his own club in 1982 and was surprised that he advocated no deviation whatsoever, no matter how much such variation might suit the physique of the bowler. The general UK view is that if change works, use it with our approval.

I pass on a warning however, Our former Empire, to use the film title, is due to Strike Back! I referred to pioneer work in Australia and Canada on bio-mechanics applied to bowls. I saw some digital print-outs in Canada in July which were on exactly the same lines as part of a report on the Australian Embassy School in Canberra by national coaching director Bob Williams. Be warned of the future of bowls and bowls coaching in this direct quotation from the report.

"One of the outstanding features we found was the force plate which was used in the Bio-mechanics Department. This gave us so much information in relation to the players delivery in long term that after another two sessions with the best players we will be getting toward some real material which will form the basis of the perfect delivery. This in turn will make more elite coaches and players."

"Three videos were taken of the player position at the same time, one from the side, one from the front and one from overhead. These pictures are transferred in data base using two computers and these computers give you a printout in graph form of weight transference, balance, consistent delivery, velocity of the bowl, giving the player a read out of difference in two bowls played trying to deliver them at the same pace, and the transfer of the body weight as each bowl is delivered."

Will this really be the basis of bowls coaching, world-wide, on delivery in the future?

Jimmy Davidson is Secretary of the World Indoor Bowls Council and former Director of Coaching.

THE 1990 SEASON

YOU'LL BE BOWLED OVER BY NATWEST'S SUPPORT

NatWest is delighted to support the game of bowls through The Middleton Cup, The British Isles Bowling Council Championship & Home International Series and The NatWest National Club Two Four's Championship.

We're also active in other sports, the Arts and Community events.

NatWest

THE ACTION BANK

National Westminster Bank PLC. Registered Office 41 Lothbury, London EC2P 2BP.

Commonwealth Games

at Pakuranga, Auckland, January 25th — February 2nd 1990
By Patrick Sullivan

Targets are an important aspect of life. We all need something to aim for if we are to achieve anything of note. To rely too heavily upon them however can also prove damaging and it may have been exactly that which cost David Bryant the Commonwealth Games Singles title on the greens at Pakuranga, Auckland.

Bryant, aiming for a record fifth gold medal in as many Games appearances, had been impressive in his section matches. The pipe was burning well, the glasses and hair glistened in the Auckland sun and where others flopped in the heat when off duty, he was busy-busy; practising, perfecting, and puffing away on the Condor.

Although engaged on a nearby rink, he kept a weather eye on the Rob Parrella-David Corkill tilt and within minutes of Corky's heroic victory, had already worked out that he required only 16 shots against the Brisbane cabbie to reach the final on shot difference. A target certainly. Sixteen shots for Bryant looked pretty easy on paper but — if you are not looking for a win at this level, it's pound to a penny you are going to lose — by how much is anyone's guess.

In the event Bryant, unable to catch the pace of a recently mown rink, chopped and changed from one hand to the other and looked desperately unhappy with both. In contrast, Parrella, who must have been surprised to find his prayers answered so comprehensively, clicked into gear at once. His draw was immaculate on short jacks and good enough to restrict Bryant to singles on almost everything else. Towards the end, a brief English recovery stalled on a full length jack. Bryant's first bowl fell short and Parrella bounced up the green, chasing, cajoling, urging his bowl on its way, ushering it towards the jack like a sheepdog with a reluctant lamb. Once there it survived a couple of Bryant drives and the match was over.

The final saw the bustling little Aussie prove too much of a handful for Hong Kong's Mark McMahon who, despite being unbeaten in his section matches, had no answer to Parrella's all-round command of the rink. When he did manage to beat his opponent to the draw, McMahon usually watched his bowls disappear into the middle of next week as they were hit by an Aussie Henselite-seeking missile.

Bryant's torture

The torture was not yet over for Bryant. In the play-off for the bronze, Edinburgh's Richard Corsie, who had played himself into form just too late, led 15-5 at fourteen ends and finally sent the world champion home empty handed from the event for the first time ever.

Australia's best For the Australians, it was their best ever team performance in a Commonwealth Games. With only one gold medal (Fours 1982) to show for their previous effort, the world's largest bowling national (450,000 registered bowlers) made up for lost time at Auckland with three gold strikes.

For England it was a disappointing experience. In the men's pairs, Gary Smith and Andy Thomson scored some heavy victories over lesser opponents but faltered against Angus Blair and Graham Robertson of Scotland, New Zealand's Rowan Brassey and Maurice Symes, and the eventual winners from Australia, Ian Schuback and Trevor Morris. The Fours went to Dennis Love, Ian Bruce, George Adrain, and Willie Wood of Scotland who went through unbeaten and proved too good for Ireland's world champions, Rod McCutcheon, John McLoughlin, Sammy Allen and Jim Baker in the final. Love and Bruce took control of the front end battle with the latter in particularly fine form, positive and accurate, he ditched the jack on the penultimate end, a move which saw the Scots finally draw clear of their opponents with a count of four.

The high hopes of England's John Ottaway, Roy Cutts, Gary Harrington and Tony Allcock survived an early two shot defeat by Australia but foundered on the rocks of Hong Kong. Holding a match winning, last end count of five which would have seen them into the final, the England four were cruelly served when the Hong Kong skip, attempting a saving draw, delivered tight and heavy, slipped past short woods to take the jack, converting five down to five up!

A jolly lady!

The women's Singles gold medallist, Geua Tau from Papua New Guinea, was a superb example to everyone who takes sport too seriously. This charming, jolly lady obviously enjoys her bowls no end. Victories over Senga McCrone, Scotland's 1986 silver medalist, Ireland's Margaret Johnston, holder of the world indoor title at the time, and the world outdoor champion, Janet Ackland from Wales in her section play gave just a hint that her game was in pretty fair condition. So too, however, was that of the Kiwi hope, Millie Khan from Matamata, boosted in her challenge by the intense home crowd, 'Going For Gold' support.

On a blisteringly hot day, Mrs Tau was coolness itself and while Mrs Khan never quite lost touch in an entertaining final, Mrs Tau from Papua New Guinea was usually in command. Minutes after the final, Mrs Khan was informed of the death of her 11 week old grandson who had been taken unconscious from the Pakuranga greens some hours before her arrival.

Widely tipped for gold, Ireland's Margaret Johnston had to settle for bronze when her lifeline to the final, world champion, Janet Ackland, fell to Mrs Tau. There was no mistaking her determination against Australia's Audrey Hefford however. The Australian was 8-0 down in the play-off before getting on the scoreboard and never fully recovered.

A place in the Pairs final narrowly evaded England's Mary Price and Jayne Roylance owing to a freak result against Zimbabwe. The English pair, after opening with a tied match against Papua New Guinea, bustled their way past Australia, Wales and Northern Ireland but, after establishing a 15-5 lead over

Zimbabwe, were pulled back and overhauled on the last end to lose by a single heartbreaking shot. To their credit, the English women stifled disappointment and earned their bronze with a spirited performance against Sarah Gourlay and Frances Whyte. The gold, though, went to New Zealand's Mary Watson and Judy Howat who, to the delight of the home crowd, scored a welcome victory over Australia's Maureen Hobbs and Edda Bonutto.

The Australia women gained their revenge and their country's gold medal when Marion Stephens, Daphne Shaw, Audrey Rutherford and Dot Roche beat their Kiwi counterparts, Marlene Castle, Adrienne Lambert, Lynette McLean and Rhoda Ryan in the final of the Fours. The English rink of Dorothy Lewis, Norma May, Norma Shaw and Mavis Steele were going well until a fifth round defeat by New Zealand and a subsequent loss to defending champions, Wales put them out of the running. For the Welsh, Ann Dainton, Linda Evans, Rita Jones and Stella Oliver, made a poor start to lose to Zimbabwe and Papua New Guinea, and it was all too late by the time they met England. Left to carry British hopes, Annette Evans, Ann Watson, Janice Maxwell and Joyce Lindores of Scotland led from the second end to the 20th against Hong Kong, in the play-off for the bronze, but lost 21-20! It's a great game, bowls — but such a cruel one at times.

Last End While Rob Parrella is to be congratulated for his superb play, he won few friends with his blatant time-wasting tactics against Ireland's David Corkill in their fifth round match. Ahead 14-1 after seven ends, and seemingly on his way to a comfortable victory, Parrella, perhaps underestimating the fighting qualities of his opponent, was rocked by a typical Corkill recovery and watched his lead dwindle to a single shot. Corkill, pride restored and body language now in large print, had turned from prey to hunter, putting his first bowl close.

Parrella then chose that moment methodically to clean every bowl at the delivery end; not just his, but the Irishman's as well! He left the green, returned, and finally delivered. The marker was baffled, the audience was baffled, the Aussie team manager was embarrassed, but Corkill sensed victory in the air and eventually finished the match with a full-house four. There will be few people in bowls who have not indulged in a little gamesmanship at one time or another. But Parrella's antics were shameful and should not have been condoned by any self-respecting umpire or, come to that, team manager, and they made the final victory taste a little sour.

Teams and Playing Order:

Men

Australia: Singles: Robert Parrella. **Pairs:** Trevor Morris, Ian Schuback. **Fours:** Denis Dalton, Rex Johnston, Dennis Katunarich, Kenneth Woods.
Botswana: Singles: Raymond Mascarenhas. **Pairs:** Thomas Foster, John Kakakis. **Fours:** John Baylis, David Murray, Clifton Richardson, John Thackray.
Canada: Singles: Burnham Gill. **Pairs:** George Boxwell, Alfred Wallace. **Fours:** William Boettger, David Brown, Peter Mutter, Robert Scullion.

Cook Islands: Singles: Philip Urlich. **Pairs:** Inatio Akaruru, Ieremia Tuteru. **Fours:** Abela Amarama, Eric Ponia, Toka Rahui, David Towgood.

England: Singles: David Bryant. **Pairs:** Gary Smith, Andrew Thomson. **Fours:** Anthony Allcock, Roydon Cutts, Gary Harrington, John Ottaway.

Guernsey: Singles: Michael Smith. **Pairs:** Michael De Carteret, Norman Le Ber.

Hong Kong: Singles: Mark McMahon. **Pairs:** Koon Leung Ho, Noel Kennedy. **Fours:** William McMahon, Roger Pickford, Melvyn Stewart, Kenneith Wallis.

India: Singles: Sreenivasa Pai. **Pairs:** Vipin Dhawan, Basant Rampuria. Fours: Rajendra Bengani, Pratap Bengani, Surya Saigai, Gopiram Sharma.

Jersey: Pairs: Marcel Coutouly, David Le Marquand.

Norfolk Island: Singles: Barry Wilson. **Pairs:** William Adams, Thornton Yager. **Fours:** John Christian, Sidney Cooper, Garry Ryan, Keith Turton.

Northern Ireland: Singles: David Corkill. **Pairs:** Victor Dallas, Ernest Parkinson. Fours: Samuel Allen, James Baker, John McCloughlin, Rodney McCutcheon.

New Zealand: Singles: Ian Dickison. **Pairs:** Rowan Brassey, Maurice Symes. **Fours:** Kevin Darling, Stewart McConnell, Peter Shaw, Philip Skoglund.

Papua New Guinea: Singles: Tau Tau. **Pairs:** Phillip Guimap, Kossy Torao. **Fours:** Albert Barakeina, Tau Nancie, Martin Seeto, Ambane Wau.

Western Samoa: Singles: Dick Hunt. **Pairs:** Peniamina Asi, Taituuga Rokeni. **Fours:** Taualeoo Faasoo, Fepuleai Sae, Tapusatele Tuatagaloa, Saivaega Vasa.

Scotland: Singles: Richard Corsie. **Pairs:** Angus Blair, Graham Robertson. **Fours:** George Adrain, Ian Bruce, Denis Love, William Wood.

Swaziland: Fours: Hayley Abrahams, David Clark, David Goddard, John Kemp.

Wales: Singles: John Price. **Pairs:** William Thomas, Robert Weale. **Fours:** Alan Beer, Trefor Mounty, David Vowles, David Wilkins.

Zambia: Fours: Ian Henderson, Cornelius Krige, Duncan Naysmith, Jacob Van Deventer.

Zimbabwe: Singles: Garin Beare. **Pairs:** William Cumming, Richard Wightman. **Fours:** Richard Hayden, Paul Kramer, Sydney Shiel, Manie Volgraaff.

Women

Australia: Singles: Audrey Hefford. **Pairs:** Edda Bonutto, Maureen Hobbs. **Fours:** Dorothy Roche, Audrey Rutherford, Daphne Shaw, Marion Stevens.

Botswana: Singles: Flora Anderson. **Pairs:** Jacqueline Rhodes, Heather Roberts. **Fours:** Shirley Baylis, Jane Mitchell, Yvonne Richards, Evelyn Thomas.

Canada: Singles: Fatima Reimer. **Pairs:** Elaine Jones, Roseann Toal. **Fours:** Dorothy Bennett, Marlene Cleutinx, Clarice Fitzpatrick, Dorothy Macey.

Cook Islands: Singles: Ngamarama Beniamina. **Pairs:** Rouru Paniani, Tereapii Urlich. **Fours:** Tangimetua Harry, Tara Pita, Makiua Tairi, Toka Tuteru.

England: Singles: Wendy Line. **Pairs:** Mary Price, Jayne Roylance. **Fours:** Dorothy Lewis, Norma May, Norma Shaw, Mavis Steele.

Guernsey: Singles: Kathleen Dodd. **Pairs:** Hazel Dorey, Sonia Murphy.

Hong Kong: Singles: Rosemary McMahon. **Pairs:** Josephine Hollis, Gillian Sperring. **Fours:** Sau Ling Chau, Yee Lai Lee, Natividad Rozario, Jenny Wallis.

Jersey: Singles: Sheila Syvret.

Norfolk Island: Singles: Emmeline Browning. **Pairs:** Anne Paton, Gabrielle Robertson. **Fours:** Carmelita Bishop, Esterlina Greenham, Beatrice Karl, Pauline Turton.

Northern Ireland: Singles: Margaret Johnston. **Pairs:** Nan Allely, Eileen Bell.

New Zealand: Singles: Millie Khan. **Pairs:** Judy Howat, Marie Watson. **Fours:** Marlene Castle, Adrienne Lambert, Lynette McLean, Rhoda Ryan.

Papua New Guinea: Singles: Gaua Tau. **Pairs:** Kathy Panap, Kathy Sigimet. **Fours:** Alu David, Mary Nancie, Walo Pisak, Norma Samba.

Western Samoa: Singles: Vaise Siaosi. **Pairs:** Marie Toalepaialii, Faaelelei Tuatagaloa. **Fours:** Leute Fua, Faamomoi Rokeni, Seupepe Sasagi, Akenese Westerlund.

Scotland: Singles: Senga McCrone. **Pairs:** Sarah Gourlay,. Frances Whyte. **Fours:** Annette Evans, Joyce Lindores, Janice Maxwell, Agnes Watson.

Swaziland: Fours: Mariana Goddard, Elizabeth James, Cynthia Thompson, Wendy Vickery.

Wales: Singles: Janet Ackland. **Pairs:** Pamela Griffiths, Mary Hughes. **Fours:** Ann Dainton, Linda Evans, Rita Jones, Stella Oliver.

Zambia: Singles: Beatrice Mali. **Fours:** Marguerite De Brito, Helen Graham, Ann Mair, Elizabeth Naysmith.

Zimbabwe: Singles: Anne Morris. **Pairs:** Winnona Butcher, Judith Penfold. **Fours:** Onei Dolphin, Joan Du Preez, Margaret Mills, Margaret Whittall.

Men's Singles

Section A: New Zealand 25, W. Samoa 20; Scotland 25, Norfolk Islands 13; Cook Islands 5, Botswana 25; Wales 12 Hong Kong 25; W. Samoa 8, Scotland 25; Norfolk Islands 25 Cook Islands 13; Botswana 6, Wales 25; New Zealand 25, Scotland 20; W. Samoa 23 Norfolk Islands 25; Scotland 25, Cook Islands 6; Norfolk Islands 25, Botswana 17; Cook Islands 12 Wales 25; Botswana 19 Hong Kong 25; New Zealand 25 Norfolk Islands 5; W. Samoa 25, Cook Islands 24; Scotland 25 Botswana 7; Norfolk Islands 19 Wales 25; Cook Islands 13 Hong Kong 25; New Zealand 25 Cook Islands 10; W. Samoa 25 Botswana 12; Scotland 25 Wales 13; Norfolk Islands 16 Hong Kong 25; New Zealand 25 Botswana 10; W. Samoa 10 Wales 25; Scotland 12 Hong Kong 25; New Zealand 20 Wales 25; W. Samoa 10 Hong Kong 25; New Zealand 17, Hong Kong 25.

Section B: Australia 25, Zimbabwe 15; Canada 25 Papua NG 15; England 25 Guernsey 9; N. Ireland 25 India 4; Zimbabwe 18, Canada 25; Papua NG 18 England 25; Guernsey 15 N. Ireland 25; Australia 25, Canada 12; Zimbabwe 25 Papua NG 13; Canada 15, England 25; Papua NG 7, Guernsey 25; England 25 N. Ireland 14; Guernsey 25, India 9; Australia 25 Papua NG 19; Zimbabwe 12, England 25; Canada 25, Guernsey 16; Papua NG 23 N. Ireland 25; England 25 India 4; Australia 25 England 14; Zimbabwe 25 Guernsey 7; Canada 19 N. Ireland 25; Papua NG 25 India 18; Australia 25 Guernsey 8; Zimbabwe 25 N. Ireland 23; Canada 25 India 5; Australia 20, N. Ireland 25; Zimbabwe 25, India 8; Australia 25, India 7.

Final: R. Parrella (Australia, gold) 25, M. McMahon (Hong Kong, silver) 14. Third/Fourth: Richard Corsie (Scotland, bronze) 25, D. Bryant (England) 17.

Men's Pairs: Section A: Scotland 20 N.Ireland 29; England 17 New Zealand 20; Zimbabwe 8 Australia 22; Papua NG 25 Guernsey 18; N. Ireland 14, England 24; New Zealand 23 Zimbabwe 13; Australia 30 Papua NG 10; Guernsey 21 Jersey 21. Scotland 19 England 13; N. Ireland 18 New Zealand 22; England 34 Zimbabwe 13; New Zealand 17 Australia 21; Zimbabwe 27 Papua NG 16; Australia 25 Guernsey 15; Papua NG 12 Jersey 32; Scotland 14 New Zealand 18; N. Ireland 17 Zimbabwe 19; England 16 Australia 24; New Zealand 31 Papua NG 10; Zimbabwe 14 Guernsey 23; Australia 35 Jersey 9; Scotland 13 Zimbabwe 27; N. Ireland 20 Australia 24; England 33 Papua NG 13; New Zealand 25 Guernsey 24; Zimbabwe 16 Jersey 14; Scotland 26 Australia 20; N. Ireland 22 Papua NG 14; England 25 Guernsey 20; New Zealand 26 Jersey 14;

Scotland 37 Papua NG 12; N. Ireland 18 Guernsey 21; England 28 Jersey 25; Scotland 24 Guernsey 25; N. Ireland 20 Jersey 26; Scotland 21 Jersey 14. Section B: Canada 21 W. Samoa 19; Wales 24 Norfolk Islands 11; Hong Kong 35 Botswana 6; Cook Islands 11 India 29; W. Samoa 17 Wales 18; Norfolk Islands 14 Kong Kong 26; Botswana 23 Cook Islands 16; Canada 26 Wales 19; W. Samoa 24 Norfolk Islands 15; Wales 18 Hong Kong 16; Norfolk Islands 12 Botswana 19; Hong Kong 40 Cook Islands 14; Botswana 18, India 32; Canada 18 Norfolk Islands 14; W. Samoa 17 Hong Kong 33; Wales 29 Botswana 19; Norfolk Islands 25 Cook Islands 15; Hong Kong 35 India 14; Canada 23 Hong Kong 16; W. Samoa 24 Botswana 15; Wales 39 Cook Islands 12; Norfolk Islands 20 India 20; Canada 27 Botswana 17; W. Samoa 41 Cook Islands 12; Wales 27 India 15; Canada 26 Cook Islands 21;W. Samoa 24 India 17; Canada 23 India 18.

Final: I. Schuback, T. Morris (Australia, gold) 23, A. Wallace, G. Boxwell (Canada, silver) 15. Third/Fourth: R. Brassey M. Symes (New Zealand, bronze) 24, R. Weale, W. Thomas (Wales) 17

Men's Fours: Section A: Wales 18 Hong Kong 20; N. Ireland 18 England 18; Zimbabwe 9 Australia 25; W. Samoa 33 Swaziland 26; Hong Kong 12 N. Ireland 19; England 29 Zimbabwe 15; Australia 38 W. Samoa 11; Swaziland 12 Norfolk Islands 35; Wales 17 N. Ireland 16; Hong Kong 21 England 14; N. Ireland 30 Zimbabwe 12; England 15 Australia 17; Zimbabwe 11 W. Samoa 24; Australia 17 Swaziland 19; W. Samoa 16 Norfolk Islands 24; Wales 6 England 26; Hong Kong 30 Zimbabwe 8; N. Ireland 17 Australia 14; England 27 W. Samoa 17; Zimbabwe 34 Swaziland 18; Australia 37 Norfolk Islands 8; Wales 22 Zimbabwe 21; Hong Kong 15 Australia 17; Northern Ireland 27 W. Samoa 17; England 26 Swaziland 14; Zimbabwe 25 Norfolk Islands 13; Wales 17 Australia 21; Hong Kong 27 W. Samoa 20; N. Ireland 35 Swaziland 13; England 25 Norfolk Islands 10; Wales 30 W. Samoa 12; Hong Kong 22 Swaziland 15; N. Ireland 16 Norfolk Islands 15; Wales 36 Swaziland 13; Hong Kong 28 Norfolk Islands 14; Wales 32 Norfolk Islands 12.
Section B: Canada 26 Zambia 12; New Zealand 22 Papua NG 23; Scotland 20 India 16; Botswana 33 Cook Islands 8; Zambia 15 New Zealand 21; Papua NG 21 Scotland 21; India 21 Botswana 22; Canada 9 New Zealand 29; Zambia 14 Papua NG 14; New Zealand 17 Scotland 18; Papua NG 34 India 5; Scotland 26 Botswana 16; India 22 Cook Islands 20; Canada 24 Papua NG 15; Zambia 10 Scotland 22; New Zealand 34 India 7; Papua NG 22 Botswana 16; Scotland 29 Cook Islands 6; Canada 15 Scotland 26; Zambia 27 India 10; New Zealand 20 Botswana 14; Papua NG 13 Cook Islands 23; Canada 25 India 22; Zambia 15 Botswana 22; New Zealand 33 Cook Islands 16; Canada 31 Botswana 10; Zambia 15 Cook islands 19; Canada 21 Cook Islands 22.

Final: D. Love, I. Bruce, G. Adrain, W. Wood (Scotland, gold) 19, R. McCutcheon, J. McCloughlin, S. Allen, J. Baker (Ireland, silver) 14. Third/Fourth: S. McConnell, J. Murtagh, P. Shaw, P. Skoglund (New Zealand, bronze) 21 K. Woods, D. Katunarich, D. Dalton R. Johnston (Australia) 13.

Women's Singles: Section A: England 25, Australia 19; Botswana 16 Hong Kong 25; Zimbabwe 19 New Zealand 25; W. Samoa 25 Jersey 22; Australia 25 Botswana 16; Hong Kong 17 Zimbabwe 25; New Zealand 25 W. Samoa 3; Jersey 25 Norfolk Islands 24; England 25, Botswana 24; Australia 25 Hong Kong 4; Botswana 22 Zimbabwe 25; Hong Kong 10 New Zealand 25; Zimbabwe 23 W. Samoa 25; New Zealand 25 Jersey 9; W. Samoa 18 Norfolk Islands 25; England 25 Hong Kong 16; Australia 25 Zimbabwe

21; Botswana 19 New Zealand 25; Hong Kong 25 W. Samoa 18; Zimbabwe 17 Jersey 25; New Zealand 25 Norfolk Islands 17; England 24 Zimbabwe 25; Australia 11 New Zealand 25; Botswana 21 W. Samoa 25; Hong Kong 17 Jersey 25; Zimbabwe 25 Norfolk Islands 10; England 22 New Zealand 25; Australia 25 W. Samoa 10; Botswana 25 Jersey 10; Hong Kong 25 Norfolk Islands 13; England 24 W. Samoa 25; Australia 25 Jersey 5; Botswana 22 Norfolk Island 25; England 25 Jersey 22; Australia 25 Norfolk Islands 5; England 25 Norfolk Islands 7.

Section B: Scotland 25 Zambia 24; Canada 20 Papua NG 25; Cook Islands 25 Guernsey 18; N. Ireland 25, Wales 21; Zambia 25 Canada 22; Papua NG 25 Cook Islands 6; Guernsey 10 N. Ireland 25; Scotland 25 Canada 17;Zambia 19 Papua NG 25; Canada 18 Cook Islands 25; Papua NG 25 Guernsey 16; Cook Islands 5 N. Ireland 25; Guernsey 25 Wales 13; Scotland 13 Papua NG 25; Zambia 25 Cook Islands 24; Canada 15 Guernsey 15; Papua NG 25 N. Ireland 19; Cook Islands 12 Wales 25; Scotland 25 Cook Islands 11; Zambia 23 Guernsey 25; Canada 12 N. Ireland 25; Papua NG 26 Wales 6; Scotland 25 Guernsey 10; Zambia 10 N. Ireland 25; Canada 12 Wales 25; Scotland 20 N. Ireland 25; Zambia 11 Wales25; Scotland 24 Wales 25.

Final: G. Tau (Papua N.G, gold) 25 M. Khan (New Zealand, silver) 18. Third/Fourth: M. Johnston (Ireland, bronze) 25 A. Hefford (Australia) 15.

Women's Pairs: Section A: N. Ireland 28 Zimbabwe 16; England 22 Papua NG 22; Wales 17 Cook Islands 18; Canada 18 Australia 27; Zimbabwe 17 England 16; Papua NG 26 Wales 18; Cook Islands 15 Canada 26; N. Ireland 14 England 20; Zimbabwe 15 Papua NG 21; England 25 Wales 15; Papua NG 19 Cook Islands 22; Wales 22 Canada 24; Cook Islands 10 Australia 29; N. Ireland 27 Papua NG 12; Zimbabwe 13 Wales 14; England 27 Cook Islands 15; Papua NG 31 Canada 16; Wales 17 Australia 24; N. Ireland 14 Wales 21; Zimbabwe 9 Cook Islands 33; England 19 Canada 14; Papua NG 24 Australia 33; N. ireland 19 Cook Islands 18; Zimbabwe 21 Canada 23; England 23 Australia 21; N. Ireland 27 Canada 14; Zimbabwe 7 Australia 34; N. Ireland 13 Australia 29.

Section B: Hong Kong 14 W. Samoa 21; New Zealand 37 Norfolk Islands 10; Scotland 29 Botswana 14; W. Samoa 15 New Zealand 32; Norfolk Islands 16 Scotland 20; Botswana 19 Guernsey 23; Hong Kong 8 New Zealand 32; W. Samoa 27 Norfolk Islands 20; New Zealand 20 Scotland 17; Norfolk Island 12 Botswana 27; Scotland 18 Guernsey 12; Hong Kong 7 Norfolk Island 25; W. Samoa 8 Scotland 22; New Zealand 15 Botswana 25; Norfolk Island 13 Guernsey 22; Hong Kong 14 Scotland 26; W. Samoa 22 Botswana 18; New Zealand 24 Guernsey 20; Hong Kong 19 Botswana 20; W. Samoa 22 Guernsey 24; Hong Kong 10 Guernsey 27.

Final: J. Howat, M. Watson (New Zealand, gold) 23, M. Hobbs, E. Bonutto (Australia, silver) 13. Third/Fourth: J. Roylance, M. Price (England, bronze) 22, S. Gourlay, F. Whyte (Scotland) 14.

Women's Fours: Section A: Wales 15 Zimbabwe 19; England 25 W. Samoa 16; New Zealand 34, Papua NG 11; Scotland 23 Norfolk Islands 13; Zimbabwe 22 England 23; W. Samoa 18 New Zealand 15; Papua NG 17 Scotland 20; Wales 21 England 17; Zimbabwe 39 W. Samoa 8; England 13 New Zealand 20; W. Samoa 14 Papua NG 25; New Zealand 29 Scotland 10; Papua NG 27 Norfolk Island 20; Wales 30 W. Samoa 17; Zimbabwe 22 New Zealand 26; England 34 Papua NG 6; W. Samoa 18 Scotland 28; New Zealand 19 Norfolk Islands 9; Wales 15, New Zealand 18; Zimbabwe 21 Papua NG 21; England 17 Scotland 19; W. Samoa 16 Norfolk Islands 22; Wales 19 Papua

NG 23; Zimbabwe 19 Scotland 22; England 18 Norfolk Islands 16; Wales 22 Scotland 19; Zimbabwe 30 Norfolk Islands 11; Wales 28 Norfolk Islands 11. Section B: Hong Kong 23 Zambia 12; Cook Islands 15 Botswana 28; Swaziland 16 Canada 25; Zambia 18 Cook Islands 21; Botswana 28 Swaziland 11; Canada 20 Australia 28; Hong Kong 21 Cook Islands 19; Zambia 13 Botswana 33; Cook Islands 21 Swaziland 13; Botswana 28 Canada 13; Swaziland 9 Australia 34; Hong Kong 22 Botswana 19; Zambia 12 Swaziland 25; Cook Islands 18 Canada 23; Botswana 14 Australia 34; Hong Kong 20 Swaziland 14; Zambia 20 Canada 19; Cook Islands 14 Australia 32; Hong Kong 25 Canada 13; Zambia 11 Australia 35; Hong Kong 12 Australia 26.

Final: M. Stevens, D. Shaw, A. Rutherford D. Roche (Australia, gold) 20, M. Castle, A. Lambert, L. McLean, R. Ryan (New Zealand, silver) 18. Third/Fourth: S.L. Chau, Y.L. Lee N. Rozario, J. Wallis (Hong Kong, bronze) 21, A. Evans, J. Lindores, J. Maxwell, A. Watson (Scotland) 20.

Internationals
By Donald Newby

A share of the 1990 honours went to all the four home countries despite England's continued domination of the British Isles international series, outdoors and indoors by both men and women.

Scotland brought gold back from the Commonwealth Games as well as bronze in the men's events, Ireland won silver and bronze, England had to be content with bronze and the Welsh though they returned from Auckland empty handed had their morale lifted a few weeks later when John Price captured the world indoor Singles title.

Young Welsh bowlers brought further pride by defeating England under-25 teams both indoors and outdoors and four successes in British Isles events, two in the women's internationals at Saundersfoot and Janet Ackland's reign as world Singles champion afforded further evidence that Welsh bowls is in good shape.

Scottish bowlers appear to fare best in Singles play at international level as their success in invitation events involving leading bowlers from other countries indicate and their success over England both in international team play — victory indoors and a tie outdoors — and in Singles challenge matches between players' teams, indicate that they only lack consistency; they have a crop of young men players who appear to get more opportunity than their English counterparts.

In Graham Robertson and Liz Wren they have talented Singles performers, neither of whose merits appear as yet to be fully recognised.

The loss of television programmes has driven the British game back into itself with visits to Australia, New Zealand and Hong Kong for a handful of selected bowlers doing little to expose the game. England still possesses three of the greatest bowlers in the world in David Bryant, Tony Allcock and Norma Shaw. Indeed the omission of Shaw from the women's world indoor event in Guernsey in 1990 made nonsense of the selection system under which this event is held. For this lady has an indoor record which is second to none.

Bristol & West One Day Internationals

at Auchinleck IBC, September 18th 1989 and Prestwick IBC, September 19th 1989

Local knowledge proved decisive in the two Bristol & West one day internationals, with Hugh Duff keeping the Auchinleck support happy in the opening event, with a 21-15 win over Gary Smith and David Gourlay Jnr, powering his way to victory over the then reigning world indoor champion Richard Corsie at Prestwick.

Duff clinched his place in the Auchinleck final with wins over England's John Bell and Tony Allcock and clubmate Neil McGhee. His final opponent was reigning UK champion Gary Smith, but Duff was always in command, leading 5-0 after two ends. Smith rallied to be one down at 6-7 after six ends and a single on the next, followed by a maximum four on the eighth end put Duff firmly in command at 12-6. He went on to win 21-15.

At Prestwick, 23-year old David Gourlay Jnr turned in impressive performances to beat John Price, Smith and Allcock, and he continued his great run in the final against Corsie, racing to a 16-1 lead after nine ends, and going on to win 21-8 six ends later.

Auchinleck: Final: H. Duff (Scotland) 21, G. Smith (England) 15. Women's Event: S. Gourlay (Scotland) 15, M. Johnston (Ireland) 13.
Prestwick: Final: D. Gourlay (Scotland) 21, R. Corsie (Scotland) 8. Women's Event: M. Lamont (Scotland) 15, J. Reid (Scotland) 12.

Players' Association International England v Scotland

at Carlisle IBC, September 30th-October 1st 1989

The third Players' association International between Scotland and England, ended with the Scots coasting to the easiest of victories, by twenty points to five. The unique format of the event brings together five top players from each country, who meet on a round robin series of singles matches.

Scotland had all but tied up victory after the opening day when they led by twelve matches to three, needing one success on the second day for overall victory. They did not have long to wait for their win, taking the penultimate session by four matches to one, and repeating that scoreline in the final session.

Results: Gary Smith (England) lost to Willie Wood (Scotland) 2-9,1-9; Tony Allcock (England) bt Jim Muir (Scotland) 9-0, 9-5; John Bell (England) lost to Hugh Duff (Scotland) 6-9, 7-9; Mike Marsden (England) lost to Richard Corsie (Scotland) 5-9, 4-9; Andy Thomson (England) lost to Angus Blair (Scotland) 2-9, 4-9. Marsden lost to Blair 9-6, 3-9, 2-9; Thomson lost to Wood 7-9, 9-8, 5-9; Smith lost to Muir 3-9, 4-9; Allcock lost to Duff 1-9, 9-6, 2-9; Bell lost to Corsie 8-9, 9-5, 4-9. Allcock bt Corsie 9-5, 9-8; Bell lost to Blair 4-9, 8-9; Marsden lost to Wood 5-9, 1-9; Thomson bt Muir 5-9, 9-8, 9-1; Smith lost to Duff 9-8, 3-9, 2-9. Thomson lost to Duff 9-5, 7-9, 4-9; Smith lost to Corsie 5-9, 8-9; Allcock bt Blair 9-1, 9-4; Bell lost to Wood 9-2, 7-9, 3-9; Marsden lost to Muir 4-9, 3-9. Bell lost to Muir 6-9, 6-9; Marsden lost to Duff 1-9, 7-9; Thomson bt Corsie 5-9, 9-5, 9-6; Smith lost to Blair 8-9, 9-7, 2-9; Allcock lost to Wood 8-9, 7-9.

CIS Insurance UK Championship

at The Guild Hall, Preston, October 28th — November 5th 1989

Prize money: £42,400. Winner £12,000. Runner-up £6,000. Losing semi finalists £3,000 each. Losing quarter finalists £1,500 each. Round 2 losers £750 each. Round 1 losers £400 each.

David Bryant's ability to wriggle out of dangerous situations enabled him to confound opponents once again and win this televised tournament.

He dropped a set in every round. After losing two to Ireland's David Corkill in the best of five sets final, and having match shot against him, he produced a remarkable delivery to obtain a three. That won him that set, and he then captured the next two to take the £12,000 first prize.

The shot that turned the tide for him was a reply to Corkill's perfectly judged delivery which left the bowl nestling behind the jack. Bryant gently edged it out, extricating himself with the same pinpoint accuracy which won him his first round game against Bill Hobart, his England colleague.

Hobart's shot to lie game seemed to be in an impregnable position. But Bryant managed to trickle in to the jack to steal the set and the game, much to Hobart's chagrin.

Shock results were common throughout the nine day event. Richard Corsie surrendered rather tamely to Hugh Duff, his predecessor as world indoor champion, in three straight sets. Then Duff was on the receiving end himself. He scored only six shots in three sets against Tony Allcock.

In the second round Allcock had had a narrow escape himself, only just avoiding defeat from the talented Irishwoman, Margaret Johnston. Keeping a constant length, Mrs Johnston levelled at two sets all and led 6-4 in the decider. Allcock then produced his best end of the game, drawing three shots on a near perfect line. Mrs Johnston failed to disturb them. In her first round she had outbowled Scotland's Ian Bruce, a world semi finalist in 1987.

Allcock finally came to grief in a semi final against Corkill who had lived dangerously in his quarter final with Jim Muir. Another Scot, Angus Blair, defeated Gary Smith, England's 1988 winner, but could not sustain his form against steady Stephen Rees, who then lost to Bryant in a four-set semi final.

When the two met in the 1986 best of nine sets final, Bryant trailed by 4-0 and hauled back to 4-4 before Rees won the decider. This time, however, Bryant was into his stride from the start and never relaxed after building a two set lead.

Round 1: Gary Smith (England) bt Michael Kent (Wales) 7-6, 7-3; Angus Blair (Scotland) bt Alan Campbell (Scotland) 7-5, 3-7, 7-4; John Wallace (Scotland) bt Wynne Richards (England) 7-4, 7-6; Stephen Rees (Wales) bt Michael Dunlop (Ireland) 1-7, 7-3, 7-6; David Bryant (England) bt Bill Hobart (England) 7-3, 0-7, 7-6; Jim Baker (Ireland) bt Raymond Weir (Ireland) 7-0, 7-6; Neil McGhee (Scotland) bt Joyce Lindores (Scotland) 7-4, 5-7, 7-5; Willie Wood (Scotland) bt Brian Rattray (Scotland) 0-7, 7-5, 7-3; David Corkill (Ireland)bt David Cox (Wales) 7-2, 7-1; John Watson (Scotland) bt Brian Kingdon (Wales) 7-2, 1-7, 7-3; Jim Muir (Scotland) bt Steven Rankin (Scotland) 7-4, 2-7, 7-5; John Price (Wales) bt Adrian Kean (Wales) 7-2, 7-2; Hugh Duff (Scotland) bt Maurice McKeown (Ireland) 7-4, 7-1; Richard Corsie (Scotland) bt Andy Thomson

(England) 7-4, 7-6; Margaret Johnston (Ireland)bt Ian Bruce (Scotland) 7-3, 1-7, 2-7; Tony Allcock bt Neil Thompson (England) 7-1, 7-1.

Round 2: Blair bt Smith 7-6 7-3, 3-7, 7-5; S. Rees bt Wallace 5-7, 4-7, 7-2, 7-5, 7-6; Bryant bt Baker 7-3, 7-1, 1-7, 7-6; McGhee bt Wood 7-2, 7-6, 3-7, 7-5; Corkill bt Watson 7-0, 7-2, 7-3; Muir bt Price 7-3, 7-6, 2-7, 6-7, 7-3; Duff bt Corsie 7-1, 7-5, 7-1; Allcock bt Johnston 6-7, 7-2, 7-6, 4-7, 7-6.

Quarter finals: Rees bt Blair 6-7, 7-0, 7-3, 7-4; Bryant bt McGhee 7-5, 7-6, 5-7, 7-4; Corkill bt Muir 5-7, 7-6, 7-5, 5-7, 7-5; Allcock bt Duff 7-0, 7-4, 7-2.

Semi finals: Bryant bt Rees 7-3, 7-4, 4-7, 7-3; Corkill bt Allcock 7-5, 1-7, 7-6, 7-4.

Final: Bryant bt Corkill 1-7, 5-7, 7-6, 7-5, 7-3.

Hong Kong Classic Singles

at Hong Kong Football Club, November 18th-19th 1989

The Souza Singles, named after one of Hong Kong's greatest ever bowls ambassadors, George Souza, is used as a curtain raiser for the Hong Kong Classic Pairs, with all the overseas competitors included in the line-up.

Played over two days, the event includes some of Hong Kong's emerging talent, but the four players who won through to the semi-finals were all established internationals. Former world champion Peter Belliss edged through to the final with a 25-20 win over England's Brett Morley, and lined up against Australia's Trevor Morris, who ended home hopes with a 25-19 win over Noel Kennedy. Belliss dominated the final, and scored a comfortable 25-16 win.

Semi-finals: P. Belliss (New Zealand) 25, B. Morley (England) 20; T. Morris (Australia) 25, N. Kennedy (Hong Kong) 19.

Final: Belliss 25, Morris 16.

Hong Kong International Bowls Classic

at Kowloon BC, Hong Kong, November 20th-26th 1989

The Hong Kong Bank International Classic Pairs went to Australia's Rex Johnston and Trevor Morris, who ended hopes of a first ever English success when they scored a 21-12 final win over Nottingham's Brett Morley and Ronnie Gass from Cumbria.

The England pair only scraped through to the knock-out stages in fourth place in their section with four wins and a draw from their nine matches. But in the quarter finals they hit back from 10-17 down with eight ends to play to beat previous winners Noel Kennedy and Mark McMahon, representing the hosts.

The Australian pair counted seven shots over the last three ends to beat Scotland's Graham Robertson and Alex Marshall 21-16, while Ireland's Jim Baker and Sammy Allen beat Canada's Alf Wallace and Graham Jarvis 22-13.

The upset of the quarter finals came with the defeat of world champions Rowan Brassey and Peter Belliss, who went down to one of the local Hong Kong club pairs Mike Abraham and Chi Chi Fernandez, who beat the Kiwis 24-20.

In the semi finals, the Aussie pair ended the run of Fernandez and Abraham with a crushing 32-11 win, while England just got the better of Ireland 19-17.

Quarter finals: Ireland (S. Allen, J. Baker) 22, Canada (A. Wallace, G. Jarvis) 13; Club de Recreio (M. Abraham, C. Fernandez) 24, New Zealand (R. Brassey, P. Belliss) 20; England R. Gass, B. Morley) 25, Hong Kong (N. Kennedy, M. McMahon) 19; Australia (R. Johnston, T. Morris) 21, Scotland (G. Robertson, A. Marshall) 16.
Semi finals: Australia 32, Club de Recreio 11; England 19, Ireland 17.
Final: Australia 21, England 12.

Mens Under 25 Indoor International. Wales v England
at Perdiswell IBC, January 21st 1990.

Wales scrambled to a one-Shot victory against England in this inaugural first event. With Mervyn King's England rink opposed to that of Welsh captain Phil Robbins on the last rink to end, the scene was set for a gripping finale. England needed a two but King, who had saved his rink time and again only held one, and with his final delivery bowled to give Wales the victory by 113-112. Play was even across the green with the well-balanced Welsh side, which contained five full internationals, constantly setting England problems. Ely's Greg Harlow was the only skip to score an English victory; his four defeated a Jeff Wilkins rink by 22-11.

England 112 Wales 113. Rink scores (England skips first): G Harlow 22, J Wilkins 11, D Holt 19, J Greenslade 20, N Smith 18, T Matthews 24, M King 19, P Robbins 20, R Vintner 18, M Prosser 20, D Ramsdale 16, S Gall 16.

Embassy World Indoor Championship
at The Guild Hall, Preston, February 20th — March 4th 1990

Prize money: Singles: Prize money £81,000 Winner £20,000. Runner-up £11,000. Losing Losing Semi finalists £5,000 each. Losing Quarter finalists £3,000 each. Round 2 losers £1,500 each. Round 1 losers £1,000 each.
Pairs: Prize money £36,000. Winners £10,000. Runners-up £6,000. Losing Semi finalists £3,000 each. Losing Quarter finalists £1,500 each. Round 1 losers £1,000 each.

Australian Ian Schuback reaped most publicity at these championships, but in the final showdown it was John Price, the slim man of bowls who became the 1990 world indoor Singles champion.

It was a popular victory for the Welsh civil servant from Port Talbot who has been close to success in major international competition on several occasions without ever reaching port. This time, however, he stayed in full sail to win a vital second set.

Play in this second set reached the highest peak of the tournament when Price was leading 4-0. Toucher after toucher was played, the lead changing five times before the shot went to Schuback. On the next end, Schuback scored two more after Price fired, only to see his wood bounce back down the green.

On the next end the Welshman could have wrapped up the set when a score of four seemed a possibility, but he missed his chance. On the next two ends he lost measures and sadly shook his head, bemoaning his misfortune. But he need not have worried. On the next end he scrambled the single he needed for the set, and having climbed this psychological barrier, cast away his fears.

Two threes helped Price to the next set in double quick time, but Schuback bounced back to win the fourth. In the fifth Price won the first two ends to lead, and then with Schuback bowling short, held four shots for the match. With his final delivery the Australian struck one out to keep in the match — but only just. Price wound a shot into the jack on the next end, and when Schuback fired wide it was all over and the title had gone once again to Wales.

Brilliant bowling was also seen in earlier games with both finalists stamping their authority against top opposition. With successive victories over Australian Stewart Davies (to whom he dropped a set), Scotland's Jim Muir, Mark McMahon from Hong Kong, and then England's Tony Allcock, Price inscribed the hallmark of a worthy champion.

Although this semi final against Allcock reached the heights, Price had already peaked — against Muir, seeded No.11. He was virtually unplayable, crushing the former British Isles indoor Singles champion. Indeed the Welsh player came within a shot of inflicting a whitewash on Muir. Leading 7-0, 7-0, 6-0, he held shot, but with his third bowl, the Scot rolled in a toucher. When Price failed to disturb it, Muir was so relieved to score, he did not bother to play his final, afraid he might give the shot away. Price scored the shot he needed on the next end.

"It was one of those days when everything goes your way," Price said later. "Jim and I have had some super games in the past, and last November he beat me by three sets to two in the UK Championship." Muir said he could play worse and win matches. "John was just in the frame of mind which made him unbeatable. I have never lost — or won — like that before. It was quite a relief to score a shot." In his quarter final, Price had to reveal tenacity and aggression against the up-and-coming McMahon, who was born in Dunfermline, but later moved to Hong Kong with his family. McMahon, aged 20, took only four ends to win the first set, and when he recovered from a 3-0 deficit to level in the second and held two more shots, he appeared likely to dominate that, too. But Price trailed the jack to restore his lead, drew shots on the next, and obtained the three he needed when the young man's running shot took out his own third shot. The use of weight saved Price in the third set when McMahon led him 5-0 and 6-1. A timely four helped to close the gap and he settled the set after striking the jack into the ditch. On his way to the final, Schuback, a Commonwealth Games Pairs gold medallist, showed his class by first defeating two former world indoor champions — Ireland's Jim Baker and England's David Bryant. Schuback - a glutton for practice as top coach Jimmy Davidson has constantly reminded us — had very little time after flying in from Australia for pre-tournament practice, but it made no difference. His third opponent was Willie Wood, the 1988 beaten finalist, who extolled Schuback's play after going the way of Baker and Bryant.

Schuback, a former tennis coach and Australian Rules footballer, who now manages the District Club at Baulkham Hills, Sydney, always appeared the likely winner, even after Wood had taken the second set.

Schuback, at this time, was also going strong in the Pairs, played alternately with the Singles matches. "He could well become the first ever player to win both titles" said Wood after his defeat. "He grounds the bowl so well and has found the green."

A player who performs with a crowd pleasing lightness of touch, Schuback pronounced his own bowling philosophy after the game. "Bowls is the friendliest game in the world," he declared. "It is also a mental game. Why not have fun? You cannot relieve your feelings in bowls as someone did to me in football and broke my jaw. But you can enjoy playing the game and entertain, too. I feel that too many bowlers in the UK are too serious and do not show enough emotion." Schuback had been quoted as a 66-1 outsider by the bookmakers before the championship and the 50-1 odds against the English champion Andy Thomson also appeared generous. According to the script, Thomson and Schuback were likely to meet in the semi final. Thomson had beaten the 1989 world title holder Richard Corsie in a second round game and appeared likely to account for his England clubmate and colleague Gary Smith in a quarter final. But Thomson saw his hopes and those of punters founder by a measure after an absorbing game.

In the fifth deciding set Thomson had climbed back from a 6-2 deficit to level at 6-all and held three shots apparently on a perfect line when Smith shaped to deliver the final shot of the game. His drive straight on target struck Thomson's holding shot and then vanished into the ditch. Both players' bowls were some distance from the jack, but Smith's was closer by an inch or two. It was a notable victory for Smith who had dominated the game in the last two sets by moving up the mat to catch Thomson out on short ends.

Both players are familiar with each other's play and the match hardly had the cutting edge of the Price-McMahon encounter. Smith just about deserved his success for his final pressure shot just when almost certain victory appeared to have eluded him.

He was unable to find the same inspiration in his semi final with Schuback, although it was close for a time with the Australian taking the second set and losing the third only by 7-5. Schuback made no mistake in the fourth however, which he won 7-0. This match took three hours and came after Schuback's three and a half hour marathon in the Pairs final with his partner Jim Yates against the holders Bryant and Allcock.

The English master bowlers won this title for the fourth time in five years, owing as much to their experience and resolution as joint good form. Before the championships began, Bryant was suffering from back trouble and even on the day of his first match — which he won — he was receiving hospital treatment.

In the final he had to take second place to Yates, but Allcock came to the rescue. After coming from behind after being 2-1 down in sets, the English pair scrambled to the title when Allcock ran the jack into the ditch to clinch it with a three.

Once again they had shown their resilience, flair and will to win. In the first round they struggled against outsiders Rod Hugh and Walton Jones of Wales after taking only three ends to win the firs set without reply and adding a second by 7-3.

The Welshmen took the next two sets each by 7-6 and led 6-5 in the decider. Unfortunately for them Hugh, in an attempt to create a favourahble position, gave a shot away and Bryant and Allcock added another on the next end to squeeze through. It had been two sets all for them in their quarter final against Ireland's Michael Dunlop and Jim Baker, but they had no difficulty in the decider. Welshman Stephen Rees and Price met them in the semi final, but the Englishmen won this in four sets.

Yates and Schuback, who won the 1988 title, also found testing opposition on their way to the final. In their opening match, the Welsh pair Jim Hoskins and Cliff Jenkins, took them to five sets and after that they were extended by the father and son combination of Adam and Graham Robertson who earlier had beaten the fellow Scots Duff and Corsie in straight sets. In their semi final the Australians lost the first set to Gerry Smyth and Steve Halmai, the England Pairs experts from Paddington, but then recovered to win the next three.

Early in the championships, players were complaining of new rulings discouraging them from frequent visits to the head. As the tournament wore on, fewer protests were made and as is usual at bowls events, confrontation between players and officials was avoided. As a bid to speed up the game, the move was to be commended, but as is so often the case in matters like this, where there is a differing point of view, settling the issue is largely a question of compromise and interpretation, and this applied on this occasion.

Singles: Round 1: Richard Corsie (Scotland) bt David Wilkins (Wales) 0-7, 7-2, 7-5, 3-7, 7-2; Andy Thomson (England) bt Maurice McKeown (Ireland) 7-4, 7-3, 7-5; Gary Smith (England) bt Clive Major (New Zealand) 7-6, 2-7, 2-7, 7-1, 7-2; Stephen Rees (Wales) bt Nick Donaldson (Channel Islands) 7-2, 7-4, 7-0; David Bryant (England) bt Robert McCulloch (Scotland) 7-4, 7-6, 4-7, 7-2; Ian Schuback (Australia) bt Jim Baker (Ireland) 7-0, 7-6, 7-2; Rowan Brassey (New Zealand) bt Neil McGhee (Scotland) 7-1, 7-1, 7-5; Willie Wood (Scotland) bt Peter Bellis (New Zealand) 7-5, 7-6, 7-3; Mark McMahon (Hong Kong) bt David Corkill (Ireland) 4-7, 7-1, 7-5, 0-7, 7-2; Cecil Bransky (Israel) bt Bryan Kingdon (Wales) 5-7, 3-7, 7-6, 7-5, 7-4; Jim Muir (Scotland) bt Pip Branfield (England) 7-2, 7-2, 0-7, 7-3; John Price (Wales) bt Stewart Davies (Australia) 7-0, 1-7, 7-2, 7-3; Hugh Duff (Scotland) bt Alex Matthews (Australia) 7-5, 7-5, 4-7, 5-7, 7-0; Wynne Richards (England) bt Clifford Craig (Ireland) 7-3, 7-2, 7-6; Steven Rankin (Scotland) bt Jim Yates (Australia) 5-7, 7-2, 7-0, 6-7, 7-5; Tony Allcock (England) bt Michael Kent (Wales) 7-5, 7-4, 4-7, 2-7, 7-3.

Round 2: Thomson bt Corsie 7-5, 7-0, 4-7, 7-6; Smith bt Rees 7-4, 7-3, 4-7, 7-2; Schuback bt Bryant 3-7, 7-4, 7-2, 7-1; Wood bt Brassey 5-7, 7-5, 7-3, 7-3; McMahon bt Bransky 7-5, 4-7, 7-2, 7-0; Price bt Muir 7-0, 7-0, 7-1; Duff bt Richards 7-2, 7-4, 7-4; Allcock bt Rankin 7-3, 7-4, 7-1.

Quarter finals: Smith bt Thomson 2-7, 7-3, 2-7, 7-2, 7-6; Schuback bt Wood 7-3, 2-7, 7-0, 7-4; Price bt McMahon 2-7, 7-3, 7-6, 0-7, 7-2; Allcock bt Duff 7-5, 7-1, 7-1.

Semi finals: Schuback bt Smith 7-5, 4-7, 7-5, 7-0; Price bt Allcock 7-6, 4-7, 7-1, 3-7, 7-2.

Final: Price bt Schuback 4-7, 7-4, 7-2, 3-7, 7-2.

Pairs: Round 1: Tony Allcock, David Bryant (England) bt Rod Hugh, Walton Jones

(Wales) 7-0, 7-3, 6-7, 6-7, 7-6; Jim Baker, Michael Dunlop (Ireland) bt Stand Espie, Barry Dunlop (Ireland) 7-5, 7-3, 7-1; Stephen Rees, John Price (Wales) bt Cecil Bransky (Israel), Mark McMahon (Hong Kong) 7-6, 7-6. 6-7, 7-5; Gary Smith, Andy Thomson (England) bt Nick Donaldson (Channel Islands), Clive Major (New Zealand) 7-1, 7-3, 4-7, 7-0; Ian Schuback, Jim Yates (Australia) bt Jim Hoskins, Clive Jenkins (Wales) 7-1, 1-7, 7-4, 3-7, 7-3; Adam Robertson, Graham Robertson (Scotland) bt Richard Corsie, Hugh Duff (Scotland) 7-5, 7-2, 7-4; Steve Halmai, Gerry Smyth (England) bt Stewart Davies, Alex Matthews (Australia) 7-1, 7-1, 7-5; Peter Bellis, Rowan Brassey (New Zealand) bt Martin Tomlin, Mick Tomlin (England) 7-2, 7-4, 7-2.

Quarter finals: Bryant, Allcock bt Dunlop, Baker 7-3, 3-7, 7-6, 6-7, 7-2; Rees, Price bt Smith, Thomson 5-7, 6-7, 7-0, 7-3, 7-4; Yates, Schuback bt Robertson, Robertson 3-7, 7-5, 7-3, 7-5; Smyth, Halmai bt Brassey, Bellis 7-4, 7-4, 1-7, 7-2.

Semi finals: Bryant, Allcock bt Rees, Price 7-6, 7-3, 4-7, 7-5; Yates, Schuback bt Smyth, Halmai 6-7, 7-5, 7-1, 7-1.

Final: Bryant, Allcock bt Yates, Schuback 3-7, 7-4, 3-7, 7-3, 7-2.

Cignet/Atlas British Isles Women's Championships

at David Bryant Indoor Bowls Centre, Cliftonville, Margate, March 19th 1990

England won only two of the four British Isles championships though qualifying for all four finals. The other two were recapture by past champions Margaret Johnston, who had also won the Singles in 1987, and Scotland's Anne McFarlane and Margaret Spink, who regained the Pairs, which they also captured in 1988.

The England victories were obtained by Boston's Dianne Wilson, Sheila King and Jean Cammack, and a Teesside four Edie McKenna, Phoebe Spence, Jenny Berry and Norma Shaw.

Margaret Johnston had to move into top gear to regain the Singles. The English champion Gill Smith led her by 11-7 after 14 ends, but on the next Mrs Johnston scored a four and after that was firmly in the driving seat.

The Scottish Pairs success came via a 30-7 win over Ireland's Belle McKeag and Marie Martin, and by 22-19 against West Cornwall's Jane Rowntree and Gloria Thomas in the final. After trailing 9-8, the Scottish pair got their act together to lead 22-11, and though losing the last four ends — a 5,1,1, and 1 - held on to win 22-19. The Boston Triples team had an easy win over their Scottish opponents in the final after surviving a scare in their semi final against Ireland's Nan Montgomery, Alice Elliott and Nan Elliott, and Mrs Shaw and her Teesside partners scored a last end four to beat Rose Neil's Kilbride team by a rather flattering eight shots in the Fours final.

Singles: Semi finals: G. Smith (England) 21 E. Wren (Scotland) 20; M. Johnston (Ireland) 21, A. Sutherland (Wales) 5.

Final: Johnston 21, Smith 12 Pairs: Semi finals: England (J. Rowntree, G. Thomas) 20, Wales (A. John, J. Ackland) 13; Scotland (A. McFarlane, M. Spink) 30, N. Ireland (B. McKeag, M. Martin) 17.

Final: Scotland 22, England 19.

Triples: Semi finals: Scotland (M. Ferguson, M. Mungall, J. Adamson) 15, Wales (M. Hopkins, J. Wason, C. Morgan) 10; England (D. Wilson, S. King, J. Cammack) 13,

N. Ireland (N. Montgomery, A. Elliott, J. Mulholland) 11.
Final: England 23, Scotland 11.
Fours: Semi finals: Scotland (M. Hosie, R. Neil Jnr., J. Fraser, R. Neil Snr) 21, Wales (S. Froud, J. Parsons, M. Jones, M. Pomeroy) 15; England (E. McKenna, P. Spence, J. Berry, N. Shaw) 27, N. Ireland (M. Tosh, A. McAleese, M. Boyd, W. Millar) 13.
Final: England 24, Scotland 16.

Cignet/Atlas British Isles Women's Indoor International Series

at David Bryant Indoor Bowls Centre, Cliftonville, Margate, March 20th-22nd 1990

England retained the series for the fifth time in seven years with an unbeaten record — although the opening game against a spirited Welsh side was very close. England won it by 117-115 after a contentious finish, the result of which undoubtedly settled the series. This game featured long serving skips, England's Mavis Steele and Margaret Pomeroy, who were in opposition on the last end to be completed. Though the Welsh team were leading 23-15, Wales were still one shot behind across the green. Miss Steele held shot but Mrs Pomeroy killed the end to keep Welsh hopes alive and force a replay. Then umpire Lucy Brownlie took a hand. She ruled that the game was over as it had gone beyond the four-hour time limit. The organisers, the British Isles Women's Indoor Bowls Council did not agree and over-ruled her, deciding the end should be replayed. With her first delivery on the replay, Miss Steele drew shot to reverse a match winning lie. Mrs Pomeroy failed to change the situation, so the match ended with England winning, just as they would have done had the umpire not been over-ruled.

Mary Price's runaway win against Stella Oliver was largely responsible for the English success, and Norma Shaw's last end three which disposed of the Welsh rink in charge of world Singles champion Janet Ackland, made hers the only other England rink to win. Wales were well served by their teams skipped by Ann Dainton and Rita Jones.

The next day Scotland had little difficulty in defeating Ireland, but went down to Wales with Janet Ackland leading the charge with a comprehensive 27-6 success over Ann Watson's four. England's 149-75 win over Ireland included another massive win for Mary Price and her colleagues Sharon Rickman, Phoebe Spence and Beryl Alderson, who scored a maximum eight in their 39-9 destruction of Nan Allely's four.

On the closing day, the Price rink routed Scotland's rink skipped by Annette Evans by 37-10 — a result in marked contrast to the Scottish four's opening game which they had won 40-9 against Ireland's luckless Marie Martin. The Price team's victory settled the England-Scottish game, for the Scots won on three other rinks, tied on one and lost by a shot on the other.

All in all England could thank Mrs Price and her partners for winning the series. During the week England won on nine rinks, lost on seven and tied on two — hardly the form of champions.

Most successful rinks, apart from Mrs Price's were those of Nan Gibson (Ireland) and Liz Wren (Scotland), who also won their three games.

Teams England: B. Alderson (Teesside), T. Barton (Croydon), M. Bennett (Richmond), E. Bessell (Yeovil), V. Branson (Darlington), P. Davis (Croydon), M. Dyer (Clevedon), G. Haney (Spalding), C. Hiom (Boston), L. Jarman (Cambridge Chesterton), W. Line (Atherley), E. Logan (Mansfield), I. Molyneux (Cherwell), M. Price (Desborough, Maidenhead), E. Read (Cherwell), S. Rickman (King George), E. Schooling (Essex County), N. Shaw (Teesside), P. Spence (Teesside), M. Steele (Egham), B. Stubbing (York), G. Thomas (West Cornwall), B. Trafford (Cherwell), P. Ward (Croydon), S. White (Picketts Lock).

Ireland: N. Allely (Belfast), E. Bell (Belfast), E. Burton (Belfast), M. Murphy (County Antrim), A. Doggart (Belfast), A. Elliott (Provincial Towns), F. Elliott (Belfast), M. Ferris (Belfast), M. Fearon (County Antrim), N. Gibson (Belfast) E. Gordon (Belfast), H. Hamilton (Belfast), M. Johnston (Provincial Towns), J. Mulholland (Provincial Towns), A. Maguiness (Belfast), K. Megrath (Belfast), M. Martin (Belfast), B. McKreag (Belfast), P. Nolan (Belfast) O. Paisley(County Antrim), M. Scott (Belfast), D. Turner (Belfast), M. Tosh (Provincial Towns), K. Toner (Belfast), M. Wilkinson (County Antrim), M. Wilson (Belfast.

Wales: J. Ackland (Vale of Glamorgan), S. Britton (Vale of Glamorgan), D. cooper (Merthyr), P. Czernecki (Merthyr), A. Dainton (Vale of Glamorgan), J. Evans (Merthyr), L. Evans (Swansea), S. Froud (Vale of Glamorgan), P. Griffiths (Merthyr), V. Howell (Merthyr), N. Hopkins (Rhondda), M. Hughes (Earlswood), A. John (Vale of Glamorgan), P. John (Cardiff), M. Jones (Cardiff), R. Jones (Merthyr), J. Mills (Rhondda), C. Morgan (Ogwr), A. Mullins (Merthyr), S. Oliver (Swansea), M. Pomeroy (Cardiff), E. Schmidt (Cardiff), N. Shipperlee (Cardiff), A. Sutherland (Torfaen), M. Greenslade (Cardiff), B. Thomas (Torfaen).

Scotland: D. Barr (Ayr), J. Beaton (Cumbernauld), J. Conlan (Midlothian), R. Dante (Prestwick), A. Evans (West of Scotland), S. Gourlay (Prestwick), M. Hastings (Edinburgh), E. Kelly (Glasgow), E. Kirkwood (Falkirk), A. Knowles (Paisley), J. Lindores (Tweedbank), H. MacDonald (West Lothian), A. MacDougall (Cowal), G. McMahon (Blantyre), M. Mackin (Auchinleck), W. Milne (Glasgow), M. Mungall (Coatbridge), R. Neil (East Kilbride), F. Pearson (Arbroath), A. Scott (Ayr), N. Stirling (Edinburgh), L. Stewart (Cowal), D. Stuart (Inverness), A. Watson (Midlothian), L. White (West of Scotland), E. Wren (Falkirk).

Scotland 135, Ireland 88: (Scotland skips first) E. Evans 40, M. Martin 9; G. McMahon 19, D. Turner 11; M. Mackin 29, N. Alleley 8; A. Watson 12, N. Gibson 26; A. Knowles 9, M. Johnston 21; E. Wren 26, E. Bell 13.

England 117, Wales 115: (England skips first) E. Logan 15, (?) Jones 28; M. Steele 16, M. Pomeroy 23; M. Price 32, S. Oliver 9; B. Stubbings 21, A. Dainton 25; N. Shaw 18, J. Ackland 15; I. Molyneux 15, M. Hughes 15.

England 149, Ireland 75: (England skips first) Price 39, Alleley 9; Logan 19, Turner 17; Molyneux 17, Gibson 18; Stubbings 28, Martin 6; Steele 26, Johnston 9; Shaw 20, Bell 16.

Wales 123, Scotland 107: (Wales skips first) Jones 17, Wren 18; Pomeroy 23, Evans 11; Dainton 15, Knowles 33; Ackland 27, Watson 6; Hughes 23, McMahon 16; Oliver 18, Mackin 23.

Wales 137, Ireland 99: (Wales skips first) Ackland 30, Martin 10; Dainton 19, Turner 15; Jones 23, Alleley 17; Hughes 20, Gibson 21; Oliver 20, Johnston 17; Pomeroy 25, Bell 19.

England 119, Scotland 107: (England skips first) Stubbings 15, Wren 19; Shaw 16, Knowles 17; Logan 18, Stewart 17; Steele 19, Mackin 19; Price 37, Evans 10; Molyneux 14, McMahon 25.

Newton Hall Ladies Classic

at Blackpool Fylde IBA, March 30th - April 1st, 1990.

This three day tournament, which offered a £500 top prize and 15 other cash awards, was sponsored by Galaxy Holiday Homes, ended in victory for Jeanette Conlan who defeated England's Norma Shaw in the final by 21-17.

Thirty two women bowlers from England and Scotland competed in the qualifying competition on the first day to find eight qualifiers to play on the second and third days against England's Mrs Shaw and Mavis Steele, Scottish Singles Champion Elizabeth Wren and Mrs Conlan, Ireland's world indoor champion Margaret Johnston, Julie Davies (Wales), Eileen Thomas the Blackpool champion, and Gloria Thomas of West Cornwall, who replaced England's Mary Price, called home because of her father's illness.

In the earlier round robin play, Barbara Rawcliffe and her mother, Doreen Ward both defeated Mrs Johnston. Mrs Wren also failed to qualify, the Scottish bowler Sandra McLeish coming through from the first day qualifier to join Mrs Shaw in their section.

Edna Bessell of Yeovil completely outbowled Miss Steele in a quarter final and showed signs of achieving another near-whitewash, against Mrs Shaw in their semi final. Mrs Shaw then climbed back to within a shot at 14-13, only to lose more ends and face defeat at 20-15. But three successive twos put her in the final.

In the other semi final Mrs Conlan led Mrs Rawcliffe 20-12, but six ones and a two enabled the Blackpool Fylde player to get on terms. The Scottish player then draw shot to go through.

Mrs Shaw could not sustain a 5-0 lead in the final and Mrs Conlan, aided by a four, was soon ahead. The Scottish player then appeared to have the title within her grasp at 18-12, but Mrs Shaw responded with a two and a three to close the gap. Then Mrs Conlan steamed ahead again to win 21-17.

Results: Section A: Norma Shaw (Teesside) 13, Sandra McLeish (Midlothian) 21, Elizabeth Wren (Falkirk) 21, Arlene Colbourne (Blackpool Borough) 7, Wren 18, McLeish 21, Shaw 21, Colbourne 14, McLeish 10, Colbourne 21, Shaw 21, Wren 20.
Section B: Margaret Johnston (Ballymoney) 20, Barbara Rawcliffe (Blackpool Fylde) 21, Eileen Thomas (Blackpool Fylde) 21, Doreen Ward (Blackpool Fylde) 13, Rawcliffe 21, Ward 13, Johnston 21, Thomas 11, Johnston 12, Ward 21, Thomas 21, Rawcliffe 14.
Section C: Diane Wilson (Boston) 18, Joyce Jones (Blackpool Borough) 21, Mavis Steele (Egham) 6, Julie Davies (Wales) 21, Steele 21, Jones 14, Davies 21, Wilson 9, Davies 21, Jones 12, Steele 21, Wilson 19.
Section D: Gloria Thomas (West Cornwall) 21, Diane Hunt (Blackpool Borough) 12, Jeanette Conlan (Midlothian) 11, Edna Bessell (Yeovil) 21, Thomas 11, Conlan 21, Hunt 18, Bessell 21, Conlan 21, Hunt 16, Thomas 16, Bessell 21.
Quarter finals: McLeish 14, Rawcliffe 21, Davies 16, Conlan 21, Thomas 13, Shaw 21, Bessell 21, Steele 2.
Semi finals: Rawcliffe 20, Conlan 21, Shaw 21, Bessell 20.
Final: Conlan 21, Shaw 17.

Look ahead

SAVINGS PLAN

TERM ASSURANCE

FAMILY IN...

WHOLE-LIFE ASSURANCE

PERSONAL PENSION PLANS

LIVERPOOL VICTORIA INSURANCE
Providing your cover

ENGLISH WOMEN'S NATIONAL BOWLING CHAMPIONSHIPS

NATIONAL MIXED FOURS COMPETITION

CIS British Isles Indoor Championships

at Prestwick April 2nd-3rd, 1990

Graham Robertson's Singles success meant that within twelve months he had won both British Singles titles. After leading all the way against English champion Andy Thomson in a semi final he overpowered Ireland's Jeff McMullen in the final by 21-7. The Scots were happy to secure another double on the day for Colin Davidson, 19, from Bainfield, who works at the Bell's whisky factory, won the junior Singles, with victories over Wyn Matthews of Wales and Neil Booth, the Irish junior champion.

Booth had surprisingly defeated Mervyn King, twice the English junior international by 21-11, but he lost his way against Davidson and was outbowled by 21-80.

England's only success was in the Fours when Andy Thomson and his all-conquering team from Cyphers Beckenham — Martyn Sekjer, Terry Heppell, Gary Smith and himself retained the title. They had to struggle, however, in both their games. Against the Welsh champions, skipped by Phil Rowlands, they had to haul back from a 12-5 deficit before winning 20-16; against Irish opponents in the final — Richard Bell, David Johnston, Marcus Craig and world Fours champion skip Jim Baker they trailed again, this time by 9-6. Then came one of their winning surges when everything falls into place for these great bowlers. They scored twelve shots while the Irish could only manage one and finished 19-13 ahead.

The father and son English champions, skip Mick Tomlin and his son Martin faced Craig and Baker, two of the Irish Fours team in the Pairs final. This produced a close game which the Irish won 17-12.

Wales had better fortune in the Triples to obtain one piece of silverware. Alan Rigby, David Mogford and Robert Price had victories over the English Triples champions from Mote Park, Maidstone led by Paul Barrett and over Jock Weir's Scottish three in the final.

Pairs: Semi finals: England (M. Tomlin Jnr, M. Tomlin Snr) 30, Wales (D. Forrester, J. Bonatti) 10; Ireland (M. Craig, J. Baker) 28, Scotland (M. Walsh, N. Gillies) 5. **Final:** Ireland 17, England 12.

Triples: Ireland (R. Bell, R. Gray, S. Allen) 16, Scotland (T. Mair, K. Williamson, J. Weir) 17; England (P. Barnicott, C. Hall, P. Barrett) 7, Wales (A. Rigby, D. Mogford, R. Price) 18.
Final: Wales 27, Scotland 16.

Fours: Semi finals: England (M. Sekjer, T. Heppell, G. Smith, A. Thomson) 20, Wales (D. Harding, K. Rowlands, N. Leigh, P. Rowlands) 16; Ireland (R. Bell, D. Johnston, M. Craig, J. Baker) 19, Scotland (J. Leckie, R. Etherington, N. Little, R. Robertson) 12.
Final: England 19, Ireland 13.

Junior Singles: Semi finals: M. King (England) 11, N. Booth (Ireland) 21; C. Davidson (Scotland 21, W. Matthews (Wales) 14.
Final: Davidson 21, Booth 8.

Singles: Semi finals: A. Thomson (England) 12, G. Robertson (Scotland) 21; J. McMullan (Ireland) 21, P. Rowlands (Wales) 15.
Final: Robertson 21, McMullan 7.

CIS British Isles Indoor Internationals

at Prestwick, April 4th-6th, 1990

England's success which gave them their seventh win in eight years was achieved though they lost by 25 shots to Scotland in the final game of the series.

Massive victories over Wales and Ireland and Scotlands defeat by Wales meant that England had only to avoid being beaten by 48 shots to retain the championship.

They achieved this for although England's rinks skipped by Pip Branfield and John Bell lost heavily to Alan Campbell and Willie Wood resepctively, those of David Bryant, David Ward and Andy Thomson all won and Allcock was only three behind, to leave the Scots well short of their target.

Earlier England had beaten Ireland by 38 shots, the foundations of this victory being laid by Bell's four who crushed David Copkill's rink by 29-10. Even a 20-17 defeat for David Bryant's four against Steven Adamson, making his debut as an Irish skip made no difference to the result.

Scotlands' were beaten by Wales the next day after a dour game with John Price's ten shot victory over Angus Blair representing the difference between the two teams. The efforts Wales made in this frame appeared to have exhausted them mentally the next day for they foundered by 153-98 to England. Only a victory by David Wilkins over John Bell lightened Welsh gloom.

The Scotland-England match was a special occasion for Bryant who was making his 75th indoor international appearance for England and was presented with a crystal decanter by EIBA President Tony Ward and team manager Peter Brimble.

England 125, Ireland 87 (England skips first) A. Thomson 20, J. Nutt 20; D. Ward 21, B. Dunlop 10; P. Branfield 18, J. Baker 15; J. Bell 29, D. Corkill 10; A. Allcock 20, S. Allen 12; D. Bryant 17, S. Adamson 20.

Wales 119 Scotland 109 (Wales skips first) G. Jones 23, R. Corsie 17; T. Sullivan 17, R. McCulloch 19; L. Webley 22, A. Campbell 17; D. Wilkins 16, W. Wood 24; P. Robins 17, R. Provan 18; J. Price 24, A. Blair 14.

England 153, Wales 98 (England skips first) A. Allcock 34, P. Robins 13; D. Bryant 26, J. Price 20; A. Thomson 30, G. Jones 11; D. Ward 23, T. Sullivan 15; P. Branfield 24, L. Webley 21; J. Bell 16, D. Wilkins 18.

Scotland 112, Ireland 101 (Scotland skips first) R. Provan 23, S. Allen 12; A. Blair 22, S. Adamson 10; R. Corsie 23, J. Nutt 19; R. McCulloch 17, B. Dunlop 21; A. Campbell 12, J. Baker 22; W. Wood 15, D. Corkill 17.

Wales 123, Ireland 114 (Wales skips first) L. Webley 23, J. Baker 15; D. Wilkins 20, D. Corkill 20; P. Robins 12, S. Allen 27; J. Price 30, S. Adamson 14; G. Jones 20, J. Nutt 19; T. Sullivan 18, B. Dunlop 19.

Scotland 134, England 109 (Scotland skips first) A. Campbell 29, P. Branfield 11; W. Wood 28, J. Bell 11; R. Provan 23, A. Allcock 20; A. Blair 18, D. Bryant 24; R. Corsie 19, A. Thomson 20; R. McCulloch 17, D. Ward 23.

England: J. Ottaway (Wymondham Dell), C. Simpson (Hartlepool), G. Harrington (Isis), J. Bell (Cumbria). S. Palmer (Ely), R. Cutts (Ipswich), W. Hobart (Boston), D. Bryant (Clevedon) D. Holt (Blackpool Borough), K. Renwick (Preston), M. King

(Hunstanton) A. Allcock (Bentham). G.R. Smith (Sunderland), R. Gass (Cumbria), G. Smith (Cyphers), A. Thomson (Cyphers). J. Rednall (Ipswich), G. Standley (Long Meadow), J. Lambert (Sunderland), D. Ward (North Walsham). B. Morley (Nottingham), M. Biggs (Thamesdown), W. Richards (Cambridge Park), P. Branfield (Clevedon). Reserves: I. Boyle (Richardsons), E. Hanger (Northampton), R. Kemp (Banister Park), J. Leeman (Stanley). Team Manager: P. Brimble Team Captain: J. Wiseman.

Ireland: S. Espie (Belfast), S. Brewster (Provincial Towns), J. McDowell (Belfast), J. Baker (County Antrim). A. Montgomery (Belfast), B. McBrien (Belfast), D. Livingstone (County Antrim), J. Nutt (Belfast). M. Dunlop (Belfast), C. Craig (Belfast), D. Gardiner (Belfast), B. Dunlop (Belfast). J. McMullan (Belfast), P. Davey (Belfast), N. Booth (County Antrim), D. Corkill (Belfast). V. Dallas (Provincial Town), S. Wylie (County Antrim), R. McCune (Provincial Town), S. Allen (County Antrim). R. McCutcheon (Belfast), B. Thompson (County Antrim), D. Newall (Belfast), S. Adamson (Belfast). Reserves: M. Craig (County Antrim), P. McGarrity (Belfast), W. Watson (Belfast), W. Loughrey (Provincial Towns). Team Manager: N. McQuay. Team Captain: D. Newall.

Scotland: N. McGhee (Auchinleck), F. Muirhead (Bainfield), B. Stillie (Cumbernauld), A. Campbell (Irvine). H. Duff (Auchinleck), W. Paul (Edinburgh), J. Muir (Irvine), A. Blair (East Lothian). W. Galloway (Edinburgh), S. Rankin (Auchinleck), A. Brown (Bainfield), R. Corsie (Edinburgh). D. Gourley Jnr (Prestwick). G. Robertson (East Lothian), P. Laidlaw (Teviotdale), W. Wood (East Lothian). B. McLelland (Galleon), J. Barclay (Glasgow), D. Clelland (East Lothian), R. McCulloch (Prestwick). W. Sullivan (Blantyre), I. Campbell (Lanarkshire), A. Marshall (Bainfield), R. Provan (Coatbridge). Reserves: D. Miller (Cumbernauld). B. Rattray (Alloa), J. Boyle (West Lothian). Team Manager: J. Summers. Team Captain: W. Wood.

Wales: J. Applegate (Rhondda), J. Wright (Vale of Glamorgan), J. Morgan (Vale ofGlamorgan) T. Sullivan (Swansea City). N. Williams (Swansea City), B. Pycroft (Vale of Glamorgan), P. Rowlands (Cardiff), P. Robins (Rhondda). W. Matthews (Llanelli), J. Wilkins (Swansea City), G. Jones (Torfaen). J. Greenslade (Cardiff), N. Collett (Cardiff), D. Wilkins (Swansea City), J. Price (Swansea City). L. Tanner (Rhondda), N. Leigh (Cardiff), J. Thomas (Rhondda), M. Jenkins (Merthyr Tydfil). D. Kingdon (Llanelli), M. Chard (Merthyr Tydfil), M. Prosser (Ogwr), L. Webley (Vale of Glamorgan). Reserves: N. Harris (Ogwr), G. Williams (Pembrokeshire), M. Hopson (Ogwr), J. Hoskins (Ogwr). Team Captain: T. Sullivan.

Carling Black Label British Mixed Pairs

at Llanelli, April 8th-9th, 1990.

All four finalists played well, but it was the magic touch of Tony Allcock that made all the difference in the final of this invitation event as he and Mary Price moved to a three sets to one victory over David Bryant and Norma Shaw. Allcock's famous running bowl was much in evidence.

Bryant chose to lead for Mrs Shaw, and gave her a good start in all three, matches. Women are not supposed to be so adept at the forcing shot, but, Norma showed once again that she can attack as well as most men. This may account for the fact that in the past decade she has beaten more leading men players than any other woman bowler.

In the final, Mary Price built good heads for her skip, and the Price-Allcock combination were always on top. They won the first two sets more easily than the score suggests, and, although they lost the third set, they regained control, and had no problem winning the fourth.

Bryant and Shaw had beaten the holders, Joyce Lindores and Willie Wood, in the semi final, and Price and Allcock gained a straight sets victory over Eileen Ball and Michael Dunlop.

Quarter finals: J Lindores and W W Wood (Scotland) bt M Johnston and J Baker (Ireland) 9-2, 6-5, D Bryant and N Shaw (England) bt A Sutherland and B Kingdom (Wales) 8-2, 11-5, M Price and T Allcock (England) bt M Mungall and H Duff (Scotland) 7-4, 7-4, E Bell and M Dunlop (Ireland) bt J Ackland and T Sullivan (Wales) 10-2, 0-10, 10-4.
Semi finals: Bryant and Shaw bt Lindores and Wood 6-4, 6-7, 11-3, Price and Allcock bt Bell and Dunlop 9-4, 8-4.
Final: Price and Allcock bt Bryant and Shaw 7-6, 7-5, 4-9, 6-3.

Women's World Indoor Championships
at Guernsey IBC, April 21st-22nd 1990

These championships moved to the Channel Islands for the first time with the superb Guernsey Indoor Club hosting the action under the sponsorship of the local Volkswagen dealership of St. Martin's Garage.

Fittingly the event was won by a local player, Fleur Bougourd, who took the title with a narrow three sets to two, to win over Scottish champion Liz Wren.

The opening day's play saw the twelve players divided into four sections of three with the top two coming through to the knock-out quarter final stages. Bougourd won both her matches in straight sets, beating Ann Sutherland from Wales and Ireland's Belle McKeag. Defending champion Margaret Johnston survived an opening match defeat from Wren to move through to the knock-out stages along with the Scottish champion, while last year's beaten finalist Mavis Steele of England also reached the quarter finals.

Bougourd then set the event alight with a three sets to one quarter final win over defending champion Margaret Johnston and then hit back in her semi final clash with Scotland's Jeanette Conlan for a best of five sets win. That put her through to a final clash with the other Scot in the field, Liz Wren, who had also recovered from two sets to one down to beat Mavis Steele. The final turned into a 40-end marathon, before the Channel Islander took the title.

Quarter finals: F. Bougourd (Guernsey) bt M. Johnston (Ireland__) 7-1,7-6,3-7,7-6; J. Conlan (Scotland) bt E. Gordon (Ireland) 7-2,7-1,7-3; E. Wren (Scotland) bt A. Sutherland (Wales) 5-7,7-4,1-7,7-2,7-4; M. Steele (England) bt S. Froud (Wales) 7-3,2-7,7-6,7-6.
Semi finals: Wren bt Steele 7-5,1-7,0-7,7-6,7-6; Bougourd bt Conlan 3-7,7-1,3-7,7-2,7-1
Final: Bougourd bt Wren 6-7,7-6,7-5,4-7,7-2.

City of Westminster International Singles
At Paddington BC, June 24th 1990

Prize money: Winner £1,500, Runner-up £600. Semi finalists £350, Others £250.

Tony Allcock proved the most consistent of twelve leading British players who contested this annual event presented and sponsored annually by Westminster City Council, supported by Otis Elevators. Throughout the day, the form book was turned upside down, sometimes from match to match, one of the factors being the nature of the green, which was rather woolly in places, following heavy rain the day before. Local experts could master it no better than the visitors. John Chubb, who won the Greater London championship on the green in September 1989, lost both his games, and home-based Gerry Smyth reseeded to the England side, also failed to reach the semi final stage.

Indeed Allcock himself had varying fortunes. He lost his opening game in his round robin section to Gary Smith, who had already been beaten by national Singles champion John Ottaway.

Allcock then secured his semi final place with a seven-shot victory over Ottaway, who had defeated him at Worthing in a national Singles semi final the year before. Allcock then paid off another old score by overwhelming Andy Thomson, allowing him only four shots. (Thomson had defeated him in the national indoor Singles final both in 1988 and 1989).

In the other half of the competition, both reigning world champions, David Bryant (outdoor) and Welshman John Price (indoor), faltered. Smyth defeated Price and both lost to the Welshman's predecessor, Scotsman Richard Corsie. Bryant, after beating Ireland's David Corkill, could manage only two shots against Rees. The Rees v Corsie semi final produced the best match of the day. Rees opened strongly and built an 11-4 lead with the aid of two fours. Then Corsie found the immaculate touch and length which won him the world indoor title in 1989, and for a time little went right for Rees. With the score standing at 14-13, Corsie drew three shots which appeared good enough for game, but the stolid Rees, unmoved, cut out two which left the score at 14-14 and all to play for on the last end. Corsie opted for a long end which suited Rees, who had tended to bowl through on shorter distances. The vital shot went to him after Corsie moved the jack in vain.

Allcock dominated the start of the final, building a 11-0 lead as Rees struggled to find length and just missed with forcing shots. A whitewash loomed. Then Rees struck form, and as he forced his way back into the game Allcock lost direction. At 12-12 Rees appeared the likely winner. Then Allcock nicked the jack, easing it to back woods for a rather surprising count of three which was decisive. Councillor David Avery, the Lord Mayor of Westminster, presented the prizes. Allcock, the winner in 1988, became the first player to win this tournament twice. Previous winners: 1985 Jim Baker (Ireland), 1986 Steve Halmai (England), 1987 Andy Thomson (England), 1989 David Bryant.

Round Robins. Section A: D. Corkill (Ireland) 12, S. Rees (Wales) 15; D. Bryant (England) 15, Corkill 10; Rees 15, Bryant 2, Rees qualified. Section B: J. Price (Wales) 11, G. Smyth (England) 15; R. Corsie (Scotland) 15, Price 13; Corsie 15, Smyth 11. Section C: W. Richards (England) 15, J. Chubb (Greater London champion) 6; A. Thomson (England) 15, Chubb 6; Thomson 15, Richards 12. Section D: G. Smith (England) 6, J. Ottaway (England) 15; A. Allcock (England) 14, Smith 15; Allcock 15, Ottaway 8.
Semi finals: Allcock 15, Thomson 4; Rees 15, Corkill 14.
Final: Allcock 15, Rees 12.

British Isles Women's International Series
at Saundersfoot BC, Dyfed, June 25th-27th 1990

England retained the Eve Trophy, winning all their three games, but they had less to spare than the final league table indicates. Ireland were without a win but came close to success each day, their total debit balance being only 19 shots.

In the first encounter of the series, Ireland recovered from a 26-shot deficit against England and very nearly stole the game. It was as well for England that Mavis Steele and her colleagues Jean Baker, Dorothy Lewis and Jayne Roylance stood firm on the last end of their game with an Irish four skipped by the charismatic Margaret Johnston, who had climbed back from 20-7 behind to level at 20-all. On the last end England's new lead Jean Baker, the 1989 Singles champion, planted one on the jack, where it survived in a close head, and the three shots England eventually scored made all the difference. From an England viewpoint, there was also an encouraging performance from another newly constituted rink which had Margaret Heggie skipping for the first time, with Brenda Atherton, Ann Erridge and Wendy Line as her partners. They recovered from 8-0 down to defeat Ireland's Hilda Hamilton, Ann McGuinness, Phyllis McDermott and Eileen Bell by 20-12.

Narrow wins for Phyl Nolan over Mary Price and for Marie Martin against Norma Shaw, plus Marie Barber's bigger success over Betty Stubbings, set alarm bells ringing in the heads of the English selectors, and the effect was visible the next day.

In the second match of the first day, Wales led 75-70 after 15 ends across the green and appeared poised for victory with only a few ends left to play. Then the Scots rallied across the green to finish 112-107 ahead. This match hinged on the game between rinks skipped by the Welsh world Singles champion Janet Ackland and Scotland's Joyce Lindores. Mrs Ackland scored a four and a six in a winning run of 12 shots, but Mrs Lindores won four of the last five ends to cut her opponent's lead from 21-10 to 21-16 and save Scotland's day.

No such deliverance came the Scottish way the next day when they met England and were defeated by 23 shots. England made five changes, four of them positional, with Val Chapman coming into the side to the exclusion of Vera Ireland. Mrs Chapman replaced Ann Pascoe, who moved over to join Mrs Stubbings, and they had a good result, as did the other England rinks with the exception of Mrs Fuller's, which had won well the previous day, but lost this one to Senga McCrone.

The Wales-Ireland match which followed was another close-run affair. The Welsh position appeared comfortable enough over five rinks with Rita Jones and Ann Dainton in command on their rinks and others holding their own. But on the sixth, Pam Griffiths was in deep trouble and it looked at one point as if skip Margaret Johnston and her colleagues Mollie Scott, Alice Elliott and Joyce Mulholland would beat Wales on their own. They led the Pam Griffiths four by 22-5, on a green requiring a little more force than skilful drawing shots played into tight heads. But Mrs Griffiths and her colleages, noting solid Welsh performance across the green, stuck grittily to their task to win five of the last six ends and cut their arrears to eleven. This, with the credit balance achieved on other rinks, was sufficient to ensure a Welsh win by 103-94.

The need for players to fight for every shot in team matches was never more evident than in the Ireland v Scotland match the following morning. Ireland were outbowling Scotland on four rinks, but Nan Allely's was being crushed by Scotland's Anne Knowles, whose team was cascading close to 40 shots. Despite this, Ireland were still ahead across the green when Mrs Knowles and Mrs Allely began their last end. Trailing 37-5 but still smiling, epitomising the indomitable spirit not only of the Irish but of love of the game itself, Mrs Allely scored two shots which won her rapturous embraces from Irish supporters. It was no easy two. The jack had been moved close to the strings but Nan found the line and weight to draw shot. When Mrs Knowles was wide Nan, scampering up the green once again behind her bowl, drew another... two more precious shots for Ireland. According to the script this should have heralded a great Irish victory. But truth is stranger than fiction and it was not to be. Two rinks had still to finish. On both Irish skips Eileen Bell and Marie Barber were winning, but their opponents, especially if they have tenancious skips like Frances Whyte and Joyce Lindores, do not easily give up. To cut this story short, the Scottish ladies collected shots on the final ends — enought to give them overall victory by three shots and afford proof, as Houdini Bryant will tell you, that you must never relax.

Welsh hopes were high when the final match of the series started. They needed a winning margin of 14 shots to take the Eve Trophy from England and had much going for them. Bringing the British Isles to little Saundersfoot had been a big success. The club's arrangements had been excellent, the beautifully kept green had played well in spite of earlier rain, drizzle from time to time, and cloud which left it spongy in the mornings. The green had been packed with people every day with no seats to spare. The cash received from sponsors had been well spent. All that was needed now was a Welsh victory.

But it was not to be. The dream soon faded. England piled up shots ruthlessly from the start. On one rink Betty Stubbings led Betty Morgan by 10-1 at five ends and 17-1 by ten — a procession of a match which finished 31-8 in England's favour. On the adjoining rink, Mavis Steele led Pam

Griffiths by seven shots after ten ends and finally won by even more than Mrs Stubbings - no less than 39-10. The other Welsh rinks were not proof against this rout and all went down except Ann Dainton who defeated Margaret Heggie by seven shots.

England: Betty Johnson (Durham), Ann Pascoe (Devon), Pam Ward (Surrey), Norma Shaw (Durham). Norma May (Cornwall), Ann Snelling (Kent), Pam Davis (Surrey), Barbara Fuller (Herts). Eileen Vigor (Surrey), Vera Ireland (Cornwall), Gwen Daniel (Cornwall), Mary Price (Bucks), Jean Baker (Derbyshire), Dorothy Lewis (Leicestershire), Jayne Roylance (Norfolk), Mavis Steele (Middlesex). Margaret Osborne (Cambridgeshire), Moira Wellington (Devon). Joy Adamson (Surrey), Betty Stubbings (Yorkshire), Brenda Atherton (Nottinghamshire), Ann Erridge (Buckinghamshire), Wendy Line (Hampshire), Margaret Heggie (Cumbria). Reserves: V. Chapman (Norfolk), P. Green (Leicestershire).

For the game against Scotland, England switched Pascoe to the Stubbings rink and Wellington to Shaw's. Chapman was introduced as No.2 to Fuller's team and Snelling played No.3, replacing Ireland in Price's rink, Daniel moving to No.2. This team remained the same for the match against Wales.

Ireland: Hilda Hamilton (Saintfield), Ann McGuinness (Divis), Phyllis McDermott (NILS), Eileen Bell (Saintfield). Audrey Doggatt (Wedderburn Park), Dorothy Kane (Moat Park), Chris O'Gorman (Blackrock). Marie Barber (Blackrock), Elsie Arlow (Coleraine), Winnie Millar (Coleraine), Margaret Ferris (Cliftonville), Nan Allely (Donaghadee). Molly Scott (Belmont), AliceElliott (Dunlace), Joyce Mulholland (Dunlace), Margaret Johnston (Ballymoney). Margaret Tosh (Portsteward), Marion Hoey (Crumlin), Doreen Turner (Holywood), Phyl Nolan (Blackrock), Maureen Montgomery (Cavehill), Kath Toner (Falls), Isa Hanna (Mossley), Marie Martin (Wingrave). Reserves: Betty Craig (Deramore), Lottie Clarke (Divis).

Against Wales, Allely's rink was reconstituted, Clarke leading and Arlow moving to No.2. In Martin's rink Craig played No.3 and Hanna moved to No.2. Millar and Toner were dropped but played the next day against England, Arlow and Scott coming out. Millar played No.2 to Johnston, Elliott moving to lead. In Bell's rink, Hamilton went to No.3, McGuinness switching to lead. Allely's rink changed once again, McDermott coming in at No.3.

Scotland: Jeanette Thomson (Overtown & Waterloo), Ellen Halldane (Melrose), Dorothy Barr (Ayr Forehill), Margaret Mackin (Muirhead). Margaret Yule (Rosehearty), Ann Watson (Loanhead MW), Janice Maxwell (Castle Douglas), Joyce Lindores (Ettrick Forest). Jan McBridge (Arthurlie), Margaret Letham (Bunbank Hamilton), Rena Dickson (Cambus), Helen Mason (Bothwell). Nan Stirling (Corstophine), Nessie Penwright (Inverness), Betty Forsyth (Blantyre), Anne Knowles (Kilbarchan). Isobel McPhee (Orbiston)m Helen Weathers (Fochabers), Sarah Gourlay (Annbank), Frances Whyte (Priorscroft). Rose-Ena Dante (Ayr Craigie), Margaret Shearer (Carnwath), Betty Smith (LWA Galston), Senga McCrone (Hawick). Reserves: Mary Reid (Ayr Northfield), Kath Methven (Ladybank).

For the match against England, Reid displaced Watson in the Lindores rink, and Methven came in for Thomson with Mackin.

Wales: Pam John (Sophia Gardens), Pat Czarnecki (Gilfach Bargoed), Mary Hughes (Skewen), Betty Morgan (Llandrindod Wells). Ann Lewis (Saundersfoot), Edwina Owen (Knighton), Val Howell (Merthyr West End), Ann Dainton (Barry Plastics). Ann Sutherland (Croesyceilog), Mair Marquiss (Tenby), Joan Warmington (Brecon), Stella Oliver (Llanelli). Jeanne Evans (Merthyr West End), Nina Shiperlee (Whitchurch), Linda Evans (Port Talbot), Rita Jones (Gilfach Bargoed). Nesta Hopkins (Porth), Eleanor

Schmidt (Sophia Gardens), Adah John (Penarth BV), Janet Ackland (Penarth). Audrey Mullins (Gilfach Bargoed), Brenda Mills (Llandrindod Wells), Margaret Rosser (Skewen), Pam Griffiths (Merthyr West).
Reserves: Marion Wintle (Aberystwyth Queens Road), Janet Bell (Knighton).
Bell replaced Pam John in Morgan's rink and Wintle took the place of Marquiss for the second game and the team then remained unchanged.
England 112, Ireland 105
Rinks (England skips first): M. Price 17, P. Nolan 19; B. Fuller 29, N. Allely 20; B. Stubbings 9, M. Barber 18; M. Steele 23, M. Johnston 20; N. Shaw 14 M. Martin 16; M. Heggie 20 E. Bell 12.
Scotland 107, Wales 100
Rinks Scotland skips first: A. Knowles 20, S. Oliver 17; H. Mason 19, A. Dainton 15; M. Mackin 14, P. Griffiths 16; S. McCrone 20, B. Morgan 12; J. Lindores 16, J. Ackland 22; F. Whyte 18, R. Jones 18.
England 119, Scotland 96
Rinks (England skips first): Fuller 15, McCrone 25; Price 25, Knowles 11; Stubbings 23, Mackin 15; Steele 19, Mason 15; Heggie 20 Lindores 19; Shaw 17, Whyte 11.
Wales 103, Ireland 94
Rinks (Wales skips first): Oliver 14, Barber 14; Ackland 14 Martin 15; Morgan 19 Bell 15; Griffiths 12 Johnston 23; Jones 23 Allely 13; Dainton 21, Nolan 14.
Scotland 115, Ireland 112
Rinks (Scotland first): McCrone 21, Martin 12; Mason 13, Johnston 25; Whyte 14, Bell 22; Macklin 16, Nolan 28; Lindores 14, Barber 18, Knowles 37, Allely 7.
Wales 92, England 157
Rinks (Wales first): Dainton 19, Heggie 12; Ackland 21, Shaw 25; Jones 21, Price 26; Oliver 13, Fuller 24; Griffiths 10, Steele 39; Morgan 8, Stubbings 31.

British Isles Women's Championships

at Saundersfoot, June 28th 1990

Liz Wren from Bonnybridge achieved a unique treble by adding the British Singles to the Scottish indoor and outdoor Singles championships she held at the time. Such a feat can be held as good a series of performances as the winning of medals at world championships at Commonwealth Games level, for it not only entails winning at grass roots level, but then beating the best.

Mrs Wren did not have matches all her own way to win at Saundersfoot. The Irish champion Phil Nolan battled all the way with great skill in their three hour marathon semi final and saved a match point before succumbing 25-23. In the other semi final England's 1989 champion Jean Baker recovered from a 22-17 deficit to win a 33-end game by a shot. In the final Mrs Wren, though finally imposing her game on Mrs Baker, had to battle for a time for every shot. Bounding up and down the green with great energy, Mrs Wren's game was in marked contrast to the more languid style of her English opponent whose drawing skills were not sufficient when under pressure. Mrs Wren constantly salvaged her position. Her 25-14 victory provided the Scots with their only success of the week, and prompted the reflection that it was strange indeed that she had not been included in the Scottish squad of 26 for the international series.

World Singles champion Janet Ackland skipped her colleagues Daisy

Wallace and Doreen Hall from Penarth Belle Vue, and Adah John to the Fours title over the Blackrock team from Dublin comprising Betty Dunne, Chris O'Gorman, Marie Barber and Alma Prodohl. The Welsh four, 18-12 behind with three ends to play, then scored 2,1,4 to scramble to the title. Mrs Prodohl unluckily gave away the vital four when the Irish champions were holding shot. There was another success for Wales in the Triples when Joan Evans, Brenda Mills and Betty Morgan from Llandrindod Wells edged ahead of England's Christine Webb, Jenny Andrews and Jayne Roylance by 15-13. The Welsh trio had been given a walk-over in their semi final as the Irish titleholders Hilda Hamilton and Eileen Bell from Saintfield were obliged to scratch because their lead Kath Megrath, omitted from the Irish team, opted not to travel to Saundersfoot for one day's play.

England won the Pairs title, Betty Johnson and Norma Shaw from Ropner Park, Stockton, defeating Irish internationals Alice Elliott and Joyce Mulholland from Dunluce by 19-16. The English pair led 13-1 but Mrs Elliott and Mrs Mulholland retrieved their position to go into the last end only two shots behind. They were holding shots, but Mrs Shaw saved the day when her delivery touched the jack, flicking it sideways to hide it and leave the Irish players in what proved an irretrievable position.

Singles:
Semi finals: Elizabeth Wren (Bonnybridge, Scotland) 25, Philis Nolan (Blackrock, Ireland) 23. Jean Baker (Derbyshire) 25, Rita Jones (Gilfach Bargoed) 24.
Final: Wren 25, Baker 14.

Pairs:
Semi finals: Alice Elliott, Joyce Mulholland (Dunluce, Ireland) 33, Marilyn Jones, Jeanne Evans (Merthyr West End, Wales) 2. Betty Johnson, Norma Shaw (Co. Durham, England) 18, June McCorkindale, Kate Chilsholm (Planefield, Scotland) 14.
Final: England 19, Ireland 16.

Triples:
Semi finals: England (Chrissie Webb, Jenny Andrews, Jayne Roylance, Norfolk) 23, Scotland (Margaret Holland, Anna Weir, Elizabeth Lessells, Cambuslang) 12. Wales (Joan Evans, Brenda Mills, Betty Morgan, Llandrindod Wells) w/o Ireland (Kath Megrath, Hilda Hamilton, Eileen Bell, Saintfield)
Final: Wales 15, England 13.

Fours:
Semi finals: Ireland (Betty Dunne, Chris O'Gorman, Marie Barber, Alma Prodohl, Blackrock) 28, England (Hazel Dobbs, Marjorie Curtis, Jo Hardy, Diane Whittingham, Sussex) 9. Scotland (M. Stevenson, A. Gallacher, A. Watson, M. Ward, Crookston) 9, Wales (Daisy Wallace, Doreen Hall, Adah John, Janet Ackland, Penarth Belle Vue) 24.
Final: Wales 19, Ireland 18.

Johnnie Walker International Singles Challenge

at Kilmarnock, Saturday June 30th, 1990.

Kilmarnock, claiming to be Scotland's oldest continuous bowling club, celebrated its 250th anniversary in 1990, and the birthday party got off to an appropriately prestigious start when eight of the top bowlers in Britain competed for the Johnnie Walker trophy.

The name-droppers of Kilmarnock will tell you that Robbie Burns enjoyed the ale if not the 'bools' at the club, and that the legendary W W Mitchell, who codified the game of bowls in the last century, delivered his first bowl on their sacred turf at the age of eleven. They can now add that their 1990 international challenge event was won by the world's greatest ever bowler for David Bryant, the world champion, looking as fresh and sprightly as ever, performed his well-known escape routine and walked off with the trophy.

Though he no longer dominates the national scene in the way he did in the 60's and 70's, Clevedon's bowling maestro can be relied on to raise his game when it comes to one-off events.

Against Jim Baker - Ireland's world championship gold medallist - in the final, Bryant ran the gamut of his extensive repertoire, winning 21-11; but had earlier qualified for the final after losing to David Corkill and only narrowly edging past Steve Rees.

Needing to beat Duff by at least six shots to head the section, his faint hopes faded even further when he slipped behind, 4-7, but a typical rearguard action brought him back into contention and eventually gave him victory by precisely the required margin, 15-9.

Section A: H Duff (Scotland) bt S Rees (Wales) 15-7, D Corkill (Ireland) bt D Bryant (England) 15-14, Bryant bt Rees 15-13, Duff bt Corkill 15-10, Bryant bt Duff 15-9, Rees bt Corkill 15-8.

Section B: J Baker (Ireland) bt T Sullivan (Wales) 15-2, T Allcock (England) bt R Corsie (Scotland) 15-9, Baker bt Allcock 15-8, Corise bt Sullivan 15-6, Baker bt Corsie 15-10, Allcock bt Sullivan 15-8.

Final: Bryant bt Baker 21-11.

3rd place play off: Allcock bt Duff 15-0.

NatWest British Isles International Championships
at Methilhill, Fife, July 2nd-3rd 1990

The hosts, Scotland, foundered in these championships, failing to reach any of the five finals. Honours were shared by England and Ireland who each won two titles, the other going to Wales.

John Ottaway, the English champion won the Singles. He has brought moving up the mat to play short ends to a fine art and used this ploy to good effect, first to overwhelm the Scottish titleholder, Colin Rae and then to edge past Ireland's Jim Baker, a former world indoor champion. The scoreline of 25-22 indicates how finely poised this match was until Ottaway's final delivery landed close to the jack. Baker, trailing 24-22 when the end began, produced a sweetly delivered drive which took out Ottaway's wood sitting on the jack. Holding two shots — the jack had remained where it was — Baker then saw Ottaway's bowl creep closer to get the single he needed. "My bowl was about a quarter of an inch from the jack when Jim drove it off, so I just had to draw another", Ottaway said later. In his semi final Baker had been fully stretched by the Welsh champion, Peter Toogood, an Englishman working in Wales.

Ottaway's success robbed Ireland of a Singles double for earlier in the day, Paul Moore from Lurgan had drawn accurately to the jack end after end, to win the junior title. His opponent, Alan Darling from Worthing was never far from the jack himself, but not quite close enough most of the time against a consistently accurate opponent. Moore nearly did not make the final. In his semi final he had trailed 21-16 to Welshman Mike Prosser, but finished with a 4,1,4, to win 25-21.

Ireland's other success came in the Triples when their international trio of Joe Whyte, Clifford Craig junior, and Ernie Parkinson from Ormeau edged out the English champions Paul Butler, Colin Knight and Andy Jordan from Southbourne by a single shot 17-16.

This was the same score the Irishmen recorded in winning their national title and one that will be etched for ever in the minds of their Southbourne opponents from a Sussex village who qualified to play for the English championship from an artificial outdoor green.

The Southbourne three, toiling behind for ten ends, began the 14th 11-7 down and won the next four with a 1,2,4 and 2 to go into the last end 16-11 ahead. Over what happened next... they will want to draw a veil. The British title slipped from their grasp. The Irish scored a six.

England took the Fours title to create a unique record for Martyn Sekjer and Terry Heppell from the Blackheath and Greenwich club. It meant that they held all four English and British Fours titles. They won the English indoor Fours title in 1990 for the fifth time in eight years as members of a Cyphers, Beckenham team in which they play in front of Gary Smith and Andy Thomson, and followed this with the British indoor championship. Heppell and Sekjer with John Chandler as lead and Jim Cross at No.2, did not find success easily. They were 19-16 down with two ends left for play in their semi final, but scored a one and two to force an extra end which they won against Ireland's Derek Mineely, Morrow Horner, Brian Sloan and Robin Horner from Belmont. Then their Welsh opponents from Abergavenny - Gethin Hill, John Evans, John Anstey, and his son Mark kept them on their toes in the final. The Welshman scored a four to cut their deficit to 22-20, to leave the Welshman requiring a three to tie on the last end. They could only score a one.

In the Pairs, the Welsh champions John Male and Mark Chard from Aberdare Harlequins were given a hard time in their semi final by Scotland's Gordon Wilson and Tommy Johnston from Winchburgh who started with a big disadvantage. Wilson's bowls were adjudged illegal and he was obliged to play with a borrowed set. He and his partner lost only by a shot. In the final, however, the Welsh combination were never headed by Gary Rees and Martin Graham from Bangor who had reached the final after a narrow victory over the English champions Paul Maynard and David McCathie from Essex County.

It was a disappointing competition for the Linlithgow club who had produced Scottish champions in two events. Both their teams lost. Billy Watson,

Graham Byrne, John Graham and Alan Old fell by a shot in a Fours semi final to the Welsh rink from Abergavenny. In the Triples, Malcolm McNichol, Ross Graham and Graham Laurie were well beaten by Parkinson's winning Irish triple.

Junior Singles:
Semi finals: Paul Moore (Lurgan, Ireland) 25, Mike Prosser (Ely Valley, Wales) 21; Alan Darling (Worthing Pavilion, England) 25 Roy Hendry (Aberdeen, Scotland) 6.
Final: Moore 25 Darling 14.

Singles:
Semi finals: John Ottaway (Wymondham Dell, England) 25 Colin Rae (Hawick Wilton, Scotland) 11; Jim Baker (Cliftonville, Ireland) 25 Pat Toogood (Bridgend, Wales) 20.
Final: Ottaway 25, Baker 22.

Pairs:
Semi finals: Wales (John Male, Mark Chard, Aberdare Harlequins) 22, Scotland (Gordon Wilson, Tommy Johnston, Winchburgh) 21; Ireland (Gary Rees, Martin Graham, Bangor) 17, England (Paul Maynard, David McCathie, Essex County) 15.
Final: Wales 21, Ireland 16.

Triples:
Semi finals: Ireland (John Whyte, Clifford Craig, Ernie Parkinson, Ormeau) 20, Scotland (Malcolm McNicol, Ross Graham, Graham Laurie, Linlithgow) 10; England (Paul Butler, Colin Knight, Andy Jordan, Southbourne) 24, Wales Mansel Hughes, Gordon Harries, Dil Harries, Aberaeron) 14.
Final: Ireland 17, England 16

Fours:
Semi finals: England (John Chandler, Jim Cross, Terry Heppell, Martyn Sekjer, Blackheath & Greenwich) 20, Ireland (Derek Mineely, Morrow Horner, Brian Sloan, Robin Horner, Belmont) 19; Scotland (Bill Watson, Graham Byrne, John Graham, Alan Old, Linlithgow) 16, Wales (Gethin Hill, John Evans, John Anstey, Mark Anstey, Abergavenny) 17.
Final: England 23, Wales 21.

NatWest British Isles International Series
at Methilhill, Fife. July 4th-6th 1990

England won the international series once again — but once again they lived dangerously. In 1988 they lost to Scotland by 22 shots, but still won the series at Larne on shots aggregate when the Scots fell unexpectedly to Wales. Then at Worthing in 1989, England defeated Scotland by a shot in the key game. This time, however, the two teams tied. Still England's victories over Wales and Ireland were larger than those obtained by Scotland, so England won again on shots.

England's overall success required application. In their first game against Wales played in steady rain, they made a dreadful start, three of their teams — those skipped by Tony Allcock, Andy Thomson and Ted Hanger — failing to register a single shot while their Welsh opponents led respectively by Trevor Mounty, Spencer Wilshire and Terry Sullivan, piled on 25.

Hanger's rink, which comprised recalled Gerry Smyth and David Holt as front men and new cap Grant Burgess at No.3, recovered splendidly from 11-0 down and with the aid of a five, got back into the game to beat Sullivan by 24-22. Allcock and Thomson, both 7-0 down, hauled back and though Thomson finished two behind that did not matter, for Allcock finished strongly at 21-16 ahead, and rinks skipped by John Bell and David Bryant also won. England's other losing rink was skipped by reserve Martyn Sekjer, the national fours winning skip, who performed creditably enough to lose by five shots to Robert Weale and his partners Nigel Williams, Mike Prosser and Malcolm Bishop.

In the second game of the first day, Ireland produced a splendid four to keep Scotland at full stretch, though they eventually went down by 20 shots. Scotland's success was based on the runaway win of Graham Hood and his colleagues Willie Paul, Bob Dick and recalled Brian Stillie. They overhwelmed the strong Irish rink led by Jim Baker, the former world indoor champion, who with his colleagues Stan Espie, Paul Moore, the new Under-25 British Isles Singles winner, and Stephen Adamson, could do little right, and lost by 35-12. The Scotsmen's tally included four threes, two fours and a five. Elsewhere the teams cancelled each other out.

The second day's opening clash between Ireland and Wales produced an absorbing game. Baker's rink redeemed itself with a 27-11 victory over Weale's four. Baker scored eight shots on the last three ends. Wales still appeared to be controlling the game but the searing Irish finish across the green had them in trouble. With one end left for play, Bryan Kingdon, the Welsh No.3 in Spencer Wilshire's rink, trailed the jack to hold a two which Willie Watson, the Irish skip just failed to disturb to leave Wales ahead by one shot 109-108.

The suspense of the day was not yet over for in the afternoon England and Scotland provided another razor edge finish. This annual confrontation, usually the one which decides the destination of the championship, is always keenly fought.

England brought David Ward back to their team for this game. He had missed the opening game against Wales owing to a back complaint and had been replaced by Sekjer, a reserve.

The match was keenly fought, with Scotland having the edge on four rinks and Willie Wood and his partners Hugh Duff, Ian Laird and George Adrain, doing best against John Bell's rink. England were bailed out by Allcock and his colleagues Alan Darling, the national Under-25 champion, Cliff Simpson, and recalled Tom Armstrong. They scored a seven to lead Doug Copland's four by 13-1 and despite dropping a five late in the game, finished 14 shots ahead. Also saving the day for England was Hanger's team which once again showed great character and scored a three on the last end with Hanger bowling a closing toucher to squeeze past Angus Blair by 19-18. The last rink to finish involved the teams of Ward and Hood who had figured in a similar situation a year earlier at Worthing. On that occasion Ward engineered the vital shot but it was Hood — No.3 in 1989, but skip this time, who scored a single which left the two countries level at 111-all. This meant that providing England and Scotland both won their closing games, the championship would be decided on shots average.

In the first of these on the third day's play, England finished 28 shots ahead of Ireland with David Bryant (restored as an England skip) and his partners striking a decisive blow with a 25-10 success over John McLoughlin. Allcock and Hanger also won to achieve 100 per cent records, and Bell, too, finishing ahead, Scotland needed a 24 shot victory over Wales in the last match to regain the title.

The task proved beyond them. Though leading by 19 shots at one stage, Wales were 82-77 ahead across the green at the 15-end mark, and though the Scots recovered in the final stages to snatch a 108-107 win, that was not enough. Once more for the eight successive year, England had won the championship — a proud record, but not as great as that of Scotland, who won every year from 1965-1977 except 1976 when there was no series.

Teams: England: John Rednall (Suffolk), Ron Gass (Cumbria),Jim Lambert (Durham), David Ward (Norfolk). John Ottaway (Norfolk), Roy Cutts (Suffolk), Gary Harrington (Oxon), John Bell (Cumbria). Gerry Smyth (Middx), David Holt (Lancs), Grant Burgess (Worcs), Ted Hanger (Bucks). Alan Darling (Sussex), Cliff Simpson (Durham), Tom Armstrong (Lancs), Tony Allcock (Glos). Brett Morley (Notts), David Taylor (Cumbria), Mervyn King (Norfolk), Andy Thomson (Kent). Iain Boyle (Yorks), Mel Biggs (Wilts), Wynne Richards (Surrey), David Bryant (Somerset). Reserves: Martyn Sekjer (Kent), Gary Smith (Kent). Team Manager: Mal Hughes (Durham).

Ireland: Stan Espie (Willowfield), Paul Moore (Lorgan), Steven Adamson (Dunbarton), Jim Baker (Cliftonville). Joe Whyte (Ormeau), Eddie McNalley (Falls), Martin Graham (Bangor), Ernie Parkinson (Ormeau). Rod McCutcheon (Bangor), David Gardiner (Belmont), Charlie Davis (Banbridge), Sammy Allen (Cliftonville). Victor Dallas (Coleraine), M. Reid (Balmoral), Jeff McMullan (Ormeau), Paul Smyth (Leinster). Clifford Craig Jnr (Ormeau), Bertie Nixon (Willowfield), John Nutt (Pickie), Willie Watson (Knock). Mervyn Jess (Banbridge), Stephen Brewster (Coleraine), Richard McDermott (Coleraine), John McCloughlin (Lisnagarvey).

Scotland: Willie Paul (Tanfield), Bobbie Dick (Duffus Park), Brian Stillie (Borestone), Gary Hood (Mauchline). Hugh Duff (Drongan), Ian Laird (Insch), George Adrain (Dreghorn), Willie Wood (Gifford). Ian Campbell (Houldsworth), Grant Knox (Armadale), Peter Laidlaw (Hawick-Wilton), Angus Blair (Haddington). Dennis Love (Dumfries), Brian Middlemass (Haddington), Richard Corsie (Craigentinny), Doug Copland (Perth-Caledonian). Willie Galloway (Gorebridge), Roy Graham (Lockerbie), G. Robertson (Tranant), Alec Marshall (Gorgie Mills). David Miller (Greenfaulds), Alan Brown (Gorgie Mills), Ian Bruce (Northern), Brian Rattray (Alve). Reserves: F. Muirhead (Deans), C. Rae (Hawick-Wilton) Team Manager: J.C. Jeans.

Wales: Nigel Williams (Gorseinon), Mike Prosser (Ely Valley), Malcolm Bishop (Brynhyfryd), Robert Weale (Presteigne). Allan McCarley (Brynhyfryd), Richard Cope (Newport Athletic), Robert Price (Brynmawr), David Wilkins (Pontrhydyfen). Gwynant Ellis (Aberystwyth), Stephen Rees (Old Landorians), Mark Anstey (Abergavenny), Terry Sullivan (Old Landorians). Andrew Atwood (Caerphilly), Alan Beer (Aberavon), Jeff Edwards (Lampeter), Trevor Mounty (Abertridwr). Philip Robins (Gorebridge), Phil Rowlands (Penhill), Bryan Kingdon (Brynhyfryd), Spencer Wilshire (Tonypandy). Dave Vowles (Dinas Powis), Ieuan Terry (Tick Tock), John Ellis (St. Fagans), Will Thomas

(Pontrhydyfen). Reserves: W. Mattews (Craig Merthyr), J. Thomas (Ystradfechan). Captain: W. Thomas. Team Manager: G. Humphreys.__

Results: Rink scores: (England skips first) Sekjer 15, Weale 20; Bell 23, Wilkins 13; Hanger 24, Sullivan 22; Allcock 21, Mounty 16; Thomson 19, Wilshire 21; Bryant 21, Thomas 16.

England 123, Wales 108.

Rink scores: (Scotland skips first) Hood 35, Baker 13; Wood 17, Parkinson 18; Blair 16, Allen 18; Copland 14, Smyth 14; Marshall 16, Watson 18; Rattray 21, McCloughlin 18, Scotland 119, Ireland 99.

Rink scores: (Wales skips first) Wilshire 23, Watson 15; Thomas 18, McCloughlin 17; Weale 11, Baker 17; Wilkins 17, Parkinson 18; Sullivan 17, Allen 18; Mounty 23, Smyth 13. Wales 109, Ireland 108.

Rink scores: (Scotland skips first) Marshall 17, Thomson 15; Rattray 20, Bryant 19; Hood 21, Ward 16; Wood 20, Bell 13; Blair 18, Hanger 19; Copland 15, Allcock 29. Scotland 111, England 111.

Rink scores: (England skips first) Hanger 25, Allen 14; Allcock 18, Smyth 17; Thomson 15, Watson 21; Bryant 25, McCloughlin 10; Ward 18, Baker 18; Bell 23 Parkinson 16. England 124, Ireland 96.

Rink scores: (Scotland skips first) Blair 15, Sullivan 12; Copland 21, Mounty 22; Marshall 19, Wilshire 18; Rattray 19, Thomas 16; Hood 17, Weale 19; Wood 17, Wilkins 20. Scotland 108 Wales 107.

Summary (table to be done at Micropress)

Civil Service Internationals

at Northfield, Ayr, July 9th — 12th 1990

England, bottom of the table in 1989, won the championship Golden Jubilee Trophy, with defending champions, Wales, sharing the runners-up place with Ireland.

Singles: John Searle (England) bt Peter Howells (Wales)

Pairs: K. Hogg, C. Williamson (N. Ireland) bt J. Courtley, T. West (England).

Triples: P. Whitely, V. Lyons, M. Gale (England) bt A. Griffiths, L. Morgan, J. Kendall (Wales).

Fours: J. Whyte, J. Cummings, G. Beggs, B. Nixon (N. Ireland) bt A. Griffiths, L. Morgan, J. Gardiner, J. Kendall (Wales).

Western Mail Double Fours Trophy: Wales beat England.

British Isles Women's Under-25 Internationals

at Stoke BC, Coventry, July 21st-23rd 1990

England overcame Scotland and Wales to win this championship for the fourth successive year but were severely tested by Scotland in their opening game.

The Scottish girls led with six ends left to play across the green, but they recovered strongly to take over. Their rink of Sandy Crampton, Judy Platter, Lynn Sandoz and Katherine Hawes turned the tide from the 16th to 20th ends, scoring 16 shots without reply from Liz Wallace's Scottish four.

Earlier Scotland had survived a late challenge from Wales who they defeated by 82-72. Welsh indoor international Louise Thomas from Pontypool led the Welsh recovery in this game scoring 13 shots without reply on the closing ends of her rink's game against a Scottish four in charge of Helen Rankin.

But Laura Jackson from East Kilbride and her colleagues Alison Blyth, Andrea Goldie and Jacqueline Rarity rescued Scotland and continued in form against England, defeating England's Jenny Tunbridge. Wales were no match for England in the closing match which England won with plenty to spare.

Scotland 82, Wales 72: (Scotland skips first): E. Wallace 19, S. Smith 17; E. Murdoch 25, S. Mainsbridge 20; H. Rankin 10, L. Thomas 24; L. Jackson 28, K. Caul 11.

England 82, Scotland 75: (England first) S. Smith 18, H. Rankin 15; J. Tunbridge 17, L. Jackson 24; C. Anton 13, E. Murdoch 19; K. Hawes 34, E. Wallace 17.

England 128, Wales 61: (England first): J. Tunbridge 36, S. Mainsbridge 18; C. Anton 25, Samantha Smith 18; Sally Smith 39, L. Thomas 13; K. Hawes 28, K. Caul 12.

Wales v London Postal Region Post Office International

at Mansfield, Highgate, August 5th 1990

Wales and the Marches Post Office team beat London Postal Region 116-114 with the last bowl of the game.

British Blind Sports UK Singles Championships

at Girvan, Ayrshire, August 13th-15th, 1990.

Men: B1 - T Angoue (Wal) bt J Pryor (Eng) 21-20, T Pyke (Eng) drew with W McLeod (Scot) 17-17, N McTavish (Wal) bt C Craig (Scot) 21-7, Angoue bt McLeod 18-17, Angoue bt Craig 21-12, Angoue bt McTavish 21-11, McLeod bt Pryor 21-14, McLeod bt Craig 21-11, MclEod bt McTavish 21-12, Pyke bt Angoue 21-10, Pyke bt Pryor 16-15, Pyke bt McTavish 21-11, Pryor bt McTavish 21-17, Pryor bt Craig 17-16, Craig bt Pyke 21-9, 1) Angoue 8 pts, 2) McLeod 7 pts, 3) Pyke 7 pts.

B2 - K Bell (Eng) bt F Creamer (Wal) 19-13, T Brown (Eng) bt D Moodie (Scot) 21-9, J Barclay (Scot) bt S Davies (Wal) 21-11, Barclay bt Creamer 21-6, Barclay bt Bell 16-13, Barclay bt Brown 20-18, Barclay bt Moodie 19-17, Brown bt Bell 18-16, Brown bt Davies 21-0, Bell bt Moodie 17-16, Bell bt Davies 21-6, Creamer bt Brown 17-14, Creamer bt Davies 21-8, Moodie bt Creamer 21-0, Moodie bt Davies 21-4, 1) Barclay 10 pts, 2) Brown 6 pts, 3) Bell 6 pts.

B3 — K Brenton (Wal) bt B Fright (Eng) 21-9, R Skeet (Scot) bt D Hayward (Eng) 20-15, B Richards (Wal) bt W Currie (Scot) 21-15, Brenton bt Hayward 21-17, Brenton bt Skeet 20-13, Brenton bt Currie 17-14, Brenton bt Richards 21-3, Currie bt Fright 21-8, Currie bt Hayward 21-7, Currie bt Skeet 21-3, Skeet bt Richards 17-14, Skeet drew with Fright 17-17, Hayward bt Richards 21-11, Richards bt Fright 21-12, Fright bt Hayward 20-15, 1) Brenton 10 ptsd, 2) Currie 6 pts, 3) Skeet 5 pts.

Women: B1 — D Brockway (Wal) bt T Groves (Eng) 21-13, S Waters (Eng) bt E Walker (Scot) 21-4, G Hopkins (Wal) bt J Marshall (Scot) 21-7, Hopkins bt Brockway 21-9,

Hopkins bt Groves 21-9, Hopkins bt Waters 19-14, Hopkins bt Walker 21-3, Waters bt Brockway 21-17, Waters bt Groves 21-14, Waters bt Marshall 17-15, Brockway bt Walker 21-13, Brockway bt Marshall 21-10, Marshall bt Walker 21-3, 1) Hopkins 10 pts, 2) Waters 8 pts, 3) Brockway 6 pts.

B2 — C Myles (Wal) bt L McTavish (Wal) 21-0, J Howard (Eng) bt J Herbert (Eng) 21-7, A Fraser (Scot) bt E Etherson (Scot) 21-13, Howard bt Myles 21-20, Howard bt McTavish 21-3, Howard bt Fraser 19-17, Howard bt Etherson 21-18, Herbert bt Myles 21-7, Herbert bt McTavish 21-7, Herbert bt Fraser 21-13, Herbert bt Etherson 18-14, Fraser bt Myles 21-17, Fraser bt McTavish 21-0, Myles bt Etherson 21-4, Etherson bt McTavish 21-12, 1) Howard 10 pts, 2) Herbert 8 pts, 3) Fraser 6 pts.

B3 - O Simpson (Eng) bt M Elias (Wal) 21-13, M Lyne (Eng) bt B Scobie (Scot) 21-7, A Dunsmuir (Scot) bt W Tudor (Wal) 21-10, Lyne bt Elias 17-14, Lyne bt Simpson 21-13, Lyne bt Dunsmuir 21-8, Lyne bt Tudor 21-2, Simpson bt Scobie 21-13, Simpson bt Dunsmuir 21-10, Simpson bt Tudor 21-6, Elias bt Scobie 21-11, Elias bt Dunsmuir 21-8, Elias bt Tudor 21-14, Scobie bt Dunsmuir 18-17, Scobie bt Dunsmuir 18-17, Scobie bt Tudor 21-2, 1) Lyne 10 pts, 2) Simpson 8 pts, 3) Elias 6 pts.

Medal Tally: Men - England — 0 gold, 1 silver, 2 bronze. Wales — 2 gold, 0 silver, 0 bronze. Scotland — 1 gold, 2 silver, 1 bronze.

Women - England — 2 gold, 3 silver, 0 bronze. Wales — 1 gold, 0 silver, 1 bronze. Scotland — 0 gold, 0 silver, 2 bronze.

Wales Civil Service v England Civil Service

at Bristol Civil Service Club, August 19th 1990

Wales retained the Swaine Trophy with a 23 shot victory, England suffering their heaviest defeat.

Wales Civil Service 130, England Civil Service 107. Rinks (Wales skips first): D. Cole 35, T. Arnold 13. B. Kenvyn 21, G. Newman 19. B. Smith 26, A. Heathcote 9. D. Stratton 19, D. Hall 23. K. Dean 18, J. Searle 16. W. Jones (President) 11, J. Masters (President) 27.

Bristol and West BS Singles Test Match, Wales v England

at Sophia Gardens, Cardiff, August 29th-30th, 1990.

John Ottaway and Tony Allcock dominated the Test Match, carrying England to their second win in succession. Allcock dropped only two sets out of twelve, and Ottaway conceded only one. The turning point came in the second session, when the green was flooded by a sudden downpour. John Price, well in control of his match with Allcock, could not adapt as well as the new English champion, lost two sets and Wales had slipped out of contention.

It was just as well for England that Ottaway and Allcock were in such supreme form, because David Bryant took only one set in each game, while Gary Smith won five sets altogether and crept into the semi final frame for the Player of the Series play-off.

Smith, an England reject in 1990, surprised Ottaway, winning by two sets to one, and seemed to have the final sewn up when he took the first two sets against Allcock. Allcock, however, fought back and levelled the match at two sets all.

Trailing 5-6 in the final set, Smith needed only to draw to within four yards of the jack for a match-winning two, but lost his bowl in the ditch. At 6-6, the last end was exciting, and well contested, but it was Allcock who scored the vital single.

First Session: Wales 12 pts, England 12: W Thomas (6pts) bt G Smith (Opts) 7-3, 7-4, 7-6; J Price (4pts) bt D J Bryant (2pts) 7-2, 3-7, 7-3; P Robins (Opts) lost to A Allcock (6pts) 5-7, 3-7, 3-7; R Weale (2pts) lost to J M Ottaway (4pts) 6-7, 6-7, 7-5.

Second Session: Wales 8pts, England 16: Thomas (4) bt Bryant (2) 7-1, 7-6, 5-7; Price (2) lost to Allcock (4) 7-4, 6-7, 5-7; Robins (0) lost to Ottaway (6) 1-7, 6-7, 0-7; Weale (2) lost to Smith (4) 7-3, 3-7, 2-7.

Third Session: Wales 8pts, England 16: Thomas (0) lost to Ottaway (6) 4-7, 3-7, 5-7; Price (4) bt Smith (2) 7-5, 5-7, 7-2; Robins (4) bt Bryant (2) 7-6, 6-7, 7-2; Weale (0) lost to Allcock (6) 4-7, 5-7, 1-7.

Fourth Session: Wales 8pts, England 16: Thomas (2) lost to Allcock (4) 6-7, 6-7, 7-6; Price (0) lost to Ottaway (6) 4-7, 2-7; 3-7; Robins (2) lost to Smith (4) 2-7, 2-7, 7-6; Weale (4) bt Bryant (2) 7-6, 1-7, 7-5.

Result: England bt Wales 60-38.

Semi finals: Smith bt Ottaway 5-7, 7-3, 7-5; Allcock bt Thomas 7-4, 7-6.

Final: Allcock bt Smith in best of five sets.

Junior International England v Wales

at Ashton Gate, Bristol, September 2nd 1990

Young Welsh bowlers excelled at Bristol against their English counterparts in this first junior international between the two countries, winning on four of the six rinks. The results came as a blow to England, whose team included a number of players with good records in their highly competitive national game.

Wales were especially well served by rinks skipped by John Applegate, Alex Meddins and Jason Greenslade who had victories over English rinks skipped respectively by Kirk Smith, Jamie Mills and Nigel Smith. Kirk Smith was runner-up to Tony Allcock in the national Singles championship at Worthing ten days earlier, but he and his colleagues were well beaten by Applegate and his partners Paul Diment, Robert Wason and John Applegate, who soared from 6-6 to lead 21-6 and finished 26-10 ahead.

Mills, a Triples finalist at the English championships, finished six short of Alex Meddins's four and Nigel Smith, who had Essex colleague Paul Maynard, an England Pairs champion in 1989 at lead, went down 21-13 to Jason Greenslade's four.

Skips Steve Tuohy (Surrey) and John Leeman (Durham) piloted their rinks to victories, but encountered spirited resistance. Leeman's four led a Welsh team in charge of Jeff Wilkins, a son of international David Wilkins by 17-6 at ten ends, but the Welshmen recovered to lose only by two. Relatives of other internationals were also in the picture. Brian Weale, a brother of Robert Weale, and David Kingdon, a son of Bryan Kingdon, were in Michael Olivers' rink which found Tuohy's four in sharp mood.

Perhaps the Welsh victory was not as surprising as some critics seemed to think however, since the size of the countries makes it easier to select a Welsh team than an English one. Welsh selectors know all the eligible candidates who live in a highly concentrated area, and the players themselves all know each other extremely well.

The English team members, in contrast, had to be introduced to each other before the game began, and there was little prospect of them gelling into a unit, however skilful they may have been as individuals.

England 108, Wales 139 Rinks: (England first): S. Letts, B. Jenkins, G. Grace, K. Smith 10, P. Diment, R. Wason, J. Langley, J. Applegate 26; N. Westlake, J. Humphrey, P. Pull, S. Airey 18, G. Williams, J. Foley, N. Collett, B. Dennis 29; R. McKie, N. Luck, R. Shelley, J. Leeman 24, I. Slade, J. Evans, P. Coles, J. Wilkins 22; P. Maynard, S. Utting, I. Daines, N. Smith 13, N. Fleming, K. Jones, A. Matthews, J. Greenslade 21; T. Lee, R. Beard, N. Connor, J. Mills 20, G. Webley, J. Britton, A. Withers, A. Meddins 26; S. Leader, J. Williams, L. Miller, S. Tuohy 23, B. Weale, J. Stephens, D. Kingdon, M. Oliver 15.

British Home Countries Paraplegic Bowls Championship

at Cwmbran Stadium August 18th-19th, 1990

Singles: J G Robertson (Scot) bt A Bailie (N Ire) 21-5, S Mitchell (Wal) bt B Bagnall (N Ire) 18-17, A Wallace (Eng) bt V Robertson (Scot) 21-5, C Gibson (Wal) bt J Sellar (Scot) 18-12, K Bridgeman (Wal) bt B Faulkner (Eng) 18-10, A Hendra (N Ire) bt H Randall (Eng) 12-10, J Gronow (Wal) bt D Peacock (Eng) 13-12, J Ure (Scot) bt P Tyler (Eng) 15-14, J Miskelly (N Ire) bt D Dowling (Wal) 19-8, F Bell (N Ire) bt I Prior (Scot) 14-13, R Daft (Eng) bt H Haydock (N Ire) 17-9, P Huball (Wal) bt A Harvey (Scot) 21-2.

Pairs: P Tyler and D Peacock (Eng) bt J Masterton and J Ure (Scot) 14-8, D Dowling and P Huball (Wal) bt A Hendra and B Bagnall (N Ire) 9-6, H Haydock and F Bell (N Ire) bt R Daft and M Vicary (Eng) 14-2, A Harvey and I Prior (Eng) bt A Bailie and F Bell (N Ire) 13-3, P Huball and C Gibson (Wal) bt B Faulkner and J Dean (Eng) 22-3, J Jones and K Bridgeman (Wal) bt H Randall and A Wallace (Eng) 12-7, V and J G Robertson (Scot) bt S Mitchell and C Gibson (Wal) 12-3, J Gronow and K Bridgeman (Wal) bt A Hendra and B Bagnall (N Ire) 12-6, H Randall and M Vicary (Eng) bt J Sellar and J Masterton (Scot) 15-7, J Ure and J G Robertson (Scot) bt A Hendra and B Bagnall (N Ire) 7-6, J Dean and D Peacock (Eng) bt J Miskelly and F Bell (N Ire) 14-8, E Arnold and J Gronow (Wal) bt J Sellar and I Prior (Scot) 20-4.

Triples: Wales (J Gronow) bt N Ireland (F Bell) 6-3, Scotland (I Prior) bt M Vicary (Eng) 17-3, England (D Peacock) bt Wales (K Bridgeman) 13-5, Scotland (J Ure) bt N Ireland (B Bagnall) 5-3, N Ireland (B Bagnall) v England (B Faulkner) 10-1, Wales (C Gibson) bt Scotland (I Prior) 11-6.

1 Wales 24 pts, 2 Scotland 14 pts, 3 England 12 pts, 4 Northern Ireland 10 pts.

England

By Donald Newby

Each of the four major English championships produced winners of a double, an extraordinary situation which has never developed before, at least not in recent years. Lack of adequate competition is hardly an explanation, for to win most England championships requires an unbeaten run of as many as 15 games throughout a season — first through success in county or area events, and then in the cockpit of a national finals week. To win two out of four or five total events with matches played on different greens under differing conditions throughout a season is a notable achievement. First to set this ball rolling were Di Wilson and Jean Cammack from Boston who won the Pairs and Triples national titles at the Englishwomen's indoor championships. While this was going on at the Luton (SMCS) club, Andy Thomson was repeating his previous year's feat at Melton Mowbray in capturing both Singles and Fours titles at the Englishmen's indoor championships.

A similar pattern was seen in the summer at the outdoor championships. Gill Fitzgerald from the Kettering Lodge club not only won the Two-Wood Singles at the Englishwomen's events at Leamington Spa, but followed it by ousting Mavis Steele in the Champion of Champions. Days later, Tony Allcock at last exorcised the outdoor hoodoo which has haunted him by winning at last a national outdoor title — the Triples — with the aid of Andrew Wills, who was 20, and Jack Drummond-Henderson, a lithe and energetic veteran of 79. With this success behind him, Allcock went on to complete a double with a masterly display in the Singles final against Buckinghamshire's Kirk Smith.

Analysis of these events suggested that the results were not so surprising as they appear at first. Andy Thomson has proved himself a superb Singles player, using his experience as a skip not only to draw a bowl 'through the eye of a needle', but also to use destructive power when being outbowled. His Fours success — the fifth in eight years — was not merely a tribute to his skill, but to that of his colleagues, Martyn Sekjer, Terry Heppell and Gary Smith, all with international experience themselves. The fact that so many good players operate from the same club raises the question as to who is likely to defeat them should they survive to reach Melton Mowbray again.

Di Wilson and Jean Cammack are clearly quality players, and after their success at Luton they went on to win the British Isles indoor Triples title in company with Sheila King. The previous year Di Wilson had won the indoor Champion of Champions title. She and Mrs Cammack might well have added the British Isles Pairs title as well had they been permitted to compete in this as well as in the Triples.

Gill Fitzgerald, a bubbling character clearly in the groove at Leamington in August, came close to recording a treble, for she and her Kettering Lodge partners also reached the Fours final. Perhaps the current vogue of multiple success in championship weeks has a psychological root, any individual achieving a success generating an aura of invincibility which transcends possible physical and mental exhaustion and diminishes opponents.

England's domination of the home internationals continues indoor and outdoor. All four series, men's and women's, indoor and outdoor, were won. Indeed, of the 32 series held in the last eight years, England men have won the championship 15 times out of a possible 16 times and English women players count is 11 out of 16, a notable achievement. The other home countries would argue that such English dominance is inevitable given numerical bowling strengths, but it is sometimes easier to produce a good team in a given sport when the range of choice is limited. England success in the past few years is, perhaps, a tribute to the success of good coaching, good discipline, good selection and good management.

'Northern Echo' Bowls Festival

at Darlington IBC, December 26th 1989 — January 1st 1990

Five hundred men and women bowlers from all over the North of England occupied this Darlington green round the clock on each of seven days. Separate competitions are held for Mixed Fours and Men's Fours, but the highlight of the week is the prestigious and keenly fought 'Top Ten' tournament, with points awarded in Singles, Pairs, Triples and Fours series. An exciting climax saw last year's winners Sunderland, and host club Darlington, finish on 29 points each. Sunderland retained the trophy with a better shots countback - plus 75 against Darlington's plus 42. The winning ten bowlers were Jim Humphrey, Richie McKie, Jim Lambert, Bill Ferry, Norman Routledge, Bert Amos, Les Clennell, Dave Gibson, Ken Briscoe and Gary Smith.

Mackeson Fylde Classic

at Blackpool Fylde IBC, December 29th-30th 1989

Wynne Richards, who plays indoors for Middlesex and outdoors for Surrey, whose speed off the mat and apparent light-hearted approach to the game can confound opponents, had a field day in this event.

He outbowled two world champions — David Bryant and Richard Corsie, the 1989 title holder, and Tony Allcock, ranked No.1 indoor bowler, all on the same day. It demanded flair, concentration, consistency, and using every shot in the book. Richards displayed them all.

This was the fourth year this event has been staged at one of the most attractive and best designed indoor bowling clubs in the country, and success was sweet indeed for Richards, who received the trophy and £1,400 of the £3,400 prize money.

"I don't suppose anyone will ever do this again... beat the game's two reigning world champions and the No.1 ranked indoor player all on the same day", said Richards after his victory.

Section A: D. Bryant (Clevedon) 21, D. Colbourne (Whitefield) 10; W. Richards (Cambridge Park, Twickenham) 21, R. Millin (Freckleton) 15; Colbourne 21, Millin 18; Bryant 21, Richards 15.

Section B: R. Corsie (Edinburgh) 21, D. Lockhart (Timperley) 19; M. Gilpin (Kendal) 21, E. Rawcliffe (Blackpool Fylde) 19; Corsie 21, Gilpin 19; Rawcliffe 21, Lockhart 17; Corsie 21, Rawcliffe 5.
Section C: W. Wood (East Lothian) 20, D. Holt (Blackpool Borough) 19; J. Ottaway (Wymondham Dell) 21, V. Lee (Blackpool Fylde) 17; Holt 21, Lee 19; Wood 21, Ottaway 19.
Section D: K. Mitchell (Bolton) 17, S. Airey (Blackpool Fylde) 15; A. Allcock (Bentham) 21, G. Booth (Bolton) 9; Airey 21, Booth 7; Allcock 21, Mitchell 16.
Quarter finals: Bryant 19, Lockhart 16 (time limit applied); Wood 21, Mitchell 13; Richards 21, Corsie 15; Allcock 21, Holt 16.
Semi finals: Richards 21, Allcock 12; Bryant 21, Wood 10.
Final: Richards 21, Bryant 17.

Ely Festival

Finals at City of Ely IBC, January 6th 1990

International Jayne Roylance (North Walsham) was outbowled by Boston's Christine Hiom in the final of the Eagle Home Interiors Women's Open. A freak shot decided the men's event. Mark Entwistle, playing on his own green, defeated Gerry Coles when his drive, on target, bounced back from the bank to finish near the jack and win the deciding set 9-8.

Eagle Home Interiors Women's Singles: Semi finals: J. Roylance (North Walsham) beat E. Tunn (Colchester) 9-3, 9-3. C. Hiom (Boston) beat G. Evans (Ely) 9-2, 9-5. Final: Hiom beat Roylance 9-4, 9-0.
Trigon Men's Open: Semi finals: G. Coles (Falcon, Chelmsford) beat D. Cornwell (Ely) 9-7, 9-5; M. Entwistle (Ely beat G. Harlow (Ely) 9-7, 4-9, 9-3.
Final: Entwistle beat Coles 3-9, 9-2, 9-8.

Anglia Secure Homes Inter-Club Championship

Semi finals and final at Havering IBC, Hornchurch
March 3rd-4th 1990

In recent years the semi finals and final of this great competition have coincided with the closing stages of the Embassy world indoor championship which tends to take the limelight away from this grass roots shoot-out. With more indoor clubs sprouting up in England the championship increases in size every years, and it is even more remarkable that the City of Ely club, by no means one of the largest in the country, should have emerged the winners twice in the last three seasons.

Their 1990 success was achieved with victories over Newcastle in a semi final and then over Dartford Stone Lodge, who were competing in the final for the first time. In both games they owed much to Andy Blair's rink. Skipping Stewart Seymour, Andrew Easy and the experienced Fred Thurling, Blair had an outstanding 30-15 win in the semi-finals against Newcastle and then ensured victory in the final with a 25-13 win over Dartford's Paul Rose, Steve Cruikshank, Tom Lawson and Barry Warren.

Trevor Lowe skipped Kevin King, David Bell and Roy Harlow to a one-shot win over Norman Evenden's rink, while Ely supremo David Cornwell and team colleague Derek Cowling, both featured in 18-all drawn games. In the semi finals Warren and Evenden were largely responsible for putting Dartford through to their first-ever final. Warren gave Torbay's former England international, John Evans a 24-11 mauling, while Evenden beat Andy Crossman 22-12, as Dartford steamed to an 81-67 victory. It was a case of mixed fortunes for Ely in their match against Newcastle. David Cornwell backed Blair's victory with a very solid performance, skipping Stephen Palmer, Mark Entwistle and Greg Harlow in a 29-14 win over Jack Ferguson's four, while Stan Lant and Ian Spoor won for Newcastle. But at the end of the day Ely won 93-80.

Ely's success was rapturously hailed by their supporters,which produced this memorable comment from the chairman of the sponsors "Ah well! That's another quiet Sunday afternoon over." Ely's record in recent seasons is quite remarkable. They reached the semi-final stage in 1987, losing by just two shots to Boston, and went out in Round 3 in 1989 to Wisbech by only one shot. Their 27 matches produced 25 wins and two defeats, the worst performance being to lose by two. During this time, a shots advantage of more than 500 was accumulated — a testimony to great club spirit. Their selectors, always firm and resolute, deserve considerable credit. All three stood down from the team, though each, in his own right, was a contender for a place.

Semi finals: Torbay 67, Dartford Stone Lodge 81: (Torbay first): A. Bratcher, I. Burrows, R. Tolchard, J. Evans 11, P. Rose, H. Louch, T. Lawson, B. Warren 24; J. Burridge, B. Target, P. Day, A. Crossman 12, G. Booth, G. Pay, M. Gaimster, N. Evenden 22; A. Bowden, P. Bright, M. Friend, L. Bowden 19, D. Coomber, J. Campbell, M. Osbourne, M. Brick 17; P. Hackett, B. Lee, L. Fisher, R. Johnson 25, P. Reeves, S. Cruikshank, J. Evenden, R. Lewing 18.

Newcastle 80, City of Ely 93 (Newcastle first): P. Duffy, S. Harvey, M. London, B. Bone 15, S. Seymour, A. Easy, F. Thurling, A. Blair 30; N. Davison, A. Johnson, R. Dougal, S. Lant 22, K. King, D. Bell, R. Harlow, T. Lowe 18; S. Proctor, S. Hubbard, R. Train, J. Ferguson 14, S. Palmer, M. Entwistle, G. Harlow, D. Cornwell 29; R. Richardson, C. Davidson, K. Bone, I. Spoor 29, S. Tutchener, N.Spittle, A. Butcher, D. Cowling 16.

Final: City of Ely 80, Dartford Stone Lodge 67 Ely: A. Blair 25, B. Warren 13; T. Lowe 19, N. Evenden 18; D. Cornwell 18, M. Brick 18; D. Cowling 18, R. Lewing 18.

English Woman's National Indoor Championships

at Luton BC, March 5th-13th, 1990.

Gill Smith who took up bowling ten years earlier at the age of 37, displayed remarkable tenacity to become the new English Singles champion. In three successive matches she was close to defeat, in each case she hauled herself back from the brink.

Trailing 15-2 in the final against Sally Franklin of Wisbech, she bounced back, first by switching play to short ends after controlling the jack and then playing her opponent at her own game over longer ends. Her recovery, which enabled her to finish 21-18 ahead after a measure on the last end, was typical of her resistance to adversity throughout the day. In her quarter final against the young Surrey international Sharon Rickman she was 16-11 behind but produced a seering finish which included a four and a three.

Then in her semi final against Mary Watson, she trailed 13-7 before scoring 14 shots without reply. "We took the game up late", said Mrs Smith's husband Arthur after her victory in the final. This was true too of the way she reached the top.

Mrs Franklin, 23, twice an outdoor under-25 champion, a former national two wood winner and outdoor international, said earlier in the day that she was retiring from bowls for a time at the end of the season. She has two young children and her decision is one which many younger women in bowls feel obliged to take.

Norma Shaw won her 13th national indoor championship when she and her Teesside partners Edie McKenna, Phoebe Spence and Jenny Berry captured the Fours title. Four of Mrs Shaw's part successes have been in Singles and her nine team championships have all been achieved in partnership with Mrs Spence.

The Teesside four outbowled Dartford Stone Lodge in the final by 26-10. It has a disappointing conclusion for the Dartford team whose players Wendy Spicer, Joan Hill, Janet Tester and Denise Batchelor had also finished runners up in 1986.

Di Wilson and Jean Cammack opted to travel over 200 miles daily from Boston in Lincolnshire to Luton in Bedfordshire, where they were involved in Pairs, Triples and Fours. Their hard work was rewarded with a rare double, and they took the Pairs and Triples trophies back up the A1.

Although they lost in the quarter final of the Fours, the experience of the Luton green stood them in good stead, and they proceeded to sweep all opposition before them in Pairs and Triples — even though they were expected to play four games a day. Their achievement in the Pairs final was quite remarkable. Against the 1988 champions, Jane Rowntree and Gloria Thomas of West Cornwall, they turned an unpromising 10-4 deficit after 10 ends into a 22-12 victory.

In the Triples, with Sheila King, Wilson, a former national indoor Champion of Champions winner, and Cammack beat the 1989 runners up from Cambridge Chesterton, skipped by Dot Rolph, by 20-6 in the semi final, and ended the hopes of Ann Moore's Egerton Park, 22-12 in the final.

Teesside, who had accounted for Cambridge Chesterton in the 1989 triples final, were skipped by Norma Shaw, and had already collected the Fours title. They reached the semi final, but were surprisingly thrashed 21-10 by Egerton Park. England international Gloria Thomas compensated for her disappointment in the Pairs when she took the Champion of Champions title, foiling in the process a bid from Colchester's Brenda Brown to add the national indoor title to the outdoor one she won in the summer of 1989. Thomas's 21-18 semi final win over Brown was one of the highlights of the championships, and her 21-5 massacre of Croydon's Jean Deacon in the final was something of an anti-climax. Erewash, the Long Eaton club who play in a converted swimming pool, won the Over 55 Triples event, and Towerlands, based in Braintree, took the Unbadged Pairs.

Singles: First round - S Rickman (King George) 21, D Mascot (Chestunt) 15, G Smith

(Bentham) 21, S Comen (Essex County) 16, M Watson (Dartford SL) 21, E Trotter (Cumbria) 16, E Vigor (Croydon) 21, B Trafford (Cherwell) 3, J Roylance (North Walsham) 21, D Taylor (Grattons, Crawley) 7, N Edwards (British Cellophane) 21, N May (West Cornwall) 11, S Franklin (Wisbech) 21, D Hall (York) 14, J Tomlin (Boston) 21, C Lloyd (Havan) 4.

Quarter final: Smith 21, Rickman 17, Watson 21, Vigor 13, Edwards 21, Roylance 19, Franklin 21, Tomlin 11.

Semi final: Franklin 21, Edwards 20, Smith 21, Watson 13.

Final: Smith 21, Franklin 18.

Fours: First round — (Skips only) N Shaw (Teesside) 26, J Little (Nailsea) 19, H Bulcock (Norfolk and Norwich) 26, D Whittingham (Preston, Brighton) 13, T Barton (Croydon) 26, R Keeling (Egham) 7, B Trafford (Cherwell) 22, P Napier (York) 16, G Thomas (West Cornwall) 30, T Bennett (Atherley, Southampton) 8, B Fuller (Tye Green) 20, A Gildert (Rugby Thornfield) 19, D Batchelor (Dartford SL) 22, M Buckley (Desborough, Northants) 10, T Cammuck (Boston) 22, E Schooling (Essex County) 18.

Quarter final: Teesside 17, Norfolk and Norwich 13, Croydon 16, Cherwell 17, West Cornwall 21, Tye Green 12, Dartford SL 22, Boston 12.

Semi final: Teesside 20, Cherwell 15, Dartford SL 21, West Cornwall 18.

Final: Teesside 26, Dartford SL 10.

Pairs: Round 1: E Read and B Trafford (Cherwell) 15, J Hellyer and L Dabbs (Angel) 9. J Nunn and G Rednall (Ipswich) 20, S Sewell and P Wynn (Cambridge Chesterton) 14. J Rowntree and G Thomas (West Cornwall) 21, A Talbot and I Younger (Gateshead) 19. P Dahlgreen and A Gildert (Rugby Thornfield) 29, J Bancroft and M Fawkes (Arun) 13. D Ferguson and M Wregglesworth (York) 21, S Langdon and J Murrell (Minehead) 20. D Wilson and J Cammack (Boston) 30, D Wickenden and A Moore (Egerton Park) 15. G Hale and A Green (Egham) 25, B Alvey and P Ward (Croydon) 19. K Bright and B Grindrod (Barking) 17, P Tarbard and J Foster (Colchester) 13.

Quarter finals: Ipswich 20, Cherwell 18. West Cornwall 26, Rugby Thornfield 12. Boston 20, York 19. Egham 22, Barking 14.

Semi-finals: West Cornwall 24, Ipswich 7. Boston 25, Egham 11.

Final: Boston 22, West Cornwall 12.

Fours

Round 1: Teesside 26, Nailsea 19; Norfolk & Norwich 26, Preston, Brighton 13; Croydon 26, Egham 7; Cherwell 22, York 16; West Cornwall 30, Atherley 8; Tye Green 20, Rugby Thornfield 19; Dartford Stone Lodge 22, Desborough, Northants 10; Boston 22, Essex County 18.

Quarter finals: Teesside (N. Shaw) 17, Norfolk & Norwich (H. Bulcock) 13; Croydon (T. Barton) 16, Cherwell (B. Trafford) 17; West Cornwall (G. Thomas) 21, Tye Green (B. Fuller) 12; Dartford Stone Lodge (D. Batchelor) 22, Boston (T. Cammuck) 12.

Semi finals: Teesside 20, Cherwell 15; Dartford Stone Lodge 22, Boston 12.

Final: Teesside (E. McKenna, J. Berry, P. Spence, N. Shaw) 26, Dartford Stone Lodge (W. Spicer, J. Hill, J. Tester, D. Batchelor) 10.

Triples: Round 1: (skips only) — Egham (M Steele, MBE) 28, Folkestone (A Snelling) 6. Boston (J Cammack) 21, Westminster (M Geary) 6. Cambridge Chesterton (D Rolph) 16, West Mersea (J Willgoss) 6. York (B Stubbings) 18, Bentham (B Carey) 11. Egerton Park (A Moore) 18, Clevedon (M Dyer) 14. Atherley (H Phillips) 24,

Diss (P Barrett) 21. Teesside (N Shaw) 16, Croydon (M James) 15. Barking (B Maisey) 17, Exonia (H Mills) 10.

Quarter finals: Boston (D Wilson, S King, J Cammack) 18, Egham (A Green, L Brownlie, M Steele) 17. Cambridge Chesterton (L Jarman, J Gazeley, D Rolph) 19, York (M Moore C Sissons, B Stubbings) 16. Egerton Park (D Wickenden, D Carpenter, A Moore) 19. Atherton (K Martin, F Guy, H Phillips) 15, Teesside (P Spence, J Berry, N Shaw) 18. Barking (S Parmenter, A Moore, B Maisey) 18.

Semi-finals: Boston 20, Cambridge Chesterton 6. Egerton Park 21, Teesside 10.

Final: Boston 22, Egerton Park 12.

Champion of Champions Singles: Round 1: M Smith (Ipswich) 21, V Branson (Darlington) 19. J Deacon (Croydon) 21, N Cannon (West Berks) 19. A Burgess (Northavon) 21, J Tomlin (Boston) 8. S Whiting (Havering) 21, D Miller (March GER) 12. S Page (Riverain) 21, J Bowles (Preston) 8. G Thomas (West Cornwall) 21, P Poole (Malvern Hills) 14. B Ansell (Kent Ladies) 21, J Searle (Moonfleet) 10. B Brown (Colchester) 21, C Griffiths (Oldham) 11.

Quarter final: Deacon 21, Smith 17. Whiting 21, Burgess 18. Thomas 21, Page 11. Brown 21, Ansell 18.

Semi final: Deacon 21, Whiting 14. Thomas 21, Brown 19.

Final: Thomas 21, Deacon 5.

Unbadged Pairs: Round 1: J Morris and J Edson (Lincoln) 22, S Hall and J Tunbridge (Cambridge Chesterton) 12. P Terrell and S O'Nians (Bridport and West Dorset) 22, J Nunn and G Rednall (Ipswich) 14. G Whatford and K Strutt (Egham) 22, W Sowerby and E Bray (Cumbria) 17. J Reynolds and G Daniel (West Cornwall) 22, B Bates and M Stokes (Dartford Stone Lodge) 12. D Lewis and J Watson (Sutton) 23, J Webb and L Noke (Thamesdown) 18. A Kerslake and B Hart (Herts) 25, B Nunns and F North (Huddersfield) 12. M Dakin and C Duckworth (Towerlands) 25, A Moore and B Maisey (Barking) 14. B Pearce and R Durrant (Preston) 22, A Burke and P Withers (Bristol) 9.

Quarter final: Bridport and West Dorset 18, Lincoln 13. Egham 28, West Cornwall 23. Sutton 22, Herts 21. Towerlands 20, Preston 13.

Semi final: Egham 20, Bridport and West Dorset 14. Towerlands 25, Sutton 13.

Final: Towerlands 18, Egham 11.

Two Wood Over 50 Triples: Round 1: County Arts 17, York 13. Cambridge Chesterton 18, Exonia 13. Nailsea 17, Isle of Wight 16. Erewash 22, Erdington Court 8. Desborough (Maidenhead) 18, Preston 17. Essex County 23, Kent Ladies 12. Hartlepool 15, Sutton 12. Tye Green 24, Whiteknights 13.

Quarter finals: Cambridge Chesterton 17, County Arts 10. Erewash 22, Nailsea 10. Essex County 20, Desborough 10. Tye Green 20, Hartlepool 13.

Semi-finals: Erewash (R Message, J Kilyon, M McHowat) 19, Cambridge Chesterton (J Morgan, J Larter, D Rolph) 12. Tye Green (E Saxby, M Sheppard, B Fuller) 20, Essex County (J Leon, D Lonergan, S Cohen) 9.

Final: Erewash bt Tye Green.

Yetton Trophy
English Women's National Club Championship

Semi finals and final at Luton, March 10th 1990

Essex County won the Trophy for the second time in the club's history, although they suffered defeats on two rinks in the semi final against Boston and final against Torbay.

Rinks skipped by Shirley Cohen and Joan Leon went down by 13 and eight shots respectively to Mary Hewison and Dorothy Quinney in the morning, but Leon's four recovered their form in the final with a crucial 18 shots credit over Torbay's Vi Cutler. Dorothy Lonergan and Evelyn Schooling steadied the ship for Essex by skipping their ranks to big wins over the Boston rinks skipped by Sheila King and Jean Cammack (who had both been part of the winning triples team the day before) and more than made up the deficit.

In the final against Torbay, Schooling kept up her winning ways — (she has never been beaten in the Yetton Trophy), returning a useful nine shots credit over Wyn Alderson, but Lonergan lost by six to Clare Bolton. Cohen's rink went down again, 22-10.

Semi finals: Essex County bt Boston 83-67.
Rink scores (Essex County skips first): J Leon 16, D Quinney 24; D Lonergan 39, S King 10; S Cohen 11, M Hewinson 24; E Schooling 17, J Cammack 9.
Torbay bt Rugby Thornfield 81-68.
Rink scores (Torbay first): V Cutler 29, M Edwards 12; C Bolton 25, J Coyles 11; J Stevens 22, D Howes 16; W Alderson 5, I Rowan 29.

Final: Essex County bt Torbay 79-70.
Rink scores (Essex County first): J LEon 26, V Cutler 8; D Lonergan 16, C Bolton 22; S Cohen 10, J Stevens 22; E Schooling 27, W Alderson 18.

Liberty Trophy (Inter-County Championship)

Final at Melton Mowbray IBC, March 18th, 1990

Middlesex, first winners of the Liberty Trophy is 1975 and runners up in 1987 and 1988, recaptured the indoor inter-county championship with a clear cut victory over Norfolk. The East Anglians, who defeated them in the 1988 final, started well enough and led across the green by a shot after five ends, but fell away later on two rinks. On one Wynne Richards and his new partners Jim Wilson, John Cooke and John Sweeney, defeated John Ottaway, Ian Daines, Gary Blake and Tom Kelly by 24-11. This match was notable for a disastrous end for Kelly, a reliable skip throughout the season. The sides were level at ten shots each after 15 ends, but two ends later Kelly took out his side's only bowl in the head to lose a six. Neither he nor his partners recovered from this shot in the foot.

Steve Halmai directed Norfolk's demise elsewhere. He and his partners Robert Ingram, Brian Phillips, Ted Barton, as well as their Norfolk opponents Ian Wones, John Youngs and Peter Sabberton, ambled and pondered ends behind other rinks, and it was Middlesex who profited from this cautious approach. Halmai and his partners scored a four and a five during the last five ends and there was no need to play the last two. By that time Halmai's four were 26-14 up and Middlesex had won the trophy with 26 shots to spare, much to the delight of their female choir, which had been in full voice long before the end of this sporting carnival.

Earlier rounds to the quarter finals were played on a round robin basis with Yorkshire, Nottinghamshire, Norfolk, Worcestershire, Wiltshire, Somerset, Suffolk and Hampshire heading their respective sections. Middlesex reached the quarter finals with an 18 shot victory over Hampshire at the Desborough club, Maidenhead. Reg Paine's rink helped turn the match Middlesex's way, climbing back from a 10-1 deficit to score 17 shots against two on the last six ends.

Middlesex then met Somerset, nine shot winners over Wiltshire at Perdiswell, Worcester. David Bryant and Peter McCall were both beaten and it was left to Pip Branfield and Ian Middlemast to clinch a Somerset success.

Norfolk had plenty to spare over Worcestershire at Luton, where John Ottaway helped Tom Kelly's four to a 34-10 win. Lancashire proved too strong for Yorkshire at Newark as they sustained a notable challenge for their first County Championship success.

In the semi finals, Norfolk overcame Lancashire and ironically it was Kelly's rink which struck the decisive blow, winning 29-14 with a late surge which produced 13 shots for them on the concluding five ends. Norfolk finished 128-110 ahead. In the other semi final, Middlesex defeated Somerset by 124-109, their success owing much to Gary Little and his partners Steve Wheeler, Chris Yelland and Mick O'Keefe who built a 25-4 lead over a rink in charge of Peter McCall, and finished 32-10 in front.

Quarter finals: (winners rinks first): Middlesex 130, Hants 112: S. Halmai 18, J. Haines 13; G. Smyth 22, R. Shelley 19; G. Little 16, G. Standley 27; W. Richards 21, P. Line 24; A. Garcia 26, N. Shelley12; R. Paine 27, D. Miller 17.

Somerset 113, Wilts 114: G. Luker 16, I. Dainford 13; P. McCall 18, A. Moore 21; A. Apsey 13, J. Aylward 18; I. Middlemast 25, B. Fernandes 14; D. Bryant 14, M. Biggs 20; P. Branfield 27, H. Pryse .

Norfolk 144, Worcs 107: B. Howes 26, R. Stanley 14; G. Duns 25, G. Readman 17; R. Thacker 19, I. Jenkins 16; T. Kelly 34, L. Whitehouse 10; D. Ward 19, G. Burgess 21; B. Taylor 21, I. Maddox 29.

Lancashire 138, Yorkshire 101: R. Millin 27, M. Harrison 22; D. Holt 26, A. Horobin 12; N. Burrows 24, M. Parker 8; B. Colbourne 19, A. Frosdick 21; K. Drury 17, A. Atkinson 23; B. Duncan 25, D. Strong 15.

Semi finals: Middlesex 124, Somerset 109: (Middx first) G. Little 32, P. McCall 10; A. Garcia 24, D. Bryant 18; W. Richards 20, G. Luker 25; G. Smyth 13, I. Middlemast 19; S. Halmai 14, P. Branfield 23; R. Paine 21, A. Apsey 14.

Norfolk 128, Lancashire 110: (Norfolk first) R. Thacker 24, D. Colbourne 17; B. Taylor 25, B. Duncan 15; M. King 13, K. Drury21; T. Kelly 29, R. Millen 14; G. Duns 19, N. Burrows 19; D. Ward 18, D. Holt 24.

Final: Middlesex 128 Norfolk 102: (Middx first) John Wilson, John Cooke, John Sweeney, Wynne Richards 24, John Ottaway, Ian Daines, Gary Blake, Tom Kelly 11; Spiro Havanis, Dave Simpson, Alan Lines, Gerry Smyth 19, Peter Harlow, Peter Richmond, Brian Howes, Brian Taylor 22; Steve Wheeler, Chris Yelland, Mick O'Keefe, Gary Little 21, Steve Ellis, Philip Barr, Dave Richmond, Mervyn King 21; Robert Ingram, Brian Phillips, Ted Barton, Steve Halmai 26, Ian Wones, John Young, Peter Sabberton, Bob Thacker 14; Bob Bass, Bob Middleton, Billy Hulbert, Reg Paine 19, John Turner, Peter Crosskill, Mel Knickle, David Ward 15; Colin Hooper, John Mildren, Bill Jones, Tony Garcia 19, Paul Webb, Wilf Graver, Tony Dunton, George Duns 19.

English National Indoor Championships
at Melton Mowbray, March 10th-17th 1990

Andy Thomson dominated these championships for the second year in succession. The only bowler in the country to qualify from the 32 areas for all four championships, he not only retained Singles and Fours, but could well have won the Pairs. He and his long-time partner, Gary Smith, went out by a shot in a quarter final to the eventual winners Terry Scott and David Webb from Gateshead.

Earlier in the week, Sunderland, Gateshead's neighbours, won the Triples. Skipped by another Gary Smith - also an international - with Richard McKie at lead and the experienced Jim Lambert, a past winner, at No.2, Sunderland had ousted Paul Nelmes, Mike Jordan and Tony Allcock, the 1986 and 1988 winners. The Allcock team which switched clubs at the start of this season from Cotswold to Bentham, had beaten Thomson and his Cyphers partners Norman Perkins and Terry Heppell on their way to that final. But Allcock found Thomson a different proposition in the Singles final, and went down 21-7. Allcock blamed the rink for his defeat, saying it was playable on only one hand, but it appeared to hold no terrors for Thomson, who mastered it effectively.

Allcock's record however, of winning the national indoor Singles twice and finishing runner-up twice in six years cannot be discounted. Thomson's record also indicates that there is no way he should ever be excluded from an indoor world championship. "Can you win all four?" he was asked at the start of these championships. "Not a chance," he replied. "There are too many good bowlers about. It's hard enough to win one." Well, two it was in 1989, and two it was in 1990.

Lodge Sports Singles

The Singles, an event which bristled with talent, was sponsored by Lodge Sports, the Lincolnshire based firm. Of the favourites Allcock was drawn in the first round against Gary Harrington, his No.3 at the Commonwealth Games, and after beating him, he tangled with Roy Cutts, his No.2 in New Zealand, and once again finished well ahead.

Robert Crawshaw, a crown green expert from Blackpool Borough, offered strong resistance in the quarter finals, but Allcock limited him to 17 shots. Making similar progress was the enterprising young Ely player, Mark Entwistle, who looked good in his early games and then dismissed Terry Perkins from the Clarrie Dunbar club, Frome, who had overcome Ted Hanger and Ron Keating. Entwistle started well enough to lead Allcock in their semi final by 9-5 after eight ends. But when he no longer enjoyed the rubs he unwisely showed his frustration and disappointment and Allcock took full advantage, stepping up the pressure to win five of the last six ends.

Bryant had a smooth ride to the quarter finals and then stayed in front of persistent Lee Shoobridge. Thomson, meanwhile, off the boil a bit in mid week after his earlier superlative form in the Fours, had an awkward second round against Jack Davies of Preston, Brighton, who led so well for his club colleagues in the Fours.

Thomson finally nailed him after living dangerously at 20-all. Following that escape, Thomson moved into top gear. Jim Moulds could only score five against him, a result that set up a Thomson-Bryant semi final. Bidding for his tenth national indoor Singles success, Bryant, whose back problems and passing years inevitably affect the smoothness of his delivery, was hard put to it to contain the champion. He used the strike on several occasions to keep in contention, but Thomson just drew and drew and drew again. "Andy was just too good for me," Bryant said later. His 21-13 victory meant a repeat of the 1989 final in which, once again, Thomson displayed mettle, class and competitive spirit.

Allcock could have led by more than 7-6 — all seven were scored in singles — while Thomson was finding line and length difficult. After resorting to clean accurate drives to hang in, Thomson found his touch, and when he did, he left Allcock stranded. Using both hands, both ways, Thomson poured shot after shot, end after end, into the head to win nine ends in a row and turn the final into a rout.

Fours

Earlier Thomson and his Cyphers, Beckenham colleagues Martin Sekjer, Terry Heppell and Gary Smith, had meted out similar summary treatment to their opponents in the Fours, winning this title for the third year in succession and for the fifth time in eight years. Some measure of their dominance is reflected in the total scoreline of their five matches. They obtained 156 and conceded only 43 shots in those games, none going the full distance of 21 ends.

First they defeated the hapless Gedling team from Nottingham by 46-7, and in their hardest game, their semi final against Wymondham Dell, they were 15 shots in front. Cyphers superiority brought fitting tributes from the beaten finalists, a workmanlike team from the Preston club, Brighton. "They are just too hot to handle," said international Keith Renwick, the Preston skip. "They are just about the best Fours team there has ever been." added Dave Williams, his No.3.

The Cyphers four blend so well it will be difficult to find a club team to come anywhere near them should they decide to stay together. Sekjer, their lead, a left handed player and the 1989 national outdoors Fours winning skip, is rarely far away from the jack, and Heppell's capacity to counter-draw and remove opponents' woods gives Smith and Thomson a solid front base. Smith provides the inspiration and motivation, and the subtle touch and leadership of Thomson, instinctively and quietly gesturing his colleagues the shot to play, sets a style which club skips everywhere would do well to follow.

Thamesdown, skipped by Mel Biggs, figured in two of the most exciting matches in the competition, one with the Ely team led by Greg Harlow, and the other against Preston, a well-balanced team with a lead in Jack Davies who was constantly on the jack, middle men Paul Lewis and Williams, both left handers, who set opponents problems, and Renwick, an efficient and intelligent skip. In the final Preston kept in the picture for a full two hours to be only 10-6 down, but after that the Cyphers bowling machine moved smoothly into top gear and did not allow them another shot.

Singles

Round 1: Tommy Appleton (Eston) 21, Ian Brewster (Bassetlaw) 17; Robert Crawshaw (Blackpool Borough) 21, Dorian Bishop (Victory) 15; Roy Cutts (Ipswich) 21, Kevin Lockyear (Riverain) 16; Tony Allcock (Bentham) 21, Gary Harrington (Isis) 11; Terry Perkins (Clarrie Dunbar, Frome) 21, Wynne Davies (East Dorset) 15; Ron Keating (Plymouth Civil Service) 21, Ten Hanger (Northampton) 17; Norman Wigg (Sole Bay) w/o Steve Halmai (Paddington); Mark Entwistle (Ely) 21, Roger Howell (Deangate Ridge) 13; Ian Daines (Wymondham Dell) 12, Terry Scott (Gateshead) 21; Bryan Lee (Torbay) 18, Lee Shoobridge (Mote Park) 21; Brett Morley (Nottingham) 12, Bill Blakemore (Coventry) 21; David Bryant (Clevedon) 21, Bob Bass (Cambridge Park, Twickenham) 12; J. Mould (Hull) 21, Martin Mills (Brit. Cellophane, Bridgwater) 12; Ray Jenkins (Desborough, Maidenhead) 21, Paul Vamvacopoulos (Wey Valley) 11; Andy Thomson (Cyphers) 21, Steve Cooper (Essex County) 17; Jack Davies (Preston, Brighton) 21, Alan Johnson (Newcastle) 17.

Round 2: Crawshaw 21, Appleton 11; Allcock 21, Cutts 10;, Perkins 21, Keating 18; Entwistle 21, Wigg 2; Shoobridge 21, Scott 10; Bryant 21, Blakemore 6; Moulds 21, Jenkins 13; Thomson 21, Davies 20.

Quarter finals: Allcock 21, Crawshaw 17; Entwistle 21, Perkins 15; Bryant 21, Shoobridge 15; Thomson 21, Moulds 5.

Semi finals: Allcock 21, Entwistle 11; Thomson 21, Bryant 13. **Final:** Thomson 21, Allcock 7.

Fours

Round 1: Wymondham Dell 29, Rushden 18; Risbygate 21, Cambridge Park 14; Huddersfield 26; Bassetlaw 8; Falcon (Chelmsford) 21, Darlington 18; Cyphers, Beckenham 46, Gedling 7; Newcastle 24, Beccles 11; Blackpool Fylde 31, Isis, Oxford 26; Whiteknights, Reading 25, Plymouth Civil Service 20; Exonia, Exeter 15, City of Ely 17; Dartford Stone Lodge 13, Clarrie Dunbar 23; Bletchley 31, Herts, Watford 12; Thamesdown 29, Sunderland 13; Preston, Brighton 30, City of Coventry 17; Atherley, Southampton 31, Wey Valley 4; Watchet, Somerset 21, Victory, Portsmouth 20; Bristol 23, Mote Park, Maidstone 10.

Round 2: Wymondham Dell 24, Risbygate 20; Falcon 23, Huddersfield 13; Cyphers 28, Newcastle 8; Blackpool Fylde 21, Whiteknights 12; Ely 25, Clarrie Dunbar 15; Thamesdown 23, Bletchley 12; Preston, Brighton 23, Atherley 19; Bristol 20, Watchet 13.

Quarter finals: Wymondham Dell (M. Overton, K. Howlett, T. Overton, I. Daines) 24, Falcon (M. Green, R. Green, F. Dowding, G. Coles) 9; Cyphers (M. Sekjer, T. Heppell, G. Smith, A. Thomson) 29, Blackpool Fylde (D. Clarkston, R. Betty, V. Macdonald, S. Airey) 10; Thamesdown (I. Jefferies, S. Cornish, D. Snell, M. Biggs) 21, Ely (S. Seymour, K. King, D. Bell, G. Harlow) 20; Preston (J. Davies, P. Lewis, D. Williams, K. Renwick) 27, Bristol (S. Sanders, M. Coles, D. Noble, A. Apsey) 14.

Semi finals: Cyphers 27, Wymondham Dell 12; Preston 16, Thamesdown 14.
Final: Cyphers 26, Preston 6.

Triples

Round 1: Bentham 20, Isis, Oxford 10; Cyphers, Beckenham 16, Arun 15; City of Ely 15, Preston, Brighton 13; Sudbury 22, Lawson Park 9; Moonfleet 22, Handy Cross 3; Darlington 22, Hull & District 15; Dolphin, Poole 21, Cumbria 7; Barking 24, Norfolk

& Norwich 15; Exonia, Exeter 17, Paddington 8; Mote Park, Maidstone 23, Wey Valley 13; Vernon Turner 22, Rushmoor, Worcester 10; Sunderland 19, Victoria, Street 9; Boston 22, Christie Miller 14; Erewash 16, County Arts, Norwich 15; Northampton 24, Blackpool Borough 12; Bodmin 16, Lewisham 7.

Round 2: Bentham 19, Cyphers 10; Ely 19, Sudbury 13; Darlington 20, Moonfleet 14; Barking 21, Dolphin 13; Exonia 16, Mote Park 15; Sunderland 19, Vernon Turner 14; Boston 17, Erewash 6; Bodmin 16, Northampton 15.

Quarter finals: Bentham (P. Nelmes, M. Jordan, A. Allcock) 18, Ely (D. King, J. Campion, T. Lowe) 16; Barking (D. Farr, G. Arnold, N. Smith) 20, Darlington (C. Houghton, M. Baines, G. Peacock) 17; Sunderland (R. McKie, J. Lambert, G. Smith) 22, Exonia (P. Firby, J. Loaring, T. Haywood) 15; Bodmin (D. Hayne, P. Bennett, S. Lane) 19, Boston (J. Forman, M. Tomlin Jnr, M. Tomlin Snr) 12.

Semi finals: Bentham 17, Barking 14; Sunderland 16, Bodmin 15.

Final: Sunderland 23, Bentham 17.

Pairs

Round 1: C. Smith, P. Vamvacopoulos (Wey Valley) 17, D. Wilkins, D. Jenkins (West Cornwall) 12; R. Fuller, G. Willis (Kettering) 13, D. Snell, M. Biggs (Thamesdown) 23; J. King, M. King (Hunstanton) 19, D. Ramsdale, D. Joyce (Darlington) 18; K. Elson, B. Jenkins (Cambridge Park) 21, R. George, G. Humphries (Christie Miller) 19; D. Farr, N. Smith (Barking) 22, A. Barnes, K. Hills (Sudbury) 14; M. Entwistle, M. Jackman (City of Ely) 20, B. Grundy, M. Milgate (Angel, Tonbridge) 18; A. Jackson, L. Whitehouse (Vernon Turner) 21, D. Williams, K, Renwick (Preston, Brighton) 19; W. Davis, R. Burch (Exmouth Madeira) 19, D. Phare, R. Jones (Desborough) 18; W. Bryce, J. Bell (Cumbria) 20, L. Eltringham, R. Mackie (Isis, Oxford) 19; B. Kirk, M. West (Hull & District) 27, N. Cheesemer, D. Roberts (Deangate Ridge) 15; N. Reeder, P. Jackson (Scunthorpe) 16, B. Collinge, A. Collinge (Blackpool Borough) 15; A. Ross, G. Standley (Longmeadow) 27, C. Brown, R. Twine (Worthing Pavilion) 8; A. Sussex, G. Smyth (Paddington) 23, D. Gall, P. Woodcock (County Arts) 19; G. Smith, A. Thomson (Cyphers) 32, G. Day, A. Day (Taunton Deane) 14; j. Allen, J. Chapman (Hatfield) 24, D. Ralph, P. Alpin (Moonfleet) 19; T. Scott, D. Webb (Gateshead) 27, R. Sutcliffe, L. Brooks (Alfreton) 17.

Round 2: Thamesdown 19, Wey Valley 18; Cambridge Park 21, Hunstanton 16; Barking 26, Ely 10; Exmouth 19, Vernon Turner 17; Hull 24, Cumbria 19; Scunthorpe 19, Longmeadow 15; Cyphers 21, Paddington 16; Gateshead 19, Hatfield 18.

Quarter finals: Thamesdown 25, Cambridge Park 7; Barking 29, Exmouth 2; Hull 21, Scunthorpe 11; Gateshead 19, Cyphers 19.

Semi finals: Thamesdown 22, Barking 21; Gateshead 30, Hull 23.

Final: Gateshead 22, Thamesdown 10.

Mackeson Mixed Pairs National Championship

at Gedling, March 23rd — 25th 1990

Norma Wilson and international Brett Morley of Nottingham won this event, but only after a number of close calls. In the final they always appeared likely to beat their Spalding opponents Kath Inglis and Rick Collins, though the margin was small. The Nottingham pair opened up a 14-9 lead after 11 ends and held on to win 19-15.

Both teams had their adventures on the way. Mrs Wilson and Morley made comfortable progress in their round robin section though Cumbria's Eleanor

Trotter and Ron Gass forced a tie with them in their last game.

In their next two matches they had narrow escapes. In the first of these they were fully extended by Joyce Richards and Barry Swannie of Croydon and had an even closer call in their semi final against Pam Garside and Arthur Hemmings of the Riverain club, Hitchin. In this game the sides finished level and an extra end was played. With Riverain holding shot, Morley ditched the jack and then drew close to the brink of the ditch to snatch the winning shot.

In their semi final, Spalding recovered from an 11-0 deficit to beat Bodmin after scoring a six. Mrs Inglis and Collins had surmounted other crises. In their round robin section they lost to Nora and Harold Clarke of Christie Miller, Melksham, but with wins in their other games, finished 14 shots up.

Running them close were Vera Lawrence and Brian Pigney of Beccles, who finished plus 12, but lost their impetus by surrendering shots on the closing ends of their final game.

In their quarter final, Spalding met the 1989 winners, Diane Sekjer and Lee Shoobridge from Mote Park, Maidstone, who had enjoyed sweeping victories in their formidable group against top class combinations — Amy Mallenby and international Cliff Simpson (Hartlepool), Malcolm and Lorraine Woodley (Desborough, Maidenhead), and Rene Notley and 1989 outdoor national Pairs champion Paul Maynard of Essex County.

The quarter final between Mrs Sekjer and Shoobridge and Mrs Inglis and Collins produced some of the best bowling of the championship with the Spalding partnership squeezing ahead by 12-11.

Quarter finals: Riverain, Hitchin (Pam Garside and Arthur Hemmings) 20, Arun, Bognor Regis (Hazel Gregory and John Walden) 11; Nottingham (Norma Wilson and Brett Morley) 16, Croydon (Joyce Richards and Barry Swannie) 14; Bodmin (Joan and Gwyn Rees) 17 , Dartford Stone Lodge (Janet Tester and Mike Brick) 16; Spalding (Kath Inglis and Rick Collins) 12, Mote Park, Maidstone (Diane Sekjer and Lee Shoobridge) 11.
Semi finals: Riverain 16, Nottingham 17; Bodmin 18, Spalding 20.
Final: Nottingham 19, Spalding 15.

Sun Life English Bowls Players Association Championships

at Wellingborough IBC, March 24th-25th, 1990

English international Steve Halmai from Paddington produced skilful drawing to the jack mixed with firm woods to win the bowlers own tournament. But he met resistance on the way, notably from the experienced Newcastle player Stan Lant in the opening round of the play-off. Halmai squeezed through in the deciding set only to meet another formidable opponent, Duncan Hayne, 20, one of the increasing number of young players from the West Country making their presence felt. Hayne won the second set before Halmai resumed control.

It was plainer sailing for Halmai after that. His accuracy, his ability to use weight, and subtle variation of length stamping him as a worthy winner of the Max Engel Trophy. He was fully extended in the second set of a final notable for the smooth delivery and flowing action of his opponent Eric

Ramsdale, a formidable Durham county player, who had enjoyed considerable success in recent years with his Pairs partner — his son David, winner of the Under-25 title in 1987. Ramsdale played well throughout the weekend, first defeating in turn the association's President, David Bryant, in straight sets, international Steve Palmer, and Paul Barnicott, the 1989 national Triples winner from Mote Park, Maidstone.

Robert Hutchinson Opticians Ltd
Masters Singles Championship

At City of Ely IBC, March 26th — 28th 1990

Stephen Rees of Swansea overcame a field which included 14 internationals to win this championship. His commanding 9-3, 9-3 victory over John Ottaway, the English national outdoor Singles champion, and earlier successes, must have afforded him special satisfaction.

No fewer than ten of the players who finished behind him were scheduled to play in the CIS British Isles international series the following week. But he was not. The Welsh selectors had dropped him and his victory was his answer to them.

Over the years David Cornwell, the architect of this tournament, has assembled a mix of invited top players and qualifiers of both sexes. This results in a good leavening of players from the host club testing their skills against some of the best bowlers in the British Isles. Ely's players have an outstanding record as a team, having won the national club championships twice in three years — and they revealed their skills once again. World outdoor champion David Bryant, five times winner of this title, was one to suffer from them. Using the athletic stance following back trouble, Bryant abandoned his familiar crouch, and lost the first game in his round robin section to Ely's Michael Jackman. Though he won his other games to finish level on points with another Ely player, Kevin King, Bryant had an inferior shots average to both.

Margaret Johnston, the 1989 women's world indoor title holder from Ireland, lost all her games; she was beaten, not only by international Roy Cutts (Ipswich) and Simon Leader from near by St. Neots, but also by local bowler Ian Brown. Scotland's 1988 world indoor champion Hugh Duff from Auchinleck, also had a tough time. He came in as replacement for No.1 seed Tony Allcock, the 1989 winner, and made a bad start losing 15-3 to Jayne Roylance, the Commonwealth Games Pairs bronze medallist.

Duff could still have qualified, but though he defeated Bill Hobart, Steve Airey of Blackpool Fylde — who performed well throughout the tournament — beat him by a shot. England skip David Ward was another who failed to reach the final stages, and so did Terry Sullivan. This meant that three former Embassy world indoor champions — Bryant, Duff and Sullivan — had no part in the second day's play.

In the first round of the knock out, Wynne Richards, who won all his round robin games, fell to Jackman who was then beaten by Norfolk's Mervyn King, the national Under-25 winner in 1988 and 1989.

Ottaway eliminated Gary Smith and then Mrs Roylance. Rees was given two good games, first by Cornwell and then by Airey, who had put out home based England international Steve Palmer.

In the semi finals, Ottaway outbowled his Norfolk county colleague Mervyn King, and the other King (Kevin) lost to Rees. Ottaway was in devastating form against Mervyn King, his machine-like accuracy in reaching the jack sweeping him to a 9-1, 6-0 lead. Though King rallied he ran out of shots.

Rees, seeded No.3, had trouble with Kevin King who captured the first set with a perfect draw and led 4-0 in the second. But the burly Rees, who never lacks inward composure, took the set with a running shot. Four successive twos in the deciding set launched him into the final where he had the measure of Ottaway.

Play Offs: Mrs J. Roylance (North Walsham) bt A. Friend (Ipswich) 9-4, 9-2; J. Ottaway (Wymondham Dell) bt G. Smith (Cyphers, Beckenham) 4-9, 9-4, 9-6; M. Jackman (Ely) bt W.Richards (Cambridge Park, Twickenham) 9-5, 5-9, 9-3; M. King (Hunstanton) bt R. Cutts (Ipswich) 9-6, 9-6; S. Rees (Swansea) bt D. Cornwell (Ely) 9-6, 2-9, 9-0; S. Airey (Blackpool Fylde) bt S. Palmer (Ely) 9-5, 9-4; S. Leader (St. Neots) bt G.Harlow (Ely) 9-3, 9-4; K. King (Ely) bt T. Lowe (Ely) 9-5, 9-3.

Quarter finals: Ottaway bt Roylance 9-7, 9-1; Rees bt Airey 9-2, 9-8; K. King bt Leader 9-6, 9-3; M. King bt Jackman 9-6, 9-0.

Semi finals: Rees bt King 7-9, 9-5, 9-5; Ottaway bt M. King 9-1, 9-5.

Final: Rees bt Ottaway 9-3, 9-3.

Bristol and West BS Champion of Champions

at Thornbury Leisure Centre April 11th-12th April, 1990

Finalists Richard Hart and Mike Freeborn, both started bowling in 1972 at the Essex County club Westcliff-on-Sea, and teamed up in the 80's to win the county indoor Triples three years in succession.

Freeborn, who skipped, has since moved to Worlingham in Suffolk, and plays for Beccles, while Hart, who led has remained at Essex County, and has been a member of the England indoor squad.

Having allowed Bob Burch, John Kenton and Steve Palmer only 29 shots while he piled up 63, Freeborn seemed to be on his way to victory when he led 16-9. Hart had appeared nervous and ill at ease up to then but recovered to accumulate 12 shots over the next six ends, while Freeborn added a single to win 21-17, and gain a title he had been close to winning on previous occasions. Both players admitted finding concentration difficult. Old friends, they said, they knew each other's play inside out, and found it hard to summon up the killer instinct.

Round 1: R Hart (Essex County) bt M Brick (Dartford Stone Lodge) 21-19; M Freeborn (Beccles) bt R Burch (Exmouth, Madeira) 21-9; G Harrington (Isis) bt A Parsons (Whiteknights) 21-6; J Kenton (Egham) bt W Ward (Avon Valley) 21-11; T Jamieson (Victory) bt E Hanger (Northampton) 21-17; S Palmer (City of Ely) bt J Hopkinson (Alfreton) 21-12; J Wickham (Dawlish) bt J Kilyon (Erewash)O 21-17; S Airey (Blackpool-Fylde) bt D Fox (Stoke Mandeville) 21-17.

Quarter finals: Hart bt Wickham 21-12; Airey bt Jamieson 21-15: Freeborn bt Kenton 21-5; Palmer bt Harrington 21-??

Semi finals: Hart bt Airey 21-17; Freeborn bt Palmer 21-15.

British Airways Open Fours

at Egham IBC, April 13th-16th 1990

Prize money: Winner £500, Runners-up £300. Losing semi finalists £100.

This four-day tournament started with round robin sections for the 72 teams, with eight qualifiers proceeding to a knock out finale. The final between rinks skipped by John Ingram (Aylesbury) and the Chris Daniels four from Atherley, Southampton, produced a razor-edge finish. Daniels, 13-9 down, picked up a four on the last end to level at 13-all and then scored the decisive single on the extra end.

Quarter finals: C. Daniels (Atherley, Southampton) 10, L. Abbett (Egham) 4; J. Ingram (Aylesbury) 8, G. Grace (Handy Cross) 4. E. Crocker (Cambridge Park, Twickenham) 7, K. Morrison (Herga, Harrow) 8.
Semi finals: Ingram 11, Kenton 10; Daniels 8, Morrison 6.
Final: G. Alford, A. Forrest, A. Anderson, C. Daniels 14, D. Plater, C. Perrotet, T. McGill, J. Ingram 13.

Famous Grouse Open Mixed Pairs

at Crystal Palace, April 14th-16th 1990

Marjorie Cook and Maldwyn Evans from the host club defeated Cynthia Still and John King from Dartford Stone Lodge in the final.
Semi finals: B. Green, L. Green 9, M. Cook, M. Evans 25, C. Still, J. King 20, M. Hilliard, J. Seaborn 16.
Final: Cook, Evans 18, Still, King 12.2

Manns Norwich Brewery Easter Triples

at North Walsham IBC, April 13th — 16th 1990
Prizes: Winners £1,200, Runners-up £600, Losing semi finalists £3,00, Losing quarter finalists £150.

Sixteen internationals from all over the country were among the competitors for this event, among them Danny Denison of Dawlish who skipped Ted Collins and Neil Franklin to a 12-9 victory in the time limit final against Norfolk's Chris and David Ward and Trevor Webb.

Quarter finals: (skips only): D. Chandler (Leicester) 9, D. Ward (North Walsham) 16; R. Harlow (Ely) 7, G. Harrington (Isis) 6; N. Jones (East Dorset) 10, D. Denison (Dawlish) 12; P. Ellis (North Walsham) 15, D. Goodley (Gt. Yarmouth) 8.
Semi finals: C. Ward, T. Webb, D. Ward 17, G. Skinner, N. Langley, R. Harlow 7; E. Collins, N. Franklin, D. Denison 14, S. Ellis D. Shorter, P. Ellis 10.
Final: Denison 12, Ward 9.

Under-25 National Mixed Double Fours

at Perdiswell, April 14th 1990

Young Cambridgeshire players from March dominated the strong East Dorset team in the final of this inaugural event, stretching their lead as the game progressed. Lee Miller's rink confirmed their form a few days later by winning the Mackeson Mixed Fours national championship at Luton.

Semi finals: March 42, Cumbria 29. Rinks (March skips first): L. Miller 17, D. Linton 14. D. Hudson 25, A. Baxter 15. East Dorset 47, Towerlands Braintree 29: Rinks (E. Dorset first): L. Pull 25, A. Popple 12; N. Smith 22, A. Cook 17.

Final: March 49, East Dorset 30. Rinks: (March first): L. Baxter, C.Miller, P. Hayes, L. Miller 23, D. Morgan, R. Bates, N. Jones, L. Pull 18. D. Gray, D. Andrew, A. Hayes, D. Hudson 26, I. Rawlinson, K. Symons, R. Gould, N. Smith 12.

Newcastle Breweries Masters Pairs

at Hartlepool IBC, April 14th — 16th 1990

Sponsored by Newcastle Breweries, this event is played on a round robin basis over two days, with the top eight pairs going forward to the knock out section on the final day.

Many fancied combinations failed to survive the round robin section, among them internationals Gerry Smyth and Steve Halmai (England), Stan Espie and Clifford Craig (Ireland), Bob Sutherland and Willie McQueen (Scotland). There was disappointment, too, for last year's winners Chris Palmer and Tommy Buller (Stanley), and Sunderland's EIBA Triples winners Richie McKie and Jimmy Lambert, who also failed to reach the quarter final stage.

The event was won by former indoor international Ron Richardson and his Newcastle clubmate Stan Lant, who only managed to reach the final day in seventh place on shots difference and needed an extra end in their quarter final clash with father and son Jeff and David Wilkins from Swansea. The winners defeated outdoor international David Kilner and Joe Gibson (Hartlepool) in the final.

Quarter finals: D. Tweddle, K. Bainbridge (Hartlepool) 13, I. Lambert, D. Webb (Durham County) 11; D. Kilner, J. Gibson (Hartlepool) 12, P. Horsey, A. Facchini (Hartlepool) 11; R. Richardson, S. Lant (Newcastle) 11, J. Wilkins, D. Wilkins (Swansea City) 9 (after extra end); N. Routledge, G. Smith (Sunderland) 16, C. Johnston, D. Bell (Hartlepool) 13.

Semi finals: Kilner, Gibson 12, Routledge, Smith 11; Richardson, Lant 16, Tweddle, Bainbridge 6.

Final: Richardson, Lant 16, Kilner, Gibson 7.

Mackeson Mixed Fours National Indoor Championship

at SMCS Luton IBC, April 20th-22nd 1990

Lee Miller's young March team which included his sister Cheryl, Louise Baxter and Paul Hayes, overcame hiccups twice against international opposition to win this title.

Opposing Paddington in a semi final, they led 17-13 and were well through the final end when time was called. Realising that a score of four or five was impossible, England player Steve Halmai, the Paddington skip struck the jack off rink to force a replay. March supporters claimed that the game was ended but umpire Peter Brimble ruled that the end should be replayed. Halmai, twice facing a similar dilemma, killed the end twice more before March triumphed.

In their semi final March had faced a different problem. With three ends' left they led 17-7 against Isis, Oxford, but then dropped a two and a five to go into the final end a mere three shots ahead. International Gary Harrington forced a last end replay by killing the end and his side then appeared likely to draw level when his No.3 Mick Gallagher found the jack. Unfortunately it trickled the wrong way and Harrington failing to change the head, March went through. Isis had won their semi final place by defeating Tony Horobin's team from Huddersfield, and though losing to a strong Boston rink at the round robin stage, survived to head their section. Boston, represented by the 1989 England Pairs champions Martin and Mick Tomlin and their partners Janet Tomlin and Christine Hiom, lost their chance by losing 16 shots to Moonfleet. Mick Tomlin killed seven ends in this game — all in vain.

Quarter finals: Wendy Barnard, Joy Stevens, Michael Friend, Les Fisher (Torbay) 11, Cheryl Miller, Louise Baxter, Paul Hayes, Lee Miller 19; Mary Mallinson, Barbara Rawcliffe, Eric Rawcliffe, Steve Airey 13, Helen Pettit, Brenda Lines, Gerry Smyth Steve Halmai (Paddington) 17; Joan Hills, Doris Batchelor, Dick Cook, Ivan Yates (Dartford Stone Lodge) 7, Jackie Harrington, Liz Read, Mick Gallagher, Gary Harrington (Isis) 27; Betty Moxon, Mary Huddlestone, Peter Huddlestone, Tony Horobin (Huddersfield) 19, Mea McHowat, Jean Kilyon, John Kilyon, Tom McHowat (Erewash) 17.

Semi finals: March 17, Paddington 15; Isis 17, Huddersfield 9.

Final: March 17, Isis 15.

Bristol & West Building Society Denny Cup

Final stages at Cambridge Park IBC, April 29th 1990

The Denny Cup started life as a two rink inter-club championship in 1935 when its donor, the late Leonard Denny of the Cambridge Park club, Twickenham, donated it for inter-club two rink competition in England. His own club won it in 1950 and again in 1959 at Thornfield, Rugby, by which time the event had become a four rink competition and an integral part of the England Indoor Bowling Association.

Then the competition was sponsored, and by the time the final stages were played in 1986, the 'Denny Cup' had changed its name to the inter-club championship, and was played for a trophy presented by the sponsors. The Denny Cup then went back to Cambridge Park and the original two rink competition was revived for the 1988-1989 indoor season, and the cup went to the Cyphers club, Beckenham. Now, once more, it is back at Cambridge Park who wrested it from Cyphers in the final.

The competition attracted 59 entries, the final stages taking place on the last Sunday of the indoor season. Cyphers had three of the National Fours champions in their team — Martin Sekjer, Terry Heppell, Andy Thomson — and were clearly capable of retaining the trophy.

They duly reached the semi finals where they were fully extended by Atherley, Southampton. With Peter Line at No.3, Norman Shelley skipped his team to a two-shot victory over John Bull's Cyphers four and on the other rink Shelley's son Richard just failed to get close enough to Thomson's team to force an extra end.

Holding one and requiring another shot to level the match overall, the younger Shelley gave away a last end shot, leaving Thomson four ahead. Meanwhile, Cambridge Park accounted comfortably for Whiteknights, Reading, largely due to the performance of Chris Yelland, Barry Jenkins, Paul Rogers and Gary Little.

This four excelled in the final, too, outbowling Thomson's rink. Killing ends, Thomson tried in vain to stem the tide, but Little is no slouch with weight himself, and he and his partners withstood a Cyphers rally.

With the Wynne Richards team routing Bull's team on the other rink, it was all over for Thomson and his men by the 19th end when they were 20-15 behind. The loss of a further five merely put the icing on the cake for Cambridge Park.

It was a great day for them, and for the organiser Ron Petch. Mrs Barbara Price, 80, daughter of the late Leonard Denny was there to see the club's victory — a thoroughly deserved one. Their two opponents on the day could however, console themselves with the thought that playing at home is a big advantage, and this must have helped Cambridge Park on the day.

Semi finals: Cyphers, Beckenham 50, Atherley 48. Rinks (Cyphers first): P. Butcher, R. Stodhart, R. Riley, J. Bull 23, C. Daniels, B. Buckle, P. Line, N. Shelley 25; I Ward, M. Sekjer, T. Heppell, A. Thomson 27, P. Ward, D. Martin, J. Keat, R. Shelley 23. Cambridge Park, Twickenham 39, Whiteknights, Reading 27. Rinks (Cambridge Park first): R. Bass, D. Kearns, N. Thompson, W. Richards 17, A. Collins, J. Ford, C. Brooks, M. Willis 18; C. Yelland, B. Jenkins, P. Rogers, G. Little 22, C. Rowe, G. Stacey, A. Cottis, K. Nash 8.

Final: Cambridge Park 44, Cyphers 21. Rinks: Richards 24, Bull 9; Little 25, Thomson 15.

Nottinghamshire Women's County Championships

at various venues and dates from May 18th — July 13th 1990

Singles: Joan Howlett (West Bridgford) bt Valerie Dexter (Players Sports).

Pairs: Jeannie Clarke, Joan Howlett (West Bridgford) bt Eileen Bird, Anne Glover (Sherwood).

Triples: Mary Ward, Winnie Reek, Norma Poole (Mansfield Colliery) bt Magdaline Hufton, Lucy Paling, Norma Wilson (Mansfield Colliery).

Fours: Margaret Maidlow, Joan Leffley, Janet Burlinson, Jeanette Wells (Balderton) bt B. Margeson, Peggy Turner, Beryl Sharpe, Enid Adams (Wilford).

Champion of Champions: Sylvia Offler (Sherwood) bt Nancy Beasley (Wollaton).

Dorset Women's County Championships

Finals at Branksome Park, May 14th, 25th, June 11th, 20th, 29th 1990

Singles: June Searle (Greenhill) 21, Janet Davison (Poole Park) 9

Pairs: Sheila Baker, Fredina Potter (Dorchester) 22, Joyce Smith, Ruth Peters (Broadstone) 13.

Triples: Rose Laming, Eve Chislett, Sue O'Nians (Melcombe Regis) 20, May Simpson, Irene Briggs, June Searle (Greenhill) 18.

Fours: Hilda Stokes, Rose Laming, Eve Chislett, Sue O'Nians (Melcombe Regis) 20, Angela Steadman, May Simpson, Irene Briggs, June Searle (Greenhill) 10.

Champion of Champions: June Searle, (Greenhill) 21, Patricia Cutler (Sherborne) 20.

Isle of Wight Women's County Championships

Finals at Cowes and Bembridge

May 11th, June 30th and July 2nd 1990

Singles: Olive Callaway (Ryde) 21, Gay Allen (Ryde) 7.
Pairs: Betty Crouch, D. Williams (Cowes) 20, Paula Benford, Pauline Proud (Cowes) 12.
Triples: Paul Benford, Chris Anderson, Pauline Proud (Cowes) 28, Marjorie Bradley, Audrey Goldsmith, Dorothy Marks (Sandown) 9.
Fours: Betty Crouch, Betty Adams, Chris Anderson, D. Williams (Cowes) 19, Vera Harris, Joyce Walker, Shireen Augustus, Audrey Sheen (Westland Aerospace) 17.
Champion of Champions: Chris Anderson (Cowes) 21, Olive Woodmore (Westland Aerospace) 19 (30 ends).
Two-Wood Singles: Paula Benford (Cowes) 20, Gladys Emery (Ryde) 8.

Cornwall Women's County Championships

at various venues

May 24th, June 22nd, July 6th & 10th, and August 30th 1990

Singles: Madge Hurrell (Lostwithiel) 21, Gwen Daniel (Penryn) 20
Pairs: Dorothy Davy, Doreen Pearce (Stratton) 20, Lilian Gardiner, Janet Newman (St. Austell) 16.
Triples: Jane Brokenshire, Gwen Daniel, Rene Kneebone (Penryn) 25, Muriel Jewell, Ann White, Audrey Richards (Falmouth) 19.
Fours: Muriel Gerry, Hester Finnamore, Jenifer Worth, Nicola Gilbert (Kensey Vale) 19, Norma May, Janet Smith, Sylvia Coak, Vera Ireland (West Cornwall) 14.
Champion of Champions: Gwen Daniel (Penryn) 21, Norma May (West Cornwall) 11.

Southport Open Pairs

at The King's Gardens, Southport, May 26th-27th 1990

Trevor Rimmer and Alec Atkinson of the host club defeated the Bolton pair, Graham Booth and Allan Higgins, to win the John James Trophy and top £220 prize. The event was one of three jointly sponsored by Dales Frozen Foods (Liverpool) and Lancashire Glass Ltd on behalf of the Lancashire County Bowling Association.

Atkinson faced defeat in the quarter final when, with one bowl left, he succeeded in taking out two bowls two feet apart to snatch victory by a shot. His opponents, Tony Gafner and Brian Hindle from Bolton, were left rooted in disbelief.

In the final, Rimmer and Atkinson were coasting comfortably to victory, when after seven ends they led 9-3 on a full length jack. On the eighth end Rimmer unaccountably delivered all of his four bowls into the ditch. Clearly suffering from shock, Atkinson failed to recover the position and lost five. All square at the tenth and last end, Rimmer redeemed himself and laid a sound foundation for the Southport pair to clinch victory by a shot and repeat their 1984 victory.

Complete outsiders Audrey Morton and Frank Raffo recorded a series of astonishing feats throughout the weekend. Among their victims were key Lancashire stars Rob Millin and David Holt, and Wiltshire's Mike Jackson and Neil Smith. In the semi final they were lying in a match winning position only to be denied by a brilliant last bowl by Allan Higgins. Frank Raffo, a last minute substitute, was playing his first ever outdoor flat green bowls' event.

Quarter finals: T. Rimmer, N. Atkinson 13, A. Gafner, B. Hindle 12; K. Mitchell, D. Colbourne 11, S. Hale, D. Ferguson 10; G. Booth, A. Higgins 14, K. Davey, A. King 3; M. Jackson, N. Smith 1, A. Morton, F. Raffo 20.
Semi finals: Rimmer, Atkinson 9, Mitchell, Colbourne 5; Booth, Higgins 8, Morton, Raffo 5.
Final: Rimmer, Atkinson 10, Booth, Higgins 9.

Durham Women's County Championships

Finals at Spennymoor, Bishop Auckland and Vane Tempest BC, June 7th and 28th, July 16th 1990

Singles: Dulcie Harbin (Hundens) 21, Gillian Jones (Consett Park) 20.
Pairs: Shirley Andrews, Sally Frith (Brinkburn Dene) 23, Elaine Ruane, Joy Powney (Durham City) 8.
Triples: Ruby Airey, Joyce Hull, Iris Lawson (Spennymoor) 31, Joan Elves, Peggy Caygill, Mary Gray (Peterlee Lowhills) 4
Fours: Shirley Andrews, Sylvia Walker, Mary Smith, Sally Frith (Brinkburn Dene) 27, Terry Ryan, Audrey Thornton, Doreen Hutton, Jean Cleet (Wheatley Hill) 17.
Champion of Champions: Betty Johnson (Houghton Dairy Lane) 21, Margaret Michison (Women's Circle) 16.

Bristol & West Building Society Teignmouth Open

At The Den and Bitton Park, Shaldon BCs, June 10th — 16th 1990
Mike Smith from Bristol won the Singles title, defeating Andy Reeson of Lincoln in the final by 21-16, and completed a double in the Triples. The Pairs holders, Andy Wickham and his father John disposed of the international combination of John Evans and Danny Denison by a single shot in an early round but were later beaten by Joe Murray and Derek Hooper in a semi final.

In the final however, Murray and Hooper were outbowled by the Taunton pair, Dennis Burch, a son of former national Singles champion Charlie Burch, and Italian-born Carmen Notaro.

The Triples title went to the Bristol trio Ernie Hill, Mike Smith and John Parker, and the daughter and mother-in-law combination of Lorraine and Margaret Hackett won the Women's Pairs. Their victory in the final was achieved over Margaret Goddard and Trixie Medland. Mrs Medland's partner in earlier rounds, Mrs Amery, fell and broke her wrist, Mrs Goddard replacing her.

Men's Singles: Semi finals: M. Smith (Gloucester) 21, N. Pook (Dawlish) 15; A. Reeson (Lincoln) 21, E. Collins (Newton Abbot) 11.
Final: Smith 21, Reeson 16.
Men's Pairs: Semi finals: J. Murray, D. Hooper (Shaldon) 24, A. Wickham (Dawlish), J. Wickham (Shaldon) 12; D. Burch, C. Notaro (Taunton) 26, B. Tibbs, B. Haywood (Shaldon) 11. **Final:** Burch, Notaro 23, Murray, Hooper 12.
Men's Triples: Semi finals: B. Tibbs (Shaldon), R. Crossman (St. Austell), B. Hayward

(Shaldon) 14, M. Marsden, A. Rees (Bristol), W. McNaughton (Teignmouth) 19; K. Smith (Bitton Park), D. Hurford, D. Beaver (Teignmouth) 14, E. Hill, M. Smith, J. Parker (Bristol) 19.

Women's Pairs: Semi finals: M. Moore (Bromsgrove), D. Cotton (Tally Ho) 14, M. Amery (Watts, Blake & Bearne), T. Medland (Totnes) 21; L. Hackett (Torquay), M. Hackett (Watts, Blake & Bearne) 14, C. Walters, B. MacKerness (Star Cross) 10. **Final:** Hackett, Hackett 24, Goddard, Medland 15.

Littlehampton 36th Open Tournament

at Norfolk and Maltravers Greens, Littlehampton, July 2nd-14th 1990
Singles:
Semi finals: M. George (Gosport) 21, Ken Armstrong (Worthing Pavilion) 14; David Murrell (Norfolk, Littlehampton) 21, Dave Herbert (Petworth) 20.
Final: George 21, Murrell 9.
Pairs
Final: Steve Hawkes (East Preston), Peter Walden (Norfolk) 24, Geoff and Ken Armstrong (Worthing Pavilion) 17.
Triples:
Final: Norman Francis, Reg Phillips, Brian Wellsted (Norfolk) 18, Joanathan Clear, Harry Hirst, Malcolm Clear (East Preston) 14.
Women's Singles:
Final: Joan Plackett (Field Place) 21, Jean McCrossen (East Preston) 11.
Women's Pairs:
Final: Susan Small, Jean Bracey (Henfield) 16, Phyllis Ridgway, Ronnie Lavelly (Lancing) 15.
Mixed Pairs:
Edna and Tommy Tucker (Horsham) 22, Janet Pidgeon,
John Dicker (East Preston) 16.

Hampshire Women's County Championships

Finals at Atherley Club, Southampton, July 6th 1990
Singles: Barbara Till (Milton Park, Portsmouth) 21, Chris Croad (Southampton Women) 16.
Pairs: Eva Dibdin, Beatrice Harrison (Romsey) 22, Wendy Line, Enid Fairhall (Southampton) 16.
Triples: Kay Martin, Freda Guy, Helen Phillips (Atherley) 24, Sheila White, Allyson Flint, Betty Sharp (Cove) 11.
Fours: Joyce Edwards, Barbara Webber, Joan Kyte, Betty Jacob (Southampton) 17, Wyn Price, 'Mo' (Maureen) Brewer, Freda Dawson, Gladys Wareham (Canoe Lake) 16.
Two-Wood Singles: Cynthia Abraham (Aldershot Underwood) 17, Diane Young (Brockenhurst) 12.
Champion of Champions: Played at Howard Park, Basingstoke, June 1st. H. Phillips (Atherley) 21, J. Brown (Royal Aircraft Establishment) 5.

Wiltshire County Championships

at Trowbridge Westbourne, Devizes & Swindon
July 9th,10th,12th,13th & September 1st, 9th, 1990
Singles: Mike Trimble (Malmesbury) 25, Mel Biggs (Wootton Bassett) 21.

Pairs: Jeff Nichols, Steve Warren (Westlecot, Swindon) 24, Andy Moore, Malcolm Webb (Spencers, Melksham) 19.
Triples: B. Shadwell, G. Shadwell, Brian Colebrook (Westbourne, Trowbridge) 16, Stephen Snell, Bert Biggs, Mel Biggs (Wootton Bassett 15.
Fours: Mark Tyler, Mick Crook, Peter White, John White (Amesbury) 28, Michael Carpenter, Clint Dean, Ian Jefferies, Steven Cornish (Rodbourne Cheney) 11.
Two-Wood Singles: David Snell (Swindon British Rail) 25, Jon Cook (Devizes) 23.
Champion of Champions: John Rothery (Marlborough) 25, Jack Grainger (Westinghouse, Chippenham) 24.
Unbadged Singles: G. House (Alderbury) 25, A. Smith (Chippenham Town) 8.

Cambridgeshire Women's County Championships

Finals at Brookland Avenue, Cambridge, Ely, and Newmarket, July 9th, 16th-18th 1990

Singles: Moira Osborne (St. Neots) 21, Pauline Ayres (March Conservative) 7.
Pairs: Cheryl Miller, Doreen Miller (March Conservative) 24, Maureen Christmas, Jenny Tunbridge (Chesterton) 17.
Triples: Ann Hammond, Joyce Blocksage, Ann Taylor (Newmarket) 20, Maureen Mallows, Daphne Hannah, Bertha Hannah (Welding Institute) 12.
Fours: Thelma Webber, Ann Halsey, Jean Hudson, Betty Edwards (March Town) 23, Jenny Gilbert, Dorothy Huckle, June George, Lily Cooper (St. Neots) 14.
Under-25 Singles: Sarah Irons (Ely City) bt Jenny Tunbridge (Chesterton).
Champion of Champions: Cheryl Miller (March Conservative) 21, Maureen Mallows (Welding Institute) 17.

Over-55s:
Singles: June Larter (Chesterton) bt Pat Bigley (Steeple Morden)
Pairs: Stella Clifton, Betty Edwards (March Town) bt Joyce Blocksage, Kathleen Bye (Newmarket)

Lancashire County Championships

at Heaton Hall, July 8th 1990

Singles: Charles Tattersall (Newton Hall) 25, John Walker (Bolton) 22.
Pairs: David Lockhart, Gordon Niven (Bolton) 21, Frederick Kershaw, Thomas Armstrong (Bolton) 20.
Triples: Bernard Milne, Alan Leach, Brian Hindle (Bolton) 20, David Lockhart, David Holt, Thomas Armstrong (Bolton) 14.
Fours: Graeme Booth, John Franklin (sub Allan Higgins), Howard Smith, Peter Huddlestone (Bolton) 14.
Under-25 Singles: Winner: Darren Gregory (Newton Hall)
Champion of Champions: Played September 15th: Alec Atkinson (Southport) 25, David Colbourne (Bolton) 10.

Woolwich Eastbourne 61st Tournament

at Princes Park, Eastbourne, July 9th-14th 1990

Leicestershire's Andrew Irons from Knighton Victoria, lifted the £100 first prize and Eastbourne Silver Challenge Cup after a runaway Singles final win, his fourth attempt at the title.

Singles: Semi finals: Andrew Irons (Knighton Victoria) 21, Arthur Small (Newick) 19; Roy Spencer (Cambridge Park) 21, Simon Riggs (Motcombe Gardens) 18. **Final:** Irons 21, Spencer 3.

Jubilee Cup (Losing semi finalists) Riggs 21, Small 13.

Pairs: final: Colin Taylor, Terry Howard (Victoria Drive) 23, R. Borthwick, M. Prentice (Bromley) 15.

Triples: final: Liam Digweed (Ventnor), Ted Gibson (Gildredge Park), David Weaver (Victoria Drive) 14, Dennis Slater (Redoubt), George Barton (Croydon), Frank Church (Redoubt) 10.

Northamptonshire County Championships
at Rushden Town and Kingsthorpe, July 10th-13th 1990

Singles: Terry James (Thrapston) bt Ernie Tredwell (Kingsthorpe).

Pairs: Ian Walker, Rodger Tansley (Kingsthorpe) bt Alan Spencer, Mick Sharpe (Kingsthorpe)

Triples: Simon Tate, Walt Winsor, Ray Gunn (Thrapston) bt Malcolm McAllister, Bill Andrew, David Brawn (Northampton County Ground)

Fours: Paul Cooke, Gordon Wright, Nev Humphrey, Don Boston (Kettering Lodge) bt Pat Hallam, Norman Mason Eric Shearsmith, J. Chapman (Kettering Midland Band).

Champion of Champions: Keith Johnson (Oundle) bt Frank Johnson (Pianoforte Supplies)

Under-25 Singles: Played September 9th: Andrew Manton (Northampton West End) bt Simon Letts (Northampton West End)

Cumbria Women's County Championships
at Silloth, July 10th and 16th 1990

Singles: Wyn Sowerby (Edenside) 21, Judy Armstrong (Edenside) 17.

Pairs: Sarah Irving, Joan Graham (Kirkbride) 25, Mattie Henderson, Cassie Walker (Dalston) 20.

Triples: Carol Studholme, Kathleen Baxter, Margaret Christie (Wigton) bt Betty Reay, Ruby Barnes, Joan Graham (Kirkbride)

Fours: Joyce Mitchell, Sally Butler, Joan Burbage, Judy Armstrong (Edenside) 21, Sheena Grayes, Ruby Baxter, Kathleen Baxter, Margaret Christie (Wigton) 17.

Champion of Champions: Played August 26th: Betty Harrison (Dalston) 21, Mary Hetherington (Aspatria) 12.

Two-Wood Singles: Pat Corps (Edenside) bt Margaret Allan (Courtfield).

Hampshire County Championships
Finals at Atherley BC, Southampton, July 13th 1990

Singles: Dorian Bishop (Alexandra) 25, Terry Chivers (Bournemouth) 21.

Pairs: John Keat, Richard Shelley (Atherley) 22, Stewart Mundy, Peter Dawson (Southbourne) 17.

Triples: Dean Morgan, Peter Pull, Russell Morgan (Boscombe Cliff) 19, Geoff Luckham, Chris Dowding, Chris Eames (Bournemouth) 10.

Fours: Mike Squires, Chris Paice, Jim Rigby, Julian Haines (Boscombe Cliff) 25, Barry Starks, Frank Middleton, Fred Harding, Ian Mackenzie (Southend Waverley) 16.

Norfolk Women's County Championships
at Carters Bowling Green, July 11th-13th, 1990

Singles: Sally Smith (North Walsham) 21, Margaret Betts (Woolpack Terrington St John) 20.

Pairs: Sandra Curtis, Susan Curtis (County Arts) 18, Geraldine Reeve, Rita Basted (County Arts) 17.

Triples: Vera Widdows, Rita Basted, Molly Woods (County Arts) 15, Edith Hall, Joan Stringfellow, Jean Gray (Browston Hall) 14.

Fours: Pamela Hood, Sybil Symonds, Elizabeth Shorter, Valerie Chapman (County Arts) 20, Margaret Hannat, Iris Flatt, Ann Gee, Dorothy Cutting (North Walsham) 17.

Champion of Champions: Jasmine Cole (East Harling) 21, Linda Bedingfield (Shouldham) 12.

Coronation Triples: Played August 21st — Vera Widdows, Madeline Ward, Pamela Calton (County Arts) 25, I Page, Margaret Betts, J Dawson (Terrington Woolpack) 7.

Benevolent Triples: C Kenwright, Eliza Norman, Joan Wilson (Shotford, Harleston) 13, P Knights, Dorothy Steward, Margaret Hannant, (North Walsham) 9.

Unbadged Pairs: H Rix, D Brown (Holt) 20, A Balls, C Rome (Hunstanton Cliff Parade) 19.

Unbadged Singles: Brenda Whitehead (St Marks) 21, B Buxton (St Marks) 12.

Lincolnshire Women's County Championships
at Railway Sports BC, Lincoln, July 12th 1990

Singles: R. Markham (Perry Sports, Kirton in Lindsey) 21, S. Dimbleby (Bourne Town) 16.

Pairs: M. Taylor, J. French (Railway, Lincoln) 23, S. Dimbleby, B. Smith (Bourne Town) 21.

Triples: M. Chester, D. Wilson, J. Cammack (Burton House, Boston) 19, A. Bellamy, C. Smith, S. Wilson (North Scarle, Lincoln) 15.

Fours: J. Toynton, E. Hoodless, J. Mews, E. Shaftoe (Swineshead, Boston) 20, D. Bines, J. Chester, M. Sanders, E. McKee (Park, Lincoln) 18.

Champion of Champions: Played on September 3rd: S. Gladwell (Clee Ladies) 21, R. Everett (Horncastle) 6.

Worcestershire Women's County Championships
at Cripplegate, July 13th, 17th, 18th 1990

Singles: Ivy Smallbone (Broadway) bt Dorothy Prior (Hewell)

Pairs: Joan Parfitt, Di Bruce (Broadway) bt Marie Borthwick, J. Taylor (Cripplegate)

Triples: Ruth Wilkes, Di Bruce, Joan Parfitt (Broadway) w/o Pat Poole, Joan Meek, Jean McPhail (Manor Park).

Fours: Joan Stanton, Dorothy Prior, Pam Boswell, Tricia Tyler (Hewell) bt B. Chinn, C. Rimmell, Vivienne Hall, Peggy Cole (Littleton).

Champion of Champions: Played at Brintons, September 18th: Vivienne Hall (Littleton) 21, June Rincher (Brintons) 16.

Lancashire Women's County Championships
at Blackpool, July 14th 1990

Singles: Margaret Marshall (Southport) 23, Arlene Colbourne (Bolton) 15.

Pairs: Margaret Powell, Arlene Colbourne (Bolton) 21, Edith Giles, Joyce Thompson (Heaton Hall) 10

Triples: Lilian Hunt, Val Holloway, Caroline Swan (Bolton) 15, Elsie Andrew, Jean Hesford, Rita Moore (Blackpool) 14.

Fours: Mary Huddlestone, Kath Bastow, Hilda Baines, Lilian Pilkington (Heaton Hall) 19, Beryl Toft, Margaret Powell, Mary Mallinson, Arlene Colbourne (Bolton) 11.

County Trophy Inter-Club (August 18th-19th):

Joint Winners: Bolton/Heaton Hall. **Runners-up:** Blackpool.

Derbyshire Women's County Championship

Finals at Ilkeston, Rutland, July 15th 1990

Singles: Christine Wealthall (Ilkeston Rutland) 21, Sheila Miller, (Silver Band) 16.

Pairs: Margaret Bonsor, Jean Baker (Alfreton) 26, Sue Jordan, Ann Selvey (Silver Band) 7

Triples: Irene Benniston, Arleen Walters, Christine Wealthall (Ilkeston Rutland) 17, Dorothy Swift, Ann Webb, June Hallam (Long Eaton Town 14.

Fours: Margaret Bonsor, Margaret Godfrey, Joan Sheppard, Jean Baker (Alfreton) 22, Jean Thompson, Audrey Lee, Glennis Haines, Jean Hill (Alfreton) 18.

Champion of Champions: Sheila Miller (Silver Band) 21, Rita Lenham (Derby West End) 14.

Margaret Bonsor and Jean Baker qualified in the Mother & Daughter competition and reached the national semi final.

Kent Women's County Championships

Finals at Clarence BC, Rochester, July 16th 1990

Singles: Ellen West (Bellingham) 21, Ann Harrison (Kearsney) 9.

Pairs: Kate Mitchell, Joyce Barnes (Whitehall) 23, Janet Stubbs, Linda Southby (Maidstone Police) 16.

Triples: Ann Harrison, Rita Vane, Ann Smith (Kearsney) 17, Rita Wilbrew, Carol Snell, Wendy Taylor (Palm Cottage) 13.

Fours: Ann Harrison, Joan Heath, Rita Vane, Ann Smith (Kearsney) 28, Johnny Nottage, Jean Sands, Millie Kent, Val Chatfield (Woolwich & Plumstead) 19.

Champion of Champions: at Maidstone BC, July 9th. Sue Miles (Hesketh Park) 21, Roz Cheeseman (Canterbury) 12.

Buckinghamshire Women's County Championships

Finals at Denham, July 16th 1990

Singles: M. Price (Burnham) 21, C. Robertson (Princes Risborough) 11.

Pairs: L. Thelwell, A. Cox (Marlow) 23, M. Dearn, P. Pye (Stony Stratford) 13.

Triples: J. Beech, C. Robertson, B. Walford (Princes Risborough) 18, G. Giles, J. Collison, M. Price (Burnham) 14.

Fours: J. Collison, V. Webb, J. Plater, M. Price (Burnham) 23, R. King, R. Gardner, J. Laing, E. Piner (Gerrards Cross) 4.

Under-25 Singles: Played at Wendover, July 24th: W. Betambeau (Wendover) 21, J. Plater (Burnham) 15.

Gloucestershire Women's County Championships

Finals at Greyfriars, July 16th 1990

Singles: M. Reeve (Caerglow) bt P. Meek (Lydney)
Pairs: J. Morris, J. Sheward (Whaddon) bt P. Tandy, S. Blackman (Pineholt)
Triples: I. Lee, P. Peachey, D. Mitchell (Glos. City) bt J. Kearsey, M. Barnaby, M. Richardson (Sir Thomas Rich's)
Fours: W. Gabb, J. Rand, A. Bradley, P. Bradley (Victory Park) bt A. Wildsmith, G. Donaldson, J. Hughes, V. Smith (Tetbury).
Champion of Champions: J. Morris (Whaddon) bt B. Poole (Falcon)

Suffolk Women's County Championships

at Ransomes BC, July 16th & 18th 1990

Singles: Pat Martin (Haverhill) 21, Lil Green (Ipswich Ladies) 20.
Pairs: Gwen Grimwood, Molly Ayers (Halesworth) 19, Mabs Podd, Margaret Smith (Roundwood) 14.
Triples: Verly Page, Norah Strong, Margaret Ashford (Beccles) 17, M. Barber, Rita Wilson Gloria Hagan (West Row) 13.
Fours: Muriel Stebbings, Eileen Baker, Isabel Morey, Janet Farrow (Otley) 18, I. Sharman, Margaret Coles, Vi Southey, Mary Bryant (Framlingham) 13.
Champion of Champions: Dorothy Panks (Hadleigh) 21, Peggy Mizon (Haverhill) 4.
Novices Singles: (Played at Rookery BC, August 30th) J. Edgar (Boxford) 17, J. Haddock (ILBC) 15.
Two-Wood Singles: Mabs Podd (Roundwood) 16, Eileen Baker (Otley) 8.

Northumberland Women's County Championships

at Burradon, July 16th 1990

Singles: Maria Shuttleworth (Ponteland) 22, Evelyne Scorer (Whitley & Monkseaton) 11.
Pairs: Mary Bruce, Joyce Down (Linton) 21, Maria Shuttleworth, Joan Graham (Ponteland) 14.
Triples: Maria Shuttleworth, Iris Fletcher, Joan Graham (Ponteland) 29, Mary Bruce, Eleanor Payntor, Connie Armstrong (Linton) 9.
Fours: Betty Parsons, Moira Neely, Sandra White, Marian Day (Seahouses) 25, Elsie Straker, Betty McNeal, Audrey Dobson, Jean Bowell (Cowden & Crofton) 9.
Champion of Champions: Ann Daley (Alnwick) 21, Olga Gasgoigne (Burradon) 15.
Two-Wood Singles: Edna Fogerty (Morpeth) 15, Norma Craig (Willington Quay) 12.

Cambridgeshire County Championships

Finals at Newnham, Cambridge, July 16th-20th 1990

Singles: Stuart Woodcock (Whittlesey Manor) 25, Trevor Lowe (Stretham) 9.
Pairs: Des Ruse, Lee Miller (March Conservative) 29, Graham Wells, John Walker (Isleham) 7.
Triples: Richard Williams, Paul Hensby, Peter Hensby (March Conservative 24, Simon Leader, Doug Berrill, Stan Worbey (St. Neots) 13.
Fours: Martin Welsford, Colin Brown, Brian Bassam, Peter Bavister (Whittlesey Manor) 27, Paul Hayes, Bill MacNamara, Maurice Miller, Lee Miller (March Conservatives) 9.
Champion of Champions: Ian McWhinney (Stretham) 25, Gordon Horry (BRSA March) 12.

Warwickshire Women's County Championships

Finals at Whitnash BC, July 18th 1990

Singles: Peggy Owen (Corley) 21, Maureen Edwards (Rugby Thornfield) 10.

Pairs: Patricia Dahlgren, Joyce Moore (GEC/AEI Rugby) 19, Vera Booth, Maureen Tims (Whitnash) 18

Triples: Carol Head, Christine Baker, Margaret Wright (British Rail, Rugby) 24, Betty Beese, Jill Brook, Elizabeth Chedgzoy (Stratford upon Avon) 14.

Fours: Sigrid Thomas, Nancy Orrell, Kathleen Adams, Maureen Edwards (Rugby Thornfield) 27, Sheila Barr, Elizabeth Allen, Dora Crewe, Beryl Cooke (Nuneaton) 11.

Champion of Champions: Maureen Tims (Whitnash) 21, Elizabeth Chedgzoy (Stratford upon Avon) 9.

Two-Wood Singles: Janet Cox (Blossomfield) 15, Iris Tough (Stoke) 12.

Nottinghamshire County Championships

at Notts EBA Headquarters, July 18th-25th 1990

Singles: Brett Morley (GPT Plessey) 25, Mick Ward (Balderton) 24.

Pairs: Dave Thomas, Phil Dickens (Players Athletic) 35, Kieran Whitmore, Bob Scott (Cotgrave) 17.

Triples: Geoff Hufton Jnr, Geoff Hufton Snr, Jamie Mills (Mansfield Colliery) 21, Trevor Lee, Terry Barker, Hedley Hill (Nottingham City) 14.

Fours: Paul Jackson, Geoff Hufton Jnr, Geoff Hufton Snr, Jamie Mills (Mansfield Colliery) 22, Paul Martlew, Mick Lukowski, Pete Goulding, Brett Morley (GPT Plessey) 14.

Somerset Women's County Championships

at Clarence BC, Weston-Super-Mare, July 18th & September 21st 1990

Singles: E. Bessell (Yeovil) 21, C. Shearing (Bloomfield, Bath) 10.

Pairs: Y. Groom, S. Nicholls (Street) 24, D. Foulkes, C. Shearing (Bloomfield) 10.

Triples: D. Gray, D. Marshall, J. Young (Taunton) 20, Y. Groom, J. Garlick, S. Nicholls (Street) 11.

Fours: M. Taylor, S. Cowcher, E. Bessell, M. Fellows (Yeovil) 19, V. Jones, G. Scott, L. Pike, H. Healey (Frome Selwood) 12.

Champion of Champions: J. Biddiscombe (Porlock) 23, P. Boynette (Norwest) 12.

Two-Wood Singles: J. Curtis (Yatton) 17, Y. Groom (Street) 11.

Fear Cup (Inter-club): West Backwell 52, Nailsea 51.

Benevolent Triples: M. Skidmore, B. Coles, S. Weaden (Ashcombe) 14, G. Ripley, H. Attfield, P. Hobbs (Keynsham) 8.

Northumberland County Championships

Finals at Alnwick and Portland, July 19th-20th 1990

Singles: Tony Kempster (Gosforth) 25, Jack Knox (Gosforth) 18.

Pairs: Terry Scott, David Webb (Summerhill) 25, Alan Johnson, George Watson (Portland) 15.

Triples: Karl Jameson, Joe Ellison, Jim Chapman (Cramlington) 24, Michael Mooney, Bob Stephenson, John Tweddle (Walker) 13.

Fours: Peter Moore, Jim Moore, Ken Elliott, Ken Conway (Wallsend) 23, Malcolm Henderson, Brian Houghton, Richard Dougal, Jack Knox (Gosforth) 10.

25 & Under Singles: Tony Kempster (Gosforth) 25, Karl Jameson (Cramlington) 22.

18 & Under Singles: David Ross (Seaton Sluice) 25, Martin Cooper (Gosforth) 16.

Lincolnshire County Championships
at Cleethorpes, July 20th and 22nd 1990

Singles: W. Hobart (Sleaford Road, Boston) 25, R. Powers (Deeping) 15.
Pairs: M. Mashford, B. GTedney (Mail Cart, Spalding) 14, R. Vinter Snr, R. Vinter Jnr (Burton House, Boston) 13.
Triples: M. Brown, J. Molson, W. Hobart (Sleaford Road, Boston) 19, B. Holden, R. Goodley, E. Houghton (Holbeach United Services) 14.
Fours: J. Laud, T. Bailey, J. Wright, R. Collins (Mail Cart, Spalding) 21, A. Norton, P. Robinson, H. Walsham, B. Christie (Cleethorpes) 20.

Suffolk County Championships
at Framlingham and Eye, July 21st, 1990.

Singles: A Chambers (Eye) 25, F Elsey (Marlborough, Ipswich) 14.
Pairs: J Barrell, R Cutts (Marlborough) 29, L Parliament, D Fey (Risbygate) 9.
Triples: B Pigney, C Moore, D Hinsley (Bungay) 18, P Jackson, E Peck, A Chambers (Eye) 15.
Fours: F Spraggons, I Parnell, R Gage, J Annis (Ipswich) 19, G McMaster, G Goodchild, O Brown, V Tricker (Roundwood) 14.
Under 25 Singles: M Parker (Marlborough) 25, P Last (Otley) 15, Played September 16th at Framlingham.
Champion of Champions: D Cooke (Crave) 25, J Jermy (Beccles Con) 18.
Over 60 Pairs: P Webber, B Crosby (Marlborough) 23, A Markwell, D Fair (Margaret Catchpole) 18, Played September 16th at Framlingham.

Durham County (EBA) Championships
Finals at Consett Park, July 21st 1990

Highlight of these events was the Singles final between the holder Eddie Henry and the man who defeated him — Cliff Simpson — the outdoor and indoor international. Simpson, who had to withstand a spirited recovery from Henry before winning 25-21, became the first man to win this title in three different decades. His previous victories were in 1979 and 1987.

Indoor international and Triples winner at Melton Mowbray, Gary R. Smith, and Hylton CW colleague John Thurlbeck took the Pairs title. The Triples went to Hartlepool Park trio Billy Ryder, Harry Dougherty and Alan Taylor, while home club Consett Park members Jim Rogan, Bob Armstrong, Alan Jones and Ron Gowland were popular winners of the rinks title.

Graham Peacock - beaten in last year's 2-Wood Singles final - went one. better this time, and Ian Jackson, a loser in the Pairs final, had consolation in winning the Junior Singles.

Singles: C. Simpson (Owton Lodge) 25, E. Henry (Houghton Dairy Lane) 21.
Pairs: J. Thurlbeck, G. Smith (Hylton CW) 23, I. Jackson, P. Stephenson (Peterlee Town) 14.
Triples: W. Ryder, H. Dougherty, A. Taylor (Hartlepool Park) 27, A. Robinson, G. Walsh, J. Horton (Sunderland Thompson Park) 12.
Fours: J. Rogan Jnr, R. Armstrong, A. Jones, R. Gowland (Consett Park) 28, R. Bell, J. Hutchinson, J. Haley, J. Stothard (Glenholme, Crook) 21.
2-Wood Singles: G. Peacock (Darlington Hundens) 25, T. Kelly (Hartlepool SDSC) 12
Junior Singles: I. Jackson (Peterlee Town) 25, A. Kirkland (Middleton St. George) 14.

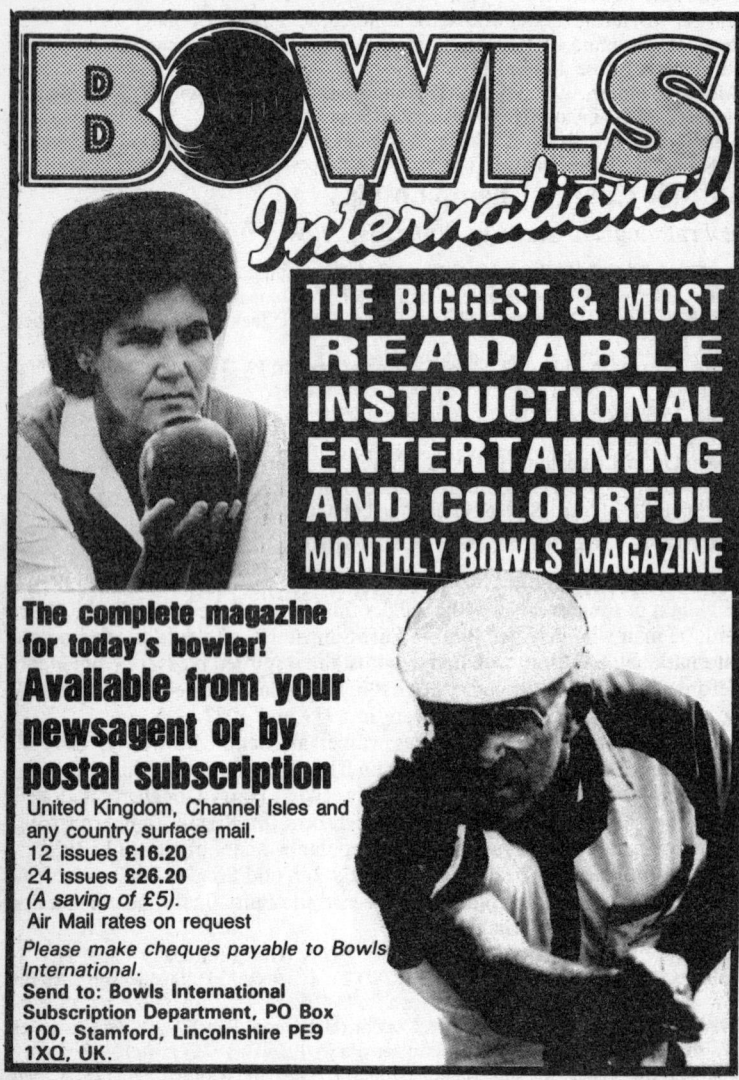

Buckinghamshire County Championships

Finals at Chesham BC, July 21st 1990

Singles: Alan Waite (Denham) 25, Kirk Smith (Denham) 16.

Pairs: Adrian Sussex, Kirk Smith (Denham) 18, William Norman, Tony Jenkins (Wolverton Town) 14.

Triples: Derek Barton, Jack Mays, Ian Harvey (Marlow) 18, John Cook, William Norman, Tony Jenkins (Wolverton Town) 14.

Fours: Peter Dickenson, Ronald Chambers, Melvyn Vickers, David Killick (Stony Stratford) 16, Ronald Oakes, Clifford Richards, Dennis Glaister, Breton Long (Slough Town) 15.

Secretaries Cup: Andy Penny (Wendover & Chiltern Hills) 25, Fred Collins (Gerrards Cross) 22.

Norfolk County Championships

at Norfolk BC, July 22nd, 1990

Singles: John Ottaway (Wymondham Dell) 25, John George (County Arts) 14.

Pairs: John Ottaway, Roger Guy (Wymondham Dell) 21, Geoffrey Roll, John George (County Arts) 12.

Triples: Mike Jarvis, John King, Mervyn King (Hunstanton EBA) 25, Carl Hipperson, David Richmond, Tony Dunton (Wymondham Dell) 10.

Fours: Cyril Smith, Trevor Reeve, David Richmond, Bob Thacker (Wymondham Dell) 24, Gerry Howes, Mal Shaw, Brian Howes, Peter Sabberton (Norfolk BC) 12.

Under-25 Singles: Mervyn King (Hunstanton EBA) 25, David Mace (Sheringham Morley) 19.

Isle of Wight County Championships

at Westland Aerospace BC, July 22nd 1990

Singles: B. Brown (Bembridge) 25, C. Baker (Newport) 14.

Pairs: K. Brown, T. Augustus (Westland Aerospace) 20, J. Young, C. Ridett (Shanklin) 12.

Triples: M. Davis, N. Carter, D. Buckley (Ventnor) 12, F. Firkins, T. Blythe, W. Mortar (Ryde) 11.

Fours: M. Davis, T. Adcock, P. Lewis, W. Best (Ventnor) 26, I. Thomas, R. Brown, A. Baker, L. Crook (Cowes Medina) 16.

Under-25 Singles: J. Davies (Ventnor) 21, C. Griffiths (Totland) 18.

Leamington Spa Men's Open

at Victoria Park, Leamington Spa, July 22nd-27th 1990

The South Warwickshire club Welford-on-Avon, secured two of the main titles at this 50th annual event. The top tournament of its kind in the Midlands, it attracted its usual maximum entry, from which Simon Davies of Welford, an England trialist, emerged to win the Singles and atone for his defeat in the final three years earlier. He defeated Calvin Carpenter of Banbury Central 21-18, after Carpenter had recovered from 17-5 down to take an 18-17 lead.

Welford trio Mick Davis, Martin Timms and Trevor Francis overwhelmed Sandy Sewell and George Jordan of Southam BC and Ian Warmington of Snitterfield BC, 31-9 in the Triples final.

Stratford on Avon players Dave Hobbis and Dave Caldwell were the Pairs champions, beating Keith Wooding and Steve Taylor of Coventry clubs Highway and Avenue respectively, 17-13 in a very good final.

Wiltshire bowler Alan Livsey of Wootton Bassett, and his nephew Mike Mattock of Loughborough won the Reprise Pairs; and a special Veterans Pairs for players who first competed in a Leamington Open at least 25 years ago, was won by Vic Walker of host club Royal Leamington Spa, and Howard Beard of Jag Daimler BC Coventry. The pair then opposed each other in a Singles match to determine an outright veteran champion, Beard winning 24-5.

Oxfordshire County Championships

Finals at South Oxford BC, July 22nd 1990

Singles: George Moon (Banbury Borough) 25, Gary Harrington (Summertown) 20.
Pairs: David Wedge, Peter Astall (Summertown) 22, Steve Beackon, Gary Harrington (Summerton) 21.
Triples: Paul Futter, Howard Watts, Steve Ellis (Oxford City & County) 29,Ian Henwood, Mark Peachey, Robert Mackie (Summertown) 9.
Fours: Roger Gotobed, Fred Roberts, Harry Williams, Peter Latter (West Witney) 25, Roger Bishop, Maurice East, John Wheeler, Robert Simpson (South Oxford) 8.

Hereford Women's County Championships

Finals at St. Martins, July 22nd 1990

Singles: Anne Russell (Leominster) 21, Betty Hackett (Leominster) 8.
Pairs: Joan Lee, Pam Hinksman (St. Martins) 19, Ann Bishop, Sue Masters (Kingsland) 14.
Triples: Netta Shakesheff, Stella Bristow, Joan Jones (Eastnor) 18, Muriel Smith, Theresa Williams, Jean Bullock (Ross on Wye) 16.
Fours: Pat York, Netta Shakesheff, Stella Bristow, Joan Jones (Eastnor) 22, Joan Lee, Lena Woodward, Del Joyce, Pam Hinksman (St. Martins) 16.

Hertfordshire Women's County Championships

Finals at Townsend BC, St. Albans, July 23rd 1990

Singles: Sue Duck (Rye Park) 21, Margaret Wiggs (Croxley) 12.
Pairs: Pat Hoare, Iris Cricket (Rosedale) 20, Peggy Saunders, Veronica Mead (Hitchin) 19.
Triples: Ann Haywood, Jill Ward, Shirley Page (Baldock) 19, Francis Chipperfield, Daphne Pratt, Barbara Groves (Sele Farm) 13.
Fours: Margaret Wiggs, Ann Walton, Audrey McLachlan, Meg Pavey (Croxley) 23, Betty Parrish, Betty Young, Mabel Sheppard, Barbara Fuller (Bishops Stortford) 18.
Champion of Champions: Played July 18th: Sue Duck (Rye Park) 21, Margaret Wiggs (Croxley) 12.

Berkshire Women's County Championships

at Maidenhead Town BC, July 23rd 1990

4-Wood Singles: Mavis Brooks (Windsor & Eton) 21, Helen Jones (Suttons) 10.
2-Wood Singles: Dot West (Reading) 10, Ruth Kennedy (Maiden Erlegh) 5.
Pairs: Joan Hawkins, Nola Bishton (Sunningdale) 20, Gwen Joice, Vera Storr (Newbury) 19.

Triples: Margaret Kozlowski, Vera Storr, Norma Cannon (Newbury) 26, Moira Weston, Jean Lambden, Janet Marriot (Woodley) 18.
Fours: Jean Clacey, Pauline Holmes, Julie Bayliss, Erica Ford (Wokingham) 26, June Essex, Brenda Clements, Margaret Hooper, Marion Aitken (Maidenhead) 18.
Champion of Champions: Shirley Sullivan (Woodley) 21, Nola Bishton (Sunningdale) 15.
Unbadged Singles: B. Clements (Maidenhead Town) bt Ann Shaw (Maidenhead Town).
Secretaries: Joan Hawkins (Sunningdale) bt Pauline Maskrey (Wallingford).

Wiltshire Women's County Championship

at Wootton Bassett, July 23rd 1990

Singles: Josie Lloyd (British Rail, Swindon) 21, Ianthea Sanders (Wilton) 16.
Pairs: Ruth Bolger, Carol Bartlett (Purton) 24, Sylvia Gerrish, Joyce Smith (Bradford on Avon) 13.
Triples: Marion Butcher, Pauline Tucker, Daphne Otridge (Devizes) 18, Ruth Bolger, Carol Bartlett, Barbara Woolford (Purton) 11.
Fours: Brenda Twine, Beverley Lane, Shirley Livsey, Dina Giongell (Wootton Bassett) 26, Joyce Jeffery, Betty Hancock, ? McMaster, Eileen Hawker (GEC Melksham) 9.
Two-Wood Singles: Ann Hayward (Westlecot) 15, Ianthea Sanders (Wilton) 13.
Champion of Champions: Played at Devizes, September 8th: Pamela Hockley (Pewsey Vale) 21, Mary Moss (Highworth) 15.

Bedfordshire County Championships

at Wilstead BC, July 23rd and Bedford Borough BC, July 29th 1990

Singles: John Jepson (Leighton Buzzard) 25. Terry Andrews (Ampthill) 16.
Pairs: Keith Thorne, John Reid (Flitwick) 26, Eric Saunders, David Randall (Electrolux) 25.
Triples: Roger Connell, Ian Oakley, Derek Hancock (Co-op Luton) 19, Bill Corless, Bill Meyrick, Gavin McLaren (Luton Town) 4.
Fours: Keith Knowles, Ken Knowles, John Sheppard, Jim Hill (Flitwick) 19, Ted Giggle, George Meyern, Keith Thorne, John Reid (Flitwick) 18.
Tomkins Singles (Officers Cup): Dave Stallan (Biggleswade Town) 25, Mervyn Brion (Leaside) 18.
Crawley Triples (Benevolent Fund): John Wildman, Terry Padgett, Roy Kitto (Eaton Socon) 19, Ken Pullan, Edward Swann, Harold Smith (Luton Town) 9.

Chandlers BMW Hove Tournament

at Western Lawns, Kingsway, Hove, July 23rd-28th 1990

There were 440 players in the four events crammed into six days, and the defending Singles champion Richard Moses, lost 21-14 to A. Gibbon (Hare and Otter) in the fifth round, playing his fourth game of the day.
Singles: Semi finals: Joe Stevens (Epsom Park) 21, Jim Bruce (Ealing Conservatives) 6; Graham Pilbrow (Epsom) 21, John Birch (South London) 18. Final: Stevens 21, Pilbrow 20.
Pairs: final: David Moses (Windlesham), Richard Moses (Hollingbury Park) 19, Bruno Wells-Brown, Terry Dade (Hove & Kingsway) 14.
Triples: David Woosnam (Mackie), Alan Clarke, Doug Whetstone (Lindfield) 25, John Hare, Fred Dent, Steve Stockley (Parsons Green) 6.
Mixed Pairs: Marjorie Curtis, Ron Savage (Hove & Kingsway) 23, Freda Page, Terry Stevens (Southwick) 9.

Middlesex Women's County Championships

Finals at Harrow BC, July 25th 1990

Singles: Ina Foote (Edmonton) 21, Ann Halliday (Masonians) 12.
Pairs: Barbara Hurst, Ann Grant (Broomfield) 19,Violet Marsh, Marjory Harwood (C & L Sports) 17.
Triples: Daphne Hobbs, Jean Baker, Doreen Lavender (Uxbridge) 15, Sandie Nailard, Olive Ratley, Betty Veal (Court Park) 14.
Fours: Pat Ketchen, Pam Watts, Irene Barber, Brenda Lines (Shepherds Bush) 24, Ann Barrett, Nonie Halse, Eileen Norris, Mary Halse (Lammas) 12.

Surrey Women's County Championships

at Southey BC, July 26th 1990

Singles: Sue King (Ashtead) 21, Betty Dudley (Southey) 14.
Pairs: Joan Cuff, Alice McKew (Horley) 20, Jenny Jarvis, Chris Wessier (Farnham Ladies) 19.
Triples: Sandra Beckett, Doreen Lewis, Jean Waton (Sutton) 22, Ann Briault, Janet Exall, Sheila Simmons (Cane Hill Hospital) 11.
Fours: Freda Starkey, Edna Gibbs, Toni Drayton, Phyl Soulsby (Epsom Park) 22, Eileen Vigor, Sheila Reeves, Muriel Kelly, Doris Stanton (Croydon) 21.
Champion of Champions: Kay Dean (Godalming) 21, Jean Watson (Sutton) 14.

Gloucestershire County Championships

Finals at Cheltenham Whaddon, July 26th,27th & 30th 1990

Singles: Tony Allcock (Cheltenham) 26, Brian Elms (Nailsworth) 19.
Pairs: Tony Allcock, Len Cooper (Cheltenham) 22, Neil Chandler, Ken Davis (Victory Park) 15.
Triples: Tim Webb, John Holmes, Martin Wynn (Cope Chat) 22, Tony Allcock, Jack Henderson, Andrew Wills (Cheltenham) 16.
Fours: John Gardiner, Terry Frost, Mike Collins, Alan Wells (Bristol Arrow) 18, Barry Fisher, John Holmes, Dave Brown, Tim Webb (Cope Chat) 17.
Under-40 Singles: Roger Hook (National Power) 25, Keith Hinder (Listers) 15.
Champion of Champions: Terry Pritchard (Bristol St. George) 25, Pat Sully (Frampton-on-Severn) 23.

Bedfordshire Women's County Championships

Finals at Bedford Borough BC, July 27th 1990

Singles: E. Rick (Bedford Women) 21, J. Bradley (Langford) 17.
Pairs: E. Shack, P. Francescon (Bedford Women) 22, P. Smith, E. Green (Kingsbury) 20.
Triples: K. Hirst, J. Larman, J. Measures (Henlow Park) 19, V. Giddins, J. Giles, A. Cruttenden (Memorial Park 15.
Fours: K. Hirst, J. Smith, J. Larman, J. Measures (Henlow Park) 23, D. Baker, T. Kilminster, R. Boston, M. Soper (Wilstead) 12.
Champion of Champions: (Played at Vauxhall Motors, September 14th) J. Mitchell (Leighton Buzzard) 21, J. Measures (Henlow Park) 12.
Unbadged Singles: J. Bradley (Langford) 21, M. Bosher (Linslade) 8.

Yorkshire County Championships

Finals at Bert Keech BC, York, July 29th 1990

Singles: Nigel Harrison (Ainsty, York) 25, Malcolm Cullingworth (King George V,

Guisborough) 24.

Pairs: Derek Boyle, Jeff Davis (Withernsea) 21, Bob Clements, John Wennington (King George V) 6

Triples: Brian Sharp, Terry Sharp, Adrian Brown (Pallister Park, Middlesbrough) 15, Brian Artingstoll, Mick Binks, Jim Moulds (Holderness) 11

Fours: Brian Chapman, John Rowan, Mick Corringham, Peter Robinson (Haxby Road, York) 25, Trevor Lea, David Roberts, Brian Sutcliffe, Eric Wilkinson (York R.I. Amateurs) 8

Under-25 Singles: Nigel Brignall (Nafferton) 25, Eamonn Addison (Scarcroft, York) 11.

Brighton 71st Open Tournament

at Preston Park, Brighton, July 30th-August 4th 1990

Singles: Semi finals: David Woosnam (Mackie) 25, Dave Herbert (Petworth) 12; John Durrant (Hollingbury Park) 25, Chris Heyward (Mitcham) 22.

Final: Woosnam 25, Durrant 17.

Pairs: final: Jim Morley, Pete Wilkinson (St. Ann's Well Gardens) 17, Harry Craig, John O'Toole (Guildford) 16.

Triples: Mike Jeffery, Steve Ponsillo, David Gaff (Woodbridge Hill) 25, Jim Turrell, Stefan Michael (Peacehaven), Alan Webb (Saltdean) 17.

Special Pairs: Ken Hodges, Angus Macdonald (Woodbridge Hill) 22, Mike Bowler, Jim McCalmont (Woodbridge Hill) 17.

Derbyshire County Championships

at Derby West End, August 1st and 10th 1990

Singles: Brian Wilkinson (Long Eaton Town) 25, John Pye (Stanton Hallam Fields) 14.

Pairs: Robert Wilson, Vernon Birtles (Elson & Robbins) 22, Brian Taylor, Tom Doig (Elson & Robbins) 14.

Triples: Glyn Barnett, Paul Harvey, John Barnett (Stanton Club House) 21, Ian Griffin, Roy Griffin, Paul Wilkinson (Long Eaton Town) 13.

Fours: Derek Larkin, Ashley Hunter, Brian Miller, Harold Scott (Long Eaton West Park) 19, Jim Morley, Chris Morley, Des Slater, Tony Lee (Long Eaton Silver Band) 15.

Secretary's Cup: Les Slater (Long Eaton Silver Band) 25, Alan Scott (Ilkeston Enterprise) 6.

Johns Trophy (Englishwomen's Inter-county championship)

Final stages at Leamington Spa, August 1st 1990

Kent surmounted their problems in the semi finals and final of this event to win for the fourth time since the competition began in 1934. Their previous successes were in 1952, 1955, and 1984.

In their semi final against Notts, Kent suffered a blow when one of their six skips, county secretary Shirley Lawrence fainted from dehydration in the heat. She recovered and continued to play, but the incident clearly affected the rink which went down by 15 shots. Kent performed well enough on other rinks, those led by Ann Snelling and Jean Lord more than redressing the adverse balance.

In the other semi final, Nottinghamshire just managed to keep ahead of Norfolk who with two ends left to finish, required five shots to tie. Their fours skipped by Jayne Roylance and Valerie Chapman both scored, but not enough to bale out their side.

Mrs Lawrence opted not to play for Kent in the afternoon's final and Diane Sekjer, wife of Martyn Sekjer, (holder of both England men's Fours titles indoor and outdoor), moved from Mrs Lawrence's No.3 to take over as skip, Beryl Reeve substituting at No.3. The reconstructed combination performed well, winning their game by six shots, and with four other Kent teams finishing ahead, this cancelled out the 21-8 victory earned by Brenda Atherton and her Notts colleagues on the remaining rink.

It was a disappointing end to a splendid season for Notts who had won all their earlier rounds with ease, but a rewarding one for Kent who had performed grittily on their way to Leamington with successive narrow victories over Middlesex, Sussex, the 1989 champions, and Surrey.

Preliminary round: Huntingdonshire 115, Suffolk 117; Leicestershire 136, Cambridgeshire 102; Isle of Wight 82, Somerset 156.

Round 1: Lincolnshire 107, Yorkshire 110; Lancashire 83, Durham 157; Northumberland 85, Nottinghamshire 154; Derbyshire 107, Cumbria 113; Suffolk 90, Leics 125; Northants 109, Oxfordshire 116; Warwickshire 98, Worcestershire 108.; Norfolk 130, Bedfordshire 105; Somerset 119, Hampshire 90; Dorset 86, Cornwall 127; Gloucestershire 106, Devon 128; Hereford 106, Wiltshire 99; Essex 120, Bucks 113; Herts 86, Surrey 115; Sussex 122, Berkshire 105; Kent 121, Middlesex 112.

Round 2: Yorks 119, Durham 122; Notts 127, Cumbria 95; Leics 110, Oxon 117; Worcs 115, Norfolk 134; Somerset 117, Cornwall 135; Devon 130, Hereford 95; Essex 106, Surrey 129, Sussex 116.

Quarter finals: Durham 105, Notts 142; Oxon 105, Norfolk 113; Cornwall 116, Devon 117; Surrey 110, Kent 117

Semi finals: Kent 124 Devon 107:

Rinks (Kent first). T. Clement, J. Cullen, D. Sekjer, S. Lawrence 15, R. Bond, M. Coates, V. Cutler, M. Powlesland 30; A. Ellis, L. Ryan, S. Haynes, B. Jones 20, A. McCambridge, M. Player, A. Pascoe, M. Gooding 16; A. Dennis, C. Branchett, Y. Wallington, E. West 14, C. Walters, B. Day, B. Harkness, M. Jenkin 19; D. Farman, J. Hellyer, J. Holliday, M. King 20, M. Elliott, R. Rimmer, B. Kilwell, P. Thomas 16; R. Vane, J. Barnes, L. Barnon, A. Snelling 28, W. Barnard, C. Theedom, C. Bolton, M. Wellington 12; S. Miles, J. Hills, D. Batchelor, J. Lord 27, H. Elliott, E. Grey, R. Dowse, H. Robertson 14.

Notts 118, Norfolk 115

Rinks (Notts first): M. Ellis, S. Lovett, J. Howlett, A. Glover 16, S. Smith, S. Symonds, C. Gapp, J. Roylance 15; M. Maidlow, G. Simpson, J. Wells, H. Morley 30, M. Carpenter, D. Steward, R. Buck, R. Norris 19; A. Pinder, S. Pollard, N. Beasley, B. Atherton 20, P. Hood, F. Moll, L. Millbank, V. Chapman 21; M. Ward, M. Johns, J. Greenfield, M. Poole 21, R. Basted, G. Reeve, V. Gibson, M. Woods 17; G. Bryan, B. Ridge, S. Offler, M. Osborne 19, J. Shepherd, B. Tuck, J. Wilson, E. Sabberton 19; E. Bird, M. Simons, G. Hofton, N. Wilson 12, M. Hannant, M. Halstead, R. Smith, J. Andrews 24.

Final: Kent 101 Notts 90
Rinks (skips only) Lord 16, Wilson 13; King 17, Glover 10; West 21, Poole 18; Jones 8, Atherton 21; Sekjer (replacing Lawrence, B. Reeves at No.3) 21, Morley 15; Snelling 18, Osborne 13.

Walker Cup (Englishwomen's National Double Rinks)

Final stages at Leamington Spa, August 2nd 1990

Oxfordshire and Devonshire contested a see-saw final in this event. After dropping the first four ends the Devon rink skipped by Mavis Wellington scored 14 shots without reply to lead 14-6. Oxfordshire's Midge Peake and her partners then captured the next seven ends to regain the lead and held on to win by one. Fortunes changed drastically on the other rink, too. Irene Molyneux and her partners trailed 10-2 to Madeline Gooding's Devon rink, but then a four launched them into a winning run of 15 shots. Leading 20-11 three ends later, their position seemed secure and with four ends to go, the Devon pair finished with a 1,3,2 and 1 to close the gap. That was not quite enough and Oxford claimed overall victory by three shots.

Semi finals: Oxon 46, Cumbria 31 Rinks (Oxford skips first): M. Peake 16, M. Allan 16; I. Molyneux 30, M. Heggie 15.

Devon 48, Kent 27 Rinks (Devon first): M. Wellington 28, A. Snelling 11; M. Gooding 20, S. Lawrence 16.

Final: Oxon 37, Devon 34. Rinks (Oxon first): A. Mainwaring, K. Hawes, S. Rogers, I. Molyneux 20, R. Bond, C. Bolton, A. Pascoe, M. Gooding 18; V. Jones, J. Franklin, M. Ellis, M. Peake 17, M. Jenkin, M. Powlesland, H. Robertson, M. Wellington 16.

North of England Festival Singles Championships

at North Marine Park, South Shields, August 2nd-11th 1990

The South Tyneside BA revived this tournament, which began in 1931 — with a £3 prize for the winner. With the South Tyneside Council and local firms, the prize money in 1990 was £1250.

Les Bolton (Leslies BC) won the men's event, with a £400 cheque and the Warwick Vase — a silver copy of the 1770 original in Warwick Castle. Runner-up Sid Johnson (Readhead West Park) received £200.

The ladies' event was won by Nell Adams (Ravensworth), who defeated Edna Atkinson (Cauldwell BC) in a dramatic final. The Junior event was won by Ian Dixon (Sutton BC) who defeated Glen Howe (Cleadon Park).

Men's quarter finals: Ian Scott 21, Doug Readman 18; Derek Bell 13, Sid Johnson 21; George Neve 21, Arthur Just 13; Maurice Dunlop 20, Les Bolton 21.

Semi finals: Johnson 21, Neve 7; Bolton 21, Scott 20. Final: Bolton 21, Johnson 18.

Ladies' semi finals: Edna Atkinson 21, Norma Thompson 20; Nell Adams 21, Edna Stevenson 17.

Final: Adams 21, Atkinson 20.

Junior Final: Ian Dixon 21, Glen Howe 17.

Kent County Championships

Finals at Folkestone Park, August 4th 1990

Singles: Mike Milgate (Tonbridge) 25, Gordon Charlton (Folkestone Park) 24.

Pairs: Dave Glazier, Arthur Cannon (Folkestone Park) 25, Dave Hilley, Mike Heppell (Cyphers) 15.

Triples: Ken Ibbotson, Brian Culver, John Armstrong (Sandwich) 19, Peter Hubbard, Mike Dutton, Frank Osbourne (Betteshanger Col.) 8

Fours: Paul Barnicott, Terry Branchett, Chris Hall, Lee Shoobridge (UK Paper, Sittingbourne) 28, Andy Smith, Clive Hunt, Stan Smith, Ron Riley (Bellingham) 8.

EWBA Competitions

at Victoria Park, Leamington Spa, August 4th-5th 1990
16-25 Singles

Catherine Anton of Peterborough and District BC, underlined her standing as England's number one junior player by winning the 16-25 title for the third time in four years.

She conceded shots on the opening two ends of the final against Bernadette Hill (24) of Billet BC, Essex, but was 8-2 in front after six ends. Her opponent secured the only three of the match on the seventh to keep in touch. From that stage, however, when she was not accumulating twos and ones herself, Miss Anton was good enough to restrict Miss Hill to singles, and she won 21-11 after 23 ends.

Although now 25, Miss Anton will be eligible to enter again in 1991 in a bid to reach her fifth final in the nine years of the competition.

Quarter finals: B. Hill (Essex) 21, H. Pettit (Middlesex) 20; D. Loveless (Sussex) 21, W. Betambeau (Bucks) 16; K. Hawes (Oxford) 21, S. Irons (Cambs) 16; C. Anton (Hunts) 21, M. Wilson (Lincs) 14.
Semi finals: Hill 21, Loveless 7; Anton 21, Hawes 14.
Final: Anton 21, Hill 11.

Mother & Daughter

Losing finalists in 1989, Joan Holliday who plays for Elton BC, and her daughter Diane Sekjer of Maidstone BC, pulled off what must have been the most dramatic win in the seven years of the competition.

With three ends to go they trailed 19-12 against Wendy Betambeau and her mother Maureen Penny from Wendover. On that 19th end the Kent players retrieved all seven shots — the seventh on a measure - to level the scores. They gained a single on the 20th, and on the last, with the Bucks pair holding, Mrs Sekjer picked up the jack with her last bowl to complete 21-19 victory.

Quarter finals: M. Bonsor, J. Baker (Derbys) 19, P. & S. Oliver (Gloucs) 14; W. Betambeau, M. Penny (Bucks) 17, S. Bailey, D. Goodwin (Surrey) 12; J. Holliday, D. Sekjer 34, V. & A. Owens (Surrey) 8; S. & C. Gapp (Norfolk) 30, S. Water, E. Cox (Essex) 14.
Semi finals: Betambeau, Penny 21, Bonsor, Baker 16; Holliday 21, Sekjer 12.
Final: Holliday, Sekjer 21, Betambeau, Penny 19.

Secretaries & Treasurers

Mavis Steele retained the Secretaries and Treasurers trophy, winning it for' the fifth time in nine years. The EWBA assistant secretary, who is also the treasurer of Middlesex, beat the Surrey treasurer Pam Davis in the final. The losing semi-finalists were Margaret Richardson, treasurer of Lincolnshire, and Pat Powell, the Hampshire secretary.

Final: M.Steele (Middx) 21, P. Davis (Surrey) 14.

Essex County Championship

at Paxmans, Colchester, August 4th 1990

Singles: Peter Ayling (Harlow) 25, Mark Christmas (Pegasus) 15.
Pairs: Rob Clark, John Watson (Chadwell St. Mary 21, David Farr, Nigel Smith (Liberty of Havering) 19.
Triples: D. Baxter, L. Freeman, R. Marrable (Thorpe le Soken) 27, Peter Demeza, Harry Musaphia, Ivan Fennell (Aldersbrook) 10.
Fours: Terry Keyworth, John Clark, Peter Sage, Roy Harrington (Old Dagenham Park) 19, Francis Raven, Tony Maples, Gary Cable, Dennis Lewis (Southend on Sea) 18.

Leicestershire County Championships

at Narborough, August 5th-6th 1990

Singles: Mick Hughes (Syston) 25, Derek Clark (Belgrave) 24.
Pairs: Sean Nicholls, John Bowman (Measham) 22, Mike Smith, Derek Clark (Belgrave) 13.
Triples: C. Bettany, George Wood, Ray Emms (Rolls Royce) 24, Lionel Moore, Russel Amies, David Shaw (Hinckley) 14.
Fours: Les Storer, Brian Crouch, Les Jinks, Roger Cooper (Leicester) 21, Mark Allison, Mike Heywood, Ron Leman, Roger Huckle (Kingscroft) 19.
Champion of Champions: Played at Knighton Victoria, September 9th: Bill Smith (Western Park) bt Ian White (Holwell Works).

Hertfordshire County Championships

Finals at Tring, August 5th 1990

Singles: M. Knowles (Cheshunt) 25, R. Jackson (Roebuck) 19.
Pairs: J. Allen, J. Chapman (Hatfield) 25, M. Knowles, D. Phillips (Cheshunt) 18.
Triples: P. Armstrong, J. Brookes, J. Cox (St. Albans Townsend) 18, T. Hayward, P. Leslie, P. Howes (Potten End) 16.
Fours: P. Spearman, C. Trussel, J. Coyne, M. Hewat (Roebuck) 24, S. Ellis, A. Warner, J. Allen, J. Chapman (Hatfield) 23.
Under-30 Singles: J. Rumball (Garston) 25, J. Allen (Hatfield) 14.
Officers Singles: A. Castle (Letchworth Garden City) 25 P. Moore (Berkhamsted) 15.
Unbadged Singles: P. Adams (Royston) 25, G. Makinson (Cheshunt) 16.

Huntingdonshire County Championships

Finals at Eynesbury, August 5th 1990

Singles: Nigel Eagle (British Rail), Charlie Lewis (Montagu) 15.
Pairs: Dave Arnold, Rick Boyd (St. Peters Municipal) 27, George Heathcote, Micky Durber (St. Peters Municipal) 13.
Triples: Peter Hammond, Ken Sansom, Pat King (Brampton Institute) 19, Peter Jessop, Derek Hinchliffe, Andy Jessop (Belvedere) 17.
Fours: Ken Ding, Rupert Cox, Trevor Collins, Peter Jessop (Belvedere) 27, Vernon Wallace, Dave Masters, Geoff Wiles, Frank Elding (GPO) 16.
Under-25 Singles: Leigh Searson (Belvedere) 25, Stephen Hill (Somersham) 17.

Warwickshire County Championships

at Nuneaton, August 5th 1990

Singles: David Caldwell (Stratford upon Avon) 25, Richard Brittan (Erdington Court) 3.

Pairs: Morgan South, Michael Caldwell (Stratford upon Avon) 19, Norman Merrett, Ernie Over (Stoke) 15.

Triples: Michael Mann, Bill Ward, Nicky Walker (Royal Leamington Spa) 17, Mick Hawkins, Dave Bennett, Simon Davies (Welford on Avon) 13.

Fours: Phil Green, Neral Brereton, Harvey Brereton, Chris Pearce (Entaco) 23, Mario Rosso, Tim Escott, Mick Hawkins, Simon Davies (Welford on Avon) 14.

Middlesex County Championships

at West London BC, August 5th 1990

Singles: Gerry Smyth (Paddington) 25, Peter Huggett (British Airways Concorde) 19.

Pairs: Joe Brook, Gerry Smyth (Paddington) 19, Colin Harman, Paul Cater (West Ealing) 16.

Triples: Colin Pink, Pat Ryan, Andy Bennett (Broomfield) 13, Kieran Day, Stan Gregory, Syd Morgan (North London) 11.

Fours: John Kelly, Chic Bruce, Lenny Cairns, Jim Fuller (Broomfield) 20, Alec Grant, Paul Lawson, Brian Phillips, Fred Hurst (Broomfield) 14.

Unbadged Singles: Bill Kirk (Hendon) 25, Ian Jenkins (Hounslow Sports) 23.

Area Champion of Champions: (Played at Mansfield BC, July 29th) David Burrowes (Hayes Park) 25, David Clare (Century) 16.

Bournemouth Open

at various Bournemouth greens, August 5th-11th 1990

Tony Allcock added his name to the roll of famous players who have won the Bournemouth Open tournament Singles, when he beat Brian Miller of Uddingston, near Glasgow, 21-14 at Meyrick Park. On his way to the final Allcock had beaten two previous winners — Bob Provan in the sixth round and David Ward in the semi finals.

Miller, who turned from football to bowls less than ten years ago, led 6-1, 10-2 and 14-10, but subsequently lost his touch as he tried to find the answer to Allcock's short-jack tactics. Allcock went ahead for the first time on the 18th end and won with a closely grouped four on the 20th. As well as the modest prize money, £250 from the sponsors, the Portman Wessex Building Society, Allcock took home a magnum of champagne presented by the tournament caterers.

The Bonsor brothers, Andrew and John, from Nottinghamshire, took the Pairs 18-17, John trailing the jack on the extra end against Chris Daniels and Peter Line. In the Triples, Dean Morgan and Russell Morgan (no relation), with Peter Pull, upheld local pride when they finished 2,2,6,1 against the Surrey combination of John Dobson, Dave Campbell and Steve Tuohy, winning 21-12 for Boscombe Cliff.

Singles: Round 6: B. Miller (Uddingston) 21, F. Williams (Kodak) 18; S. Tuohy (Mitcham) 21, R. Thomas (Barry Athletic) 8; D. Bishop (Alexandra) 21, G. Morgan (Mid-Surrey) 11; P. Vamvacopoulos (West Wimbledon) 21, J. Stanley (Rugby Thornfield) 12; A. Allcock (Cheltenham) 21, R. Provan (Airdrie) 15; W. Davies (Blandford) 21, A. Berry (Taunton) 18; D. Ward (Cromer) 21, A. Redfern (Tally Ho) 10; I. Bond (Crediton) 21, A. Atkinson (Southport) 19.

Quarter finals: Miller 21, Tuohy 12; Vamvacopoulos 21, Bishop 12; Allcock 21, Davies 8; Ward 21, Bond 14.

Semi finals: Miller 21, Vamvacopoulos 17; Allcock 21, Ward 15.
Final: Allcock 21, Miller 14

Pairs: Final: A. Bonsor, J. Bonsor (Huthwaite Park) 18, C. Daniels, P. Line (Atherley) 17 (after extra end)

Triples: Final: D. Morgan, P. Pull, R. Morgan (Boscombe Cliff) 21, J. Dobson, D. Campbell (both Old Dean), S. Tuohy (Mitcham) 12.

Windlesham (Hove) Tournament

at Windlesham Club, Hove, August 6th-11th 1990

Club members, antique dealers David Wigdor and Tony Dade sponsored the event.

Singles:
semi finals: Roy Hockley (Hurstpierpoint) 25, Glen Holly (Preston) 15; Bruno Wells-Brown (Hove & Kingsway) 25, Bill Wareham (Worthing Pavilion) 20.
Final: Wells-Brown 25, Hockley 22.

Pairs:
Final: Alan Webb, Jim Morley (Saltdean) 22, John Stevens (West Hoathly), Ian Watson (Lindfield) 18.

Triples: Mervyn Fyffe, Roy Pocock, Ron Savage (Hove & Kingsway) 21, Eddie Vince, Joe Moses, Dave Moses (Windlesham) 10.

Brighton 48th Women's Open

at Preston Park, Brighton, August 6th-11th 1990

Sue Drummond, Brighton Borough Council's organiser of both the town's men's and women's tournaments welcomed the Mayor, Mrs C. Simpson for the presentations.

Singles:
Semi finals: June Cain (J.E. Hall) 21, Helen Keating (Popesmead) 16; Doreen Smith (Streatham Park) 21, Mary Perrett (BAA Heathrow) 10.
Final: Cain 21, Smith 11.

Pairs:
Final: Glenda Jones (Hampton), Irene Ellins (Masonians) 22, Doreen Smith (Streatham Park), Eileen Knight (Redhill) 15.

Mixed Pairs:
Final: Eileen Knight, Len Deadman (Redhill) 21, Sue Small (Henfield), Geoff Cresswell (Hove & Kingsway) 18.

EWBA Champion of Champions

at Victoria Park, Leamington Spa, August 6th-8th 1990

This competition, in only its second season, was notable for a second title for Gill Fitzgerald. Having won the Two-Wood Singles with great style she switched smoothly to the four-wood game and bore out what she said after her two-wood triumph: "My favourite game is the four-wood."

Mrs Fitzgerald, 41, plays for Kettering Lodge BC, and 21-13 and 21-15 wins against York and Leominster opponents respectively, preceded a classic quarter final tie against Linda Bedingfield from Shouldham, Norfolk, who delivered some superb drawing woods to retrieve a 17-11 deficit and make

it 20-20 after 26 ends. Mrs Bedingfield then trailed the jack, as did Mrs Fitzgerald, under great pressure, to win 21-20. By contrast her 21-13 semi final win against Sheila Offler of Sherwood, Notts, was smooth.

On a complementary path to the final was none other than Mavis Steele, doyenne of the women's game, and still as astute a bowler as ever. The Sunbury Sports player proved this in her semi final against the talented Edna Bessell from Yeovil who was losing 19-18 but holding four shots on the 20th end. With her final wood Miss Steele took out three of them, and then cooly drew the two she wanted for 21-19 victory on the 21st.

Both players found a dry green producing inconsistency in the final. Miss Steele seemed to be in control when she led 14-9, but Mrs Fitzgerald was undaunted by her opponent's record and skill. Four consecutive draws gave her a 16-14 lead. Miss Steele hit back with a three. Again the Northants player responded, and three and two gave her 21-17 victory, and the double.

The result reversed the 21-15 defeat Miss Steele inflicted on Mrs Fitzgerald in the last 16 of the national indoor singles at York in 1989.

Round 1: E. Bessell (Yeovil) 22, P. Sturgeon (Priory, Southend) 18; C. Anderson (Cowes) 21, J. O'Donnell (Worcester) 15; P. Ward (West Oxford) 21, S. Duck (Rye Park Hoddesdon) 12.

Round 2: Bessell 21, Ward 5; S. Miles (Hesketh Park, Dartford) 21, Anderson 11; W. Barnard (Brixham) 21, P. Elliott (Princes Risborough) 14; B. Johnson (Houghton Dairy Lane, Durham) 21, B. Noble (Luton Town) 14; G. Acland (Liskeard) 21, P. Owen (Corley, Coventry) 20; G. Fitzgerald (Kettering Lodge) 21, A. Leeman (Dunnington York) 13; M. Day (Seahouses Northumberland) 21, L. Murden (Silver Band Long Eaton) 18; L. Bedingfield (Shouldham, Norfolk) 21, H. Ashton (Heaton Hall Manchester) 15; J. Chapman (Hemingford Hunts) 21, S. Sullivan (Woodley Berks) 20; S. Offler (Sherwood Notts) 21, E. Evans (Gloucester City) 12; J. Searle (Greenhill Weymouth) 21, J. Haines (Melton Town) 16; P. Strong (BRSA Lincoln) 21, C. Miller (March Conservatives Cambs) 7; D. Panks (Hadleigh) 21, C. Duarte (South London) 10; B. Hackett (Leominster) 21, M. Allan (Courtfield Carlisle) 14; M. Steele (Sunbury Sports) 21, L. Kemp (Bexhill) 16.

Round 3: Offler 21, Panks 10; Strong 21, Searle 18; Johnson 21, Acland 14; Bedingfield 21, Chapman 14; Fitzgerald 21, Hackett 15; Bessell 21, Miles 17; Day 21, Barnard 18; Steele 21, Bartlett 16.

Quarter finals: Bessell 21, Day 9; Fitzgerald 21, Bedingfield 20; Offler 21, Strong 18; Steele 21, Johnson 15.

Semi finals: Fitzgerald 21, Offler 13; Steele 21, Bessell 19.

Final: Fitzgerald 21, Steele 17.

Standard Life Open

at Clevedon, August 6th-11th, 1990

David Bryant, keen to enliven an unusually quiet summer, almost took the Standard Life Open title at home in Clevedon, but went down in the final to Chris Messer a promising newcomer from Cambridge Chesterton. Messer, 21, on the opening day of the tournament, learned his bowls at Clevedon from the likes of Bryant himself and his England colleague, Pip Branfield, but has matured a great deal since his family moved to Cambridge.

Singles: Semi final: — D J Bryant (Clevedon) 21 C Notaro (Taunton) 7, C Messer (Cambridge Chesterton) 21 G Hazell (Cardiff Ath) 15.
Final: Messer 21, Bryant 18.
Pairs: Semi final: W Davy, A Gadd (Clevedon) 23, G Screen, R George (Redland Green) 18, P Wootten, E Seaville (Robinson) 16, M Rowsell, S Harvey (Clevedon Promenade) 15.
Final: Wootten, Seaville 24, Davy, Gadd 14.
Triples: Semi final: J Packer, R Hughes, C Jones (Robinsons) 20, A, N and C Pearce (Portishead RBL) 15, R Sweet, R Pitts, K Frost (Clevedon) 21, D Harrison, P Iles and W Gunningham (Avondale) 16.
Final: Sweets, Pitts and Frost 16, Packer, Hughes and Jones 15.

Tunbridge Wells Men's Tournament

at Tunbridge Wells, August 6th-11th 1990
Singles:
Semi finals: D. Corke (Grove) 17, R. Dinham (Borough Green) 21; C. Dann (Grosvenor) 21, J. Smith (Wadhurst) 6.
Final: Dann 21, Dinham 10
Pairs:
Semi finals: L. Yeomanson (Tunbridge Wells), D. Yeomanson (Grove) 18, M. & N. Aers (Clare Park) 19; J.A. & J. Dunn 24, G. Bailey, K. Tadd (Tunbridge Wells) 12.
Final: Dunns 22, Aers 10

Triples:
Semi finals: R. Day, O. Fryer, J. Tuff (Hunton) 15, H. Bryant, L. Aldred, L. Jarvis (Culverden) 24; J. Smith, W. Crittle, J. Picknell (Wadhurst) 17, M. Ward, D. Lott, J. Worsell (Tunbridge Wells) 13.
Final: Smith, Crittle, Picknell 17, Bryant, Aldred, Jarvis 14.

Bexhill 53rd Tournament

at Polegrove, Bexhill, August 6th-11th 1990
Singles:
Semi finals: Tim Baker (Sidley Martlets) 21, Vince Valenzuela (Sidley Martlets) 3; Mick French (Bexhill) 21, Stan Howe (Sidley Martlets) 16. Final: Baker 21, French 17.
Pairs:
Final: David Dignum (Severalls, Colchester), Charles Stock (Gullivers) 29, Eric Allen, Bert Oettle (Bexhill) 8.
Triples:
Final: Alan Evans, Gordon Moore, Peter Fitzsimmons (Sidley Martlets) 17, Jack Humphrey (Gullivers), David Dignum (Severall), Charles Stock (Gullivers) 10.

Surrey County Championships

Finals at Croydon, August 9th 1990
Singles: Wynne Richards (Mid-Surrey) 25, Bill Short (Old Dean) 12.
Pairs: James Howick, Andrew Hawes (Croydon) 21, Terence Honnor, Gary Little (Mid-Surrey) 14.
Triples: J. Pullen, R., Buckle, R. Lamdin (Sub. N. Hezzell) (Woking Park) 19, M. Tuck, J. Hempston, P. Vamvacopoulos (West Wimbledon) 15.
Fours: B. Willingham, B. Badgery, L. Dickson, G. Nicholls (Wimbledon Durnsford) 20, M. Flaherty, H. Punjabi, A. Nuttall, P. Hunt (Old Couldson) 13.

Champion of Champions: Joe Stevens (Epsom Park) 21, John McDonnell (Gonville) 12.
Unbadged Singles: Andrew Mitchell (Guildford) 22, Michael Sigamoney (North Sheen) 13.
Secretaries Singles: John Hawes (Putney) 9, Graham Jenkins (Putney Town) 21.

Somerset County Championships

Finals at Victoria BC, Weston-Super-Mare, August 11th 1990

Singles: Peter Mattravers (Ilminster) 25, Jim Hobday (West Backwell) 13.
Pairs: Peter Owens, Alan Apsey (Bristol) 23, Paul Davies, Mike Martin (Banwell) 12.
Triples: Bob Johnson, Selwyn Jones, Peter McCall (Bristol) 16, G. Flyng, Dave Coles, Ivan Danford (Bristol) 12.
Fours: Neil Westlake, Chris Ratcliffe, Mike Roberts, Colin Westlake (Winscombe) 20, Steve Gait, Derek Chivers, Terry Perkins, Ian Middlemast (Bath) 18.
Under-25 Singles: N. Draper (Eastover Park) 25, T. Trent (Willmott Park) 3.

Berkshire County Championships

Finals at Reading, August 11th 1990

Singles: Gary Stacey (Huntley & Palmers) 25, Michael Newman (Reading) 17.
Pairs: John Smith, Jim Clarke (Wokingham) 20, Robert Newman, Michael Newman (Reading) 12.
Triples: Fred Moore, Peter Heayns, Paul Ryman (Hagbourne) 18, Robert Newman, Adam Graves, Michael Newman (Reading) 13.
Fours: Les Rowe, Keith Hawkins, Colin Brooks, Ken Nash (Suttons) 24, John Walker, Colin Harrison, Gordon Ballantyne, Neil Haines (Thatcham) 22.
Champion of Champions: Gary Stacey (Huntley & Palmers) 26, Colin Brooks (Suttons) 16.

Woolwich EBA National Championships

at Beach House Park, Worthing, August 12th-24th 1990

Tony Allcock's double success, the excellent condition of the Worthing greens and the introduction of admission fees to the greens to watch the championships were all milestones in the history of the championships, writes Donald Newby.

The success of Allcock, aged 35, in both Triples and Singles, was significant, for although it is 18 years since he first qualified for the championships, he had never before won a title.

It was a welcome surprise to both players and supporters of the game to discover the greens at Beach House Park in such good condition. Worthing Borough Council enjoys a close and helpful association with the English Bowling Association, and has made considerable efforts to provide facilities for bowlers, but it would be idle to pretend that the greens in recent years have been up to standard for national and international play. But since the 1989 championships the greens had been improved beyond all recognition, their green and velvety condition causing favourable comment on all sides.

To assist increased costs of upkeep of the greens a charge of £1 a day was imposed in the area of the park containing the four greens, and though there were a few grumbles, the system worked well and appeared justified. The crowds were the thickest ever, though it has to be said that this could have been due in some measure to the almost constant sunshine spectators enjoyed.

Fours

A team from Bath, skipped by Ian Middlemast, a university research officer who reached the Singles final in 1988, won the Fours, the traditional opening event of the championships.

Middlemast and his partners, Steve Gait, Derek Chivers and Terry Perkins, had a six-shot victory over a Nottingham team, GPT Beeston, in a semi final and then had seven shots to spare against Mansfield Colliery, the other Nottinghamshire team in the final.

The comparative ease of Bath's victory over GPT Beeston came as something of a surprise, for the Notts team in charge of England lead Brett Morley — who has developed into a highly competent skip — had a number of easy victories in the earlier rounds. Bath completely outbowled them, building an 18-8 lead which proved unassailable.

Triples

The wide age range of competitors provoked considerable interest in the Triples, much being made of the fact that one of the Sussex qualifiers, Oliver Ovett, playing for Preston Manor club was only 14 years old and one of the winners, Jack Drummond-Henderson a veteran of 79.

Sporting an ear-ring, Ovett, a cousin of the athlete Steve, and a couple of weeks from his 15th birthday, played well enough, but in company with his partners Ian Blake and Leigh Prince, lost a close first round against Andy Bennett's Broomfield team who had three shots to spare.

More impressive on the green than Ovett, however, were the two other young players, Graham Shadwell from the Trowbridge, Westbourne club and Robert Newman of Reading. Shadwell, only a month older than Ovett, assisted his father Brian and skip Alan Colebrooke to a first round victory over a Dorset triple from the West Moors Memorial club, but were dismissed in the second round. Newman, who had his 15th birthday earlier in the year, made more substantial progress leading. With Tony Graves at No.2 and his father Mike skipping, Robert reached the quarter finals with a runaway victory over Wootton Bassett (skipped by international Mel Biggs), and then successes over Marlow and Bristol. Reading then met their match against a first class team from Poole Park — Brian Shepherd, Ron Porter and John Kingdon — whose victims had included Hunstanton, skipped by Mervyn King, one of England's latest internationals. Poole Park recovered from a 9-6 deficit against Reading to win nine consecutive ends and end young Robert's dream of a national title on his first appearance at Worthing.

Young teenagers had certainly made their mark in the Triples, but they could not match the septuagenarians who occupied the limelight throughout this event. One of these was Bob Stephenson, aged 73, who, with his Walker (Northumberland) colleagues, reached the semi finals. Stephenson's appearance at these championships evoked memories of four years earlier when he and his partner had reached the final of the world indoor Pairs only to lose to David Bryant and Tony Allcock. Stephenson illustrated that he had not lost any of his skill with the passage of the years. The Walker three failed to reach the final, finding their Welford-on-Avon opponents, Mick Hawkins, Dave Bennett and Simon Davies too strong. Davies, in particular, was in scintillating form for Welford, his final deliveries, end after end, keeping his team out of trouble.

Stephenson had done well, but not so well as Drummond-Henderson from the upbeat Gloucestershire club from Suffolk Square, Cheltenham, playing No.2 to Tony Allcock. This sprightly veteran frequently raced up the green behind his deliveries, belying his years, and kept his energy and concentration over three days to play a vital part in assisting Allcock to his first championship.

The Cheltenmham trio, Andy Wills, 20, Drummond-Henderson, and Allcock displayed tremendous form as the event progressed. Wills, who has made a coaching video with Allcock, is a lead of great promise and Drummond-Henderson did all that was asked of him at No.2.

In the final, Cheltenham led Welford by 14-4 and then 17-6 with only five ends left for play. But the Warwickshire side had an inspired skip in Davies, whose form throughout the week must have impressed the England selectors. He contrived a four, then a three and a two to leave his side only two shots adrift with two ends left. Welford then moved the mat further up the green to exploit Cheltenham's discomfiture over short ends, but Hawkin's jack was too short. It went back to Wills, who played a long end, and Cheltenham scored a single to leave Welford requiring a last-end three to tie.

Both sides responded to the pressure, but Drummond-Henderson's astutely placed back woods and a timely last wood by Allcock saw Cheltenham through. Welford won the end, but a single was not enough.

Pairs

John Ottaway, the 1989 Singles champion, and his skip Roger Guy from Wymondham Dell, emerged from a top class field to win this title. After the second round it was never easy for them, but each time they withstood the challenge. Ian Reeves and international David Taylor from British Rail, Carlisle, led them 11-10 in a quarter final, but with four ends left, the Wymondham pair were seven shots ahead, and that was a sufficient cushion depsite the loss of a four on the 20th end.

They then met the Reading father and son combination of Mike Newman skipping his 15-year-old son Robert, whose exploits deserve attention. In the third round, the Newmans recovered from 17-10 down to defeat Norman Merrett and Ernie Over of the Stoke Club, Coventry. Over the last five ends they scored a four and a three, and after a tie, added and five and a single to win 26-17.

In their next encounter the Newmans met Middlesex qualifiers, international Gerry Smyth and his lead Joe Brook from the Paddington club, and by the half-way stage, had built a seven-shot lead. Then Brook had the better of matters with young Newman, and with Smyth also finding good touch and not sparing his forcing shots, a tight finish seemed inevitable. Smyth buried the jack to score four and disaster loomed for the Newmans two ends later when Paddington held six shots. But they lost them all when Mike Newmans's running shot rolled the jack close to the strings to earn him a three. Brook and Smyth tried everything they knew on the closing ends, but the Newmans finished 23-14 ahead.

The Wymondham-Reading semi final clash produced a cracking match. Ottaway and Guy built an 11-1 lead, but schoolboy Robert and his father were not done yet. Their fight back began with a four when Robert outdrew Ottaway and his father planted 'policemen' to protect the head. They went on to take a 17-16 lead, but the Norfolk pair battled back to go ahead 19-18 with one end left for play. The Newmans held shot on the final end, but Guy had the last word to give the Norfolk pair a passport to the final.

In the other half of the draw, the other Middlesex quarter finalists Colin Harman and Paul Cater from West Ealing club figured in one of the best matches of the championship fortnight. Their opponents, Ron Keating and David Cutler, both former EBA Singles champions from the Plymouth Civil Service Club led by 16-10, only to lose 14 shots in a row. Two fours helped the Plymouth pair to force an extra end. West Ealing held shot when Cutler played his final wood — a near perfect last wood. It rocked the West Ealing shot bowl, but failed to displace it from the jack. So the Londoners were through to the semi final.

The form of Geoff Roll and John George from the County Arts club, Norwich, had suggested the possibility of an all-Norfolk final. Their quarter final against Alan Johnson and George Watson from Portland, Northumberland, produced a drawing match of high quality, and the Norfolk side finished a shot up to reach the last fours.

Their semi final with West Ealing produced another close game. County Arts slipped up in the middle of it, dropping two fours to fall 16-10 behind. Norfolk hauled themselves back into the game but despite skilful skipping by George, they finished two shots behind. A five and a three on the two opening ends had put the Norfolk pair firmly in control, but Harman and Cater battled all the way. On the 15th end Ottaway delivered four bowls short and West Ealing scored a one to reduce the gap to 14-12. That Ottaway lapse, however, was only temporary. On the next end Ottaway rolled three shots within a foot of the jack. Although Cater moved it, Guy did too, to give Wymondham a single. Cater suffered on the next end when, with woods at the back, his drive bounced the jack back from the ditch to give Wymondham shot and a lead of 171-13. West Ealing picked up singles on the next three ends, but Wymondham held firm on the final shoot-out when Ottaway trapped the jack to take the title.

Singles

Tony Allcock's first Singles success at these championships should be considered against the background of his record of the past few years. It was the third time in four years he had qualified from Gloucestershire toreach the last four, and one previous occasions he had been beaten, once in the

LEFT: Tony Allcock proudly displays the EBA Singles trophy. Picture: Steven Line.
RIGHT: Welshman John Price poised for the shot that won him the Embassy World
indoor title. Picture: Duncan Cubitt.

Australian Ian Schuback in action,
outdoors and indoors. Soon after
winning gold in the Commonwealth
Games pairs, he was at Preston seeking
further honours. He reached the finals in
both events, the singles and pairs but
was beaten in both. Pictures: Duncan
Cubitt.

ABOVE: Australian Rob Parrella, Commonwealth Games singles winner chats with David Bryant, who lost his bid to win a fifth Commonwealth Games Singles Gold. Picture: Duncan Cubitt.
RIGHT: Mark McMahon, runner-up to Parrella watches his bowl down the purpose built rink at Preston in the World Indoor singles. Picture: Kevin Chevis.

Gill Fitzgerald, elated with her victory in the Englishwomen's national two wood singles. She also won the Champion of Champions title and was in the Kettering Lodge team, runner-up in the National Fours. Picture: Dave Shopland.

Liz Wren, skipping for Scotland in the British Isles women's indoor internationals won all her games. Picture: Kevin Chevis.

BELOW: Barbara Till, the grandmother who won the Liverpool & National Insurance Englishwomen's national singles at Leamington. Picture: Kevin Chevis. Catherine Anton (right) who won the Englishwomen's national under-25 title for the third time in four years. Picture: Dave Shopland.

The graceful delivery of Richard Corsie, the brilliant young Scottish bowler in play at Preston Guild Hall where he lost his world indoor Singles title. Corsie, back from New Zealand, defeated David Bryant to win a second successive Commonwealth Games bronze medal. Picture: Kevin Chevis.

Elation from Andy Thomson, who won the English indoor singles title for the second successive year. Picture: Duncan Cubitt.

Elation from John Price when he realised he was world indoor singles champion. Pictures: Duncan Cubitt.

Elation from Norma Shaw at the moment of winning the British Isles women's pairs title with Betty Johnson (left). Picture: Kevin Chevis.

John Ottaway (ABOVE extreme left) looking concerned, explains to his Pairs partner and skip Roger Guy what he has to do. Guy obliges and the pair become the National Pairs champions. They celebrated at Worthing (right above). Ian Middleton of Bath skipping his Fours team in the same championship looks concerned too. Picture: Stephen Goodger. But it all came right for him for Bath won the title and are seen (BELOW) with Woolwich marketing services manager Mr Roger Ham. Picture: Stephen Line.

ABOVE: England's national triples winners Jack Drummond-Henderson, 89, Tony Allcock, 35 and Andrew Wills, 20, receive the Triples trophy from Mr Neil McMahon, general manager Woolwich Administration.

BELOW: The scene at Worthing during the final at the Woolwich National championships as Kirk Smith waits for the next delivery from the eventual national singles winner Tony Allcock. Picture: Stephen Line.

LEFT: Smiles from the winners of the Ashbourne Homes Scottish Mixed Pairs.

ABOVE: Smiles, too, from the British Isles women's championship winners Joan Evans, Betty Morgan and Brenda Mills from Wales.

BELOW: Smiles from President Kath Horncastle and other England officers, celebrating their team's Eve Trophy success, also at Saundersfoot. Pictures: Kevin Chevis.

ABOVE: Thamesdown skip Mel Biggs gets down to it at the English indoor pairs championships at Melton Mowbray. Picture: Duncan Cubitt.
RIGHT: Martin O'Kane celebrates a winning shot for Cleator Moor during a first round fours match at the Woolwich championships. Picture: Dave Shopland.

LEFT: Gill Smith, England's indoor singles champion (Picture: Kevin Chevis) and Wendy and Peter Line winning partners in the McCarthy & Stone Mixed Pairs. Picture: Stephen Goodger.

ABOVE: Winners and runners-up in the two-wood Singles and Fours English women's championships at Leamington with Mr Ken Wilkinson, chairman of the sponsors, Liverpool Victoria Insurance. BELOW: England hail their Nat West British Isles outdoor international victory for the eighth successive year.

TOP LEFT: Oliver Ovett, 14 at the time, and youngest ever competitor in the EBA championships. TOP RIGHT: The oldest champion in play at Worthing in August, 79 at the time. ABOVE (left) Kirk Smith, runner up to Tony Allcock watches his delivery. Pictures: Stephen Goodger. RIGHT: Gary Harrington, beaten finalist, describes how he managed to lose the Toshiba tournament at Tiverton to winner John Evans (right). Picture: Castle Photographers.

ABOVE: Norma Wilson and Brett Morley, winners of the Makeson National Mixed Pairs receive their trophy from EIBA President Tony Ward and Mackeson branch manager Tony Watson. RIGHT: Irish happiness during the Ireland v Scotland international at Sandersfoot. Picture: Kevin Chevis. BELOW: Bowls in Spain at Bena Vista. One green is carpet, the other grass. Picture: Chris Mills.

RIGHT: Robert Montgomery, President 1990-1991 of the World Indoor Bowls Council, a former Irish international.

BELOW: The women's and men's winners at the Scottish championships. Pictures: Gordon Hyslop.

ABOVE: Action in a semi-final of the Middleton Cup. LEFT: A tense moment in the final. Pictures: Stephen Goodger.

BELOW: Yorkshire celebrate their Middleton Cup victory; their last success in the county championship was in 1978. Picture: Stephen Goodger.

semi final against Ottaway in 1989, and in the final against David Holt in 1987. Following successes in the national indoor Singles in 1985 and 1987, he reached the finals again in 1989 and 1990, only to be tamed each time by Andy Thomson.

Such a record, whilst indicating that Allcock was undoubtedly a Singles bowler of the very highest class, suggested also vulnerability when it comes to the crunch, and the Singles for which he had qualified once again appeared wide open with a number of his international contemporaries in contention. In Allcock's half of the draw were internationals Wynne Richards, Bill Hobart, Mel Biggs and Brett Morley and he defeated them all with flair and style.

After winning the title, Allcock said he felt his most difficult game ofall was against Wiltshire's Mel Biggs, now an experienced England front player, who is never very far away in national championships and competitions. The 25-17 quarter final scoreline in favour of Allcock may have been rather flattering, but his closing touch was sure.

Brett Morley, the fourth international Allcock had to face playing in his second semi final — he reached that stage in the Fours — gave him less trouble. So Allcock was in the final.

The possible finalists in the other half of the draw included John Ottaway, the reigning champion, Gary Harrington, and Jim Hobday who won a Triples gold medal with Allcock and David Bryant at the 1980 world championships.

Harrington was tumbled out in the first round by Mick Harris of the Preston club, Brighton, who was then mastered by Alf Chambers, an ebullient, crowd pleasing character from Suffolk. After his Pairs success which involved two long games, Ottaway was called on to a preliminary round of the Singles. He won this to end an exhausting day, but the mental effort and concentration his Pairs victory and this Singles match entailed were clearly visible the following morning when Dave Caldwell from Stratford-on-Avon edged him out. Caldwell, however, was outbowled in the next round by Terry James, a newsagent from Thrapston, Northants, a tenacious opponent clearly intent on making the news himself. James finally reached the semi finals with a handsome victory over Hobday.

Chambers, constantly racing up the green, also reached the quarter finals where he faced Kirk Smith, 23, a junior international and former winner of the indoor Cockney Classic from Dedham. Smith proved too sharp for Chambers and his 25-13 victory won him a semi final place against James, who appeared a good prospect for the final when leading 12-6 and holding four shots. Smith however, killed the end and scored three on the replay, later running into a closing purple patch which earned him three successive threes and a 25-20 win.

Smith found Allcock on song in the final. An opening four gave the Gloucestershire maestro a flying start. By the 11th end, he led 15-6, and after conceding a four, took complete control. Displaying precise control of length, moving up the mat and flicking his woods to the jack in a style all his own, Allcock kept his young opponent constantly under pressure. "He was absolutely brilliant", Smith said after his 25-12 defeat.

Fours

Quarter finals: Mansfield Colliery,(P. Jackson, G.B. Hufton, G. Hufton, J. Mills) 20, West Witney (R. Gotobed, F. Roberts, H. Williams, P. Latter) 17; Topsham (M. Osborne, P. Durrant, A. Elson, D. Tucker) 28, Thatcham (J. Walker, C. Harrison, G. Ballantyne, N. Haines) 22; Bath (S. Gait, D. Chivers, T. Perkins, I. Middlemast)' 20, Glenholme (R. Bell, J. Hutchinson, J.Haley, J. Stothard) 10; GPT (P. Martlew, M. Lukowski, P. Goulding, K. Morley) 18, Belvedere (K. Ding, R. Cox, T. Collins, P. Jessop) 17.
Semi finals: Mansfield Colliery 27, Topsham 18; Bath 23, GPT 17.
Final: Bath 20, Mansfield Colliery 13.

Triples

Quarter finals: Welford-on-Avon (M. Hawkins, D. Bennett, S. Davies) 20, Woking Park (J. Pullen, R. Buckler, N. Hezzell) 18; Walker (M. Mooney, R. Stephenson, J. Tweddle) 21, Bolton (B. Milne, A. Leach, B. Hindle) 13; Cheltenham (A. Wills, J. Henderson, A. Allcock) 22, St. Albans Townsend (P. Armstrong, J. Brookes, J. Cox) 5; Poole Park (B. Shepherd, R. Porter, J. Kingdon) 19, Reading (R. Newman, A. Graves, M. Newman) 9.
Semi finals: Welford-on-Avon 17 Walker 8; Cheltenham 17 Poole Park 13.
Final: Cheltenham 18 Welford-on-Avon 16

Pairs

Quarter finals: W. Ealing (C. Harman, P. Cater) 26, Plymouth CS (R. Keating, D. Cutler) 25; County Arts (G. Roll, J. George) 17, Portland (A. Johnson, G. Watson) 16; Wymondham Dell (John Ottaway, R. Guy) 21, British Rail (I. Reeves, D. Taylor) 17; Reading (R & M Newman) 23, Paddington (J. Brook, G. Smyth) 14.
Semi finals: Harman, Cater 18, Roll, George 16; Ottaway, Guy 20, Newman, Newman 18.
Final: Ottaway, Guy 19, Harman, Cater 15 (???)

Singles

Quarter finals: K. Smith (Denham) 25, C. Chambers (Eye) 13; T. James (Thrapston) 25, J. Hobday (West Blackwell) 20; A. Allcock (Cheltenham) 25, M. Biggs (Wootton Bassett) 17; B. Morley (GPT Notts) 25, G. Stacey (Huntley & Palmer, Berks) 18.
Semi finals: Smith 25, James 20; Allcock 25, Morley 12.
Final: Allcock 25, Smith 12.

Hastings 72nd Open Tournament

at White Rock Gardens, Hastings, August 13th-25th 1990

Singles:
Semi finals: David Colbourne (Bolton) 21 David Kennedy (West Barnes, Dunbar) 19; John Hooker (White Rock) 21, Tony Cottis (Bracknell) 13. Final: Colbourne 21, Hooker 20.
Triples:
Final: L. Ellis, P. Hanger (Rochester) B. Diplock (Bat & Ball, Gravesend) 26, H. King, D. Yeomanson, M. Luker (The Grove, Tunbridge Wells) 5.
Fred Turk Trophy Singles (last 16 losers) final: B. Balfour (West Barnes, Dunbar) 21, Charlie Aries (Hastings Rosemount) 11.
Pairs:
Final: J. Davies (Preston Manor), Alan Mayne (Bolton) 30, Robert Curry, George Young (Glen Park, Dunston) 11.

Fours:
Final: D. King, L. Flyn, L. Dickson, G. Nicholls (Wimbledon Durnsford) 19, J. Moore, N. Ives, G. Evans, V. Page (White Rock) 13.
Consolation Triples:
Final: M. Southouse, D.Southouse (Hailsham), D. Ashby (S. Norwood) 20m, A. Short, S. McClelland (Leam Lane, Gateshead, H. Wade (Brogborough) 19.

Liverpool Victoria Insurance
English Women's National Championships

at Victoria Park, Leamington Spa, August 1st-11th 1990

No recent English Women's Championships, not even those of the previous year, basked in such glorious weather, writes Doug Hughes With temperatures well into the 90s on the opening four days, the voice of EWBA secretary Nancie Colling using the public address system to urge green-side supporters to keep their players well supplied with suitable drinks, was regularly heard. It says much for the endurance of women bowlers - and much perhaps, for the often maligned uniform, particularly the hat — that only one player had to retire through heat exhaustion.

Reputations count for little in these championships. Norma Shaw did not qualify from her county competitions, Mary Price fell at four hurdles, failing to get beyond quarter finals, and internationals generally were given short shrift.

The outstanding individual player was 41-year-old Gill Fitzgerald of Kettering Lodge. She won both the Two-Wood Singles and the Champion of Champions Singles and was a losing finalist in the fours with three Kettering colleagues. Mrs Fitzgerald's achievements underlined Northamptonshire's most successful ever national championships. She was involved in 16 consecutive victories before losing in the Fours final.

Pairs

The gradually increasing awareness of young women in the sport was reflected in the semi-finals line up. Three of the pairings comprised mother and daughter combinations, and two of them moved on to contest the final.

The EWBA's Mother & Daughter competition itself first prompted Maureen Christmas and her daughter Jenny Tunbridge from Chesterton, Cambridge, to join competitive forces in 1987. They have yet to make an impact in it, which is surprising in view of the skilful bowls they played during the four days it took them to become the 1990 senior champions at Leamington.

Victories of relative comfort against opponents from Derbyshire, Worcestershire, Northants and Essex, carried them into a semi final against Audrey Cox and Lynn Thelwell of Marlow who started their campaign in the preliminary round and were playing their sixth match in little over 50 hours. They led until the 15th end, and then conceded a five to trail 15-11, an advantage which Mrs Christmas and Mrs Tunbridge seized upon. Thw Cambridge pair could afford to drop three shots on the 19th end before winning 18-16.

In the other half of the draw, Margaret Bonsor and her daughter Jean Baker, the 1989 Singles champion from Alfreton, negotiated their stiffest hurdle in round one, scoring a three on the final end to defeat the former England player Irene Molyneux and Audrey Mainwaring of Oxford City and County 20-19.

The Derbyshire pair conceded only 26 more shots in beating opponents from Northumberland, Norfolk and Northants. In the semi finals they faced the third mother and daughter, Doreen and Cheryl Miller from another Cambridgeshire club, March Conservatives, who were winners of the Mother & Daughter competition in 1989. Mrs Bonsor and Mrs Baker opened a 7-0 lead after three ends, and a four on the fifth made it 11-1. There was no way back for the Millers who eventually lost 26-11.

It seemed the final might follow a similar pattern when the Alfreton duo drew three opening end shots. Two more on the third made it 5-1. Mrs Christmas and Mrs Tunbridge then found their mark, and six shots on the next three gave them a 7-5 lead. A two on the tenth pulled Mrs Bonsor and Mrs Baker back to 8-10 in arrears and the match was simmering.

But on the next two ends the superb lead woods of Mrs Christmas were capitalised upon by her skip and junior international daughter. Four shots were secured each time, and Cambridgeshire was on the way towards its first senior national title for many years, the final scoreline was 24-12.

Triples

Three Baldock bowlers secured Hertfordshire's first major title for four years, and deservedly so after three days of very consistent play.

Ann Haywood, Jill Ward and skip Shirley Page, produced a string of performances so precise that in three of their six matches the 18th ends did not have to be played. Long Eaton Town 20-12, and Falmouth 28-10 were their early successes, before they faced England's Mary Price and her Burnham Bucks colleagues.

Leading 16-8 with three ends to go, the game looked safe for Baldock. Mrs Price then inspired a typical fight back. She needed three shots to draw level on the last end, and was holding them — plus a possible measured fourth — until Mrs Page delivered a stunning last wood to bisect Burnham's first shot and the jack and gain shot herself for a 17-13 victory. There could have been no better wood in the entire championships.

Another Buckinghamshire team from Princes Risborough opened an 8-2 lead against Baldock in the quarter finals - but were overwhelmed 21-11 by the 17th end. The Uxbridge three Daphne Hobbs, Jean Baker and Doreen Lavender had also played well up to the semi finals where they succumbed 18-7 to the Hertfordshire trio.

The other finalists were from Lincoln and the North Scarle club, which had, at the start of the season, a membership of just eight. Ann Bellamy, Cath Smith and Sheila Wilson did their small club proud. They were run close by Brixham (18-13), by Oxford City and County (18-16), and even closer by Memorial Park Luton, who saw a 16-11 lead vanish. North Scarle scored five on the 17th, and one on the last end to win 17-16.

Quarter final opponents from Bolton were comfortably beaten 22-11, and that brought them up against England junior captain Catherine Anton from Peterborough, skipping her mother Ivy, and England junior team mate Mandy Brundle. At that stage, these three were favourites for the title, and even stronger ones when they led 7-0 at three ends. The Lincoln team countered by scoring on nine of the next eleven ends, and then hold off a late Peterborough charge to win 18-16.

The final lived up to the reputations the two teams had by now forged for themselves. The lead switched several times up to the 15th end when the contest was poised at 13-13. Baldock then drew a crucial three, and followed it with a four. North Scarle required seven on the last end to save the match. They obtained four but that was not enough.

The most remarkable match of the competition was in the first round. Mary Bruce, Eleanor Paynter and Connie Armstrong from Linton Morpeth club in Northumberland, and first won their preliminary round crushing their West Row, Mildenhall opponents by 24-7. Then they crashed themselves, losing 25-1 to Cumbria's Wigton trio of Carole Studholme, Kathleen Baxter and Margaret Christie.

Two-Wood Singles

Elegant, six-foot tall Gillian Fitzgerald brought Northamptonshire its first major EWBA title for many years when she overwhelmed Beryl Noble of neighbouring Bedfordshire 18-8 in the final.

After nine ends it looked as if Mrs Fitzgerald would whitewash her opponent. Six maximum draws and three singles gave her a 15-0 lead. Mrs Noble of Luton Town got off the mark on the tenth end. She wanted twos to have any chance of retrieving the situation, but Mrs Fitzgerald allied confidence with style and accuracy to maintain control, and as soon as Mrs Noble erred again, she swooped to pick up two championship clinching shots on the 17th end.

It was Mrs Fitzgerald's third successive visit to Leamington as Northants county champion. She lost in the first round on each previous occasion, first against Jayne Roylance of North Walsham, Norfolk, who went on to win the title in 1988.

Fours

Starcross and District, a club which stands on the estuary of the River Exe in Devon, trod an up and down path on the way to this triumph. Yet the club's ladies section only affiliated to the EWBA in 1988; until then only the Starcross men had played competitive bowls.

Sheila Turner, a Devonian, Jill Gush, a Starcross member for 25 years, Carol Walters, whose origins are Scottish, and Betty Mackerness who played her first bowls in Middlesex, have played as a rink since 1988, and only missed qualifying for Leamington in that first year because the EWBA annulled the rule that losing semi-finalists from the larger counties were also eligible to play.

The 1989 Starcross lost their first round county tie, but a year later reached the final, journeyed to Leamington, and crushed Blyth opponents Cowpen and Crofton 30-11 to open the campaign. Starcross then survived a precarious last five ends against Lammas Ealing whom they beat 22-20. In round three against Henlow Park from Bedfordshire, they conceded five on the first end, and recovered to win 29-23. A late evening quarter-final against Redditch club, Hewell, was won 18-14 thanks to six shots on the last three ends. The following morning Somerset neighbours Yeovil were comfortably beaten 22-10 in the semi finals.

Opponents in the final were Kettering Lodge four Brenda Wills — 17 years' at the club, Sue Bagshaw — her first time at Leamington, Gill Fitzgerald, and skip Mavis Buckby, a veteran of all the national competitions. But it was a particularly significant final for Mrs Fitzgerald, already winner of the Two-Wood Singles, and the Champion of Champions. A third title would have been unprecedented.

Singles

Barbara Till, aged 56, a grandmother of seven from Portsmouth, took the title back to Hampshire for the first time since 1982. She moved through the early rounds largely unnoticed as the achievements of others tended attract attention. Especially so was a quarter-final,in which Joan Howlett of West Bridgford in Nottinghamshire overcame the favourite, and 1988 champion, Mary Price of Burnham, Bucks. A three on the 29th end gave Mrs Howlett a dramatic 21-19 victory after an enthralling match which earned spontaneous applause as the players left the green.

But Mrs Till was also claiming a notable quarter-final victim in another England player, Gwen Daniel of Penryn, who was outplayed to the tune of 21-9. That same 21-9 scoreline prevailed in both semi finals. Mrs Till, who plays for Milton Park BC, eventually proved too skilful for 24-year-old Sally Smith from Norfolk, who was the EWBA's first Under-25 champion in 1983. After seeing an early six shots lead whittled down to one, Mrs Till regained control and scored on six consecutive ends to complete victory in 18 ends.

Mrs Howlett (57), also required 18 to defeat Arlene Colbourne from Bolton who went on to the green barely 30 minutes after overwhelming Dorothy Prior from Hewell, Redditch 21-4 in a quarter-final which was delayed by the non-stop progress both players had enjoyed in Singles and Fours during the two previous days. Mrs Colbourne started the semi final by drawing a three and a two, but only scored on three ends thereafter as Mrs Howlett found a relentless length and accuracy, and clinched her win with a four.

The Nottinghamshire player — runner-up in the Two-Wood Singles in 1987 — drew the opening shot, and then conceded singles on the next three ends. Mrs Till built on her lead with some immaculate bowling, and a four on the 13th put her 14-5 in front, which she increased to 15-5 and 17-6. Mrs Howlett then called on the grit she had shown against Mrs Price, and a three and four in succession made it 17-13 and had the crowd really buzzing. Mrs Till in turn, did not lose her composure; she replied with a three, and two ends later secured the one she wanted for her 21-15 triumph.

A 'bowls widow' until ten years ago, Mrs Till then decided to follow in her husband Cyril's steps, and quickly became a devotee. In 1987 she reached the indoor Singles final and was beaten by Norma Shaw. One of the first things she did after winning at Leamington was to telephone her son-in-law in Australia. "He often rings me to say how well he and my grandson are bowling," said Mrs Till. "Now I shall be able to tell him he is speaking to a national champion!"

Pairs

Quarter finals: A. Cox, L. Thewell (Marlow) 28, E. Bird, A. Glover (Sherwood, Notts) 8; M. Christmas, J. Tunbridge (Chesterton) 24, D. Chenery, V. Young (Colchester) 17; M. Bonsor, J. Baker (Alfreton) 32, S. Drage, V. Bird (British Timken, Norhtants) 8; C. Miller, D. Miller (March Conservative) 20, S. Baker, F. Potter (Dorchester) 19.
Semi finals: Christmas, Tunbridge 18, Cox, Thewell 18; Bonsor, Baker 26, Miller, Miller 11.
Final: Christmas, Tunbridge 24, Bonsor, Baker 12.

Triples

Quarter finals: Uxbridge (D. Hobbs, J. Baker, D. Lavender) 19, Spennymoor (R. Airey, J. Hull, I. Lawson) 14; Baldock (A. Hayward, J. Ward, S. Page) 21, Princes Risborough (J. Beech, C. Robertson, B. Walford) 11; Peterborough & District (I. Anton, M. Brundle, C. Anton) 25, Ilkeston, Rutland (I. Benniston, A. Walters, C. Wealthall) 4; North Scarle (A. Bellamy, C. Smith, S. Wilson) 22, Bolton (L. Hunt, V. Holloway, C. Swan) 11.
Semi finals: Baldock 18, Uxbridge 7; North Scarle 18, Peterborough 16.
Final: Baldock 20, North Scarle 17.

Two-Wood Singles

Quarter finals: I. Molyneux (Oxford C & C) 15, Y. Groom (Street) 6; B. Noble (Luton) 15, D. Davy (Stratton, Bude) 12; J. Roylance (N. Walsham) 16, J. Curtis (Yatton, Somerset) 9; G. Fitzgerald (Kettering Lodge) 18, S. Chamberlain (Connaught, Chingford) 3.
Semi finals: Noble 15, Molyneux 12; Fitzgerald 16, Roylance 12.
Final: Fitzgerald 18, Noble 8.

Fours:

Quarter finals: Braintree (R. Collett, A. Beale, L. Cowell, C. Duckworth) 19, St. Neots (J. Gilbert, D. Huckle, J. George, L. Cooper) 9; Kettering Lodge (B. Wills, S. Bagshaw, G. Fitzgerald, M. Buckby) 21, Bolton (B. Toft, M. Powell, M. Mallinson, A. Colbourne) 13; Yeovil (M. Taylor, S. Cowcher, E. Bessell, M. Fellows) 22, Peterborough (I. Anton, V. Newson, M. Brundle, C. Anton) 19; Starcross (S. Turner, J. Gush, C. Walters, B. Mackerness) 18, Hewell (J. Stanton, D. Prior, P. Boswell, T. Tyler) 14.
Semi finals: Kettering Lodge 19, Braintree 17; Starcross 22, Yeovil 10.
Final: Starcross 20, Kettering Lodge 14.

Singles

Quarter finals: S. Smith (N. Walsham) 21, M. Osbourne (St. Neots) 13; B. Till (Milton Park, Hants) 21, G. Daniel (Penryn) 9; J. Howlett (West Bridgford) 21, M. Price (Burnham, Bucks) 19. A. Colbourne (Bolton) 21, D. Prior (Hewell) 4.
Semi finals: Till 21, Smith 9; Howlett 21, Colbourne 9.
Final: Till 21, Howlett 15.

Hartlepool Open Pairs

at Brinkburn and Greyfields Bowling Greens, August 18th-19th 1990
The Hartlepool Open Pairs forms an integral part of the annual Town Show, a two-day event that attracts more than 20,000 visitors. Entries were received from 140 pairs from England and Scotland. Local club bowlers contested

a dramatic final when John Sharp and Eddie Leck (Foggy Furze) scored a, four count on the 21st end to level with Ray Clementson and Steven Hutchinson (Hartlepool Boilermakers). Leck again faced defeat on the extra end, but his running bowl took a fortunate deflection to finish shot.

Semi finals: John Sharp, Eddie Leck 13, Tony Macey, Ian Fletcher 9; Ray Clementson, Steven Hutchinson 15, Enid and John Parkes 8.

Final: Sharp, Leck 20, Clementson, Hutchinson 19.

Bolton Open Pairs

Finals day at Bolton, August 18th 1990

After struggling for nine ends in the final, Brian Oakes and Bill Cropper snatched a last end three to win the £300 top prize. Their opponents and club colleagues David Lockhart and international David Holt took the runners up prize of £150.

Section 1: W. Counsell, J. Howe 6, G. Haslam, F. Harrison 10; M. Axford, A. Higgs 3, A. Locke, G. Niven 10; Counsell, Howe 5, Locke, Niven 5; Haslam, Harrison 10, Axford, Higgs 5; Counsell, Howe 7, Axford, Higgs 7; Haslam, Harrison 8, Locke, Niven 6.

Winners: Haslam and Harrison.

Section 2: C & J Walker 6, T. Barber, R. Vaughan 12; F. Hamer, K. Bradshaw 5, J. Twemlow, J. Simpson 5; Walkers 4, Twemlow, Simpson 7; Barber, Vaughan 8, Hamer, Bradshaw 6; Walkers 7, Hamer, Bradshaw 5; Barber, Vaughan 4, Twemlow, Simpson 5.

Winners: Twemlow and Simpson

Section 3: A. Shurmer, G. Schofield 11, J. Colling, H. Hargreaves 2; D. Counsell, R. Millin 5, D. Lockhart, D. Holt 13; Shurmer, Schofield 8, Lockhart, Holt 7; Colling, Hargreaves 11, Counsell, Millin 5; Shurmer, Schofield 6, Counsell, Millin 9; Colling, Hargreaves 5, Lockhart, Holt 9.

Winners: Lockhart and Holt.

Section 4: J. Finnerty, C. Greenwood 10, D & A Herd 9; M & A Baker 4, B. Oakes, W. Cropper 9; Finnerty, Greenwood 9, Oakes, Cropper 5; Herds 17, Bakers 5; Finnerty, Greenwood 4, Bakers 10; Herds 7, Oakes, Cropper 16.

Winners: Oakes and Cropper Semi finals: Lockhart, Holt 14, Haslam, Harrison 4; Oakes, Cropper 15, Twemlow, Simpson 4.

Final: Lockhart, Holt 6, Oakes, Cropper 7.

Huntingdonshire Women's County Championships

at Ramsey BC, August 18th 1990

4-Wood Singles: Catherine Anton (Peterborough & District) 22, Mandy Brundle (Peterborough & District) 20.

2-Wood Singles: Val Newson (Peterborough & Dist) 14, Edna Housden (Ramsey) 11.

Pairs: Mary Palmer, Ann Ashmore (Hemingford) 25, Margaret Manchett, Meg Fisher (Warboys) 20.

Triples: Ivy Anton, Mandy Brundle, Catherine Anton (Peterborough & Dist) 18, Joyce Anthony, Betty Morton, Val Newson (Peterborough & Dist) 13.

Fours: Joyce Foster, Nancy Lilley, Peggy Aldcroft, Lorna Lewthwaite (Wittering) 22, Ivy Anton, Val Newson, Mandy Brundle, Catherine Anton (Peterborough & Dist) 21.

Champion of Champions: Catherine Anton (Peterborough & Dist) 21, Joan Wakefield (Wittering) 15.

Sussex Women's County Championships

at Lewes, August 20th 1990

Singles: Kathie Herrington (Petworth) 21, Trixie Moore (Royal Parade) 17.

Pairs: Iris Grice, Joan Meek (Kingsway) 27, Freda Linberry, Marjorie Martin (Field Place) 12.

Triples: Marjorie Curtis, Jo Hardy, Diana Whittingham (Kingsway) 19, Maggie Woodcock, Joan Parker, Doris Blunt (Worthing Pavilion) 14.

Fours: Val Burr, Trixie Moore, Ann Rose, Pat Bain (Royal Parade) 30, Terry Thatcher, Isabel Fisher, Pat Pearce, Jean Bowles (Preston Park) 15.

Champion of Champions: Lorraine Kemp (Bexhill) 21, Diana Whittingham (Kingsway) 10.

Two-Wood Singles: Sue Walter (Nutley) 17, Freda Linberry (Field Place) 9.

Bristol and West Women's Open

at Weston-Super-Mare, August 20th-25th 1990.

August 20th-25th, 1990.

Wendy Slatter of ICI, Gloucester, beat four internationals on her way to the title, her most notable scalp being that of England's Mary Price in a Singles semi final. Peggy Edwards and Barbara Carey, practising for their successful bid to regain the all-England Over 55 Pairs title, swept everything before them — and even accounted for the current world outdoor Singles champion, Janet Ackland, in a semi final of the Pairs.

Singles semi final: W S Slatter (ICI, Gloucester) bt M Price (Burnham) 21-16, V Howell (Merthyr West End) bt M B Cawley (Port Talbot) 21-16.

Final: Slatter bt Howell 21-15.

Pairs semi finals: D Woodley (Swindon) and D Mitchell (Gloucester City) bt F Tovey (Ashcombe) and B Atherton (Nottingham) 25-13, P Edwards and B Carey (Bentham) bt J Ackland (Penarth Belle Vue) and D Roberts (Sully) 19-9.

Final: Edwards and Carey bt Woodley and Mitchell 28-10.

Mixed Pairs semi finals: L and M Thomas (Pontypool) bt D Parker and H Langley (Nailsea) 26-12, E Humphries (Stony Stratford) and R Joyes (Ashcombe) bt J Wilkinson (Bristol South) and R Wilkinson (Greville Smyth) 19-11.

Final: Thomas and Thomes bt Humphries and Joyes 26-17.

Yorkshire Women's County Championships

at Bert Keech, York, August 21st 1990

Singles: Anita Haw (Bert Keech) 21, June Foster (Nafferton) 16.

Pairs: Hilary Cooke, Jean Pindar (Springhead, Hull) 25, Barbara Constable, Peggy Madden (Marske) 12.

Triples: Marjorie Zimnoch, Anita Haw, Pat Napier (Bert Keech) 23, Jean Landers, June Kay, Nilar Hey (Selby-Brayton) 6.

Fours: Janet Hague, Hilary Cooke, Mary Blackburn, Jean Pindar (Springhead) 29, Pat Melling, Marjorie Porteous, Margaret Turner, Shirley Sharket (Reckitts, Hull) 12.

Champion of Champions: Jenny McCluskey (Eston) 21, June Hartley (Nafferton) 8.

Essex Women's County Championships

at Woodford, August 23rd 1990

Singles: Penny Else (Rayleigh) 21, Carol Duckworth (Braintree) 18.

Pairs: Penny Else, Evelyn Schooling (Rayleigh) 21, Diane Chenery, Vivian Young (Colchester) 11.

Triples: Sheila Hennessy, Delia Searle, Valerie Wade (Wickford) 26, Jean Bridge, Doris King, Elsie Herron (Liberty of Havering) 9.

Fours: Ruth Collett, Ann Beale, Lois Cowell, Carol Duckworth (Braintree) 24, Janice White, Angela Pease, Sylvia Clarke, Pat McGuinn (Billet) 23.

Champion of Champions: (Played at Falcon BC, August 30th) Evelyn Schooling (Rayleigh) 21, Alma Willcox (Orford House) 14.

Northamptonshire Women's County Championships

at Corby Grampian BC and Wellingborough,
July 18th, 25th, and August 24th 1990

Singles: Maria Gearey (PSL Roade) 21, Val Wade (Kingsthorpe) 20.

Pairs: Marilyn Patterson, Cathy Kyle (Stewart & Lloyd, Corby) 21, Sheila Drage, Vi Bird (British Timken) 17.

Triples: Adele Gearey, Diane Bowtle, Maria Gearey (PSL Roade) 18, Isabel Brown, Sylvia Brown, Christine Barlow (Abington Park Ladies) 13.

Fours: Brena Wills, Susan Baghsaw, Gil Fitzgerald, Mavis Buckby (Kettering Lodge) 22, Marlene Beck, Wendy Bishop, Blanche Cox, Edna Payne (Rushden Town) 18.

Champion of Champions: Val Wade (Kingsthorpe) 21, Mary Moseley (West End) 15.

Two-Wood Singles: Played at Abington Park BC, 18th June: Gil Fitzgerald (Kettering Lodge) 14, Diana Bowtle (PSL Roade) 12.

Oxfordshire Women's County Championships

at South Oxford BC, August 20th-21st 1990

Singles: B. Trafford (City & County) 22, I. Molyneux (City & County) 12.

Pairs: A. Mainwaring, I. Molyneux (City & County) 18, G. Winstone, S. Rogers (City & County) 13.

Triples: I. Molyneux, G. Winstone, M. Ellis (City & County) 23, G. Blackmore, G. Clarke, B. Trafford (City & County) 7.

Fours: A. Allmond, G. Ward, V. Jones, M. Peake (Thame) 19, P. Empson, J. Jarrow, H. Woodward, J. Fawdrey (Charlbury) 15.

Champion of Champions: Played at Oxford City & County, May 19th) P. Ward (West Oxford) bt G. Harris (South Oxford).

NatWest Middleton Cup

Semi finals and final at Beach House Park, Worthing,
August 25th 1990

Yorkshire's sixth Middleton Cup victory since this inter-county competition was launched in 1911, followed steady progress earlier in the season to head what is probably the hardest round robin section of any to win.

Northumberland had won the title in 1985 and 1988, Lancashire were runners-up in 1989, and Durham, though not quite so successful outdoors have proved the most consistent indoor county during the past decade with four Liberty Trophy successes during the past nine years.

But Yorkshire emerged from the three to head their section and reach the quarter finals, at which stage they outbowled Nottinghamshire. It was clear therefore, that they could be serious challengers for the title when the last four counties, Essex, Buckinghamshire, Dorset and Yorkshire, converged on Beach House Park, Worthing, to shout and shoot it out for the cup at the end of the national championships.

Logical it may have been to consider Yorkshire likely winners, but the manner of their triumph defied logic and description. One rink won the championship almost on their own — that skipped by Yorkshire president Geoff Mooring who crowned his year of office with a runaway 44-4 victory over a hapless Dorset rink in the charge of John Searle.

Yorkshire's avalanche of four fours and a five on this rink left Dorset little hope of rescue from other rinks despite the form of Brian Shepherd, Ron Blake, Ron Porter and John Kingdon, who won their game against Ray Graham's four by 20 shots. Shepherd, Porter and Kingdon confirmed the class they had shown a few days earlier in the Triples and Fours in the National Championships.

So it was Yorkshire's cup. "This is the biggest win of my life, and what a way and what a day to do it," said Mooring, who is 60 and plays at the Bert Keech club, York.

This game, as well as being a mortifying experience for Searle and his partners, was a great blow to the army of Dorset supporters who had introduced a carnival atmosphere to the lush green lawns of placid Beach House Park, seeking Dorset's first Middleton Cup triumph for 52 years.

Quarter finals: Yorks 134, Notts 98 (at Burton House, Boston); Essex 125 Warwicks 107 (at St. Neots); Bucks 130 Oxon 111 (at Croydon); Somerset 112 Dorset 127 (at Westlecot, Swindon).

Teams for final stages: Yorkshire: Mark Walton, Charlie Bateman, Iain Boyle, Geoff Mooring. Brian Chapman, Nigel Brignell, Ian Farrar, Ray Graham. Steve Sanderson, David Harrison, Nigel Watson, Mick Parker. Anthony Scruton, David Carr, Bill Rodham, Ted Boyle. Eddie Gill, Brian Tennant, John Stroughair, David Stroughair. Simon Archer, David Coulson, Malcolm Harrison, Richard Hudson. Buckinghamshire: David Parr, Malcolm Giles, Kirk Smith, Michael Richardson. Mark Bantock, Andy Wise, Denis Glaister, John West. Derek Barton, Adrian Sussex, Breton Long, Tony Jenkins. David Gee, Ron Oakes, Melvin Vickers, Bill Vincent. William Norman, William Gee, Gary Grace, Ted Hanger. Denis Robertson, Claude Stimpson, Geoffrey Springell, Ian Harvey. Essex: Paul Maynard, Ken Blackman, Steve Pickford, Lionel Lee. Rob Morris, David Jarrold,. Norman Groves, Warren Whiteman. Ian Barker, Ray Marshall Alan McEl;rea, Derek Parsonson. Derek Ross Richard Hart, David Wakefield, Graham Brinley. Pat Watford, Peter Ayling, Andy Cooper, Tony Nimmo. David Farr, David McCathie, Nigel Smith, Joe Stamper. Dorset: Alec McKenzie, Mike Stapleton, M. Tomberry, A. Tidby. Sid Brice, Wayne Garnett, Chris Martin, Wynne Davies. Stuart Morgan, Barry Pattison, John Crabb, Phil Aplin. Ben Steadman, Dave Ralph, Ben Baker, John Searle. Brian Shepherd, Ross Blake, Ron Porter, John Kingdon. Richard Oliver, Mike Goddard, Peter Clarke, R. Freeman.

Semi finals: Yorks 117 Bucks 104. Rinks (Yorks first):
G. Mooring 21, M. Richardson 21; R. Graham 22 J. West 13; M. Parker 20 T. Jenkins 17; E. Boyle 18 W. Vincent 17; D. Stroughair 20 E. Hanger 16; R. Hudson 16 J. Harvey 20. Essex 104 Dorset 121. Rinks (Essex first):
L. Lee 8, A. Tidby 27; W. Whiteman 21, W. Davies 24; D. Parsonson 16, P. Aplin 16; G. Brinkley 17, J. Searle 19; A. Nimmo 15, J. Kingdon 22; J. Stamper 27 R. Freeman 13.

Final: Yorks 136 Dorset 113. Rinks (Yorks first) Hudson 14, Davies 13; Stroughair 27 R. Freeman 19; Mooring 44 Searle 4; Parker 19 Tidby 20; Graham 14 Kingdon 34; Boyle 18 Aplin 13.

Group 4:

Section A: Somerset 122 Gloucestershire 82; Devon 112 Worcestershire 114; Somerset 107 Devon 135; Worcs.100 Glos 120; Glos 129 Devon 125; Worcs 101 Somerset 120. Section, winner Somerset

Section B: Herefordshire 104 Dorset 138; Cornwall 111 Wiltshire 112; Heref 105 Cornwall 103; Wilts 109 Dorset 123; Dorset 150 Cornwall 88; Wilts 123 Heref 110. Section winner Dorset.

Cumbria County Championships

at Dalston, August 26th 1990

Singles: Ian Carruthers (Dalston) 25, Ron Little (Subscription) 18.

Pairs: Ian Reeves, David Taylor (British Rail) 18, Iain Howe, Ron McMath (Longtown) 17

Triples: Ian Carruthers, Graeme Vipond, John Willis (Dalston) 23, Ray McCarron, James Cowan, George Grearson (Workington) 8.

Fours: Paul Barlow, Andrew Baxter, Ron Gass, John Bell (Wigton) 30, Martin O'Kane, Clive Allison, John Brew, Malcolm Brew (Cleator Moor) 3.

Under-25 Singles: Richard Sampson (Appleby) 25, Stuart Airey (Workington) 9.

Under-18 Singles: Steven Dalziel (Wigton) 25, Richard Sampson (Appleby) 22.

Two-Wood Singles: Ron Gass (Wigton) 21, John Nicholson (Port Carlisle) 11.

Champion of Champions: Played at Edenside, September 9th. Anthony Little (Edenside) 25, Ron Gass (Wigton) 18.

Sussex County Championships

at Preston, Brighton, August 26th 1990

Singles: D. Whetstone (Lindfield) 25, M. Harris (Preston) 16.

Pairs: G. Knight, L. Prince (Preston Manor) 25, K. Holden, R. Owen (Hangleton) 15.

Triples: O. Ovett, I. Blake, L. Prince (Preston Manor) 23, K. Vickers, M. Chiappori, I. Puddick (Crawley Post Office) 15.

Fours: C. Wright, K. Cheetham, S. Jeapes, S. Walters (White Rock) 20, G. Leaman, D. Robinault, B. Spears, A. Hall 17.

Double Fours: T. Howard, F. Breach, C. Taylor, D. Weaver (Victoria Drive) 30, J. Foate, R. Jarrett, R. Edwards, J. Arthur (British Rail) 5.

Unbadged Singles: K. Bryder (Worthing) 25, K. Bayfield (Chichester) 17.

Champion of Champions: M. Smith (Tarring Priory) 27, A. Burchett (Motcombe Gardens) 11.

Woolwich Worthing Tournament

at Beach House Park, Worthing, August 27th — September 8th 1990

Dave Dennis of Portsmouth Civil Service, a member of the EBA coaching team, raced to 16-1 ahead after nine ends in the final and defeated Jack Davies (Preston Manor) by 21-14 to record his first open Singles title.

Former England player Peter Line put in a 4, 2, 1, finish to take the Triples and John Norman's team from the Portsmouth area won the Fours on an extra end. The Pairs ended in a clear cut win for Ben Norman and Peter Lazenby.

Singles:
Semi finals: D. Dennis (Portsmouth CS) 21, B. Bass (Mid Surrey) 11; J. Davies (Preston Manor) 21, W. Charles (Alexandra) 16.
Final: Dennis 21, Davies 14.
Pairs:
Semi finals: B. Norwell (Peterborough), N. Lazonby (Maryport) 24, P. Rees, G. Edward (DRG Shendish) 17; F. Varns, M. Bunyan (Merrow) 25, R. Gibson (Supreme), P. Wessier (Southey) 19.
Final: Norwell, Lazonby 26, Varns, Bunyan 16.
Triples:
Final: D. Bishop (Alexandra), D. Dennis, Peter Line (Atherley) 23, M. Crocker (Mid Surrey), R. Gibson, E. Crocker (Mid Surrey) 22.
Fours:
Final: J. Lee (College Park), R. Welch, I. Stephens (Copnor), J. Norman (Alexandra) 22, I. Morgan (Cwmavon), G. Knight (Preston Manor), T. Delaney (York Scarcroft), G. Lingwood (Norfolk, Norwich) 21.

Leicestershire Women's County Championships

at Narborough, August 24th 1990

Singles: Sue Jones (Hinckley Spa Lane) bt Janet Aitheson (Hinckley Sweet Pea)
Pairs: Zoe Eisler, Eve Duncan (North Kilworth) bt Olive Herbert, Dorothy Bannister (Barwell)
Triples: Chris Percial, Jenny Sutcliffe, Clare Cheney (Colinsthorpe) bt Lyn Green, Connie Beard, June Bentoft (Shepshed)
Fours: Betty Gale, Cynthia Wormleighton, Rene Langley, Joan Freeman (Belgrave) bt Enid Corby, Audrey Morring, Pat Blair, Dorothy Corby, (Blaby).
Champion of Champions: Ena Clarke (Countesthorpe) bt Maureen Gray (Westcotes).
Two Wood Singles: Marjorie Kilby (Oakham) bt Kath Fudger (Earl Shilton).

Herefordshire County Championships

at Kingsland and Hereford, August 26, September 8th-9th 1990

Singles: R. Perry (Bulmer) 25, R. Gardiner (Ledbury) 18.
Pairs: M. Elton, G. Sandford (Weobley) 22, T. Wear, S. Eden (Ross-on-Wye) 15.
Triples: P. Johnson, G. Griffiths, R. Perry (Bulmer) 22, B. Read, I. Maddox, M. Smith (Ledbury) 15.
Fours: P. Johnson, P. Griffiths, G. Griffiths, R. Perry (Bulmer) 22, T. Pritchard, B. Bradley, V. Shears, F. Williams (Leominster) 16.
Champion of Champions: L. Bethel (Hereford), S. Smith (Ledbury) 18.
Three Counties Champion of Champions: Winners: Bulmers, Herefordshire. **Runners-up:** Gloucestershire, Worcestershire.

Woolwich English Civil Service Championships

at Victoria Park, Leamington Spa, August 26th-30th 1990

Keen competition was again seen at these championships contested by the winners from 25 counties. John Searle (Dorset) retained the Singles, defeating Willy McCay of Cheltenham in the final by 25-21 and a Lancashire Middleton Cup trio also repeated their 1989 success.
Singles: Quarter finals: J. Searle (Dorset) beat D. Heath (Gloucester) 25-20. J.

Stringfellow (Plymouth) beat C. Kiddy (Londfon) 25-21. B. Gilmore (Waterside) beat D. McCalden (Farnborough) 25-10. W. McCay (Cheltenham) beat G. Newman (Birmingham) 25-23.
Semi finals: Searle beat Stringfellow 25-12. McCay beat Gillmore 25-11.
Final: Searle bt McCay 25-21
Pairs: Semi finals: E. Bateman, E. Gill (Yorkshire) bt G. Newman, R. Smith (Birmingham). N. Lewis, M. Elton (Worcestershire) beat S. Brice, J. Burns (Dorset) 19-18.
Final: Bateman, Gill beat Lewis, Elton 25-11.
Triples: Quarter finals: Notts beat Dorset 12-10; Lancs beat Thames Vakket 22-17; Bristol beat Farnborough 19-14; Birmingham beat Yorkshire 17-11.
Semi finals: Lancs beat Notts 21-12. Birmingham beat Bristol 23-17.
Final: P. Whiteley, V. Lyons, M. Gale (Lancashire) beat F. Maund, R. Smith, G. Newman (Birmingham) 18-15.
Fours: Quarter finals: London beat Birmingham 17-16; Bristol beat Yorkshire 19-15; Newcastle beat Durham 25-14; Farnborough beat Gloucester 20-12.
Semi finals: Bristol beat London 22-18; Newcastle beat Farnborough 25-10.
Final: W. Davy, B. Sandell, M. Collins, S. Meyrick (Bristol) beat E. Ewen, I. Peacock, A. McKenzie, R. Train (Newcastle) 20-17.

South Western Counties Championships

at Wellington, August 26th-27th 1990

Spectators anticipating the previous year's high standard were not disappointed. This was evident in the Singles with a preliminary round in which Stephen Rowse (Stenalees, Cornwall) defeated Roy Hawker (Spencer's, Melksham, Wiltshire) 25-24. After the first end there was never more than two shots difference between the two. Rowse then played Grahame Luker (Clevedon, Somerset) in a semi final. It was a nip and tuck game once again, Luker finally winning 25-24 after a marathon 33-ends match.

Nicky Jones (Bournemouth, Hampshire) had little difficulty qualifying for a semi final place, defeating Syd Brice (Wellworthy, Dorset) 25-9, and looked certain of a place in the final when he led Danny Denison (Newton Abbot, Devon) 14-3 after 10 ends, and 20-10 after 18, but a magnificent recovery by Denison over the next nine ends, during which he scored a four, a three, three twos and two singles to two single by Jones, assured him a place in the final by 25-22. In the final, Luker established a 4-3 lead after six ends, but following a two and a three by Denison on the next two ends, Luker's effort to get back into the match came to naught, Denison eventually winning 25-17.

The Pairs title went to Dorset (Dave Hanger and Syd Brice, Wellworthy), who defeated Ron Sparkes and Peter Shearing (Bournemouth) 25-17. Dick Foord and Peter Day (Brixham St. Mary's Park, Devon) must still be wondering how they missed out on a place in the final. Leading 21-12 at 18 ends in a semi final against Hanger and Brice, they dropped 1,6,3 to be squeezed out 22-21.

The Bristol (Somerset) Triple of Bob Johnson, Selwyn Jones and Peter McCall defeated Fred Tiddy, Monty Hawken and Eddie Whitburn (Perrantporth, Cornwall) 14-13 after an extra end to win the Triples, and the Totnes (Devon) four Norman Western, Ernie Knight, Bill Doble and Roy

Johnson proved too strong for Chris Ward, Mike Davies, Barry Taylor and John Davies (Banwell, Somerset), winning 22-11.

President Sam Mulligan (Shaftesbury, Dorset), presenting trophies and replicas expressed thanks to Gordon Fernley, Financial Services Consultant, Albany Life Assurance Co. Ltd. for generous sponsorship.

League Championship: Winners Cornwall, Runners-up Devon.

Singles: Danny Denison (Newton Abbot, Devon) beat Grahame Luker (Clevedon, Somerset) 25-17.

Pairs: Dave Hanger, Syd Brice (Wellworthy, Dorset) beat Ron Sparkes, Peter Shearing (Bournemouth, Hampshire) 25-17

Triples: Bob Johnson, Selwyn Jones, Peter McCall (Bristol, Somerset) beat Fred Tiddy, Monty Hawken, Eddie Whitburn (Perranporth, Cornwall) 14-13.

Fours: Norman Western, Ernie Knight, Bill Doble, Roy Johnson (Totnes, Devon) beat Chris Ward, Mike Davies, Barry Taylor, John Davies (Banwell, Somerset) 22-11.

Bristol & West Building Society
EBA Champion of Champions

at Bath, September 1st-2nd, 1990

Mike Bennett, 34, a former golf professional, from West Witney, Oxfordshire, who had been bowling for only five years, won his first major title here. Bennett had played golf professionally for 13 years, in tournaments all over Europe, and, although he did not win any event of note, he reckoned, prior to the final against Surrey police officer John Dobson, 41 from Guildford, that his experience of pressure on the golf course was proving to be a useful asset on the bowling green.

In the semi-finals, Bennett called upon that experience to halt the flamboyant charge of Italian born Carmine Notaro, 61, from Taunton, who learned to bowl when he played bocce in his native Naples. Bennett won 25-19.

Detective Sergeant John Dobson sank to his knees in mock relief after delivering a toucher to finish off the tenacions Andrew Jessop (Belvedere, Peterborough) 25-18 in the other semi-final.

Last 16: C Rowe (Tothill, Devon) 25, J Goode (Grantham, Lincs) 19, J Dobson (Guildford) 25, D Wilkinson (Cramlington, Northumberland) 7, A Jessop (Belvedere, Peterborough) 25, K Knowles (Flitwick, Beds) 14, P Bull (Boscombe Cliff, Hampshire) 25, L James (Shell, Essex) 10, C Notaro (Taunton) 25, S King (Hinckley, Leics) 18, D Cook (Billericay, Essex) 25, M Lill (Rugby) 23, M Bennett (West Witney) 25, R Holbrook (Canford, Gloucs) 23, D Burrowes (Hayes Park, Middlesex) 25, D Tynan (Ditton, Kent) 23.

Quarter finals: Dobson 25, Rowe 15; Jessop 25, Pull 16; Notaro 25, Cook 11; Bennett 25, Burrowes 21.

Semi finals: Dobson 25, Jessop 18; Bennett 25, Notaro 19.

Final: Bennett 25, Dobson 23.

Devon County Championships

at Tavistock, September 1st 1990

Singles: John Kelly (Plymouth Civil Service) 26, Andrew Knowles (Tiverton Borough) 20.

Pairs: Bill Powell, Danny Denison (Newton Abbot) 19, Ron Keating, David Cutler (Plymouth CS) 16
Triples: Bill Jones, Jack Boobier, Peter Curgenven (Tiverton Borough) 15, Bernie Blatchford, Barry Fletcher, Colin Rice (Mount Gould) 11.
Fours: Norman Western, Ernie Knight, Bill Doble, Ernie Knight (Totnes) 30, Mike Osborne, David Durrant, Adrian Elson, David Tucker (Topsham) 13.

Cornwall County Championships

at Kensey Vale, September 1st 1990

Singles: Harry Cattran (Penlee) 25, Alan Bray (Porthleven) 19.
Pairs: Peter Trusler, Albert Leaford (Bodmin) 23, Charles Edwards, Peter Towers (Looe) 20
Triples: John Lawer, Stephen Lawer, Bill Lawer (Carnon Down) 13, Peter O'Mahoney, Sidney Jones, Tony Smith (West Cornwall) 12.
Fours: Mike Cummins, Len Beckman, Norman Scott, Albert James (Liskeard) 21, Paul Sturtridge, Norman Coad, Mike Sturtridge, Steve Bray (St. Austell) 19.
Champion of Champions: Played September 13th: Ian Spreadborough (Saltash) 25, Brian James (Camborne) 15.

R. F.Taylor Northern Counties Championships

Finals at Kingston, Hull, September 1st-2nd 1990

Nigel Harrison from Ainsty club, York, had a comfortable victory in the Singles final to provide Yorkshire's only championship success from an appearance in four of the five finals. Kingston is the home green of Northern Counties chairman, Brian Reeve. The championships were again sponsored by the Northern Counties patron, EBA Past President, Fred Taylor.
Finals: Singles: Ian Carruthers (Dalston, Cumbria) 15, Nigel Harrison (Ainsty, York) 25.
Pairs: Terry Scott, David Webb (Summerhill, Newcastle, Northumberland) 21, Dennis Boyle, Jeff Davies (Withernsea, Yorkshire) 14.
Triples: Bill Ryder, Harry Dougherty, Alan Taylor (Hartlepool Park, Durham) 22, Karl Jamieson, Ronnie Keir, Joe Ellison (Astley Park, Northumberland) 10.
Fours: Graham Booth, John Franklin, Howard Smith, Peter Huddlestone (Bolton, Lancs) 26, Brian Chapman, John Rowan, Mick Corringham, Peter Robinson (Haxby Road, York) 18
Under-26 Singles: Ian Jackson (Peterlee, Durham) 125, Nigel Brignall (Nafferton, Yorkshire) 18.

Dorset County Championships

at West Moors BC, July 24th-25th, September 2nd & 8th 1990

Singles: Terry Baumber (Gillingham) 25, James Holloway (Shaftesbury) 10.
Pairs: Alec McKenzie, Bob Atkins (Poole Park) 21, Mark Tomberry, Adam Tidby (Poole Park) 19.
Triples: Stan Barnett, Stan Nelson, Bob Tappin (West Moors Memorial) 18, Brian Shepherd, Ron Porter, John Kingdon (Poole Park) 17.
Fours: Brian Shepherd, Peter Lovell, Ron Porter, John Kingdon (Poole Park) 21, Eddie Young, Richard Oliver, Ken Richards, Ben Baker (Dorchester) 20.

Under-25 Singles: Chris Pearce (Melcombe Regis) 25, Martin Patterson (Wellworthy) 9.
18s & Under Singles: Martin Patterson (Wellworthy) 25, Jamie Redman (Poole Park) 17.

Leamington Spa Ladies Open

at Victoria Park, Leamington Spa, September 3rd-8th 1990

There was an all-West Country Singles final in this 45th event, which, apart from the opening day, was completed in splendid weather. The defending champion, Wendy Anderson from Swindon, again reached the final having defeated Erica Humphries of Milton Keynes, winner of the title twice in previous years, by 21-13 in a semi final. Jill Price of Burnham-on-Sea defeated Leamington player Bridget Hay 21-14 in the other semi final, and then trailed 7-2 in the final. But the Somerset player recovered to 10-10 , and after a struggle, drew a 3 on the 21st end to win 21-17.

Experienced Rugby pair Pat Dahlgren of the GEC club, and Audrey Gilbert of Thornfield, beat Eileen Braidwood and Christine Hart of Leamington Avenue 24-18 in the Pairs final, after coming from 18-15 behind. Two more local players, Pam Morbey (Leamington Avenue) and Tony Van Spall of the town's Home Guard club, defeated Lynn and Alan Jones of Wolvey, Coventry 15-14 in the closest and best final, the Mixed Pairs. Warwickshire men's champion Dave Caldwell of Stratford, skipped his mother Wyn and Moira Honor to a 23-20 Mixed Triples victory against Maureen and Eddie Tims (Whitnash, Leamington) and Alice Macpherson (Banbury).

After eight years as tournament secretary, Mrs Tessa Stock has retired and been replaced by Mrs Val Steele of Southam.

Great Yarmouth Open Bowls Festival

at Great Yarmouth September 3rd-14th, 1990

Finals: British Gas/Gt Yarmouth Holiday Assocation Singles: — D Baird (Notts) 21, J George (County Arts, Norwich) 13.
Grant Drylining Mens Pairs: R Thacker, A Hart (Wymondham Dell) 17, J Weddall, D Wrigthson (North Walsham) 15.
Sandy Mobbs Sports Mens Triples: J Harns, M Butler, R London (Trethorpe/County Arts Norwich) 21, A Hill, F Vertigan, L Gutteridge (Downham/Gaywood Park) 15.
Butler and Blazey Mens Fours: J Barratt, M Chapman, W Miller, I Crook (Worksop Park/Rugby) 25, J Hawkins, M Gunton, J Wieson, P Wilson (Plumstead/County Arts) 9.
Martwell Ladies Pairs: R Buck, R Ward (Acle) 22. J Roylance, C Cragg (North Walsham) 13.
R Thacker Ladies Triples: M Moll, L Robinson, A Read (Norfolk County Council) 17, R Norns, A Dowe, V Atthowe (County Arts) 14.
Gt Yarmouth Holiday Association Mixed Pairs: D Ward, C Webb (Cromer) D Dougal, J Chilvers (Omnipac/Fleggburgh) 9.

Devon Women's County Championships

at Torquay, September 6th 1990

Singles: Mary Plater (Plymstock) 21, Anita Harris (Yealmpton) 16.

Pairs: Lucy Budge, Anne Pascoe (Plymouth Hoe) 25, Ali Thomas, Doreen Nightingale (Budleigh Salterton) 4.

Triples: Jenny Moore, Nora Baines, Wendy Barnard (Brixham) 27, Lilian Sparks, Phillis Osborne, Eileen Perrett (Plymouth Civil Service) 15.

Fours: Sheila Turner, Gill Gush, Carol Walters, Betty Mackerness (Starcross) 19, Dee. Lane, Betty Pennell, Sheila O'Connell, Ann McCambridge (Exonia) 18.

Champion of Champions: Played at Topsham, September 10th: Lorna Hackett (Kings) 22, Ann McCambridge (Exonia) 16.

NatWest Two Fours National Championship

at Oxford C & C, September 8th-9th 1990

Bolton twice showed great tenacity in semi final and final to overcome top England players and scramble to this title. After defeating Malmesbury in a quarter final they accounted for Clevedon by five shots with Tom Armstrong's rink defeating Pip Branfield's Clevedon four by six shots, while David Bryant and David Holt battled it out on the other rink in a drawn out game which included several dead ends. Bryant's advantage of one was insufficient to save Clevedon.

In the other semi final between Marlow and Blackheath & Greenwich, Ian Harvey's 21-12 victory over Gary Smith failed to cancel out Andy Thomson's 13 shot success over Jack Mays. Thomson scored a six on the 17th end and a five on the 19th.

With two of the national indoor Fours champions in each of the Blackheath rinks — Terry Heppell and Gary Smith in one, and Martyn Sekjer and Andy Thomson in the other, Blackheath had always appeared strong challengers and their route to the final was via Preston Manor, Brighton, who they defeated comfortably, and Marlow, who gave them a close game. Smith's four went down to Ian Harvey's team by nine shots, but Thomson's 27-14 win over Jack May left Blackheath four ahead.

The final produced a knife-edge finish with Bolton winning both games by a single shot. Holt and Smith were the first to finish, leaving everything to play for between Armstrong and Smith on the last end. Blackheath had held three shots until Tony Horobin, Armstrong's No.3 produced a perfect delivery which cut them all out. The skips failed to change the position, Thomson twice using weight in vain to leave Bolton champions by two shots.

Quarter finals: Blackheath & Greenwich 56, Preston Manor, Brighton 32. Rinks (Blackheath first):

A. Thomson 32, D. Ovett 12; G. Smith 24, W. Hayward 20.

Marlow 37, Cromer 34; Rinks (Marlow first):

I. Harvey 21, C. Ward 13; J. Mays 16, D. Ward 21,

Bolton 43, Malmesbury 29; Rinks (Bolton first):

T. Armstrong 19, M. Trimble 18; D. Holt 24, C. Exton 11.

Clevedon 43, Boston Sleaford Road 31, Rinks (Clevedon first):

P. Bramfield 20, W. Hobart 16; D. Bryant 23, R. Hall 15.

Semi finals:

Blackheath & Greenwich 39, Marlow 35. Rinks (Blackheath first):

Graham Booth, Tom Beasley, Martyn Sekjer, Andy Thomson 27, Dereck Barton, Andy

Wise, Geoff Springell, Jack Mays 14; John Chandler, Ken Lewis, Terry Heppell, Gary Smith 12, Jim Kirk, John Gamlin, Dave White, Ian Harvey 21.
Bolton 38, Clevedon 33. Rinks (Bolton first):
Steve Airey, Robert Millen, Tony Horobin, Tom Armstrong 22, Sid Apsey, Ray Pitts, Graham Luker, Pip Branfield 16; Bernard Milne, Karl Mitchell, David Colbourne, David Holt 16, Ken Frost, Hugh Hayter, John Freeman, David Bryant 17.
Final:
Bolton 38, Blackheath & Greenwich 36. Rinks (Bolton first):
T. Armstrong 19, A. Thomson 18; D. Holt 19, G. Smith 18.

Toshiba International Singles Challenge

at Tiverton, September 8th-9th, 1990.
The format of this event pits 16 in-form grass roots bowlers, survivors of the summer's qualifying rounds, against 16 invited internationals from England and Wales. Early exits were made by British Isles champion, John Ottaway and new England title holder, Tony Allcock, and the previous year's winner, Danny Denison, and runner up, Gerry Smyth, were also first-round casualties. The final had a footballing flavour, because John Evans and Gary Harrington had given up promising soccer careers in their early twenties to concentrate on bowls. Evans played inside forward for Torquay United in the 60's, and Harrington, 28, was a prolific goalscorer for Oxford City before he hung up his boots eight years ago. Both have gone on to win top honours at bowls, and both have represented England at Commonwealth Games. Evans won a silver medal in the Pairs in 1974, Harrington played in the fours at Auckland in 1990.

The former international beat the current England player in the final, which, in the best soccer tradition was a game of two halves, Harrington holding his own for the first ten ends, and Evans taking control thereafter.

Round 1: S Evans (Plymouth) bt D Denison (England) 25-23, M de Carteret (Guernsey) bt D Rhys Jones (England) 26-16, J Ottaway (England) bt E Furze (Clevedon Promenade) 25-19, P McCall (England) bt D Le Marquand (Jersey) 25-16, P A Line (England) bt I Mitchell (Shepton Mallet) 25-16, M Biggs (England) bt B Seabourne (Newquay Trenance) 25-3, M Prosser (Wales) bt R Osmant (Tiverton West End) 25-3, R Withers (Bristol St Andrews) bt G Smyth (England) 25-24, J Evans (England) bt L Fisher (Torbay) 25-7, J Haines (England) bt S Brice (Weymouth) 25-12, G P Harrington (England) bt M Osborne) 25-9, R Kivell (England) bt W Bell (Shepton Mallet) 25-20, W Richards (England) bt J Smith-Harris (Exeter St Thomas) 25-5, D Burch (Wellington) bt A Allcock (England) 25-24, T Mounty (Wales) bt A Knowles (Tiverton Borough) 25-18, M Bishop (Wales) bt D Bryant (Hatherleigh) 25-20.
Round 2: McCall bt Ottaway 25-23, S Evans bt de Carteret 25-20, Harrington bt Kivell 25-10, Haines bt Withers 25-20, Biggs bt Line 25-19, Mounty bt Burch 25-23, J Evans bt Prosser 25-14, Richards bt Bishop 25-23.
Quarter finals: McCall bt S Evans 25-18, Harrington bt Biggs 25-19, Richards bt Mounty 25-19, J Evans bt Haines 25-22.
Semi finals: Harrington bt McCall 25-16, Evans bt Richards 25-19.
Final: Evans bt Harrington 25-14.

London Parks BA Championships

at Barking Borough BC, September 8th, 1990.

Finals: Singles: P Cook (Pymmes Park) 21, D Beckett (Morden BC) 10.
Pairs: J Pring, C Brown (Hook and Southborough) 23, M Richfield, A Wiltsher (Culver).
Triples: D Bolton, J Walshe, D Field (Stormont) G Stimpson, P Lidbury, R Dixon (Ilford).
Champion of Champions: T Brooks (Shadwell) 21, R Dennison (Andre) 16.
Secretaries: J Brookes (Shadwell) 8, P Fuller (Surbiton Legion) 21.
Fours: W Cook, L Boswell, E Atkins, T Daden (Victoria Park) 20, A Rigby, L Weadman, A Wright, A Driver (Thornton) 16.
Jacksons Shield: Valentines Park 58, Wimbledon Durnsford 61.

Woolwich Broadstairs & St. Peters Open

at Broadstairs, September 9th-22nd 1990

Denis Edmeades of Herne Bay won the men's Singles title with two narrow victories, the first in a semi final over George Yandle, who later skipped the winning Mixed Fours. Irene Grace of Horton Kirby was another who narrowly missed a double. She was beaten by Doreen Hankin (Farnham) in the ladies Singles finals, but won the Mixed Pairs with Ron Acott after going ahead for the first time on the last end in the final.

Men's Singles:
Semi finals: D. Davey (Faversham) 21, N. Bishop (Northfleet) 20; D. Edmeades (Herne Bay) 21, G. Yandle (Ramsgate) 19.
Final: Edmeades 21, Davey 17.
Ladies Singles:
Semi finals: I. Grace (Horton Kirby) 21, M. Webster (Thanet) 17; D. Hankin (Farnham) 21, P. Selwyn (Magdalen Park) 17.
Final: Hankin 21, Grace 19.
Mixed Pairs:
Semi finals: I. Grace, R. Acott (Horton Kirby) 26, R & C Coleman (Victoria Park) 7; E & P Wathen (Heathfield) 17, H & A Thorpe (Chelmsford) 15.
Final: Grace, Acott 19, Wathens 17.

NatWest National 18s and Under

at Oxford C & C, September 9th 1990

Stuart Airey of Workington, who reached the final of the national 16 and Under national championship in 1987 won this title, after an interesting clash with Ian Bond of Crediton who had reached the last four a year earlier.

At 18 ends the score was 12-all, but Airey then surged to a 22-13 lead. Bond hit back to win the next four ends, but Airey put paid to this recovery by scoring a three. Both players had won their semi finals comfortably. Among those who failed to qualify at the regional finals were Nicky Jones, the 1989 Hants county Singles champion, Stuart Nelmes of Ardagh BC, Gloucestershire, who was 14 at the time and Oliver Ovett, a month older than Nelmes — who qualified in August for the national Triples, to become the youngest player ever to challenge at Worthing for an England title.

Semi finals: Stuart Airey (Workington) 25, Steve Cooper (Essex County) 9; Ian Bond (Crediton) 25, Ian Bunday (British Transport, Swaythling) 12.
Final: Airey 25, Bond 19.

Midland Counties Championships

at Nottingham, September 9th 1990

Singles: T. James (Northants) bt W. Hobart (Lincs) 25-19.
Pairs: D. Thomas, P. Dickens (Notts) bt I. Walker, R. Tansley (Northants).
Triples: W. Gill, D. Ludwig, R. Morris (Worcs) bt M. Mann, W. Ward, N. Walker (Warwicks)
Fours: P. Green, N. Brereton, H. Brereton, P. Pearce (Warwicks) bt D. Larkin, N. Hunter, B. Miller, H. Scott (Derbyshire) 24-6.
Secretaries: J. Ades (Warwickshire) bt N. Deeprose (Worcs) 25-21.

Warner Bembridge - County Club Over 55's National Championships

at Westlands BC, Earl Cowes, IOW, September 11th-13th, 1990

David Bryant, the star attraction at these championships, won the men's singles rather more easily then he had done the previous year, *writes Don MacQuarrie.* Torrential rain halted the 1989 final with Bryant trailing Barney Fernandes 11-12, but when the replay took place at Bath a week later, the world champion won 25-23.

This time the weather was perfect and Bryant, hungry for yet another title, drew away from the effervescent Alf Chambers, from Eye, Suffolk, to win the final 25-13. Chambers had made an impact in the Woolwich National Championships at Worthing the previous month, when he reached the Singles quarter finals.

Fernandes returned to the title trail at Westlands, when he and his Swindon clubmate Reg Jackson won the men's pairs, sweeping home 22-12 against Ray Watson (Ashford, Middlesex) and former England international Reg Paine (Feltham Ex-serviceman) in the final.

Paine had an eventful second day. As he prepared to drive off from the Warner Bembridge Bowls and Country Club to play his pairs semi-final, he realised he had locked himself out of his Rover. Maggie Siequien, the country club's booking supervisor, moved swiftly to the rescue — summoning a taxi which whisked Reg ten miles to Westlands.

He capped his day in style, scoring four shots with a superb bowl to topple the favourites Bob Jack (Southport) and Ken Drury (Newton Hall, Blackpool) 20-19 in a semi final. Jack, the EBA treasurer, and Drury had sparkled in the quarter-finals, defeating Dennis Griffiths and Rex Pike, from Clevedon Promenade, by 20-9. Drury, 62, who was manager of the overseas players in the Woolwich Masters tournament at Worthing, was surprised to find himself in the semi-finals. "I didn't even know I was playing in this championship until Bob came and told me he had entered us!" he said.

Betty Edwards, an attractive 61 year old from the March Conservative Club, Cambridgeshire, completed an unusual double, which spanned 45 years. At the country club on the eve of the championships, she won the Miss Warner title! That success prompted her to recall, "Back in 1945, when I was 16, I was Miss Chatteris in Cambridgeshire. I reckon I'll be able to dine out on the fact that I'm Miss Warner for the next year!".

On the bowling green there was further joy for her when she and Stella Clifton edged out Betty Pennell and Sheila O'Connell (Exonia, Exeter) 20-19 to reach the Women's Pairs semi-finals. Clifton and Edwards lost 14-23 in the semi-finals to Peggy Edwards and Barbara Carey, of Bentham, Gloucester, who took the title for the second time in three years when they defeated England International Irene Molyneux and Margaret Ellis (Oxford City and County) 24-17 in the final.

Iris Roberts, of Langford Playing Fields, Bedfordshire, six times winner of her club singles, cruised to the women's singles title with a 21-11 victory over Margaret Ketley, of Hatfield, Hertfordshire.

Results: Men's Pairs Quarter Finals - R Watson (Ashford, Middlesex), R Paine (Feltham Ex-servicemen) 22, B Everton, J Coates (Vines Park, Worcs) 16. B Jack (Southport), K Drury (Newton Hall) 20, D Griffiths, R Pike (Clevedon Promenade) 9. R Jackson, B Fernandes (Swindon) 23, G Williamson, J Hedley (Felixstowe) 16. B Francis, P Lundy (Herts) 27, D Gosling (Burgess Hill, Sussex), J Wilkins (Newick) 20.
Semi finals: Watson, Paine 20, Jack, Drury 19. Jackson, Fernandes 23, Francis, Lundy 20.
Final: Jackson, Fernandes 22, Watson, Paine 12.
Men's Singles: Quarter finals: D Bryant (Clevedon, Somerset) 25, H Clark (Seaton Sluice, Northumberland) 5. T Andrews (Ampthill, Beds) 25, T Wilden (Handsworth Wood, Warks) 20. R Watson (Ashford) 25, M Goddard (Greenhill, Weymouth) 22. A Chambers (Borough of Eye, Suffolk) 25, L Bull (Eastbourne) 22.
Semi-finals: Bryant 25, Andrews 10. Chambers 25, Watson 12.
Final: Bryant 25, Chambers 13.
Women's Pairs: Quarter finals: R Airey, I Lawson (Spennymoor, Co Durham) 20, S Everett, A Williams (Desborough, Berks) 18. I Molyneux, M Ellis (Oxford C & C) 23, E Cullen, B Dingley (Magdalen Park, London) 8. S Clifton, B Edwards (March Conservatives) 20, B Pennell, S O'Connell (Exonia, Exeter) 19. P Edwards, B Carey (Bentham, Gloucester) 21, M Richardson, M Chester (Boston Burton House) 19.
Semi-finals: Molyneux, Ellis 17, Airey, Lawson 14. Edwards, Carey 23, Clifton, Edwards 14.
Final: Edwards, Carey 24, Molyneux, Ellis 17.
Women's Singles: Quarter finals: I Roberts (Langford Playing Fields, Beds) 21, M Rome (Caldbeck, Cumbria) 20. E Bird (Sherwood, Nottingham) 21, F Tovey (Ashcombe, Somerset) 17. M Ketley (Hatfield, Herts) 21, J Scoular (Southbourne, Hants) 13. J Thomson (Avenue, Leamington Spa) 21, G Kite (Southall Conservatives, Middlesex) 9.
Semi finals: Roberts 21, Bird 18. Ketley 21, Thomson 5.
Final: Roberts 21, Ketley 11.

Bristol and West B.S. Under 25 Singles Championship
at Bristol, September 15th-16th, 1990

Neil Westlake, from Winscombe, aged 25, but elegible when entering, finally won a title he had been seeking for almost ten years. He led Mark Bantock, a 20 year old surveyor from Gerrards Cross, throughout the final, but was relieved to score the winning single on the 31st end after Bantock threatened to catch him.

In his semi final against Wellingborough's Paul Broderick, Westlake saw a 21-2 lead slip to 24-17 before clinching a place in the final. David Holt, the favourite, had lost his quarter final to David Harding of Cheltenham Spa after leading 17-6.

Harding now lives in Wales, and had helped St Fagans win the Welsh Private Greens team title the day before. He was hoping to qualify for a unique British Isles junior Singles clash with his pairs partner, Jason Greenslade, who won the Welsh junior title at Ebbw Vale, but was outbowled by Bantock.

Quarter finals: D Harding (Cheltenha Spa) bt D Holt (Bolton) 25-23; M Bantock (Gerrards Cross) bt J Durrant (Hollingbury Park) 25-17; P Broderick (Wellingborough) bt A Brown (Whitwick Park) 25-4.

Semi finals: Bantock bt Harding 25-9; Westlake bt Broderick 25-17.

Finals: Westlake bt Bantock 25-21.

Liverpool Victoria Insurance National Mixed Fours

Final stages at Swindon BC, September 18th-19th 1990

Prize money: Winners £2,000. Runners up £1000. Losing semi finalists £500.

This competition originally attracted 1,051 teams, eight of whom qualified for the final stages to compete for a £2,000 top prize. Players were invited to seek sponsorship of games from their friends for the Cancer Research Campaign, which also benefitted from the sponsorship of Liverpool Victoria Insurance.

Many well known players were dismissed in the first seven rounds of the competition, and only one international player survived to the final stages — Norma May, the 1987 national Singles champion from the Bickford Smith club, Camborne. Playing lead in a rink skipped by her husband Tony, with another married couple, Sylvia and Howard Strutt at Nos 2 and 3, Mrs May played a notable part in their comfortable victory in the final against an Oakley, Basingstoke four.

Bickford Smith's hardest game at Swindon, however, was against North Walsham in a quarter final, the eventual scoreline of 25-15 hardly flattering the Norfolk team. Leading 17-15, but with shots against them, Bickford Smith kept their advantage when Tony May killed the end, scored a four on the replay, and added another four on the final end. In their semi final, the Cornish club finished 11 shots ahead of Princes Risborough who had Beryl Walford skipping her husband and son. To reach that stage Princes Risborough had built an unassailable lead of 17-2 against White Rock, Hastings.

Oakley's disappointing performance in the final when they failed to master a stiff cross wind blowing in gusts across a swinging green, came after spirited play in their two earlier games, first against Welford, who caught them on the 20th end but lost a last end three , and then over a combination of three players from Kings Chase, Brentwood and John Rodwell Jnr., the Essex Middleton Cup manager who plays at the Liberty of Havering club. The Essex four led Oakley by 16-10 in that semi final, but surrendered ten shots on the last three ends. Rodwell and the King's Chase three, Beryl Hope, Jean Williams and skip Lionel Lee, had also figured in an extraordinary quarter final against Thatcham, whose skip Derek Crouch crashed the jack off rink six times — fireworks which availed him little against the experience of Rodwell and Lee.

Bickford Smith, ably skipped by Tony May and energetic Howard Strutt, outstanding at No.3, adapted best to the windy conditions which tended to offset the advantages offered on a splendid green, and thoroughly deserved their £2,000 top prize.

Quarter finals: Oakley Basingstoke (Nancie Goosey, Bill and Mary Britchford, Eric Rodgers) 23, Welford (Lisa and Yvonne Francis, Martin Timms, Trevor Francis) 20. Kings Chase, Brentwood (Beryl Hope, Jean Williams, John Rodwell (Liberty of Havering), Lionel Lee) 25, Thatcham (Beryl Reynolds, Keith Faulkner, Ken Bowers, Derek Crouch) 15. Princes Risborough (Craig Walford, Stella Curry, Tom and Beryl Walford) 25, White Rock, Hastings (Christine Marsh, Daphne Foster, Tony Monk, Derek Foster) 16. Bickford Smith, Camborne (Norma May, Sylvia Strutt, Howard Strutt, Tony May) 25, North Walsham (Janet Brawn, Lilian Smith, George McElveen, David Brawn) 15.
Semi finals: Oakley 20, Kings Chase 16. Bickford Smith 23, Princes Risborough 12.
Final: Bickford Smith 31, Oakley 9.

McCarthy and Stone National Mixed Pairs

Finals at Atherley BC, Southampton, September 22nd-23rd, 1990

Prize money: £6,000

Husband and wife, Peter and Wendy Line, who finished runners-up in this competition in 1987 and 1989, reached the final again and toppled the number one attraction, Tony Allcock and Pat Bradley, from Gloucestershire, 23-16 to take the title.

Peter Line is a member of the Atherley club at Southampton and the noticeboard faithfully records his achievements, England international honours and a prolific collection of titles, including — with Wendy — the national indoor mixed pairs in 1986. Wendy, of the Southampton Ladies club, is also an England international and has won many titles, notably the Women's Singles gold medal at the 1986 Commonwealth Games.

In these semi-finals, the Lines had to call up all their experience to edge out the flamboyant Lee Shoobridge and Ann Lawrance, from Sittingbourne, after an extra end.

The Lines led 22-17 with two ends to play, but Shoobridge, the 1989 Kent Singles champion, conjured a brilliant finish, scoring a four and a single to draw level at 22-22, forcing the match into an extra end.

Even Shoobridge could not dislodge the Lines' shot bowl and the Southampton pair advanced to the final.

Tony Allcock arrived at Atherley in a winning groove, having taken the

Westminster Classic, the Bournemouth Open Singles and the Woolwich English National Singles and Triples titles in a glorious summer of success.

With his partner, Pat Bradley, from Victory Park, Stroud, he cruised to the final, defeating Colin and Kay Deans of Godalming by 31-14, and John and Maria Gearey (Roade, Northampton) by 34-11.

In the final, however, Allcock and Bradley were soon in trouble. The Lines led 10-1 after five ends and 14-5 after the eight. A Bradley-Allcock revival was expected and it duly arrived. They battled back to draw level at 15-15 after 15 ends.

The Lines, however, banished thoughts of a third defeat in this final and with calm and decisive bowling, took five of the last six ends to win 23-16.

A record total of 3,655 pairs entered the competition. The £6,000 prize money was distributed as follows: Regional finals, eight winners £100 per pair, eight runners up £50 per pair, eight club contributions £100 per pair.

Final stages: Quarter finals — four winners £150 per pair, four runners up £100 per pair, four club contributions £150 per pair. Semi-finals - two winners £250 per pair, two runners up £200 per pair, two club contributions £150 per win. Final - winners £500, runners up £300, two club contributions £200 per pair.

Quarter finals: Peter Line (Atherley), Wendy Line (Southampton Ladies) 26, David and Susan Swan (Laceby, Grimsby) 10. Lee Shoobridge (UK Paper, Sittingbourne), Ann Lawrance (St George's) 26, Derek Shorter (North Walsham), Elizabeth Shorter (County Arts) 8. John and Maria Gearey (Pianoforte, Roade) 18, James Fuller (Broomfield, Middlesex), Barbara Fuller (Bishops Stortford) 13, Tony Allcock MBE (Cheltenham), Pat Bradley (Victory Park, Stroud) 31, Colin and Kay Deans (Goldalming, Surrey) 14.

Semi-finals: Line and Line 23, Shoobridge and Lawrance 22. Allcock and Bradley 34, Gearey and Gearey 11.

Final: Line and Line 23, Allcock and Bradley 16.

Simba Home Counties Championships
played during the 1990 season

Kent won the Simba league for the second year in succession with a record points score. Buckinghamshire just failed to oust Middlesex from second place despite a late surge. The winners received £500 from Simba Security Systems and runners-up £250 for their county funds. Keith Renwick (Sussex) won the Singles championship, overwhelming George Moon (Oxfordshire) in the final by 21-3 after a narrow 21-20 semi-final success over international Gerry Smyth (Middlesex) by 21-20.

Greene King League
Finals at Broomfield, September 16th, 1990

This Middlesex based league resulted in a run for Broomfield for the second successive year. The section winners were Hounslow Sports, Uxbridge, Broomfield and West Ealing who played off for the title.

Ireland

By Ronnie Harper

It was not such a bad year after all for Irish bowls. The fears of going in to the outdoor international series with an extra rink proved unfounded and the results turned out quite heartening.

Jim Baker became the first home-based player to lift the prestigious Bushmills Whiskey Irish International Masters at Ballymoney, and came very close to winning the British Isles outdoor Singles title against John Ottaway (England) at Methilhill. However, there was British Isles championship joy for Joe Whyte, Clifford Craig and Ernie Parkinson of the Ormeau club.

The Northern Ireland Bowling Association and Irish champions took a count of seven on the last end to win by a shot over the English Fours champions and young Paul Moore of Lurgan turned in a magnificent exhibition to win the British Isles junior title, completely outbowling England hope, Alan Darling.

The ladies, too, had one of their best years in recent times in the outdoor international series in Saundersfoot, but both indoor teams once again found the going tough as they sought their respective trophies.

And of course there was joy in the Commonwealth Games with the Northern Ireland rink of Rodney McCutcheon, John McCloughlin, Sammy Allen and Jim Baker bringing home the Fours silver medal, and Margaret Johnston coming back from New Zealand with a Singles bronze.

In the indoor internationals the ladies finished up with the wooden spoon after losing at Margate — Scotland 135-88, England 149-75 and 137-99 against Wales. But Margaret Johnston did give them something to celebrate with her British Isles championship winning performance (21-5) against Ann Sutherland of Wales.

The men fared little better at Prestwick, which turned out to be a pointless exercise after losing to England (125-87), Scotland (112-101) and Wales (123-114). The County Antrim pair of Marcus Craig and Jim Baker won the British Isles Pairs title with a 17-12 win over Martin and Mick Tomlin.

The Irish ladies finished propping up the other three countries in the outdoor international table, but it could have been very different. Ireland produced a very good performance when losing to England (112-105), Wales (103-94) and Scotland (115-112). It has been a long time since Ireland finished the outdoor championship only 19 shots down.

And the men's international series at Methilhill did not exactly turn out the ogre many thought it would. The new six rinks format meant that the Irish selectors had to find new players, and indeed they can feel happy with the performances of the team, especially that of new caps. All three games were lost - Scotland (119-99), Wales (109-108) and England (124-96), but in none was Ireland disgraced.

Bushmills Whiskey Irish Masters Championship

at Provincial Towns IBC, Ballymoney, January 3rd-7th 1990

Jim Baker became the first home based player to life this prestigious championship, televised by BBC Northern Ireland, with a magnificent display of bowls. After dispensing with former world champion and defending title-holder, Hugh Duff (Scotland), 3-7, 7-3, 7-6 in the opening round, Baker went on to score a 7-4, 7-4, 7-4 win over fellow Irish international Michael Dunlop in the semi final and then beat Scotland's Richard Corsie 7-1, 7-5, 2-7, 7-6 in the final. "That was the best I have played for a long while", said Baker.

His performance in Ballymoney saw him hit the sort of form that made him one of the best indoor bowlers in the British Isles. Once again the championship was a resounding success, played to packed houses every session, and event which is quickly becoming the best 'Masters' in the British Isles. Baker took the 1750 first prize with Corsie lifting 850. Dunlop and Allcock picked up 400 each and Duff, Wood, Corkill and Burrows 200.

Round 1: Jim Baker (Ireland) bt Hugh Duff (Scotland) 3-7, 7-3, 7-6; Michael Dunlop (Ireland) bt Willie Wood (Scotland) 7-6, 7-1; Richard Corsie (Scotland) bt David Corkill (Ireland) 7-2, 7-5. Tony Allcock (England) bt Noel Burrows (England) 7-6, 2-7, 7-0.
Semi finals: Baker bt Dunlop 7-3, 7-4, 7-4; Corsie bt Allcock 7-5, 7-1, 7-6.
Final: Baker bt Corsie 7-1, 7-5, 2-7, 7-6.

Bushmills Whiskey Irish National Indoor Championships

at County Antrim, February 16th-18th 1990

Jeff McMullan of Belfast upset the applecart when he went in to Jim Baker's den at Parkgate and beat the County Antrim champion 21-14 to win this event for the first time. Baker had no answer to the deadly drawing of the Belfast club champion in a match which failed to live up to expectation.

Neil Booth of County Antrim took the Under-25 title with a 21-16 win over Iam McClure of Provincial Towns, and the Triples went to County Antrim's Richard Bell, Robin Gray and Marcus Craig who beat Damian Ophert, Ali Roukottaya and Dickie Hughes (Provincials) 25-7.

The Fours championship was also won by County Antrim with Jim Baker's rink of Richard Bell, David Johnston and Marcus Craig beating Gary McCloy's four from Provincial Towns 19-12. Baker won a third Irish title when he lifted the Pairs title, partnered by Marcus Craig. They defeated Noel Metcalf and Stevie Adamson (Belfast) by 20-12 in the final.

Under-25 Singles:
Semi finals: N. Graham (Belfast) 16, I. McClure (Provincial Towns) 21; N. Booth (County Antrim) 21.
Final: McClure 16, Booth 21.
Open Singles: J. Baker (County Antrim) 21, I. McClure (Provincial Towns) 14; J. McMullan (Belfast) bye.
Final: McMullan 21, Baker 15.

Pairs: J. Craig, J. Baker (County Antrim) 18, U. Brewster, S. Brewster (Provincial Towns) 17, N. Metcalf, S. Adamson (Belfast) bye.
Final: Craig, Baker 20, Metcalf, Adamson 12.

Triples: R. Bell, R. Gray, J. Craig (County Antrim) 21, C. Craig, M. Dunlop, B. Dunlop (Belfast) 10; D. Olphert, A. Roukottaya, R. Hughes (Provincial Towns) bye.
Final: County Antrim 25, Provincial Towns 7.

Fours: R. Bell, D. Johnston, J. Craig, J. Baker (County Antrim) 19, R. Millar, C. Hogg, J. Smyth, G. McCloy (Provincial Towns) 12; J. McMullan, P. Davey, M. Dunlop, D. Hamilton (Belfast) bye.
Final: County Antrim 27, Belfast 9.

Irish Bushmills Whiskey Inter-Club Championship
Played on various dates during the season.

Belfast IBC once again won the Irish Bushmills Whisky inter-club championship when they pipped County Antrim on shots up. With only three clubs competing this season due to the demise of the North Down club, the championship lost a little of its appeal.

Country Antrim got their season off to a good start in their opening home leg game against the Provincials, coasting to a comfortable 118-100 victory. When Belfast travelled to Ballymoney, however, they had to battle hard for their opening win in the championship, beating the Provincials by 10 shots (105-95). In the return leg County Antrim won at Ballymoney, beating the Provincials 126-97, but came unstuck at Shaw's Bridge where Belfast won 135-98.

The Provincials fared no better against Belfast at Shaw's Bridge, losing 142-104 which left County Antrim having to win their last game at Parkgate against the defending champions. County Antrim won by 12 shots but that was not enough to divest Belfast of the title.

County Antrim 118, Provincial Towns 100.
Rinks (County Antrim first): J. Baker 29, T. Smith 15; J. Craig 21, H. Elliott 12; D. Johnston 15, W. Loughrey 16; S. Allen 23, C. Mearns 14; D. Livingstone 17, R. McCune 18; J. Cairns 13, K. O'Neill 24.

Provincial Towns 95, Belfast 105.
Rinks (Provincial Towns first): H. Elliott 12, W. Watson 16; K. O'Neill 21, S. Elliman 24; V. Mullan 7, S. Elliman 24; R. McCune 18, J. Nutt 13; W. Loughrey 16, J. McCloughlin 16; T. Smith 20, S. Adamson 14.

Provincial Towns 97, County Antrim 106.
Rinks (Provincial Towns first) H. Elliott 15, D. Livingstone 27; T. Smith 10, G. Scott 26; J. Irwin 15, A. Murphy 24; R. McCune 20, J. Craig 20; W. Loughrey 16, S. Wylie 13; K. O'Neill 21, D. Johnstone 20.

Belfast 135, County Antrim 98.
Rinks (Belfast first): D. Corkill 18, D. Livingstone 17; B. Dunlop 21, S. Allen 21; J.

McCloughlin 20, D. Johnston 17; W. Watson 24, G. Scott 18; S. Elliman 21, J. Baker 13; J. Nutt 31, J. Craig 12.

Country Antrim 111, Belfast 99.
Rinks (Belfast first): S. Elliman 10, S. Wylie 26; D. Corkill 22, J. Craig 12; J. McCloughlin 10, S. Allen 26; B. Dunlop 18, D. Johnston 15; W. Watson 19, J. Baker 15; J. Nutt 20, D. Livingstone 17. Belfast 142, Provincial Towns 104. Rinks (Belfast first): D. Corkill 23, J. Irwin 12; B. Dunlop 32, L. Loughrey 15; J. McCloughlin 24, T. Smith 12; J. Nutt 24, K. O'Neill 17; S. Elliman 24, R. McCune 24; W. Watson 15, H. Elliott 24.

Irish Ladies Indoor Championships
at Ballymoney, February 16th-18th 1990

As expected, Ireland's top lady bowler Margaret Johnston won the Singles championship with a one way victory 21-3 over the inexperienced Geraldine Law of County Antrim. Miss Law was playing in her first Singles championship final and just did not have the armoury to handle the powerful Johnston.

Singles: M. Johnston (Provincial Towns) 21, G. Law (County Antrim) 3.
Pairs: B. McKeag, M. Martin (Belfast) 24, B. Cameron, O. Paisley (County Antrim) 10.
Triples: J. Mulholland (Provincial Towns) 21, E. Bell (Belfast) 16.
Fours: W. Miller (Provincial Towns) 22, B. Cameron (County Antrim) 14.

Northern Ireland Bowling Association Championships
at Carrickfergus, Ausut 2nd-4th 1990

Bangor's international Rodney McCutcheon became the first Parks player to win all five of his association's championships when he took the Open Singles title for the first time in the Park Travel sponsored event. After beating Irish indoor champion Jeff McMullan of Ormeau in a last bowl cliff hanger in the semi final of the event, McCutcheon went on to defeat Clifton Quinn, a 17-year-old Bainbridge player, who is also in the Irish Under 18 hockey team.

McCutcheon also won the Fours title, playing third in the Bangor rink skipped by Gary Scott, making it a memorable day for the experienced Irish international.

Junior Singles:
Semi finals: S. Denley (Bangor) 25, A. Frazer (Garvey) 13; G. Francey (Musgrave) 23, M. McHugh (Whitehead) 25.
Final: McHugh 25, Denley 3.

Open Singles:
Semi finals: G. Scott (Bangor), C. Quinn (Bainbridge) 25; J. McMullan (Ormeau) 23, R. McCutcheon (Bangor) 25.
Final: McCutcheon 25, Quinn 18

Pairs:
Semi finals: McHugh, McHugh (Whitehead 8, Walker, Johnston (Musgrave) 28; Bell, Barnard (Dungannon) 12, Killough, Graham (Lisnagarvey) 18.
Final: Killough, Graham 32, Walker, Johnston 13

Triples:
Semi finals: E. McVeigh (Balmoral) 17, A. Irwin (Garvey) 22; R. Johnston (Musgrave) 22, M. Reid (Balmoral) 10.
Final: Johnston 18, Irwin 12.
Fours:
Semi finals: G. Scott (Bangor) 26, C. Davis (Banbridge) 17; P. McMenemy (Dungannon) 20, T. Stewart (Clarendon) 15.
Final: Scott 21, McMenemy 16.

ICL Northern Ireland Provincial B.A. Championships

at Coleraine, August 3rd-4th 1990

Young Liam McHugh of Cookstown took the Under-26 Singles championship with a sparkling display against Russell Miller of Portrush in the final. The Singles title went to Willie Smith of Magherafelt who disposed of Ron Milliken of Ballymoney 25-10.

Nigel and Hugh Shannon, the father and son combination from Ballymoney, came unstuck in the Pairs final when they were beaten 22-20 by Barry Moffatt and Jeremy Henry of Portrush. Gary McCloy of Portrush won the Triples with a 23-3 win of clubmate Dickie Hughes. A Dunluce rink skipped by Fred Murray had a 34-9 win over Alan Stewart's four from Portstewart.

Finals: Under-26 Singles: L. McHugh (Cookstown) 25, R. Miller (Portrush) 23.
Open Singles: W. Smith (Magherafelt) 25, W. Milliken (Ballymoney) 10.
Pairs: N. Shannon, H. Shannon (Ballymoney) 20, B. Moffett, J. Benry (Portrush) 22.
Triples: G. McCloy (Portrush) 23, R. Hughes (Portrush) 3.
Fours: F. Murray (Dunluce) 34, A. Stewart (Portstewart) 19.

ICL Private Greens League Championships

Finals at Pickie, August 4th 1990

Stevie Adamson, the Irish international from Dunbarton won the Singles championship with a 25-20 victory over his clubmate Myles Greenfield in the final at Pickie.

There was an interesting confrontation in the final of the Under 26 Singles when Annesley Harrison of Willowfield met his younger brother Phillip (Knock). Annesley won 25-13.

The Cliftonville triple who won the British Isles championship in Worthing two years earlier repeated their PGL success when the three Davids (Carson, Heatley and Johnstone) scored a one-sided 26-3 victory over a trio in charge of Stevie Adamson. Jim Baker's experienced rink of Carson, McDonnell and Porter took the Fours title with a 25-30 win over the Old Bleach four skipped by Sam Wylie.

In the best match of the championships, brothers David and Brendan Thompson scored a great last-end two shot victory over the strong father and son combination of Brian and Marcus Craig (Cliftonville).

Open Singles:
Semi finals: C. Porter (Cliftonville) 23, S. Adamson (Dunbarton) 25; M. Greenfield (Dunbarton) 25, A. Harrison (Willowfield) 7.
Final: Adamson 25, Greenfield 20.

Pairs:
Semi finals: D. Forsythe, K. Lynn (NICS) 10, B. Craig, J. Craig (Cliftonville) 27; D. Thompson, B. Thompson (Transport) 20, J. McCormick, J. Ralph (Cliftonville) 8.
Final: Thompsons 25, Craigs 23.

Triples:
Semi finals: K. McKeown, S. Hoy, R. McReavie (Forth River) 15, D. Carson, D. Heatley, D. Johnston (Cliftonville) 16; D. Peden, N. Metcalf, S. Adamson (Dunbarton) 25, N. McBratney, J. McKinley, J. McCreight (Shorts) 17.
Final: Carson, Heatley, Johnston 26, B. Gribbon (sub), Metcalf, Adamson 3.

Fours:
Semi finals: C. Wilson, D. Burrows, A. Campbell, S,. Wylie (Old Bleach) 21, G. McDowell, D. White, G. Mitchell, T. Henderson (Belmont) 17. D. Carson, J. McDonnell, C. Porter, J. Baker (Cliftonville) 23, D. Heatley, D. Johnston, J.M. Craig, J. Craig (Cliftonville) 22.
Final: Cliftonville 25, Old Bleach 20.

Northern Ireland Women's Bowling Association Championships
at Carr's Glen, August 8th 1990

Finals: Singles: Connie McKee (Ward Park) 21, Lottie Clarke (Divis) 19.
Pairs: Belle McKeag, Marie Martin (Wingrave) 25, Alice Cameron, Olive Paisley (Whitehead) 9.
Triples: Glynis Campbell, Lucy Palmer, Eileen Higgins (Moat Park) 19, Sadie Boyd, Lettie Murdock, Doreen Turner (Holywood) 16.
Fours: Dorothy Marsden, Vi Huston, Sadie Donald, Nancy Gibson (Lisnagarvey) 23, Nan Barnes, Lela Russell, Belle McKeag, Marie Martin (Wingrave) 19.

Northern Ireland Women's Private Greens League Championships
at Hilden, August 14th 1990

Freda Elliott, the former Commonwealth Games Pairs champion, made it a first for her new club Knock, when she won the Singles in her first year with the club. She took the title with a 21-13 win over Rita McCandless of Shaftesbury.

Maureen Montgomery and Lilian Johnston of Cavehill were bidding for two titles, but had to settle for one. They won the Pairs against Hilda Hamilton and Eileen Bell of Saintfield (20-16), but Montgomery, Johnston and Isobel Bell lost the Triples final to Lela Boal, Margaret Hardy and June Wilson of Pickie (16-14). Kathleen Toner's rink won the all-Falls battle against Margaret McGarrity's four.

Singles: Semi finals: F. Elliott (Knock) 21, J. McCaughey (Comber) 18, R. McCandless (Shaftesbury) w/o.
Final: Elliott 21, McCandless 13.
Pairs: Semi finals: M. Montgomery, L. Johnston (Cavehill) 28; M. Morrison, K. Thompson (Saintfield) 11; H. Hamilton, E. Bell (Saintfield) 26; L. Hanna, P. Dillon (Owenbeg) 16.
Final: Maureen Montgomery, Lilian Johnston (Cavehill) 20; Hilda Hamilton, Eileen Bell (Saintfield) 16.
Triples: Semi finals: N. McGhee (Salisbury) 11; J. Wilson (Pickie) 18; I. Bell (Cavehill) 14; K. Thompson (Saintfield) 13.
Final: Lisabeth Boal, Margaret Hardy, June Wilson (Pickie) 21; Maureen Montgomery, Lilian Johnston, Isobel Bell (Cavehill) 16.
Fours: Semi finals: K. Toner (Falls) 21; Y. Ross (NICS) 13; M. McGarrity (Falls) 20; A. McMillen (Comber) 15.
Final: Kathleen Duffin, May Laverty, Lottie Donelly, Kath Toner (Falls) 21; Ann Dillon, Maureen Webb, Ita Rogan, Margaret McGarrity (Falls) 13.

Park Travel Irish Women's Bowling Association Championships
at Cliftonville, August 29th-30th 1990

Irish international bowler Marie Barber of Blackrock, Dublin, upset the apple-cart when she beat hot favourite Margaret Johnston in the Singles final. Marie received a bye into the final owing to her opponent Connie McKee of Ward Park being away on holiday. Margaret Johnston coasted to her place with a comfortable 21-7 win over Freda Elliott of Knock, who led for her when they won the Commonwealth Games Pairs gold medal in Edinburgh. But in the final it was Marie Barber who produced better bowls for a deserved 21-16 win.

Singles:
Semi finals: M. Johnston (Ballymoney) 21, F. Elliott (Knock) 7; M. Barber (Blackrock) w/o C. McKee (Ward Park).
Final: Barber 21, Johnston 16.

Pairs:
Semi finals: M. Montgomery, L. Johnston (Cavehill) 17; B. McKeag, M. Martin (Wingrave) 18 (after tie end); L. Hill, B. Dunne (Blackrock) 15; M. Boyd, E. Arlow (Coleraine) 20.
Final: McKeag, Martin 26; M. Boyd, E. Arlow 22.

Triples
Semi finals: B. Dunne, M. Schofield, P. Nolan (Blackrock) 15; N. Montgomery, A. Elliott, J. Mulholland (Dunluce) 16; E. Boal, M. Hardy, J. Wilson (Pickie) 11; G. Campbell, L. Palmer, E. Higginson (Moat Park) 18.
Final: Dunluce 26, Moat Park 18.

Fours:
Semi finals: K. Duffin, M. Laverty, L. Donnelly, K. Toner (Falls) 21; J. Spencer, L. McNulty, M. Sullivan, A. Tunny (Kenilworth) 24; D. Marsden, V. Houston, S. Donald, N. Gibson (Lisnagarvey) 18; N. Montgomery, F. Chestnutt, A. Elliott, J. Mulholland (Dunluce) 30.
Final: Dunluce 19, Kenilworth 17.

Old Bushmills Irish National Championships
at Belmont, August 31st — September 1st 1990

Barry Moffett and Jeremy Henry, two 16-year-olds from the Portrush club made history when they became the youngest players to win an Irish national championship. These Provincial champions turned up trumps at Belmont when they won the final of the Pairs 25-16 against the much fancied Private Greens League champions, David and Brendan Thompson from the Ulster Transport club. It was a good championship all round for the Portrush club, for their trio of Russell Millar, Colin Hogg and Gary McCloy won the Triples with an 18-11 win over the former national and British Isles title holders from Cliftonville, David Carson, David Heatley and David Johnston.

Rodney McCutcheon, the Irish international, failed to win his first Irish Open Singles when he was beaten in the semi final by Magherafelt's Willie Smyth. Willie just missed out on the title when he was pipped 25-22 by Stevie Adamson of Dunbarton in the final. This was the first time the Gilford club have won a national title.

Under-26 Singles:
Semi finals: B. Somers (Bray) 25, L. McHugh (Cookstown) 16; M. McHugh (Whitehead) 24, A. Harrison (Willowfield) 8.
Final: McHugh 25, Somers 21

Open Singles:
Semi finals: S. Adamson (Dunbarton) 25, E. Hilton (Blackrock) 24; W. Smyth (Magherafelt) 24, R. McCutcheon (Bangor) 23.
Final: Adamson 25, Smyth 22.

Pairs:
Semi finals: D. Thompson, B. Thompson (Ulster Transport) 28; J. McCarthy, A. Davis (Herbert Park) 14. B. Moffett, J. Henry (Portrush) 24, J. Killough, N. Graham (Lisnagarvey) 16.
Final: Thompsons 16, Moffet, Henry 25.

Triples:
Semi finals: C. Murphy, s. Tate, E. Hilton (Blackrock) 15, D. Carson, D. Heatley, D. Johnston (Cliftonville) 16; R. Walker, W. McKee, R. Johnston, (Musgrave) 15, R. Millar, C. Hogg, G. McCloy (Portrush) 16.
Final: McCloy 18, Johnston 11.

Fours:
Semi finals: P. Heade, R. Darcy, P. Moorehead, P. Smyth (Leinster) 8; J. Nelson, R. Hastings, R. McCutcheon, G. Scott (Bangor) 26; J. McClaughlin, F. McHardy, J. McAfee, F. Murray (Dunluce) 12, D. Carson, J. McDonnell, C. Porter, J. Baker (Cliftonville) 21.
Final: Scott 18, Baker 11.

Scotland

By Gordon Dunwoodie

The highlight of the Scottish bowls year came on the other side of the world when Denis Love, Ian Bruce, George Adrain and Willie Wood left behind the January snows to make the long journey to New Zealand, and return with Commonwealth gold.

The Scots quartet saved their best performance for last at the plush three green Pakuranga club, where they counted a timely four on the penultimate end of their final clash with Jim Baker's Irish rink to take a six shot cushion into the last end. A nervy performance from the front end was retrieved by Adrain and the Scots were happy to concede a single and take the gold medal.

For Adrain and Wood, it was their second Commonwealth triumph, Wood having won the Singles in 1982 and Adrain the Pairs at Edinburgh four years later.

The remainder of the international season proved disappointing for the Scots. After Hugh Duff's indoor success in 1988 and Richard Corsie's the following year, Scotland surrendered their hold on the title at Preston's Guild Hall in February when John Price claimed the crown.

The home international championship again eluded Scotland, both indoors and outdoors. In the indoor series at Prestwick defeat at the hands of Wales left Scotland requiring a 45-shot win over England to take the title. They did win, and at one stage the margin rose to 34 shots, but the damage had been done in the defeat by Wales. Outdoors it was a similar story, with Scotland beating Ireland and Wales, and tieing with England, results that left them in second place, losing to England on shots aggregate.

On the women's front, Scotland failed to halt England's dominance of both the indoor and outdoor series, but Liz Wren gained consolation for her defeat in the British indoor championship at Margate when she took the outdoor equivalent at Saundersfoot with a 25-14 final win over English champion Jean Baker. Earlier in the year Wren had gone down to home club player Fleur Bougourd in the final of the women's world indoor championship in Guernsey.

The inaugural CIS Insurance Scottish Indoor Masters went to East Lothian's Angus Blair, who also completed a double when he retained the Players' Association championship. East Lothian made it a double success when Graham Robertson lifted the Scottish Indoor Singles championship, and Robertson went on to take the British championship at Prestwick.

One bright note on the international front came on the Players' Association International at Carlisle where the Scots overwhelmed the 'Auld Enemy' with a crushing 20 matches to 5 win.

The Woolwich Scottish Masters saw Willie Wood end the memory of his last end defeat at the hands of Peter Bellis in the World Singles final at Aberdeen's Westburn Park in 1984, when Wood returned to the Granite City and took the title with a final victory over England's Wynne Richards.

A break from tradition came in August, when the Scottish championship finals ended a 96-year association with the Queen's Park Club in Glasgow to move down the Ayrshire coast to the five green Northfield complex. The move, while greeted with less than enthusiasm in some quarters, proved to be a winner, with all six events coming under the umbrella of the same venue for the first time ever.

On the domestic front, the Kilmarnock club celebrated their 250th anniversary with nine days of festivities that included invitation international Singles events for both men and women, and their organising committee can look back with justifiable pride on their efforts to commemorate a landmark in Scottish bowling.

CIS Insurance Scottish Indoor Singles Championship

at Coatbridge IBC November 14th 1989

Once again the Scottish Indoor Singles Championship was divorced from the other national championships to allow television to cover the action. This time the event was used as a curtain raiser for the inaugural CIS Scottish Masters.

For the first time ever, the championship was decided using the sets format and Graham Robertson from East Lothian confirmed his growing status as the top Singles player in the country. He had little difficulty scoring a straight sets win over Bainfield's Alex Marshall, but was pushed to the limit by Inverclyde's Tom McLees in the final, having to come from two sets to one down before clinching victory.

Semi finals: G. Robertson (East Lothian) bt A. Marshall (Bainfield) 7-1, 7-5; T. McClees (Inverclyde) bt G. Ritchie (Stirling) 7-3, 3-7, 7-3.
Final: Robertson bt McLees 7-3, 4-7, 6-7, 7-3, 7-4.

CIS Insurance Scottish Masters Championship

at Coatbridge IBC, November 15th-16th 1989

The newest event to the indoor scene in Scotland, the Scottish Masters, brought together eight top United Kingdom players to battle for a £1,500 first prize, and the Scottish Masters title. Angus Blair, after surviving a first round scare against East Lothian clubmate Willie Wood, produced two devastating performances to crush David Bryant 7-1, 7-0 and then add a straight sets final win over Port Talbot's John Price, who later in the season won the world title.

Tweedbank's Joyce Lindores lined up as the only woman in the event and after shocking Belfast's David Corkill in the first round, went down at the semi-final stage to Price.

Round 1: Joyce Lindores (Scotland) bt David Corkill (Ireland) 7-3, 6-7, 7-4; John Price (Wales) bt Hugh Duff (Scotland) 7-2, 7-4; David Bryant (England) bt Richard Corsie (Scotland) 7-4, 7-1; Angus Blair (Scotland) bt Willie Wood (Scotland) 7-6, 6-7, 7-4.
Semi finals: Price bt Lindores 7-1,7-3; Blair bt Bryant 7-1, 7-0.
Final: Blair bt Price 7-6, 7-5, 7-5.

Coral Bingo Scottish Indoor Bowls Players Association Championship

at Coatbridge IBC, January 11th 1990

Twenty-four year old Angus Blair became the first player to successfully defend this championship when he returned to the Coatbridge stadium two months after his Scottish Masters sucess. Blair won through to a final clash with Irvine's Jim Muir, when he disposed of another young up and coming star, Prestwick's David Gourlay Jnr., in straight sets. He then beat off a determined challenge from Muir to retain the title 7-5, 7-3.

Semi finals: Angus Blair (East Lothian) bt David Gourlay (Prestwick) 7-4, 7-4; Jim Muir (Irvine) bt Frazer Muirhead (Bainfield) 7-0, 7-1.
Final: Blair bt Muir 7-5, 7-3.

Apex Construction SWIBA Championships

at Arbroath IBC, February 3rd 1990

International Liz Wren from Falkirk won the title for the second time, and became one of the few players to have completed the double of indoor and outdoor Singles titles, when she held off a fightback from Midlothian's Jeanette Conlan to win 21-16. Wren saw a 16-4 lead disappear as Conlan picked up 12 shots in five ends to tie at 16-all, but a finishing burst of 2,2 and 1 gave Wren the title.

In the Pairs, Headwell's Anne McFarlane and Margaret Spink recaptured the title they won two years ago when they edged home 21-20 after an extra end over Garioch's Wilma Forbes and Minnie Naismith. There was further disappointment for Garioch when they went down 25-16 to Coatbridge in the Triples final.

Singles: Semi finals: E. Wren (Falkirk) 21, F. Pearson (Arbroath) 16; J. Conlan (Midlothian) 21, L. Jackson (East Kilbride) 18.
Final: Wren 21, Conlan 16.
Pairs: Semi finals: Headwell (A. McFarlane, M. Spink) 28, Glasgow (J. McGregor, I. Walker) 22; Garioch (W. Forbes, M. Naismith) 26, Auchinleck (J. Burley, J. Sykes) 22.
Final: Headwell 21, Garioch 20 (after extra end)
Triples: Semi finals: Coatbridge (M. Ferguson, M. Mungall, J. Adamson) 22, Inverclyde (M. McArdle, V. Johnstone, C. Cairns) 9; Garioch (A. Bissett, A. Thom, P. Clark) 22, East Kilbride (J. McIntosh, E. Brewster, M. Douglas) 15
Final: Coatbridge 25, Garioch 16.
Fours: Semi finals: East Kilbride (M. Hosie, R. Neil Jnr, J. Fraser, R. Neil) 20, Midlothian (A. Yule, M. Ferguson, N. Carson, S. Morrison) 16. Aberdeen (K. Watt, H. Lees, D. Baxter, D. Dick) 22, Cowal (E. Whyte, A. Galloway, D. McGarvie, McEwan) 17.
Final: East Kilbride 24, Aberdeen 8.

CIS Insurance Scottish Indoor Championships

at Ardrossan IBC February 10th-11th 1990

Bainfield's Alec Ross and Alex Marshall suffered a double blow, going down in both the Pairs and Fours. It was particularly frustrating for Marshall, who earlier in the season, lost in the national Singles at the semi final stage.

In the Fours, Ross and Marshall linked with clubmates Charlie Adamson and Robert Marshall, but went down 24-22 to Raymond Robertson's Whiteinch rink, and later the Bainfield pair found Paisley's Mike Walsh and Neil Gilles too much of a handful in the Pairs final. The Paisley duo repeated their win of 1986.

The Junior Singles gave Bainfield some consolation for their defeats in the Pairs and Fours, when nineteen year old factory worker Colin Davidson defeated Craig Murray from the Galleon club in Kilmarnock by 21-17.

Past world indoor champion Hugh Duff won his first ever national title when he and Auchinleck clubmate Steven Rankin became the inaugural holders of the new Two Bowl Pairs Championship, with an 8-3, 6-4 win over Allander's Tom Stewart and Andy McGrandle. Lanarkshire managed a double, with victories in both the Triples and Senior Fours.

Junior Singles: Semi finals: C. Davidson (Bainfield) 21, K. Cairnie (N. Stewart) 10; C. Murray (Galleon) 21, G. Stuart (Aberdeen) 9.
Final: Davidson 21, Murray 17.
Pairs: Semi finals: Paisley (M. Walsh, N. Gillies) 25, Edinburgh (W. Galloway, R. Corsie) 13; Bainfield (A. Ross, A. Marshall) 27, Fintry (A. McColl, A. Stevenson) 11.
Final: Paisley 26, Bainfield 19.
Triples: Semi finals: Lanarkshire (T. Mair, K. Williamson, J. Weir) 17, Ardrossan (G. McCulloch, W. Reilly, J. Cran) 14; Inverness (F. MacKenzie, F. Lee, G. MacLeod) 25, Midlothian (A. Kirk, J. Russell, R. Campbell) 5.
Final: Lanarkshire 23, Inverness 15.
Fours: Semi finals: Bainfield (R. Marshall, C. Adamson, A. Ross, A. Marshall) 18, Lanarkshire (M. McGowan, A. McIntyre, I. Campbell, A. McIntyre) 14; Whiteinch (J. Leckie, R. Etherington, N. Little, R. Robertson) 26, Falkirk (I. Stewart, J. Kerr, J. Cochrane, J. Hunter) 20.
Final: Whiteinch 24, Bainfield 22.
Senior Fours: Final: Lanarkshire (J. Cassidy, D. Williamson, T. Horton, J. Girdwood) 18, Coatbridge (J. Laird, J. Mackie, W. Graham, R. Stewart) 14.
Two Bowl Pairs: Semi finals: Auchinleck (S. Rankin, H. Duff) bt Blantyre (B. Miller, J. Murray) 5-3, 10-0. Allander (T. Stewart, A. McGrandle) bt Aberdeen (A. Milne, W. Morrice) 8-6, 10-0.
Final: Auchinleck bt Allander 8-3, 6-4.

CIS Insurance Scottish Women's Inter Club League

at Arbroath February 17th 1990

Paisley retained their Women's Inter Club League title when they edged home 80-78 winners over Aberdeen, though they had to go an extra end. The sides were locked together at 77-77 after the allotted ends, but on the extra one Paisley picked up singles from Netta Dunlop, Annie Knowles and Frances Whyte to offset Eleanor Bartlett's counter for Aberdeen.

Paisley 80 Aberdeen 78
F. Whyte 27, S. Stott 13; N. Dunlop 24, E. Sainsbury 15; A.Knowles 13, W. Jeffrey 30; H. Wylie 16, E. Bartlett 20.

CIS Insurance Scottish Inter Club League Final

at Ardrossan IBC February 24th 1990

Blantyre regained the CIS Insurance Scottish Indoor league title they last held in 1987, when they beat off a Prestwick fightback to win 88-81. Blantyre raced to a 34-10 lead after just five ends, but Prestwick, bidding for a record eighth win, hit back to move 56-54 ahead after 14 ends. On the 15th end, however Blantyre picked up 12 shots without reply to move ahead again at 66-56 and from then they always held the upper hand.

Blantyre 88 Prestwick 81

G. Sullivan 20, J. Reid 24; S. McCall 18, C. Eade 22; J.Cameron 27, R. McCulloch 19; I. Steele 23, D. Gourlay Snr. 16.

CIS Insurance Senior Fours League Final

at Aberdeen IBC March 17th 1990

Lanarkshire bridged a 15-year gap since their only previous success in the Senior Fours National League, when they powered their way to an 82-52 win over Paisley. Paisley led briefly 5-4 after the opening end, but by the five end mark, Lanarkshire had raced to a 29-9 lead and were always in command. They finished ahead on three of the four rinks for a convincing 30-shot win.

Lanarkshire 82 Paisley 52

K. Williamson 16, A. Whyte 13; T. Horton 26, E. Blair 9; J. Girdwood 17, J. Dunlop 19; D. Johnston 23, J. Ritchie 11.

Lodge Sports Scottish Indoor Team Championship

at East Lothian IBC March 24th 1990

Lanarkshire ended the dream of Turriff of winning a first major indoor title when they took this event by 81-73 after the sides had finished all square at four points all.

The final revolved around the pairs encounter between Lanarkshire's Wendy Grant and international Ian Campbell and the Turriff pairing of Mary and George Morrison. With Turriff needing a draw or better to take the title, they looked as if their dream might come to fruition when the Morrisons edged into an 19-16 lead after 18 ends. Campbell however produced the shot of the match on the next end, removing a Turriff bowl to count four, and a double on the penultimate end followed by a single gave Lanarkshire a 23-18 victory. Lanarkshire's other points came in the Fours when Robert Grant's rink crushed Jeff Robertson's team 28-12.

Turriff's consolation wins came in the Singles where Alistair Campbell beat Alan Clark 21-15 and in the Triples where Isobel Gordon, David Anderson and Mike Stephen defeated Nancy Smith, Jim Cassidy and John Girdwood 22-15.

Lanarkshire 4 points (81 shots) Turriff 4 points (73 shots).

Singles: Alan Clark 15, Alistair Campbell 21.

Pairs: Lanarkshire 23 Turriff 18.

Triples: Lanarkshire 15 Turriff 22.

Fours: Lanarkshire 28 Turriff 22.

Dundee Masters

at Dundee IBC, April 14th-15th 1990

Willie Killens, aged 25, from the Inverclyde Club in Greenock scored a surprise win in the Tennents Masters, emerging victorious from a star studded 48-strong field. Killens won through to the competition proper when he beat Lanarkshire's Alan Clark 21-16 in the knock-out round, and then finished his opening day group matches with two wins and a defeat. Killens beat Duncan MacDougall from Teviotdale 15-12, but went down 15-10 to Welsh champion Phil Rowlands, but a 15-0 whitewash of Scottish international skip Robert McCulloch put him through to the final day.

Killens then reeled off wins over international Willie Galloway (Edinburgh), Midlothian's David Peacock and Marshall Presly from Aberdeen to push him through to a final clash with 1984 winner Jim Bright.

Killens opened up a 17-9 lead after 7 ends, but the Perth man hit back with seven shots over the next three ends to close the gap to just one at 17-16. Killens however steadied and two successive singles and a double gave him the title.

Final: W. Killens (Inverclyde) 21, J. Bright (Perth) 16; 3rd D. Peacock (Midlothian) 21, I. Bell (East Lothian) 7; 5th J. Jackson (East Kilbride) 21, W. Galloway (Edinburgh) 15; 7th J. Price (Wales) 21, M. Presley (Aberdeen) 5.

CIS Insurance Scottish Cup Final

at Ardrossan IBC, April 21st 1990

West Lothian finished the indoor season on a high note when they took the Cup with a comfortable 84-61 final win over Auchinleck.

West Lothian made the best start, and raced into a 21-9 lead after five ends, but Auchinleck hit back and by the halfway mark had edged in front 35-32. West Lothian led 52-47 at the close of the 15th end and then piled on the pressure over the last quarter to pull away for a convincing 23-shot win.

Ronnie Erskine counted on the last seven ends, to turn a 15-8 lead over Sam McKenzie into a 26-8 win and Davie McCormick recovered from 4-12 down at nine ends to beat Tommy Woods 21-17. West Lothian's third victory came from Grant Knox who picked up a double on the last end to beat George Speirs 20-18. Auchinleck's consolation win came from Jim Fleming, who edged out Jim Boyle 18-17.

West Lothian 84, Auchinleck 61
D. McCormick 21, T. Woods 17; G. Knox 20, G. Speirs 18; R. Erskine 26, S. McKenzie 8; J. Boyle 17, J. Fleming 18.

CIS Insurance Scottish Counties Championships

at Sighthill, Edinburgh, 24th June, 1990

Ayrshire rewrote the record books when they won the CIS Insurance Scottish Counties Championship for the tenth time, after a surprisingly easy 30 shot final win over East Lothian. Ayrshire finished ahead on all five rinks for a comprehensive victory.

They survived a scare the previous day in their semi-final clash with Bon Accord at Auchterarder, only a late flourish taking them to a 99-87 win, while East Lothian were coming through their last four clash with a 19 shot win over Stirlingshire.

Semi final at Auchterarder 23rd June: Ayrshire 99, Bon Accord 87. (Ayrshire skips score first) Gary Hood 24, Steven Henry 10, Tommy Campbell 22, Alec Mearns 18, George Adrain 24, Alan Pirie 16, David Gourlay Snr 9, Tom MacDonald 29, Jock Fleming 20, Ted Mowat 14.

Semi final at Linlithgow: East Lothian 105, Stirlingshire 86. (East Lothian skips score first) Angus Blair 24, Alec Stirling 19, Willie Wood 23, Brian Stillie 15, Graham Robertson 18, Peter Lyons 17, Jock Greig 16, Jim Blevins 20, Brian Middlemass 24, John Pryde 15.

Final at Sighthill: Ayrshire 115, East Lothian 85. (Ayrshire skips first) David Gourlay Snr 18, Angus Blair 15, Jock Fleming 21, Jock Greig 20, Gary Hood 21, Brian Middlemass 16, George Adrain 27, Willie Wood 20, Tommy Campbell 28, Graham Robertson 14.

Glasgow BA 'Kilglass' Championships
at Killermont June 30th, 1990.

George Farquhar missed out on his son's wedding to take the Glasgow Singles Championship back to Victoria Park for the first time ever, when he picked up two shots on the deciding end to edge out Arthur King from Cathcart 21-19. Victoria Park made it a double celebration when Derek Thomson picked up ten shots over the last five ends of the Junior Singles for a 21-11 win over Kirkhill's Gordon Cunningham.

Singles Final: George Farquhar (Victoria Park) 21, Arthur King (Cathcart) 19.
Pairs: Cumbernauld (Dan Elliot & Adam Shaw) 19, Drumoyne (Jim Leckie and Robert Etherington) 15.
Triples: Rutherglen (John McCann, Stewart Caldwell, Jim Walker) 13, Titwood (Tom Duncan, Ian Boyd, Robert Moles) 11.
Fours: Bishopbriggs (Nat Galloway, George Graham, William Hamilton and Hugh Davidson) 20. Shawlands (Mike Lang, Hugh Thomson, Edward Boyd and Edward Broadfoot) 7.
Senior Fours: Mearns (Bob Nichols, Frank Martin, Ted Howard and Hugh Drummond) 13, Baillieston (Wm Walmsley, Mike Johnstone, Wm Thomson and Pat Tierney) 11.
Junior Singles: Derek Thomson (Victoria Park) 21, Gordon Cunningham (Kirkhill) 11.

Edinburgh 'Isle of Skye' Open
at Balgreen, Edinburgh 9th-14th July, 1990

Alex Marshall completed a record equalling third win in the Edinburgh Open Singles, when he added to his victories of 1986 and 1988, with a runaway 21-5 success over Gala Waverley's Ralph Nicholson. Nicholson also tasted defeat in the Pairs final when he and Gala Waverley clubmate Brian Blackwood lost 21-10 to Gorebridge's Alec Cox and Ian Hutchison.

Singles Final: Alex Marshall (Gorgie Mills) 21, Ralph Nicholson (Gala Waverley) 5.
Pairs: Alec Cox and Ian Hutchison (Gorebridge) 12, Ralph Nicholson and Brian Blackwood (Gala Waverley) 10.

Woolwich Scottish Masters

at Westburn Park, Aberdeen, July 28th-29th, 1990

Willie Wood finally laid to rest the ghost of his last end World Singles Championship defeat at the hands of Peter Belliss in 1984 when he returned to Aberdeen's Westburn Park, and took the Scottish Masters title, with a dramatic last end victory over England's Wynne Richards.

Richards dominated the deciding set, but when leading 6-3 sliced the jack with his final bowl to leave Wood lying three shots and with acres of room to add a title winning fourth, Wood duly obliged, much to the delight of the home support at Westburn Park.

Section 1 Winner: Wynne Richards (England) lost to Hugh Duff (Scotland) 7-3, 6-7, 3-7, bt George Adrain (Scotland) 7-6, 7-5, bt Stephen Rees (Wales) 3-7, 7-4, 7-3.

Section 2 Winner: Dennis Love (Scotland) bt David Bryant (England) 4-7, 7-2, 7-0, lost to Richard Corsie (Scotland) 5-7, 7-0, 4-7, bt Jim Baker (Ireland) 7-4, 7-1.

Section 3 Winner: Willie Wood (Scotland) bt Ian Bruce (Scotland) 7-3, 7-5, bt Colin Rae (Scotland) 5-7, 7-0, 7-4, bt Graham Robertson (Scotland) 7-5, 7-4.

Section 4 Winner: Angus Blair (Scotland) bt Roy Henry (Scotland) 7-6, 7-0, bt David Corkill (Ireland) 7-2, 4-7, 7-6, bt John Price (Wales) 7-5, 2-7, 7-6.

Semi finals: Richards bt Love 7-3, 7-4. Wood bt Blair 2-7, 7-6, 7-5.

Final: Wood bt Richards 5-7, 7-0, 7-6.

Avon Insurance 'Jack High' Scottish BA Championships

at Northfield, Ayr, 2nd-4th August, 1990

The Scottish championships moved to a new venue this year, breaking a ninety-seven year association with the Queen's Park Club in Glasgow, with a journey into Ayrshire, and the five green Northfield Complex in Ayr.

The Singles final brought together two of the country's younger players, 22-year-old Simon Thomson from the Adrian Club in Falkirk and his namesake, Steven Thomson, 25, from Castlepark.

Steven made the best start and led 7-1 after six ends, but Simon, a past winner of the Scottish Junior Indoor Championship, hit back to take the title, with a 21-18 win.

Alistair Will, a past beaten finalist in both the Singles and Pairs, made it third time lucky when he teamed up with Maud clubmate Ian Emslie to take the Pairs and Alex Marshall skipped his Gorgie Mills side to a crushing 27-4 win over a Haddington trio skipped by international Angus Blair.

Craigentinny, skipped by SBA Councillor and Scotland's Commonwealth Games team manager, Jack Jeans, took the Fours with a 22-15 win over Maryhill, and Inverurie took the Senior Fours with a 19-14 win over Priorscroft. Port Glasgow's Willie Killens who earlier in the year won the Tennents Masters indoor title, lifted the Junior Singles, with a 21-9 win over Alan Clydesdale from Macmerry.

Singles: Semi finals: Simon Thomson (Adrain) 21, Alan Poole (Pilrig) 15. Steven Thomson (Castlepark) 21, John Dolan (Inkerman) 16.

Final: Simon Thompson 21, Steven Thomson 18.

Pairs Semi Finals: Maud (Ian Emslie and Alistair Will) 17, Birkmyre Park (T Johnstone and A Wotherspoon) 7. Grangemouth (Ken Dobson and Ian Todd) 13, Spittalmyre (John Mackintosh and Neil Robertson) 12.

Final: Maud 20, Grangemouth 9.

Triples: Semi finals: Gorgie Mills (Alex Hurry, Willie Dyet, Alex Marshall) 20, Balgay (Ron Turfus, Alex McGurk, Jack Brodie) 10, Haddington (Davie Logan, Keith Rutherford, Angus Blair) 24, Kilmaurs (Rusty Dunlop, Harry Bennett, Andy Gilmour) 2.

Final: Gorgie Mills 27, Haddington 4.

Fours: Semi Finals: Craigentinny (Dave Curran, Alex Handerson, John Fraser and Jack Jeans) 16, West Barns (Ian Knox, Bill Aitken, Dougie Kennedy, John Kennedy) 11. Maryhill (Willie McVicar, Cameron Adam, Ian Coutts, Cyril Bell) 20, Crossgates (Stewart Anderson, David Murray, Willie Bathgate and David Cuthbert) 17 ex end.

Final: Craigentinny 22, Maryhill 15.

Senior Fours: Semi finals: Inverurie (George Barclay, Jim Thom, Jim Knowles, Alex Simpson) 16, Newbattle (Steve Potter, Norman Anderson, John Noble, Dick Wishart) 13. Priorscroft (Willie Todd, John Gribben, Bobby Shaw, Alan Whyte) 18, Whitecraigs (Tom Maxwell, Jim Young, Peter Brogan, Ted Clark) 17 ex end.

Final: Inverurie 19, Priorscroft 14.

Junior Singles: Semi finals: Wm Killens (Port Glasgow) 21, Robert Bruce (Easthouses) 15. Alan Clydesdale (Macmerry) 21, Gary Craig (Polmaise) 20.

Final: Killens 21, Clydesdale 9.

Women's Pairs: Semi final: Greta Boyle (Irvine Winton) and Doreen Jeffrey (Springhill) 16, Dorothy Barr (Ayr Forehill) and Margaret Agnew (Ayr Craigie) 8. Rose-ena Dante (Ary Craigie) and Mary Reid (Northfield) 15, Ann Brown and Dianne Colville (Crooksmoss) 13.

Final: Boyle and Jeffrey 14, Dante and Reid 13.

Junior Boys Championship (Under 16's): Semi finals: — Mark Dunlop (Irvine Park) 21, Eddie Ecrepont (Ayr Wattfield) 13. Jim Glenn (Meikleriggs) 21, Ally Fleming (Drongan) 9.

Final: Dunlop 21, Glenn 20.

Junior Girls Championship (Under 16's) Semi finals: Arlene Aitken (Drongan) 21, Kelly Bell (Northfield) 16. Jane Campbell (Crooksmoss) 21, Kirsty Broadfoot (Drongan) 8.

Final: Aitken 21, Campbell 10.

Tennant's Ayr Open Tournament

at Northfield, Ayr, August 6th-11th, 1990

Alec Kelly, 18, from Stranraer, whose mother Susan played in the Scottish Women's international side in the mid-80's emerged triumphant from a field of 550 to take Scotland's most prestigious open tournament title after a 21-16 final win over Tom McLarty from Crooksmoss.

The Women's Singles title went to junior international Helen Duff, wife of past World Indoor Champion Hugh, who beat past winner and Scottish International, Dorothy Barr, 21-14.

Men's Singles: Semi finals: Alec Kelly (Stranraer) 21, Brian Cavers (Northfield) 9, Tom McLarty (Crookmoss) 21, Donnie McWhirter (Dailly) 17.

Final: Kelly 21, McLarty 16.

Men's Pairs: Semi final: Willie Clark (Riccaton) and Bob Martin (Tarbolton) 10, Tom Maxwell and Steve Conchar (Castle Douglas) 8, Colin Alexander and Willie Kennedy (Littlemill) 14, Davie Crawford and Robert McCulloch (Maybole) 10.

Final: Clark and Martin 16, Alexander and Kennedy 14.
Women's Singles: Semi finals: Helen Duff (Coylton) 21, Jean Sykes (Cumnock) 8, Dorothy Barr (Ayr Forehill) 21, Sarah Gourlay (Annbank) 12.
Final: Duff 21, Barr 14.

East of Scotland WBA Championships
at Seafield BC, Edinburgh, August 10th, 1990

Winners:
Singles: P Johnstone (Zetland) 21, A Farmer (Lutton Place) 12.
Pairs: Blairgowrie (J Campbell and F Beedie) 19, Castle Park (E Leigh and T Gordon) 10.
Fours: Colinton (A Dick, J Anderson, J MacDonald, J Fairley) 24, Wardie (C Millan, K Beveridge, M Allan, V Ritchie) 16.
R G Lawrie Trophy: Winners: Postal (I McVittie, M Nimmo, M Turnbull, E Rodger) 20 shots up.
Runners Up: Loanhead Miners Welfare (H Easson, B Phillips, C Higgins, J Hope) 17 shots up.
Isobel Murphy Triples: Winners: Currie (M Strickland, M Dougal, J Ballantine) 39 shots up.
Runners Up: Arniston (P Higgs, J Jones, D McKinnon) 33 shots up.
Olive Smith Fours: Winners: Linlothgow (W Hyslop, E Stobie, J Glover, R Greenlaw) 29 shots up, extra ends +3 and −3.
Runners Up: Whitburn (I Imrie, I Cunningham, N Kerr, M Halliday) 29 shots up, extra ends +1 and -2.

Scottish Women's BA Championships
at Northfield, Ayr, August 16th-18th, 1990

Margaret Ritchie from the Wishaw South Club, emerged as the surprise winner of the Scottish Women's Singles Championship. Ritchie, a 52 year old housewife won through to the final with a 25-20 win over Kelty's Rosina Wilson and lined up against Sheila Mann from the Braid Club in Edinburgh, who had accounted for the favourite Margaret Letham from Burnbank Hamilton, a past winner of the Scottish Indoor Singles title, in her semi final.

After scoring three shots on the opening end Ritchie was never behind, as she went on to complete a 25-13 win in 24 ends.

International Dorothy Barr skipped her Forehill rink to the Fours title, Joan Gordon and Helen Cullen took the pairs after beating 1988 runners up Isobel Dockrell and Agnes Blackmore, 23-10, and Lochwinnoch took the Triples with a narrow 14-13 win over Muirkirk.

Anne Brown from Crooksmoss lifted the Junior Singles with a 25-15 win over Elaine McLelland, helped by three maximum counts four.

Singles: Semi final: Margaret Ritchie (Wishaw South) 25, Rosina Wilson (Kelty) 20, Sheila Mann (Braid) 25, Margaret Letham (Burnbank, Hamilton) 19.
Final: Ritchie 25, Mann 13.
Pairs: Semi finals: Milngavie (Joan Gordon and Helen Cullen) 20, Argyll (Betty McCallum and Douglas McKerral) 19. Ardrossan (Isobel Dockrell and Agnes Blackmore) 19, Whitburn (Jean Thomson and Anne Grant) 14.
Final: Milngavie 22, Ardrossan 10.

Triples: Semi final: Lochwinnoch (May McAvoy, Isobel Pratt, Helen Wylie) 18, Thurso (Moira Connell, Cath Swanson, Ann Sinclair) 7. Muirkirk (Marion Muir, Jean Holden, Betty Little) 22, Milton of Campsie (Nina Marshall, Sadie McKean, Nancy Reid) 6. **Final:** Lochwinnoch 14, Muirkirk 13.

Fours: Semi final: Forehill (Bertha Baker, Margaret Taylor, Sarah McKechnie, Dorothy Barr) 30, Irvine Fullarton (Mary Brown, Doreen Bennett, Helen Craig, Susan Crawford) 13. Hawthorn (Kath McFarlane, Marie Millar, Mary Macleod, Helen Crichton) 23 , Queen's Park (Florence Rae, Helen Fairbairn, Nancy Dunsmuir, Bett Urquhart) 13. **Final:** Forehill 29, Hawthorn 13.

Junior Singles Semi final: Anne Brown (Crooksmore) 25, Sharon Leitch (Livingston Letham) 12. Elaine McLelland (Ardrossan) 25, Alison Jenkins (Carron and Carronshore) 17.

Final: Brown 25, McLelland 15.

West of Scotland Women's BA Championships

Semi-Finals at Mount Florida, Glasgow August 22nd, 1990

Finals at Yarrow Recreation, Glasgow 23rd August, 1990

Annette Evans repeated her win of 1987, when she recaptured the West of Scotland Women's Singles Championship, with a 21-18 success over international colleague Janette Thomson from Overtown and Waterloo. Kirn took the Pairs, and Ayrshire notched up a double success, with Newmilns capturing the Triples and Ardrossan the Fours.

Singles: Semi-Finals: Annette Evans (Willowbank) 21, Rita Wishart (Ardeer Recreation) 12. Janette Thomson (Overtown and Waterloo) 21, Rita Vernall (Kingston) 13. **Final:** Evans 21, Thomson 18.

Pairs: Semi-Finals: Kirn and Hunters Quay (Dot McGarvie and Audrey McDougal) 18, Castlemilk (Eleanor Molloy and Rose Hunter) 13. Carnwath (Jenny Armstrong and Mgt Shearer) 24, Hillington (Ian Millar and Grace Palmer) 5. **Final:** Kirn and Hunters Quay 17, Carnwath 8.

Triples: Semi-Finals: Newmilns (Anne Borland, Annie Pollock and Lottie Gilmour) 28, Willowbank (Isobel Drynen, Irene Pullen and Evelyn Smith) 6. Drumoyne (Cathie McDingall, Anne Blair and Greta Crawford)25. Thornliebank (Margo Cox, Betty Scoular and Sadie Hamilton) 7. **Finals:** Newmilns 21, Drumoyne 10.

Fours: Semi-Finals: Ardrossan (Jean Gillies, Nan Cramb, Isabel Dockrell and Agnes Blackmore) 24. Gourock Park (Jane Findlay, Myra Beattie, Jessie Donnachie and Ella Craig) 5. Torrance Victoria (Sadie McMonagle, May McLellan, Irene Campbell and Janet McBride) 22. Wishaw (Sadie St John, Emma Waldie, Cathie McNulty and Betty Denholm) 16. **Final:** Ardrossan 21, Torrance Victoria 8.

East Renfrewshire Women's BA Championships

Semi-Finals at Mearns BC Glasgow, Finals at Drymoyne, August 29th-30th, 1990

Singles: Semi Finals: Raydan Wilson (Busby) 21, Mary Cossar (Mearns) 18, Liz Wilson (Neilston) 21, Rena Carlton (Nitshill) 17.

Final: Raydan Wilson 21, Liz Wilson 17.

Pairs: Semi Finals: Cardonald (Mae McLean and Mai Hood) 23, Mosspark (Mary Holmes and Isa Lindsay) 6. Clarkston (Renee McGhee and Evelyn Craig) 12, Cathcart (Betty Brownlee and Betty Davison) 11.

Final: Cardonald 21, Clarkston 11.

Triples: Semi Finals: Castlemilk (Anne McNeil, Rose Hunter and Cath Vine) 21, Hampden (Mary Gardner, Nancy Fitzpatrick and Mary Logan) 8. Fairfield (Nancy O'Donnell, Mgt Kelly Ann Balfe) 15, St John's (Mgt Smith, Angela Rowand, Mattie Watson) 13.

Final: Castlemilk 14, Fairfield 10.

Fours: Semi Finals: Drumoyne (Cathy McDougall, Chris Lea, Anne Blair and Greta Crawford) 21. Nitshill (Christine Forrester, Isa Montgomeray, Christine Hughes and Mgt Morris) 15. Kings Park (Connie Bremner, Isobel Bryce, Ann Proudfoot and Betty Balfour) 19. Kingswood (Sheila Cumming, Nan Finlay, Jane Muir and Christine Arthur) 10.

Final: Drymoyne 20, Kings Park 7.

Ashbourne Homes Mixed Pairs

at Queensberry, Edinburgh, Sunday September 2nd 1990

Thurso's Moira Connell and Keith MacKay clocked up more than two thousand miles on their way to victory in the Scottish Mixed Pairs.

They took the title with a 20-14 win over the hot favourites, past Scottish outdoor Singles champion Sheila Valentine and past indoor Scottish champion Steve Rankin from Lugar. Thurso led 15-13 with three ends to play, and counted a double on the fifteenth end, followed by a three on the penultimate end, to give them a seven shot cushion, and they were happy to concede a single on the last end, and still run out convincing 20-14 winners.

Semi-finals: Thurso (M. Conell, K. McKay) 16, Newbridge (I. Pollock, Al Allan) 15. Lugar (S. Valentine, S. Rankin) 14, Scotstounhill (E. & S. Livingstone) 12.

Final: Thurso 20, Lugar 14.

Third place play-off: Newbridge 21, Scotstounhill 10.

Wales

by Stuart Dorney-Kingdom

Welsh bowlers brought no medals back from the Commonwealth Games in New Zealand despite a brave attempt by Will Thomas and Robert Weale who finished runners-up in their Pairs section, but lost the play off for the bronze medal to New Zealand's Rowan Brassey and Maurice Symes. John Price, too, went close, losing the chance of a play off for bronze on shots aggregate after defeats by Mark McMahon from New Zealand and Scotland's Richard Corsie who both won medals.

Back in Britain, Price crowned devastating form in the Singles at the Embassy world indoor championships at Preston, defeating Australia's Ian Schuback in the final to lift the title and claim £20,000, the largest prize ever offered in the game. This feat gave the Principality the distinction of holding two key world championships - for Janet Ackland holds the women's world title until 1992.

Janet also distinguished herself in the British Isles international championships at Saundersfoot, hosted by the Welsh Women's BA and the local Saundersfoot club. Aided by Doreen Wallace, Doreen Hall and Adah John from the Penarth Belle Vue club, Mrs Ackland won the Fours title for the second year in succession. The same day the Welsh Triples team from Llandrindod Wells Joan Evans, Brenda Mills and Betty Morgan defeated the England champions from North Walsham to give Wales another British title. There was yet another British Isles success for Wales when John Male and Mark Chard captured the Pairs at Methilhill, Fife at the men's championships.

It was a good year for Will Thomas, who won the Welsh Singles title for the first time as well as the Porthcawl Open for the third. He and Weale were representing Wales in the Hong Kong Classic in November and Mrs Ackland was off to New Zealand with a British party.

One of the most significant features of the Welsh year was the success of their younger players in the Under-25 internationals. The Welsh lads won the indoor match at Perdiswell by a shot and improved on this in the outdoor match at Bristol when they finished 21 shots ahead.

On the indoor front, Weale, who plays at the English club Park Hall Wormelow (Hereford), won all four club championships - Singles, Pairs, Triples and Fours. He also reached the Area Fours semi finals for the English indoor championships and just lost a place in the last 32 of the Singles at Melton Mowbray. It would have been ironic if this Singles standard bearer for Wales had won an English title.

A new indoor club nearer to Weale was opening in Llandrindod Wells, and another was due at Port Talbot, which will further increase interest in the Welsh indoor game.

Welsh Brewers Champions All

at Earlswood, December 2nd-3rd, 1989.

John Price, Swansea, who won the title, did not lose a set in four games over the two days of the tournament. He defeated Jason Greenslade, 20, in the final and won every end against David Newth, Ogwr, in the semi final.

Round 1: Jason Greenslade bt Malcolm Thomas, Torfaen, 7-1, 7-3, Peter Howells, Pembroke, bt Brian Kingdon, Llanelli, 7-4, 5-7, 7-3, John Power, Taff Ely bt Rod Hugh, Llanelli, 7-6, 2-7, 7-2, John Bonatti, Sealand, bt Phil Robins, Rhondda, 7-5, 4-7, 7-6, Mark Hopson, Ogwr, bt Ann Sutherland, Torfaen, 7-3, 7-5, David Newth, Ogwr, bt Alan Davies, Merthyr Tydfil, 7-1, 7-3, John Price, Swansea, bt Gary Williams, Vale of Glamorgan, 7-1, 7-3, Jeff Wright, Vale of Glam, bt Clive Williams, Earlswood 7-0, 7-3.

Round 2: Greenslade bt Howells 7-6, 7-2, Power bt Bonatti 7-1, 7-4, Newth bt Hopson 7-5, 2-7, 7-6, Price bt Wright 7-5, 7-2.

Semi finals: Greenslade bt Power 7-2, 6-7, 7-6, Price bt Newth 7-0, 7-0.

Final: Price bt Greenslade 7-4, 7-5.

CIS Insurance Welsh Indoor Championships

Finals at Ogwr, Bridgend, January 22nd-23rd 1990
(Singles & Under-25 Singles)
and Merthyr Tydfil, January 27th-28th 1990

Phil Rowlands of Cardiff scored a notable double in the CIS Insurance Welsh indoor national championships, recording victories in the Singles and Fours. A brilliantly drawn shot enabled him to defeat double international Michael Kent in the Singles final 21-20 at Ogwr.

It was a bitter blow for Kent, who had reached the final for the second year in succession. In 1989 he was ousted by Brian Kingdon who went on to win the British Isles championship.

Kent, playing on his home green, recovered from a shaky start to score nine shots in a row and lead 14-11. Rowlands took over again with the aid of a four and a three, but a timely three put Kent one shot away from the title. Rowlands climbed back once more and held shot for the match. Kent's final running shot split the head, but Rowlands was still holding shot.

Six days after his national Singles success at Ogwr, Rowlands skipped his partners, David Harding, Keith Rowlands (his father) and Nigel Leigh to a 17-15 Fours win at Merthyr Tydfil against another Cardiff rink comprising David Cox, Frank Schmidt, Brian Sage and Gary Cox. In their semi finals the winners had overwhelmed a Swansea four weakened by the absence of John Price, representing Wales in New Zealand in the Commonwealth Games.

The Pairs title went to Dick Forrester and John Bonatti from the newly established Sealand club in North Wales. They proved too accurate for Merthyr's John Downey and Carl Lewis, whose power driving killed one end six times.

The trio of Alan Rigby, David Mogford and Robert Price made full use of home advantage to take the Triples, outbowling their semi final and final opponents with some ease.

The Under-25 Singles went to Wyn Mathews, who defeated clubmate David Kingdon — son of the 1989 Welsh champion — in the final at Ogwr by 21-7.

Singles:
Semi finals: P. Rowlands (Cardiff) 21, S. Evans (Pembrokeshire) 18; M. Kent (Ogwr) 21, I. Terry (Earlswood) 11.
Final: Rowlands 21, Kent 20.

Under-25 Singles:
Semi finals: D. Kingdon (Llanelli) 21, A. Withers (Rhondda) 10; W. Mathews (Llanelli) 21, J. Stephens (Merthyr Tydfil) 15.
Final: Mathews 21, Kingdon 7.

Pairs:
Semi finals: D. Forrester, J. Bonatti (Sealand) 21, P. Evans, M. Thomas (Torfaen) 18; J. Downey, C. Lewis (Merthyr) 21, M. Thomas, T. Docton 20.
Final: Forrester, Bonatti 24, Downey, Lewis 10.

Triples:
Semi finals: (skips) P. Jenkins (Llanelli) 18, P. Jones (Rhondda) 13; R. Price (Merthyr) 20, I. Fraser (Vale of Glamorgan) 7.
Final: A. Rigby, D. Mogford, R. Price 23, P. Jenkins, M. Morgan, W. Samuel 12.

Fours:
Semi finals: (skips) G. Cox (Cardiff) 24, J. Wilkins (Swansea) 13; P. Rowlands (Cardiff) 25, H. Thomas (Swansea) 6.
Final: D. Harding, K. Rowlands, N. Leigh, P. Rowlands 17, D. Cox, F. Schmidt, B. Sage, G. Cox 15.

South Wales Electricity Welsh Ladies Indoor Championships

at various venues November 1989 — February 1990

Ann Sutherland of Torfaen won the Singles title at Merthyr Tydfil, with victories over Merthyr's Dot Cooper in a semi final, and then Pam John (Cardiff) in the final. Ann reached the indoor final for the first time, but has been Croesyceiliog outdoor Singles champion for eight years (1983-1988) and was runner up in 1989.

Mrs Ackland took the Pairs title at Llanelli in partnership with Adah John. After a closely contested semi final with Jean Evans and Val Howell, they had a comfortable victory over another Merthyr Tydfil pair, Helen Jones and her mother Marilyn Jones. In their semi final Miss Jones, 17, and her mother led all the way against experienced internationals Pam John and Gill Miles, but in the final they were outbowled by their Vale of Glamorgan opponents who led 12-1 at one point and were always in control.

Shirley Proctor and Margaret Pomeroy (Cardiff), who won the British Isles Pairs outdoor championship in 1989 but were omitted from the Welsh Commonwealth Games team, picked up two more titles in these championships.

They were in commanding form all day at Bridgend to finish easy winners of the Triples and complete a double by winning the Fours, defeating a Vale of Glamorgan rink which included the 1989 world outdoor Singles champion

Janet Ackland and Sylvia Froud, the 1989 indoor Singles titleholder.

Singles: Semi finals: A. Sutherland (Torfaen) 21, D. Cooper (Merthyr Tydfil) 6; P. John (Cardiff) 21, S. Williams (Swansea) 13.
Final: Ann Sutherland 21, Pam John 9.
Pairs: Semi finals: A. John, J. Ackland (Vale of Glamorgan) 28, J. Evans, V. Howell (Merthyr) 24. H & M Jones (Merthyr) 21, P. John, G. Miles (Cardiff) 16.
Final: Adah John, Janet Ackland 28, Helen Jones, Marilyn Jones 10.
Triples: Semi finals: M. Hopkin, J. Wason, C. Morgan (Ogwr) 19, N. Parsons, C. Pearce, I. Williams (Earlswood) 12. S. Proctor, M. Jones, M. Pomeroy (Cardiff) 23, R. James, A. Davies, A. Mullins (Merthyr Tydfil) 8.
Final: Cardiff 28, Ogwr 8.
Fours: Semi finals: D. Hall, D. Wallace, J. Ackland, S. Froud (Vale of Glamorgan) 20, A. Toms, J. Lovett, D. Blackmore, J. Ward (Cardiff) 14. S. Proctor, J. Parsons, M. Jones, M. Pomeroy (Cardiff) 23, F. Humphreys, D. Aretsen, A. Smith, N.Shipperlee (Cardiff) 13.
Final: Cardiff 17, Vale of Glamorgan 14.

Jewsons Welsh Indoor Championship

Swansea City, captained by former world champion, Terry Sullivan, won the title for the seventh time in eight years, this being last time for the 11 clubs to play each other home and away. This season the completion has been zoned into East and West sections:

East, comprises Cardiff, Merthyr Tydfil, Rhondda, Vale of Glamorgan, Torfaen and Taff Ely, and the West — Swanseam Llanelli, Ogwr, Earlswood and Pembroke. The new system prepares for the future introduction of new clubs into the championship for the 1991/92 season.

Jewson's National Team Championship East v West

Final at Earlswood, April 15th 1990.

Ystadyfodwg one of Rhondda's two teams won the title for the fourth time when they beat Caswell, one of Swansea's three teams in a game featuring two great recoveries. Caswell's Richard Allen, 17-5 down to Phil Robins, levelled the score 17 all at finish, and Rhondda's Lyn Tanner cut his seven shot arrears to a one shot deficit. Spencer Wilshire's seven shot victory over Stephen Rees, ensured Ystradyfodwg's victory.

Ystradyfodwg 75, Caswell 70.

Rinks: (Ystradyfodwg first): S Wilshire 22, S Rees 17, P Robins 17, R Allen 17, J E Thomas 21, J Squires 20, L Tanner 15, R Gough 16.

Brains Brewery Welsh Open Singles

at Dinas Powis, May 28th — June 3rd 1990

Idris Jones (Cardiff Athletic) won the £400 first prize with a three shot victory in the final over Fred Phillips from Cadoxton, after leading 20-10. In his semi final Jones recovered from a 17-13 deficit against Alan Mathias to win 21-18.

Semi finals: I. Jones (Cardiff Athletic) 21, A. Mathias (Penarth Belle Vue) 18; F. Phillips (Cadoxton) 21, R. Lewis (Whitchurch) 9.
Final: I. Jones 21, F. Phillips 18.

Welsh Private Greens Gwalia Cup

at Penarth, June 6th 1990

East Wales, captained by president John Taylor (Rhiwbina), beat West Wales Private Greens (president Rhys Asher, I.N.C.O. BC) to retain the Cup which was first presented for competition in 1939.

Welsh PG East 127, Welsh PG West 97.

Futureglaze Windows Open Mixed Pairs

at Pontyclun BC, June 4th-10th, 1990.

Judith and Andrew Wason, Chepstow, defeated Pengelli's Marion Evans and Ivor Bassett who dropped a six on the tenth and never recovered.

Semi finals: J and A Wason, (Chepstow) 20, B and D Francis, (Pontyclun) 11, M Evans, I Bassett, (Pengelli) 16, G and H Gillard, (Pengelli) 15.

Final: J and A Wason 28, Evans, Bassett 12.

Brecon Open Singles

at Brecon, June 9th-16th 1990

Tommy Cannon (Ynysangharad, Pontypridd) had a narrow victory over Dave Jones (Mount Pleasant, Neath) in the final.

Semi finals: T. Cannon (Ynysangharad) 21, R. Aherne (Brecon) 6; D. Jones (Mount Pleasant) 21, P. Carpenter (Aberfan) 16.

Final: Cannon 21, Jones 19.

Pilkington Insulation Torfaen Open Singles

Final at Pilkington, June 29th 1990

Pilkington's Bill Jones celebrated his 67th birthday, winning the title, just as his mother, aged 93, a former clairvoyant, had predicted from her hospital bed. But he won his quarter final and semi final only by one-shot margins.

Semi finals: W. Jones (Pilkington) 21, H. Hill (Croesyceiliog) 20; H. Rees (Panteg House) 21, G. Morgan (Croesyceiliog) 14.

Final: W. Jones 21, H. Rees 13.

Warmlite Windows Swansea City Open

at Victoria Park, Swansea, July 22nd — August 11th 1990

Robin Burden (Kidwelly) won the £300 first prize, defeating Garfield Phillips (unattached), who led most of the way, till reaching 15-14 when Burden took command.

In the Pairs Wyn Mathews and Stephen Thomas (Graig Merthyr) led by five going into the last end against Roy Murray (Briton Ferry Steel) and Islwyn Morgan (Cwmavon) who held four shots and just lost the measures for another two which could have won them the game. The Women's Singles was won by Ceri Piper of Aberavon.

Pairs:
Semi finals: W. Mathews, S. Thomas (Graig Merthyr) 24, D. Turner, J. Lee (Salisbury) 14; R. Murray (Briton Ferry Steel) I. Morgan (Cwmavon) 21, W. Storey, E. Evans (Bonymaen) 17.
Final: Mathews, Thomas 18, Murray, Morgan 17.

Mixed Pairs:
Semi finals: L. Evans (Port Talbot), T. King (Old Landorians) 23, L & D James (Salisbury) 12; T & T Bendle (Loughor) 16, S. Williams (Gorseinon), C. Taylor (Old Landorians) 15.
Final: Evans, King 20, Bendle, Bendle 17.

Women's Singles:
Semi finals: C. Piper (Aberavon) 21, P. Washer (Trallwyn) 8; M. Cawley (Port Talbot) 21, D. Thompson (Swansea) 9.
Final: Piper 21, Cawley 18.

Llanelli Open

at Parc Howard, Llanelli and other greens, July 23rd-28th 1990

This tournament was sponsored by Llanelli Borough Council. Colin Forey (Tyfran) won the Robert Rolfe Cup and £500 first prize with a two-shot victory over Adrian Evans (Brynhyfryd Llanelli) who gained the £200 runner-up award.

Robert Blacklaw of Parc Howard won the Stacey Cup and £300 first prize, with Mel Griffiths (St. Gabriels) receiving the £150 runner-up award. A feature of the Stacey Cup and Mercury Triples this year was the entry of three wheelchair bowlers, Stuart Mitchell (Cwmbran), John Gronow (Cardiff) and Paul Huball (Pontardulais). Though they lost their first rounds they offered their services as markers, though unable to measure. Stuart Mitchell lost the first round of the Stacey 21-14 to the eventual runner-up Mel Griffiths after a creditable performance, and taking an early lead of 9-7.

Brothers Gareth Jones (Loughor) and Kevin Jones (Rhondda), and Jos. Whitefoot (Haverfordwest), won the Mercury Cup Triples and £480 first prize, defeating another Gareth Jones, Hafod Thomas, and Dev. Davies (Loughor), who received the £240 runners-up award.

Robert Rolfe Cup:
Semi finals: C. Forey (Tyfran) 21, C. Piper (Vivian Park) 19; A. McCarley (Brynhyfryd) 17, A. Evans (Brynhyfryd) 21.
Final: C. Forey 21, A. Evans 19.

A.J. Stacey Cup:
Semi finals: M. Griffiths (St. Gabriels) 21, G. Jones (Tumble) 18; R. Blacklaw (Parc Howard) 21, J. Forey (Brynhyfryd) 17.
Final: Blacklaw 21, Griffiths 15.

Mercury Cup Triples:
Semi finals: G. Jones, H. Thomas, D. Davies (Loughor) 19, R. Burden, P. Jenkins, W. Samuel (Kidwelly) 17; G. Jones (Neyland), K. Jones (Rhondda), J. Whitefoot (Haverfordwest) bt O. Colwill & Co. (Kidwelly).
Final: Jones, Jones, Whitefoot 17, Jones, Thomas, Davies 14.

Croeso Cup

Welsh Private Green v London Southern Counties Tour
at six Welsh venues, July 23rd — 28th 1990

London and Southern Counties, captained by John Morgan-Griffiths, a Welshman now a member of Atherley BC, Southampton, brought a tour party representing six English counties to play six matches for the Croeso Cup. The Welsh Private Green teams won all the matches, played at Rhiwbina, Llanelli, Llanbradach, INCO, Clydach, Penarth and Ynys, Port Talbot, to retain the trophy, scoring a total 805 shots against 596.

Ansells Brewers 67th annual Tenby Open

at Tenby July 28th — August 4th 1990

Ken Hewling, a Tenby music teacher won the coveted Gold Cup and £200 top prize, defeating Mike Owen who won the Cup in 1987 when living at Carmarthen, and who now teaches in London. Hewling ran out winner with a 3,4,1, after Owen led 15-13. Incidentally, Hewling won his quarter final by seven shots over Mike Owen's father, tournament experienced Arnallt Owen (Carmarthen).

Keran Peregrine, 22, from Ammanford Park, beat David Daniel (Maesteg Celtic), Gold Cup winner two years ago, to win the Silver Bowl. Daniel found the tables turned on him in the final after his dominating semi final victory.

Gold Cup semi finals: K. Hewling (Tenby) 21, M. Davies (Loughor) 9; M. Owen (Hounslow Sports) 21, C. Davies (Carmarthen) 4.
Final: Hewling 21, Owen 15.

Silver Cup semi finals: K. Peregrine (Ammanford Park) 21, Simon Evans (Saundersfoot) 16; D. Daniel (Maesteg Celtic) 21, A. Brain (Saundersfoot) 5.
Final: Peregrine 21, Daniel 3.

Five Arches Cup semi finals: K. Barnett (Fishguard) 21, J. Lawler (Bristol) 14; R. Cowling (Tenby) 21, S. Harris (Tumble) 20
Final: Barnett 21, Cowling 15.

Aberdare Open

at Aberdare Park, July 29th — August 5th 1990

Peter Jones (Gelli Park) won the Gwyrdd Memorial Cup and £200 first prize, surging from a 12-12 scoreline to defeat Welsh international Carl Lewis, Merthyr West End by eight shots in the final.

Semi finals: C.Lewis (Merthyr West End) 21, J. Stone (Maerdy) 8; P. Jones (Gelli Park) 21, C. Cooper (Harlequins) 15.
Final: P. Jones 21, C. Lewis 13.

Penylan Open

at Penylan, July 30th — August 4th 1990

For the second time in four years, Peter Evans, 58, of Cardiff Athletic won the Harry Jones Bowl and £200 first prize, comfortably defeating Cyril

Williamson (Barry Plastics) in the final after a narrow semi final victory over Brian Rich (Penylan) by 19-18.

Semi finals: P. Evans (Cardiff Athletic) 21, B. Rich (Barry Plastics) 18; C. Williamson (Barry Plastics) 21, A. Rowe (Cardiff Athletic) 19.

Final: Evans 21, Williamson 8.

Whitbread Open Ladies Pairs

at Rhydycar BC, Merthyr Tydfil, August 5th-12th, 1990

Beryl Hawkins and Vera Haines, (Cynon Parc), became the first holders of the Whitbread Cup, in this inaugural event, organised by the newly formed Merthyr Tydfil Ladies on their new synthetic outdoor green, and played over 15 ends throughout.

Semi-finals: B Hawkins, V Haines (Cynon Park), J Rowlands, D Patterson 14, D Cooper (Gilfach Bargoed), A Davies (Guest Memorial) 30, T Rees, M Budden (Merthyr Tydfil) 10.

Final: Hawkins, Haines 13, Cooper, Davies 11.

Jewsons Open Singles

at Llandovery, August 6th-11th 1990

International Robert Weale, Presteigne, was beaten in the final by his brother, David Weale, a Welsh trialist. David won the Jewson Cup and £500 first prize to complete a double, for he had also beaten Robert in the final of the Llandrindod Cup at Llandrindod Open June tournament.

Semi finals: D. Weale (Presteigne) 21, A. Jenkins (Builth Wells) 12; R. Weale (Presteigne) 21, G. Phillips (Presteigne) 19

Final: D. Weale 21, R. Weale 16.

Miss Savegar Memorial Cup

Final at Rectory Road, Penarth, August 8th 1990

Welsh Women's BA donated the Miss Savergar Memorial Cup for contest between the four county associations to commemorate Miss Gertrude Savegar (Abergavenny Nevil), who was Welsh WBA treasurer 1953-1963 and secretary 1963 until her death in 1980.

Glamorgan beat West Wales 132-90 in the final, with 31 of their 42 shot win coming from the rink skipped by Adah John (Penarth Belle Vue).

Glamorgan County WBA 132, West Wales CWBA 90

Glamorgan skips first: A. John 33, S. Mainbridge 2; R. Jones 28, N. Evans 13; N. Shipperlee 18, M. Marquess 19; J. Ackland 17, D. Davis 21; A. Dainton 14, A. Lewis 19; J. Whalley 22, A. John 16.

Porthcawl Open

at Griffin Park, Porthcawl on August 13th-25th, 1990

Arthur Applegate, (Ely Valley), won the W J Griffin Singles Cup and £300 first prize, to capture his first tournament title. The Builders Cup Singles went to Singles champion Will Thomas, the Welsh captain for the last three years. He scored on seven of the last eight ends of the final to defeat Peter

Rinks (Brynhyfryd skips first): E Oliver 21, G Williams 14, D Richards 23, J R Evans 16, M Bishop 23, J A Morgan 15, B Kingdom 33, S Humphreys 17.
Old Landorians bt Presteigne 81-65?
Rinks (Old Landorians skips first): S Rees 19, E Gummer 18, C Taylor 18, R Weale 26, P J Bailey 32, D Weale 13, T Sullivan 22, W Weale 18.
Final:
Brynhyfryd bt Old Landorians.
Rinks (Brynhyfryd skips first): E Oliver 28, P J Bailey 11, B Kingdom 24, S Rees 14, M Bishop 19, T Sullivan 19, D Richards 11, C Taylor 25.

NatWest Carruthers Shield

at RTB, Ebbw Vale, August 18th 1990

Brynhyfryd, Llanelli, won the Shield for the first time since their formation 52 years ago, defeating Old Landorians in the final.
Semi finals: Brynhyfryd 100, Barry Athletic 62: Rinks: (Brynhyfryd first) E. Oliver 21, G. Williams 14; D. Richards 23, R. Evans 16; M. Bishop 23, J Morgan 15; B. Kingdon 33, S. Humphreys 17. Old Landorians 91, Presteigne 75: (Old Landorians first) T. Sullivan 23, W. Weale 18; P. Bailey 32, D. Weale 13; C. Taylor 18, R. Weale 26; S. Rees 19, E. Gummer 18.
Final: Brynhyfryd 82, Old Landorians 68 (Brynhyfryd first): Richards 11, Taylor 25; Kingdon 25, Rees 14; Oliver 28, Bailey 10; Bishop 19, Sullivan 19.

WBA Under 18 Singles Championship

at Ynysangharad Park, Pontypridd, August 25th-26th, 1990.

Johnathan Stephens of Aberdare Harlequins tore through the field at Ynysangharad Park, scoring 105 shots and conceding only 45 on his way to the Welsh Under 18 championship.

Martyn Snow, from Swansea's Mount Pleasant Club, who faced Johnathan in the final, seemed to have shot his bolt in the semi final, when he was involved in a titanic struggle with Stuart "Sarge" Sargent of Bedwas.
Round 1: B Evans (Pontryhydyfen) bt C Smith (Llantrisant) 21-19; D Holt (Machynlleth) bt J Davies (Gwynfi) 21-20; N Jones (Llantwit Major) bt T Watkins (Bedwellty Park) 21-10; G Williams (Pembroke Dock) bt K Egan (Aberavon) 21-13; J Stephens (Aberdare Harlequins) bt C Jenkins (Penclawdd) 21-7; R Phillips (Cardigan) bt M Gravell (Kidwelly) 21-16; G Davies (Aberavon) bt A Jones (Llandovery) 21-10; J Webley (Dinas Powis) bt G Howard (Caldicot) 21-10; R Walters (Bedwellty Park) bt J Matthews (Neath Town) 21-18; J Flynn (Aberavon) bt D Pearce (Ystradfechan) 21-11; D Richards (Abergavenny) bt C Thomas (Tenby) 21-14; M Snow (Mount Pleasant) bt A Bushell (Cross Keys) 21-16; M Gaskell (Machynlleth) bt J Britton (Pontrhydyfen) 21-18; M Letman (St Fagans) w/o J Rogers (Gwynfi) scr; M Williams (Llandrindod Wells) w/o, D Jones (Llandysul) scr; S Sargent (Bedwas) bt E Jones (Kidwelly) 21-5.
Round 2: Evans bt Holt 21-9; Jones bt Williams 21-6; Stephens bt Phillips 21-8; Webley bt Davies 21-6; Flynn bt Walters 21-10; Snow bt Richards 21-17; Letman bt Gaskell 21-17; Sargent bt Williams 21-10.
Quarter finals: Evans bt Jones 21-12; Stephens by Webley 21-14; Snow bt Flynn 21-10; Sargent bt Letman 21-17.
Semi finals: Stephens bt Evans 21-8; Snow bt Sargent 21-19.
Final: Johnathan Stephens bt Martyn Snow 21-8.

Warmlite Welsh Bowling Association Mixed Pairs Championship

at Victoria Park, Swanse, August 23rd-24th 1990

Islwyn Morgan and Louie Davies from Port Talbot won the shield presented by Swansea City Council for this inaugural event. They scored a seven on the 15th end of the final against David Weale (Presteigne) and Mary Davies (Llandrindod), the 1988 Welsh WBA President, which set them on the way to their 23-14 victory. They had dominated their semi final with Fred and Pauline Took of Chepstow and had a narrow escape after dropping an eight to Robert Weale (Presteigne) and Betty Morgan (Llandrindod) at the quarter final stage. The teams were level at 21-all going into the last end, but Morgan and Davies went through by scoring a three.

Round 1: I. Morgan, L. Davies (Port Talbot) 26, L. Webley, D. Thompson (Barry) 23; R. Weale (Presteigne), B. Morgan (Llandrindod) 30, D & J. King-Thomas (Pendine) 11; F & P Took (Chepstow) 26, R & B Hopkins (Abertridwr) 14; A & W Lamb (Pendine) 21, E & C Taylor (Aberdare) 12; D. Price, G. Lappage (Neath) 19, G. Morgan, D. Thorne (Llandovery) 17; D. Weale (Presteigne), M. Davies (Llandrindod) 18, D & T Wilton (Pontymister) 15; N. Collett, M. Jones (Cardiff) 33, K & M Walding (Blackwood) 18; J. Wright, S. Britton (Barry) 28, D. Richards, D. Lewis (Llanelli) 12.

Quarter finals: Morgan, Davies 24, Weale, Morgan 21; Tooks 21, Lambs 12; Weale, Davies 27, Price, Lappage 13; Collett, Jones 19, Wright, Britton 16.

Semi finals: Morgan, Davies 31, Tooks 10; Weale, Davies 19, Collett, Jones 17.

Final: Morgan, Davies 23, Weale, Davies 14.

Penarth Belle Vue Open

at Penarth Belle Vue BC, August 26th — September 2nd 1990

Prizes: £200, £100, two of £50

Welsh international, David Vowles (Dinas Powis) won the £200 first prize, defeating tournament organiser Robert Ackland in the final with a last end three. Sponsors: Tern Construction Group.

Semi finals: D. Vowles (Dinas Powis) 21, R. Osborne (St. Fagans) 14; R. Ackland (Penarth Belle Vue) 21, E. Roberts (Barry Plastics) 20.

Final: Vowles 21, Ackland 18.

Merthyr West End Open Singles

at Merthyr West End BC, August 25th-September 2nd 1990

Former Welsh indoor team captain, John E. Thomas (Ystradfechan) won the £500 first price when he beat Les Chard, 73, of Aberdare Harlequins who had led 20-17/ When Thomas led 17-16, Chard took a four, looked at the score-board, thought he was on 17 and had won. His disappointment resulted in his bowling a loose end, enabling Thomas to pick up a three and then a single on the next end, to win the title for the third time. The tournament was sponsored by Dragon Ford (Merthyr Tydfil).

Semi finals: J. Thomas (Ystradfechan) 21, I. Bishop (Guest Memorial) 12; L. Chard (Aberdare Harlequins) 21, D. Osling (Cardiff Athletic) 17.

Final: J. Thomas 21, L. Chard 20.

Evans and take the £300 top prize. Thomas climbed back from defeat of 18-5 and 20-17 to win his semi final against Michael Kent, Keith Davies and Trevor Evans of Cofn Cribbwr, semi finalists last year, won £300 and the Sir Leslie Joseph Pairs Cups with a run-away victory in the final.

The Ron Harris Memorial Juniors Trophy was changed to a Mixed Pairs event this year, and won by Iris and Ronald Loveridge.

Welsh Bowling Association Championships

at BSC (Tinplate), Ebbw Vale, August 15th-17th, 1990.

Ebbw Vale, preparing to host the national garden festival in 1991, became the hothouse of Welsh bowls for a week, when more Welsh internationals than ever before qualified to play in the national championships.

Len Platts, a former Middleton Cup player from Kent, made a strong bid to become the second Englishman in succession to win the Singles title — Bristolian, Pat Toogood, the holder, had gone out in the first round at Bridgend — but lost his touch in the semi final.

The Singles was won by Will Thomas, who has earned medals at Commonwealth Games (fours gold in 1986) and at World championship level (pairs bronze in 1988) — but, like Tony Allcock, had to wait until 1990 to win his first national outdoor title.

From Pontryhydyfen, Thomas was part of a veritable takeover by West Wales, for it was only Jason Greenslade of St Fagans in the Junior Singles and Trevor Mounty's Abertridwr rink who produced wins for the eastern counties.

Terry Sullivan and Steve Rees, well-known for their exploits in televised events, teamed up to win the Pairs for Old Landorians. Though Rees has won a number of junior titles, this was their first senior national title on grass.

A young trio from Pontardulais, Wyn Matthews, Huw and Steve Thomas of the Graig Merthyr club surprised three Tonypandy internationals, Eric John, Lyn Tanner and Spencer Wilshire, winning the Triples final, 19-3.

The shift of power to the west was underlined when Old Landorians from Swansea met Brynhyfryd from Llanelli in the final of the NatWest inter-club team championship for the Carruthers Shield, Brynhyfryd winning the title for the first time. Old Landorians had defeated Mid Wale's Presteigne — who fielded five members of the Weale family — in the semi final, while Brynhyfryd overwhelmed Barry Athletic, one of the Vale of Glamorgan's most powerful clubs.

Singles: Round 1. R Treherne (Llandbradach) bt C Lewis (Merthyr West End) 21-19, W Millar (Tyrfran, Llanelli) w/o, M Chard (Aberdare Harlequins) scr; L Platts (Aberavon) bt J Bullock (Penhill) 21-12, I Slade (Abercarn) bt A Davies (Parc Howard, Llanelli) 21-11, R H Morgan (Aberystwyth) bt G Lewis (Griffin Pack) 21-8, R Cowling (Barry Athletic) bt G Cavell (Saundersfoot) 21-20, W Thomas (Pontryhydyfen) bt M Davies (Knighton) 21-12, W Pugh (Welshpool) bt M Anstey (Abergavenny) 21-19.
Quarter finals: Treherne bt Millar 21-19, Platts bt Slade 21-7, Morgan bt Cowling 21-20, Thomas bt Pugh 21-13,.
Semi finals: Treherne bt Platts 21-8, Thomas bt Morgan 21-9.
Final: Will Thomas (Pontrhydyfen) bt Robert Treherne (Llandbradach) 21-14.

Under 25 Singles: Round 1. M Lewis (Pontymister Athletic) bt E Thomas (Pontrhydyfen) 21-12, J Wilkins (Pontrhydyfen) bt I Slade (Abercarn) 21-8, J Greenslade (St Fagans) bt J Stevens (Aberdare Harlequins) 21-10, A Muskett (Tenby) bt B Weale (Presteigne) 21-19, J Webley (Dinas Powis) w/o, M Chard (Aberdare Harlequins) scr, A Jones (Tumble) w/o, J Applegate (Ely Valley) scr, A Price (Ammanford) bt G Ellis (Aberystwyth) 21-4.

Quarter finals: Wilkins bt Lewis 21-10, Greenslade bt Muskett 21-12, Webley bt Atwood 21-17, Price bt Jones 21-19.

Semi finals: Greenslade bt Wilkins 21-9, Price bt Webley 21-17.

Final: Jason Greenslade (St Fagans) bt Adrian Price (Ammanford) 21-9.

Pairs: Round 1. Dinas Powis (P Coles and A R Dibble) bt Pontrhydyfen (I Shepherd and K Parfitt) 24-22, Old Landorians (T Sullivan and S Rees) bt Machynlleth (A Fleming and J Davies) 18-17, Pontymister Athletic (G and D Wilton) bt Pembroke Dock (G Williams and L H Davies 16-15, Brynhyfryd, Llanelli (D Kingdom and D Richards) bt Merthyr West End (C Lewis and M Jenkins) 22-12, Rhymney Gwent (J K Evans and N Tippett) bt Wheatsheaf, Llanelli (P Richardson and G David) 27-14, St Fagans (W Letman and J Ellis) bt Cardiff (G Taylor and M Cox) 30-11, Brecon (M Padmore and L H E Thomas) bt Aberystwyth (G Gravell and R H Morgan) 21-10, Caerau (D Jenkins and D Brace) bt Penygraig (D Robins and E Walton) 23-12.

Quarter finals: Old landorians bt Dinas Powis 25-16, Pontymister Athletic bt Brynhyfryd 23-18, St Fagans bt Rhymney Gwent 22-12, Brecon bt Caerau 25-12.

Semi finals: Old Landorians bt Pontymister Athletic 26-13, St Fagans bt Brecon 20-18.

Final: Terry Sullivan and Steve Rees (Old Landorians) bt Wayne Letman and John Ellis (St Fagans) 30-12.

Triples: Round 1. Llanfair (D Edwards) bt Penhill (E Edwards) 16-15, Tonypandy (S Wilshire) bt Wheatsheaf (G David) 16-11, Queens Road, Aberystwyth (E Salmon) bt Blaenrhondda (A Collins) 22-15, Old Landorians (T King) bt New Tredegar (R Morris) 22-4, Pembroke Dock (R Bastin) bt Porthcawl (M Kent) 18-14, Barry Althetic (J R Thomas) bt Skewen (G Mellor) 16-13, Graig Merthyr (S Thomas) bt Knighton (G Moorhouse) 18-16, Caerphilly (B Llewellyn) bt Llanwern (T Williams) 21-15.

Quarter finals: Tonypandy bt Llanfair 29-3, Old Landorians bt Queens Road 17-12, Pembroke Dock bt Barry Althetic 13-12, Graig Merthyr bt Caerphilly 14-13.

Semi finals: Tonypandy bt Old Landorians 20-17, Graig Merthyr bt Pembroke Dock 21-13.

Final: Wyn Matthews/Huw Thomas/Steve Thomas (Graig Merthyr) bt Eric John/Lyn Tanner/Spencer Wilshire (Tonypandy) 19-3.

Fours: Round 1. Tonypandy (L Perkins) bt Cwmafan (L Davies) 20-18, Standard Telephone (B Cork) bt Cardiff (M Maunder) 24-14, Milford Haven (D Griffiths) bt Penclawdd (D Palmer) 22-18, Tonypandy (S Wilshire) bt Machynlleth (M Caskell) 21-19, Lampeter (J Edwards) bt RTB, Ebbw Vale (B Willis) 21-16, Barry Athletic (G Humphreys) bt Llandrindod Wells (P Rowlands) 22-13, Porthcawl (M Kent) bt Ammanford (R Anthoney) 27-8, Abertridwr (T Mounty) bt Brynhyfryd, Llanelli (D Richards) 23-17.

Quarter finals: Tonypandy (L Perkins) bt Standard Telephone 19-10, Tonypandy (S Wilshire) bt Milford Haven 25-8, Lampeter bt Barry Athletic 25-10, Abertridwr bt Porthcawl 24-17.)

Semi finals: Tonypandy (L Perkins) bt Tonypandy (S Wilshire) 19-18, Abertridwr bt Lampeter 27-13.

Final: Gareth Griffiths/Gwynmor Hopkins/Gwyn Roberts/Trevor Mounty (Abertridwr) bt Roy Thomas/Mike Young/Vic Dimond/Lyn Perkins (Tonypandy) 16-15.

Ely Valley Open Pairs

at Ely Valley BC, August 26th — September 2nd 1990

Prizes: 1st: £500, 2nd: £250, 3rd & 4th: £100

Welsh Open Singles champion, Idris Jones (Cardiff Athletic), joined up with his former Coal Board colleague, Jim Hoskins, Bridgend, to win the Cup and £500 first prize, beating Tonypandy's Eric John and Welsh international Spencer Wilshire by three shots in the final, after leading throughout, and by a massive 24 shot advantage in the semi final. The tournament was sponsored by Norman Harris Printers (Porthcawl).

Semi finals: I. Jones (Cardiff Athletic), J. Hoskins (Bridgend) 31, M. Davies, C. Evans (Ystradfechan) 7; E. John, S. Wilshire (Tonypandy) 23, P. Robins (Penygraig) I. Buckley (Ely Valley) 18.

Final: Jones, Hoskins 21, John, Wilshire 18.

Wales & the Marches Post Office Finals

at Hereford, September 2nd 1990

Singles: Brian Davies (Aberystwyth) 21, Brian Sage 20.
Pairs: Colin Cooper, Len Cummings (Aberdare) 30, Aldryd James, Bob Walls (Builth Wells) 7.
Fours: Brian Fender, Dave Riseley, Nicky Miller, Stephen Rees (Swansea) bt Len Buse, Roy Rees, Clive Holmes, Alan Denis (Swansea).

Welsh Women's Championships

Semi finals and finals at Gilfach Bargoed, September 3rd and 6th 1990

Eileen Thomas (Port Talbot), aged 65, a former double international, won the Singles title for the second time, shared in Port Talbot's double rink success, and was runner up in the Fours. She defeated Nesta Hopkins (Porth) after surging to a 14-0 lead.

Rita Jones (Gilfach Bargoes), the 1989 Singles champion, again qualified for three titles. She won the Two-Wood against Adah John (Penarth Belle Vue), but lost in the Pairs and Triples finals. Marlene Burns and Mair Marquis (Tenby) won the Pairs after leading 26-10 and 26-23. Going into the last end against Gilfach Bargoed, who held four shots for game, Marquis's last delivery glanced off a side wood to rest out the opposition for a single. Llandrindod's Doreen Rowlands, Shirley King, and the 1988 Welsh president, Mary Davies, won the Triples.

Pam Skinner, Val Mitchell and Joy Watts (Pontypool), brilliantly skipped by 25-year-old junior international, Louise Thomas, won the Fours. Louise was moving later to Lethworth with her baby son and husband Malcolm, who has played indoor for Wales.

Port Talbot had little difficulty in defeating Parc Cynon (Abercycnon) 57-30 in the Double Rinks final.

Singles: Semi finals: E. Thomas (Port Talbot) 21, J. Harris (Saundersfoot) 12. N. Hopkins (Porthcawl) 21, P. Griffiths (Merthyr West End) 13.
Final: E. Thomas 21, N. Hopkins 12.
Two Wood Singles: Semi finals: A. John (Penarth Belle Vue) 15, E. Smith (Sophia

Gardens, Cardiff) 10. R. Jones (Gilfach Bargoed) 16, W. Morris (Port Talbot) 6.
Final: R. Jones 17, A. John 3.
Pairs: M. Burns, M. Marquis (Tenby) 24, S. Proctor, M. Pomeroy (Sophia Gardens) 21. A. Mullins, R. Jones (Gilfach Bargoed) 20, C. Stinchcombe, L. Parker (Knighton) 11.
Final: Burns, Marquis 27, Mullins, Jones 23.
Triples: Semi finals: Gilfach Bargoed 20, Aberystwyth (M. Wintle) 15. Llandrindod 17, Sophia Gardens (E. Schmidt) 14.
Final: Llandrindod Wells (S. King, D. Rowlands, M. Davies) 14, Gilfach Bargoed (G. Saunders, A. Mullins, R. Jones) 9.
Fours: Semi finals: Port Talbot 23, Merthyr West End (V. Howell) 13. Pontypool 21, Llandrindod (S. Gough) 13.
Final: Pontypool (P. Skinner, V. Mitchell, J. Watts, L. Thomas) 21, Port Talbot (M. Cawley, W. Morris, L. Evans, E. Thomas) 12.
Double Rinks: Semi finals: Parc Cynon (Abercynon) 44, Pendine 39. Port Talbot 47, Llansawel 40.
Final: Port Talbot 57, Parc Cynon (Abercynon) 30.

Welsh Private Greens 1 & 2 Club Championships
at Barry Athletic (PG1) and Rhiwbina (PG2), September 8th 1990

St. Fagans won the title and William Tucker Cup for the second time, thwarting Cardiff's hopes of winning for the third successive year. St. Fagans won on three rinks, with their teenage rink, skipped by Jason Greenslade, performing brilliantly. Cardiff had reached the PG2 final also, and looking for a double, lost this as well, beaten by Barry Athletic whose Ron Thomas, in superb form, must have saved at least 25 shots in his victory over Wyn Jones.

William Tucker Cup: St Fagans 98, Cardiff 75. Rinks (St. Fagans first): J. Ellis 29, G. Cox 19; B. Nicholas 25, N. Leigh 14; J. Greenslade 29, A. Pearce 15; M. Greenslade, 15, H. Davies 27.
G.H. Morgan Cup: Barry Athletic 87, Cardiff 76. Rinks (Barry first): N. Wheeler 28, J. Taylor 17; R. Thomas 23, W. Jones 14; G. Thomas 15, B. Blackmore 26; W. Thomas 21, V. Willis 19.

Civil Service, Wales, Championships
Finals at Cardiff Athletic BC, September 9th and 16th 1990

Singles: Semi finals: D. Gough (East Wales) 21, R. John (West) 19; L. Culley (Pembroke) 21, W. Jones (East) 20.
Final: Gough 21, Culley 10.
Pairs: Semi finals: E. Johnson, B. Owen (East) 23, C. Phillips, D. Gough (East) 11; B. Kenvyn, R. Bowdler (East) 26, A. Wood, E. Sturley (Pembs) 14.
Final: Johnson, Owen 16, Kenvyn, Bowdler 14.
Triples: Semi finals: M. Smith, P. Harris, P. Howells (Pembs) 19, K. Myatt, A. Marshall, S. Jackson (East) 14; M. Mitchell, N. Collett, W. Jones (East) 17, R. Blewitt, P. Jones, J. Gibbons (West) 14.
Final: Smith, Harris, Howells 21, Mitchell, Collett, Jones 16.
Fours: Semi finals: D. Gough, R. Bowdler, B. Kenvyn, W. Jones (East) 20, P. Jones, R. Blewitt, E. Chard, J. Gibbons (West) 17; M. Smith, M. Jenkins, P. Harris, P. Howells (Pembs) 25, R. Osborne, M. Chapple, M. Allen, G. Hazell (East) 16.
Final: Gough, Bowdler, Jones 23, Smith, Jenkins, Harris, Howells 20.

Visually Handicapped Pairs (Cardiff Rotary District)

at Cardiff IBC, September 9th 1990

Twenty four pairs entered from Ammanford, Cardigan, Swansea, Cardiff and Newport, the event being organised by Ron Thomas (Barry Athletic), chairman of the Welsh Visually Handicapped Committee.

Semi finals: Laura and Neville McTavish (Swansea) 5, Dorothy Brockway, Frank Cremer (Cardiff) 2; Llewellyn and Ron Williams 8, Len Jones, Tom Wright (Newport) 2.
Final: McTavish 5, Williams 2.

Welsh Private Green Club Championships

at I.N.C.O, Clydach, September 15th 1990

St. Fagans, East section champions, won the Evans Bevan Cup for the second time when they beat West section champions, I.N.C.O., who had aspired to avenge their 1987 defeat at St. Fagans when St. Fagans won the cup for the first time. I.N.C.O. led 19-17 at the fifth, St. Fagans edging to a 41-40 lead at the tenth, steadily increasing their advantage to 10 at the 15th, and 18 at the finish.

Cliff Williams, I.N.C.O., West section Singles champion, a Welsh international 1979-1982, was in outstanding form against East section champion, Arthur Marshall (Llanbradach) who bowled immaculately to the jack, only for Cliff Williams to take out the offending shots to win 21-4.

Evans Bevan Cup: St. Fagans 82, I.N.C.O. 64. Rinks (St. Fagans first): John Ellis 25, R. Allen 15; R. Greenslade 15, W. Evans 20; M. Greenslade (capt) 23, K. Beale 14; J. Greenslade 19, C. Williams 15.
R.B. Southall Singles Cup: Cliff Williams (I.N.C.O.) 21, Arthur Marshall (Llanbradach) 4.

Tennents Lager Invitation Classic

at Ogwr, Bridgend, September 22nd — 23rd 1990

Scottish international Angus Blair made a flying start to his indoor season, winning the Tennents Lager Invitation Classic at Ogwr, Bridgend with successive victories over Michael Dunlop (Ireland), Stephen Rees (Wales) and Andy Thomson (England).

Rees was lying game in a semi final but Blair drew perfectly to win a third decisive set. In the final, with the score at 6-all in the second set, Blair planted one on the jack which Thomson failed to disturb.

Quarter finals: S. Rees (Wales) bt W. Richards (England 7-2, 7-4. A. Blair (Scotland) bt M. Dunlop (Ireland) 7-5, 7-6. J. Baker (Ireland) bt R. Corsie (Scotland) 7-0, 7-6. A. Thomson (England) bt P. Rowlands (Wales) 7-1, 7-5.
Semi finals: Blair bt Rees 3-7, 7-3, 7-5. Thomson bt Baker 4-7, 7-2, 7-3.
Final: Blair bt Thomson 7-5, 7-6.

Federation

English Bowling Federation
National Indoor Championships

Northern Play-offs at South Tyneside March 24th, 1990

In the northern area play-off, the singles was won by 68 year old Robert Curry, who has an artificial hip. Giving a great display of drawing, he outplayed Gerry Fulstow, 21-15, in the final.

Barney Clifford and Gary Whiting of Humberside won the northern pairs play-off, beating Norman Rutter and Glen Mitchell of Durham by 18 shots to 11, while former EBA Commonwealth Games player, Harry Taylor, partnered Colin Cairns and Brian Watson to a 30-8 win over Norman Curtis, Reg Emmitt and Norman Furniss in the rinks.

Singles: Semi final: Fulstow (Humbs) bt H Blacklock (Nland) 21-13.
Final: R Curry (Drham) bt Fulstow 21-15.
Pairs: Semi final: N Rutter & G Mitchell (Drham) bt H Taylor & C Cairns (Nland) 19-16.
Final: B Clifford & G Whiting (Humbs) bt Durham 18-11
Rinks: Semi final: N Curtis, R Emmitt, N Furniss (Humbs) bt R Knights, J Stidolph, D Maughan (Drham) 23-8.
Final: H Taylor, C Cairns, B Watson (Nland) bt Humbs 30-8.
Team events: Derbyshire Trophy (Northern section): final league positions: 1. Durham (38 points); 2. Cleveland (19); 3. Humberside (9)
Eversley Trophy (Northern section)
Final league positions: 1. Humberside (40 points); 2. Cleveland (36); 3. Durham (36); 4. Northumberland (20); 5. Nottinghamshire (8)

Southern Play-offs at Peterborough, March 24th-25th, 1990

North Walsham's Ian Wones, a 29 year old accountant with an insurance company, overwhelmed Darren Want, a 17 year old wool-grader from Peterborough. Only a single on the 7th end averted a whitewash as Wones got home in ten ends.

Wones, a Norfolk Middleton Cup player who divides his time between federation and association bowls, had beaten the pairs winner, Don Griffin of Hunts, 21-9, in the semi final, while Want had mastered England (EIBA) Under 25 international, Neil Bowden, 21-11.

Bowden had qualified for all three events, throwing the schedule into chaos — but he was below his best and failed to win any of them.

Brian Arnold came in as a last minute substitute for Peter Cossey, and partnered Don Griffin to a great win in the pairs. Griffin was outstanding in Hunts' demolition of former champions, Maurice Stratton and Jeff Newson, playing on their own green.

Newson gave up his position of skip in the Northants rink, and asked 21 year old electrician, Stuart Popple, to take over. Such a switch is permissible in federation bowls, and it worked a treat. Northants powered their way past North Cambs, and scored a tremendous 20-19 win over Hunts in the final.

Singles: Semi finals: I Wones (Norfolk) bt D Griffin (Hunts) 21-9.
D Want (Nhants) bt N Bowden (Lincs) 21-11.
Final: Wones bt Want 2-1.
Pairs: Quarter final: N Bowden and D Boone (Lincs) bt J Smith & N Ward (Norfolk) 23-18.
Semi finals: B Arnold & D Griffin (Hunts) bt Bowden & Boone (Lincs) 22-12.
M Stratton & J Newson (Nhants) bt J Goult & C Cousins (NCamb) 26-3.
Final: Hunts bt Nhants 190-8.
Rinks: Quarter final: P Black, S Popple, J Newson (Nhants) bt G Hardisty, N Bowden, D Boone (Lincs) 26-10.
Semi finals: Black, Popple, Newson (Nhants) bt M Carter, R Jackson, S Smith 24-8.
P Boyd, T McCormack, D Arnold (Hunts) bt R Sparrow, S Willoughby, S Bensley (Norfolk) 24-19.
Final: Nhants bt Hunts 20-19.
Team events: Derbyshire Trophy (Southern section) - final league positions: 1. Lincolnshire (51 points); 2. Norfolk (40); 3. Northants (31); 4. North Cambridgeshire (10)
Eversley Trophy (Southern section)
Final league positions: 1. Northants (64 points); 2. Norfolk (36); 3. Suffolk (36); 4. Lincolnshire (20); 5. N Cambs (18); 6. Hunts (8)

Finals at Lincoln April 21st, 1990

Robert Curry, who says he has spent a lifetime in bowls, used his vast experience to overcome the youthful challenge of Ian Wones of North Walsham in the singles final.

Curry, a sprightly 68 year old, has been secretary of Durham's Glan Park club for over 30 years and is forty years older than Wones, a regular Middleton Cup player for Norfolk.

Wones, the favourite, got off to a good start, and led 6-1, but was caught then overhauled by the gritty Curry, who seemed to have the knack of escaping from tight corners.

Gary Whiting and Barney Clifford of Hull and District bought Humberside their first national indoor title, beating Brian Arnold and Don Griffin of Huntingdonshire by the narrowest of margins in an exciting pairs final.

Jeff Newson of Peterborough became the first man to win all three individual championships - singles, pairs and rinks — when he partnered Stuart Popple and Peter Black to the rinks title.

In the major team event, Durham, who had won the Derbyshire Trophy five times on the trot, fell from grace, beaten by twenty shots by the home county, Lincolnshire, while Humberside notched up their first Eversley Trophy success.

Singles: R Curry (Durham) bt I Wones (Norfolk) 21-19.
Pairs: R Whiting & B Clifford (Humbs) bt B Arnold & D Griffin (Hunts) 17-16.
Rinks: S Popple, P Black, J Newson (Northants) bt B Watson, C Cairns, H Taylor (Northumberland) 20-15.
Team events: Eversley trophy: Humberside bt Northants 116-82.

Rink scores (Humberside skips first): C Glover 36, R Morton 13:
E Killgallon 28, I Eagle 16:
H Dixon 25, D Duffy 24: M Penny 27, J Newson 29.
Derbyshire trophy: Lincolnshire bt Durham 144-124.
Rink scores (Lincolnshire skips first): G Morris 31, D Russell 15; D Skelton 16, A Hunter 26; A Hall 24, T Martin 17; A North 36, C Evans 23; D Boone 19, M Talbot 25; N Bowden 18, A Moffat 18.

British Gas Skegness Tournament

At Skegness June 3rd-8th 1990

The finals of this event were played on the Sun Castle greens, and for the first time in the 46-year history of the competition there was a chance that the male dominance of the Open Singles would be broken. Margaret Archer of Woodhall Spa reached the final, but could not quite make it, and was beaten 21-16 by Philip Garrick of Metheringham.

Open Singles:
Semi finals: M. Archer (Woodhall Spa) 21, J. Cox (Horncastle) 15; P. Garrick(Metheringham)21, R. Robinson (Stapleford) 14.
Final: Garrick 21, Archer 16.

Open Pairs:
Semi finals: J. Wilson, D. Wilson (Collingham) 18, D. Brown, M. Bradshaw (Sutton-on-Sea) 16; R. Colton, K. Barker (Mansfield) 4, T. Hudson, D. Sharpe (Billinghay, Woodhall Spa) 22.
Final: Hudson, Sharpe 18, Wilson, Wilson 13.

Triples:
Semi finals: F & F. Swannick (Isle of Man) D. Brown (Sutton-on-Sea) 25, T. Pollard, R. Millar, R. Thornley (Coalville) 7; M. Swift, D. Boyfield, R. Bainbridge (Bardney) 11, J. Corby, P. Corby, R. Taylor (Sleaford) 24.
Final: Corby, P. Squires, Taylor 28, Swannicks, Brown 9.

Mixed Pairs:
Semi finals: E. Elsam, D. Tryner (Mansfield) 12, J. Paulger, R. Paulger (Branston) 19; E. Jarrett, J. Jarrett (Edwinstowe) 16, S. Simpson-Shaw, W. Barton (Boston) 21.
Final: Paulgers 19, Simpson-Shaw, Barton 10.

National Garden Festival Open Mixed Triples

at Saltwell Park, Gateshead, June 25th-30th 1990

This was probably the biggest tournament ever held in the North East with 150 mixed triples playing to the rules of the English Bowling Federation with more than £2,000 prize money at stake.

Supported by the sports conscious Gateshead Metropolitan Borough and sponsored by local business including Cameron Hall Developments and Federation Breweries, the tournament was a huge success and hopes are high that this can become an annual event.

A competitive week's bowling ended in a most exciting final which was won — after an extra end — by Sylvia Lewars, George Shaw and Paddy Buchan of Northumberland, who defeated the Saltwell Park trio of Ena Clarke, John Wilson and Harry Parking.

Cleveland Men's County Championships

Finals at John Whitehead Park, Billingham-on-Tees, July 21st 1990

Cleveland county is one of the more recent associations to join the English Bowling Federation, and more than 1,000 members competed leading to the finals. The winners of all events, except the Fours and the team event for the club championship, qualified for the national finals at Skegness.

Two Bowl Singles: E. York (Elm Tree) 21, Paul Harrison (Ropner Park) 16.
Four Bowl Singles: K. Price (Elm Tree) 21, L. Jackson (Pallister Park) 11.
Under-25 Singles: G. Storr (Stockton) 21, J. Walker (Ropner Park) 17.
Senior Singles: F. Thomas (Ropner Park) 21, D. Grove (Stockton) 20
Secretary's Singles: E. Redfearn (Locke Park) 21, F. Gatenby (Smiths Dock) 16.
Two Bowl Pairs: C & C. Bowes (Elm Tree) 21, W. Gallagher, P. Clinton (Stockton) 14
Two Bowl Triples: B. Picot, R. Nesbitt, T. Addison (Smiths Dock) 20, J. Pearce, R. Ashby, K. Lamb (West End) 12.
Three Bowl Triples: J. Whitmarsh, R. Walker, A. Cordukes (Ropner Park) 14, E. York, W. Ridley, J. Place (Elm Tree) 13.
Fours: G. Storr Jnr, W. Orr, D. Grove, G. Storr Snr (Stockton) 35, D. Wrightson, J. Sables, W. Gallagher, L. Parnell (Stockton) 7.
Club Championship: John Whitehead Park 80, Thornaby 74. Mixed Pairs: N. Robinson, K. Price (Elm Tree) 19, E. & R. Nesbitt (Smiths Dock) 18.
Mixed Triples for Marie Denny Trophy: G. Adamson, D. Todd, R. Walker (Hartlepool) 25, N. Scotson, D. Grove, W. Orr (Stockton) 19.

Cleveland Women's County Championships

Finals at Hartlepool Park, July 27th 1990

Four Bowl Singles: M. Judson (Eldon Grove) 21, O. Wilson (Middlesbrough Ladies) 19.
Two Bowl Singles: P. Packham (Hartlepool Park) 21, M. Stark (Billingham-on-Tees) 20
Senior Singles (2 bowl): K. Geddes (Locke Park, Redcar) 21, J. Richardson (Teesside) 17
Two Bowl Pairs: N. Scotson, P. Blackwell (Stockton) 17, M. Judson, M. Williamson (Eldon Grove, Hartlepool) 13.
Two Bowl Rinks: E. Partridge, L. Young, B. Bartram (Smiths Dock Park) 15, E. Hunt, O. Wilson, E. Dowson (Middlesbrough Ladies) 12.
Three Bowl Rinks: C. Clements, B. Picot, S. Moreman (Smiths Dock Park) 15, B. Lamb, M. Thomas, S. Whitehouse (Elm Tree, Stockton) 10.

English Bowling Federation National Championships
at Suncastle Greens, Skegness, August 28th-September 1st 1990

The Lincolnshire resort of Skegness has been the home of the EBF Championships since 1957, but it is doubtful if any of the previous 33 'weeks' — as the event is known amongst Federation devotees — would have bettered this year's spectacle, writes Ron Hails. With 16 individual championships and five team events to fit into five days, one of the most important ingredients for success is the weather, and 1990 was without blemish in that respect.

The Suncastle greens form a natural amphitheatre, and large crowds each day had much to keep them interested, particularly on the opening day when the Under-25 team event between Lincolnshire and Nottinghamshire was not settled until the 124th and final end when Lincolnshire celebrated s single shot victory. On the same day, Cleadon Park, Durham, going for a third successive title, trailed 18-9 going to the last end of the three bowl rinks — and scored a maximum of nine. Despite that mighty blow, Durham's hopes ended sadly on the extra end.

A feature of Federation bowling in recent years has been the emergence of young players, and both Under-25 Singles winners in 1990 were 17 years of age. Add to this the fact that Emma Barker, a 16-year-old from Norfolk reached the semi final stage, and that Graham Storr from Cleveland is just 14, and it will be appreciated that the future of the game in the 13 counties of the EBF is bright indeed.

Other performances of note included the women's Two-bowl Singles success of Nottinghamshire's Gill Restall — she first won this event in 1973 — and the feat of her county colleagues Jeanette Wells and Margaret Maidlow who retained the Pairs title won last year. An honourable mention too for Tom Greetham (Derbyshire), whose victory in the men's Cets Singles meant he became the first man to win the trophy three times. And in his 74th year!

Men's Results

Proctor Cup (Two-Bowl Singles): The winner of the Proctor Cup, Brian Ball (Derbyshire) had a razor-edge 21-20 first round victory over Ian Baker (Hunts), and was taken to 33 ends by Norfolk's Ian Wones. The hard work paid off however, and in the final he gained a 21-13 victory over Barry Plowman (Northants).

Semi finals: B. Plowman (Northants) 21, K. Deeks (N. Essex) 17; B. Ball (Derbys) 21, A. Holden (Suffolk) 16.
Final: Ball 21, Plowman 13.

Lincolnshire Cup (Four-Bowl Singles): Andrew Bird from Sleaford had arranged his wedding day for September 1st, but found himself in the Four-Bowl Singles final on that day. Brian Miller, his opponent, readily agreed to play the final 24 hours earlier. Andrew, a model of consistency throughout, was able to present his bride with the Lincolnshire Cup.

Semi finals: B. Miller (Derbys) 21, M. Ward (Notts)12; A. Bird (Lincs) 21, G. Emery (Northumberland) 18.
Final: Bird 21, Miller 11.

Men's Under-25 Singles (Jim Pratt Trophy): Neil Cammack, 17, from Burton House, Boston, has a bowlers pedigree, for earlier this year at Luton, his mother Jean won the English Women's Pairs and Triples title. Neil displayed maturity and tactical awareness in the final when he defeated Darrell Cantwell (Suffolk), although the 21-12 scoreline did less than justice to the loser.

Semi finals: N. Cammack (Lincs) 21, A. Croft (Notts) 11; D. Cantwell (Suffolk) 21, R. Coleman (Hunts) 12.
Final: Cammack 21, Cantwell 12.

Men's Vets Singles (A.J. Ludlam Trophy): Tom Greetham, 73, a robust veteran from Worksop Park, was in commanding form in each of his four matches, and became the first man to win this event three times when he defeated sprightly Stanley Brown from Cleadon Park in the North East, in the final.

Semi finals: T. Greetham (Derbys) 21, F. Barker (Northumberland) 12; S. Brown (Durham) 21, J. Frost (N. Cambs) 17.
Final: Greetham 21, Brown 13.

Men's Pairs (Gratton Cup): Alan Ayre won the Two-Bowl Singles in 1985 and teamed up with his Sutton Colliery club mate Ian Bailey to take the Gratton Cup back to Nottinghamshire. They defeated the experienced Ashley Nelson and Eric Clarke — winners of the Frank Holmes Shield in 1980 and 1984 — 18-12 in a well fought final.

Semi finals: A. Nelson, E.Clarke (N. Cambs) 22, J. Johnstone, R. Williamson (Lincs) 7; A. Ayre, I. Bailey (Notts) 18, R. Wright, D. Filby (Norfolk) 11.
Final: Notts 18, N. Cambs 12.

Two-Bowl Rinks (Stoddard Trophy): Humberside — relative newcomers to the EBF — gained their first men's championship (though Jeff Davis has won the Mixed Pairs and the Non-championship Secretaries Cup). Davis joined Bob Thompson and Dennis Boyle to defeat North Cambs trio Paul Bennett, Michael Pope and Tony Perfect in the final.

Semi finals: P. Bennett, M. Pope, D. Boyle (N. Cambs) 19, R. Picot, R. Nesbitt, T. Addison (Cleveland) 14; J. Davis, R. Thompson, D. Boyle (Humberside) 18, M. Elliott, S. Elliott, B. Grint (Norfolk) 16.
Final: Humberside 24, N. Cambs 18.

Two-Bowl Rinks (Frank Holmes Shield): Northamptonshire had not won a rinks title since 1976, and Tony Morton, Maurice Stratton and Jeff Newson only just made it this time, after scraping their quarter final tie against Norfolk 21-20 after an extra end. However, they showed good form in the final and defeated Clarrie Nellist, Phil Blackburn and Mal Penny (Humberside).

Semi finals: T.Morton, M. Stratton, J. Newson (Northants) 20, E. Delaney, J. Largen, A. Largent (Suffolk) 10; C. Nellist, P. Blackburn, M. Penny (Humberside) 15, S. Chamberlain, C. Balding, I. White (Lincs) 12.
Final: Northants 20, Humberside 12.

Women's Events

Two-Bowl Singles (Paul Howard Trophy): Gill Restall from Newstead, Notts, is no stranger to championships. She won this event in 1973, and the Four-Bowl title in 1978. Her opponent was Sandra Curtis from Norfolk — winner of the Pairs in 1987. Both players had displayed impressive form to reach the final, but the Notts player had the surer touch.
Semi finals: S. Curtis (Norfolk) 21, J. Watson (Derbyshire) 15; G. Restall (Notts) 21, Jayne Taylor (Suffolk) 19.
Final: Restall 21, Curtis 13.

Four-Bowl Singles (Wyand Trophy): Peterborough indoor international Gloria Haney, winner of the Three-Bowl Rinks in 1986, looked to be on her way to defeat in the final when she trailed Olive Henderson (Durham) by 16-8. But Mrs Hanley got to grips with the problem to such good effect that her opponent from Saltwell Park, Gateshead, who won this title in 1984, scored only two more shots.
Semi finals: O. Henderson (Durham) 21, M. Nicholls (Suffolk) 20; G. Haney (Northants) 21, M. Presswood (Derbyshire) 12.
Final: Haney 21, Henderson 18.

Under-25 Singles (Hilda Carver Trophy): Anne Savage, a 17-year-old student went into this final already a national champion, for on the previous evening she won the Two-Bowl Rinks in partnership with her mother and an aunt. She faced a formidable taske in the junior event against the reigning champion Debbie Turner (Brigg Town). Trailing 13-18, Miss Savage made a spirited recovery to climb back to 19-20 and clinched victory with a two on the next end.
Semi finals: A. Savage (N. Cambs) 21, S. Hopkinson (Derbyshire) 13; D. Turner (Humberside) 21, E. Barker (Norfolk) 17.
Final: Savage 21, Turner 20

Senior Singles (Anne Saint Trophy): Doreen Cooper, a retired clerk from Ilkeston, completed a notable senior double for Derbyshire when she gained a 21-15 victory over Pauline Leslie from Seaton Delaval.
Semi finals: P. Leslie (Northumberland) 21, L. Green (Suffolk) 9; D. Cooper (Derbyshire) 21, R. Stenhouse (Durham) 14.
Final: Cooper 21, Leslie 15.

Women's Pairs (Alice Rice Trophy): Nottinghamshire's Jeanette Wells and Margaret Maidlow won this title in 1989 and never looked likely to relinquish their crown in 1990. Only quarter final opponents Humberside got within six shots of the Balderton pair, and they reclaimed the title in style with a 22-9 victory over Daphne Cooper and Rita Allin (Hunts).
Semi finals: J. Wells, M. Maidlow (Notts) 35, M. Emmonds, R. Doyle (Northumberland) 5; D. Cooper, R. Allin (Hunts) 18, L. Whitehead, B. Whitehead (Norfolk) 12.
Final: Notts 22, Hunts 9.

Three-Bowl Rinks (G.W. Jones Trophy): Jackie Hearle and Janet Savage won thistrophy in 1985 with Caroline Quinney, and this year they introduced Ann

Savage, 17, Janet's daughter. The move was successful, for they outplayed the home trio of Jill Newcombe, Lorna Tinkler and Laura Bland on their own Skegness green.

Semi finals: J. Hearle, A. Savage, J. Savage (N. Cambs) 21, B. Tickle, C. Brodie, V. Gibson (Norfolk) 8; J. Newcombe, L. Tinkler, L. Bland (Lincs) 24, R. Allin, N. Bailey, D. Cooper (Hunts) 7.
Final: North Cambridgeshire 24, Lincolnshire 11.

Three-Bowl Rinks (Shepperson & Brown Trophy): The Mansfield (Notts) trio of Joan Beardsley, Anne Hallam and Audrey Pinder, needed much resolve to win the final, for they had three single shot victories, including one of 16-15 in the final against Gwen Hanson, Meg Fisher and Margaret Manchett from Warboys White Hart.

Semi finals: J. Beardsley, A. Hallam, A. Pinder (Notts) 12, G. Hancock, M. Presswood, R. Bannister (Derbyshire) 11; G. Henson, M. Fisher, M. Manchett (Hunts) 23, P. Watson, D. Dicker, A. Johnson (Humberside) 14
Final: Notts 16, Hunts 15.

Lodge Sports Mixed Pairs (A.J. Ludlam Trophy): The Lodge Sports Mixed Pairs brought a second championship success for Joan Beardsley when she joined Nottinghamshire colleague Steve Woodward in defeating Peterborough's Joyce Holden and Albert Horton in the final.

Semi finals: J. Holden, A. Horton (Northants) 18, C. Gapp, R. Haddingham (Norfolk) 11; J. Beardsley, S. Woodward (Notts) 20, J. Savage, E. Clarke (N. Cambs) 17.
Final: Notts 20, Northants 15.

Mixed Rinks (Marie Denny Trophy): The North Essex trio Jim Thompson, Joan Webb and John Orbell (Haverhill) won an entertaining final when they scored a one shot victory over John Haigh, Alma and Maurice Talbot (Glen Park, Durham).

Semi finals: J. Haigh, A. Talbot, M. Talbot (Durham) 19, H. Ward, P. Baumber, M. Ward (Notts) 17; J. Thompson, J. Webb, J. Orbell (N. Essex) 30, V. Newson, G. Polson, J. Newson (Northants) 18.
Final: North Essex 18, Durham 17.

Non Championship Events

Men's Secretaries Singles (Jim Dunn Trophy): Northumberland's George Emery was just beaten in the Four-Bowl Singles, but he made no mistake when he gained a 21-4 victory over Arthur Martindale (Players Athletic) in the final.

Semi finals: G. Emery (Northumberland) 21, B. Nicholls (Norfolk) 20; A. Martindale (Notts) 21, G. Prior (Hunts) 18.
Final: Emery 21, Martindale 4.

Women's Secretaries Singles: Kath Scatliffe won the Two-Bowl Singles title in 1988 and showed she had lost none of her touch by becoming the first winner of this event. She was given a tremendous battle, however by Pat Watson (Melbourne, Humberside) in the final.

Semi finals: P. Watson (Humberside) 21, B. Ketteringham (N. Cambs) 20; K. Scatliffe (Lincs) 21, L. Francis (Hunts) 1.
Final: Scatliffe 21, Watson 20.

Men's Team Events

NatWest Adams Trophy: A 'rink' in the Federation game is of three players with two bowls each, and the men's events are played over 31 ends. Suffolk, holders of the Adams Trophy, made a good start but were soon overtaken by a Nottingham team which went on to a handsome victory, although their opponents won on two rinks and led on a third. This was Nottinghamshire's fourth win in five years and their 15th overall — a record second only to Durham.

Notts 180, Suffolk 140
Rinks: (Notts skips first): G. Hufton 25, B. Thorpe 27; J. Bowers 23, R. Paternoster 23; J. Brooks 38, S. Ayres 18; T. Lee 30, J. Summons 24; B. Edmonds 37, A. Mills 19; K. Eames 27, I. Meikle 29.

Newton Trophy: Lincolnshire appeared to be coasting to victory but a determined Humberside fought back to within two shots, then a couple of late 'five counts' gave Lincolnshire victory.

Lincolnshire 172, Humberside 158
Rinks: (Lincs first): J. Lewis 32, C. Fulstow 28; E. Codd 30, A. Hutchinson 30; G. Lamplough 26, M. Penny 31; D. Dickinson 27, N. Gibson 27; M. Asplen 22, J. Davis 24; P. Hurton 35, G. White 18.

Reg Wright Trophy (Under 25s Men): This is a four rink game of 31 ends and Lincolnshire and Nottinghamshire produced magnificent game. With three games finished, the Wayne Tomlinson-Steve Wright game was left to decide the issue. Lincs were one shot in the lead but their opponents drew level on the replayed penultimate end. Lincolnshire's Andrew Limb settled the issue when he trailed the jack through the head.

Lincolnshire 120, Nottinghamshire 119.
Rinks: (Lincs skips first): G. Smith 28, P. Talbot 32; N. Bowden 32, D. Tomlinson 32; S. Wright 30, W. Tomlinson 28; G. Morris 30, M. Egginton 27.

Women's Team Events

The strength of the ladies' game in Norfolk is proven by the fact that the East Anglians repeated last year's double in both team events, again with plenty to spare.

Donald Steward Trophy: Norfolk 154, Nottinghamshire 94
Rinks: (Norfolk skips first): L. Smith 23, O. Frith 18; P. Calton 34, M. Simons 11; J. Wilson 25, J. Barks 12; L. Millbank 18, G. Restall 20; B. Annison 26, M. Allam 13; V. Chapman 21, M. Osborne 20.

Silver Jubilee Vase: Norfolk 158, Cleveland 104
Rinks: Norfolk skips first: N. Melton 26, J. Hails 16; M. Norton 24, B. Barthram 16; V. Gibson 39, S. Willgress 12; M. Smith 25, K. Dodd 20; V. Atthowe 23, A. Ingham 15; J. Bullock 21, J. York 25.

The Victor Ludorum Trophy is awarded to the county with most championship points. Lincolnshire and Nottinghamshire share the Victrix Ludorum Trophy.

Crown Green

By Geoff Clare

In last year's edition attention was drawn to the fact that the year had been somewhat strange in that there had been a huge number of new tournaments at a time when media coverage was going downhill. Little did I think, twelve months later, that 1990 would be a repetition of what had gone before with press coverage still on the wane and television cover almost down to nil.

Sports editors, more than ever, simply refuse to accept just how popular the game is, and the BBC's decision to drop the almost sacred Waterloo was almost beyond the belief of Northern enthusiasts. On the box, the game just manages to keep a foot in the door thanks to Granada's Paul Doherty and the television powers that be must believe that he is out on a limb. Crown enthusiasts prefer to think that he is the only one in step.

Competitions increase in number month by month, but we could be close to a time when quality should outpace quantity. There is, however, a bright side. The bread and butter player can now get a game of bowls with his or her club in any number of local leagues, can enter scores of tournaments at local, county or national level, and if good enough, can get in the county side or perhaps win a way to the finals of the Yorkshire Bank, the Waterloo, the Isle of Man, the All England, or even the Bass Masters.

Perhaps, then, the game should look inwards, and with the BCGBA tightening its grip through club and individual registrations it could be time for a Crown HQ with its own offices and full time staff. It is not the end of the world if the press and TV are currently looking in other directions, but if we endeavour to show them just how good we are, the situation could change. With more money in the game than ever before, the opportunities for improvement are there and the game's leadership must be prepared to rise to the occasion.

The 1990 season was a fine one because of the lovely summer, though few new names emerged. Brian Duncan is still 'king' of the game and his great achievement in 1990 was to collect the Bass Masters for the second time. He went close to making it a fifth Waterloo but with a five handicap it was like a class racehorse giving away too much weight. He fell to Hyde's John Bancroft who started the season with a splendid win in the Midshire's collected the Waterloo in his stride and almost took the Champion of Champions when he fell at the last hurdle.

For me he was the outstanding Player of the Year. It was nice to see Mike Leach and Noel Burrows back in the honours and Gary Wallis being there or thereabouts so many times.

The Birmingham Midshire Open

at the Meole Brace Club, Shrewsbury.
Finals Day, April 28th, 1990.
Prize money: £6,000.

The importance of the "Midshire" was certainly confirmed with an increase in prize money, over the previous year, of some £2,500 and there was an entry of over 800 with almost all the game's top players taking part.

Indeed the programme for finals day was almost like a "Who's Who" of crown green bowls with players from most of the leading counties there. In the end there was personal success for Hyde's John Bancroft and it turned out to be a pipe opener for the Cheshire star who went on to have his best season to date.

John's victim on his way to the final included Roy Price, Stan Frith, Bob Hitchen and Gary Wallis and somewhat amazingly when he reached the close he should find himself up against his 16 year old team mate, Tommy King.

King promptly proceeded to show just why it is that he is one of the most promising youngsters in the game and he must have worried Bancroft as he went into leads of 8-3 and 12-9. Bancroft stuck to his task however, and with all the skills expected of him these days wore down his younger opponent to take the £1,000 first prize on a 21-16 scoreline.

Quarter finals: J Bancroft (Hyde) 21, R Hitchen (Halifax) 16. G Wallis (Doncaster) 21, K Perks (Shrewsbury) 15. M Winnington (Northwich) 21, B Burlinson (Warrington) 18. T King (Hyde) 21, K Wainwright (Warrington) 17.
Semi final: Bancroft 21, Wallis 13. King 21, Winnington 11.
Final: Bancroft 21, King 16.

The Stones Bitter British
Crown Green Team Championship.

Finals at the British Steel Club, Irlam, Manchester
April 29th, 1990.
Prize money: £2,100.

The 1990 battle for the top club title lived up to the expectations of the qualifying clubs, and the weather and a huge crowd made it a day to remember. Pundits made it a Sale Excelsior/Brighouse final and it worked out that way. Brighouse, however, had to work hard for their opening win. Sportsmans of Leigh pushed them to a mere four shots in the quarter finals and though Wharton Conservatives looked likely to repeat the dose in the semi finals, Brighouse went through by 26 shots.

In the other half of the draw, Sale were in scintilating form and after a mammoth, 93 shot victory over Telford St George, their final place was secured by a win over Touchers by 28.

Robert Crawshaw's opening 21-13 return for Sale in the final tie was very much the card on which the Excelsior win was based for though the eventual result was close, Brighouse could not get their noses in front. But two

Yorkshire wins from the last three cards meant that anchor man Chris Morrison could take no chances and his cliff hanging 21-20 scoreline gave the Cheshire side an overall advantage by just four shots.

Quarter final: Brighouse (Yorkshire) 148, Sportsmans Leigh (Lancashire) 144. Wharton Conservatives (Cheshire) 161, M and B Hilton (Staffs) 135. Sale Excelsior (Cheshire) 168, St Georges (Shropshire) 75. Touchers (Cheshire) 147, Black Horse (Merseyside) 136. **Semi final:** Brighouse 147, Wharton Cons 106. Sale Excelsior 162, Touchers 134. **Final:** Sale Excelsior 147, Brighouse 143.

The Spring Waterloo

at the Waterloo Hotel, Blackpool. Finals day, May 5th, 1990. Prize money: £5,020.

Tommy Heyes, the diminutive Hyde bowler, proved to be one of the most popular "Spring" winners to date especially in view of his many near misses in the past. After withstanding challenges from Alan Broadhurst and Tommy Johnstone in the quarter and semi finals, there were several occasions in the final when he seemed destined to be a bridesmaid yet again.

Local bowler Alan Ward looked very much a winner following leads of 12-5 and 19-15 especially when the Blackpool player lay two at the next end with Heyes, seemingly, playing the last wood. Tommy, however, promptly brought the house down by playing through on the jack and with Ward not seeing the jack again, it was a splendid win for Heyes at 21-19 and a cheque for £1,000.

Quarter final: T Heyes (Hyde) 21, A Broadhurst (Wigan) 18. T Johnstone (Warrington) 21, J Cooper (Chester) 17. A Ward (Blackpool) 21, M Robinson (Liversedge) 10. M Gilpin (Kendal) 21, D Wright (Wem) 9. **Semi final:** Heyes 21, Johnstone 12. Ward 21, Gilpin 14. **Final:** Heyes 21, Ward 19.

The Chetwode Arms Classic

at Lower Whitley, Cheshire. May 26th, 1990. Prize money: £6,000.

After only three years, this event has leaped into a position as one of the game's top events and the very consistent Glyn Cookson made it two in a row when he collected the £1,600 winners award after a superb final between him and Cheshire County colleague Stan Frith.

In the semis finals it seemed that Cookson would have the tougher task when he came up against Gary Wallis but though the pair were level over the first half a dozen ends, Glyn came through with colours flying to win 21-13.

Frith's hopes of an easier path against Barry Kirk seemed well founded when he thundered to a 16-8 lead but Kirk scored nine in a row before a relieved Frith took charge again to win 21-18.

There was never much in it in the final, but Cookson held a slight lead almost throughout. Frith caught him at nineteens but Cookson was not to be denied amd a two at the next end gave him a memorable double.

Quarter final: B Kirk (Biddulph) 21, T Kelly (Leeds) 19. S Frith (Northwich) 21, M

Walker (Stoke) 14. G Cookson (Winsford) 21, S Copeland (Oldham) 17. G Wallis (Doncaster) 21, D Grant (Telford) 13.
Semi final: Frith 21, Kirk 18. Cookson 21, Wallis 13.
Final: Cookson 21, Frith 19.

The Isle of Man Summer Festival.

Finals at the Villa Marina Green, Douglas, June 15th, 1990.
Prize money: Men £7,000, Ladies £2,750.

Men: Nearly six hundred competitors entered the 1990 holiday tournament and the final produced two bowlers who knew a little bit about each other's play having met a couple of times in the previous year or so. Colin Price of Stockport started with the advantage of a couple of wins over the younger Kevan Shaw but it was the 20 year old Bolton bowler who came up trumps this time.

Price started well by taking a 9-6 lead but six successive shots by Shaw gave him advantage; then Price came again to lead 14-13 but Shaw then managed to gain superiority and at 19-14 he was looking a winner. That was confirmed by the closing 21-17 scoreline.

Ladies: The Ladies final produced an enthralling match between Cumbria's Joyce Foxcroft and Wirral's Margaret Browning who won the title in 1981. The ex champion looked in good form as she sped to a 10-6 advantage but Foxcroft won the block at this point and dominated on a long mark down the side of the green to go to 15-10. The pair were level at sixteens and seventeens before Browning looked poised for a double at 20-19. She slipped at the next two ends but then added singles to take the top prize.

Mens Quarter final: K Shaw (Bolton) 21, T King (Hyde) 12. F Hulme (Stockport) 21, G Wallis (Lower Hopton) 20. C Price (Stockport) 21, G Telford (Timperley) 10. D Kelly (Peel) 21, A Stretch (Urmston) 17.
Semi final: Shaw 21, Hulme 7. Price 21, Kelly 11.
Final: Shaw 21, Price 17.
Ladies Semi final: J Foxcroft (Hale) 21, J Jones (Wirral) 19. M Browning (Wirral) 21, B Cameron (Southport) 18.
Final: Foxcroft 21, Browning 20.

The Bunbury Open Classic

at The Bunbury BC, Cheshire. Finals June 24th, 1990.
Prize money: £4,200.

Allen Broadhurst and Tony Poole, exponents of the long and short games of crown green bowling respectively, combined to make the Bunbury final an entertaining affair.

A field of six had produced an excellent assembly for Finals Day and, in the main, all the games produced reasonably close encounters. The exception was the Broadhurst/Mike Leach, quarter final clash in which Allen produced marvellous corner play to win 21-5 before a tight 21-19 win over Ronnie Bradshaw took him to the final.

Meanwhile, Tony Poole was involved in two great games with Peter

Richardson, whom he beat 21-20 in the last eight, and Jeremy Muff in the semi finals whom he beat by a similar score.

Both Richardson and Poole led to their favourite marks when winning the jack in the final and though, from 13 across, Poole took a slight advantage at 16-14, Allen was not to be outdone and rallied to 20-16. Poole's last fling gave him a single at the next end but Broadhurst sensed the £1,000 winner's cheque and duly collected it.

Quarter final: A Poole (Shrewsbury) 21, P Richardson (Wigan) 20. G Muff (Yorkshire) 21, S Frith (Northwich) 16. A Broadhurst (Wigan) 21, M Leach (Fylde) 5. R Belshaw (Wigan) 21, M Chamberlain (Stockport) 20.
Semi final: Poole 21, Muff 20. Broadhurst 21, Belshaw 19.
Final: Broadhurst 21, Poole 17.

The Yorkshire Bank Crown King Championship.

Final stages at the Waterloo Hotel, Blackpool, June 30th, 1990. Prize money: £3,500.

Mike Leach, after his semi final defeat in the Crown King in 1989, reached the final and it looked as though he might be celebrating a triumphant return. But he ran up against the consistant Bob Hitchen and the Yorkshireman pipped him on the post.

Leach's progress to the final had been competent with only Tony Bracken of Warwick and Worcester, in the quarter finals, giving him much trouble in a game which ended 21-19. Hitchen, on the other hand, survived 21-20 games in the last 16 and again in the quarter finals. In his game against the Isle of Man's David Kelly, there was never a hint of the drama to come when the Halifax left hander went into 7-0 and 17-11 leads but Kelly came back to level at 20 across and lay game at the next end.

Hitchen's decision to strike must have been one of the most vital he has ever made and in just managing to brush his opponent's wood aside he squeezed his way through to the semi finals.

Leach, following a 21-12 win against Ian Damms, started well in the final with advantages of 7-3 and 12-8 but six singles put Hitchen ahead before the two peeled at fourteens. But Leach faded from this point.

Quarter final: M Leach (North Lancs and Fylde) 21, A Bracken (Warick and Worcs) 19. I Damms (Sth Yorkshire) 21, M Britton (Lancashire) 19. R Hitchen (Yorkshire) 21, D Kelly (Isle of Man) 20. J Morgan (Wales) 21, E Crawford (Derbyshire) 13.
Semi final: Leach 21, Damms 12. Hitchen 21, Morgan 14.
Final: Hitchen 21, Leach 15.

The Whitbread Liverpool Echo Masters

Final stages at Black Horse Hotel, Old Swan, Liverpool July 6th, 1990.

Prize money: £2,700

Three times winner Brian Duncan was in the field once again and with no local win since the Black Horse became the venue in 1979 it looked as though there would be no change in the pattern.

There was, however, an excellent blend of local and national talent at the last eight stage and though three of the four Merseyside bowlers went out at the quarter final point, county player Gerald Gregson was in real form and went on to win the title.

Duncan had no difficulty in the semi finals where he defeated Peter Marrow but Gerald had a tough time against Tommy Johnstone who led 25-21. But four doubles in five ends had the crowd on tenderhooks and Gregson swept to the final.

The final was one of the best ever with Gregson down in the early stages at 7-10 and 11-14 in spite of his superb bowling. His splendid play brought eventual reward and with a run of nine shots he went to 20-14. At 29-23 he was close to home but a typical Duncan charge now became evident and at 29-27 one wondered if Gregson could hold on. But he did.

Quarter finals: G Gregson (Eagle and Child) 31, K Shaw (Halliwell Lodge) 1. T Johnstone (Touchers) 31, H Fielding (Coronation Park) 23. B Duncan (Baxi) 31, G Cookson (Winsford) 19. P Marrow (Hinds Head) 31, J Fielding (Coronation Park) 14.
Semi finals: Gregson 31, Johnstone 27. Duncan 31, Marrow 23.
Final: Gregson 31, Duncan 27.

The Bowlers World/Greenall Whitley Classic

Finals at the Black Bull Hotel, St Helens Day July 20th, 1990.
Prize money: £2000+

Outsider Julian Fullerton caused something of a shock in a field which included the celebrated Len Higginbottom and he completed all of his closing three matches with something in hand. Left handed Fullerton, a former Merseyside county champion, is rapidly become well known on the circuit but this was his first big win and it gave him entry into the Bass Masters and the Champion of Champions as well as a cheque for £750.

In his opening game, Fullerton lagged behind Stockport's Andy Proctor for some time but once he caught up at 15 across, he allowed his opponent only one more shot. Julian again played second fiddle in the opening stages of his semi final meeting with Welshman, Ivor Gwyn Williams but from 13-15 he took full command.

Meanwhile, Bill Hilton of Wigan had a titanic struggle against the current Merseyside Champion, Paul Gartside and was in danger of defeat at 16-20. At the next end, Gartside lay game but an accurate strike by Hilton did the trick and a three singles and a double took him through.

Fullerton reversed the trend in the final with the advantage being his early on.

Quarter final: J Fullerton (Wirral) 21, A Proctor (Stockport) 16. I G Williams (Denbigh) 21, C Bebbington (Warrington) 16. P Gartside (St Helens) 21, P Hammond (Liverpool) 14. W Hilton (Wigan) 21, L Higginbottom (Atherton) 20.
Semi final: Fullerton 21, Williams 15. Hilton 21, Gartside 20.
Final: Fullerton 21, Hilton 15.

The Yorkshire Bank Golden Lady Classic.

Final stages at the Waterloo Hotel, Blackpool, July 21st 1990.
Prize money: £1600

The Yorkshire Bank decided to play their Ladies Classic on the same lines as the men's event with the preliminaries taking part in the various counties and the last 32 playing off on the Waterloo. Karen Johnstone of Warrington, a superb left hander, took the title for the second time after what turned out to be an "old girls" final between her and the 1989 winner, Lesley Smith of Padgate.

Both of the finalists had to work hard to get through a field which included many of the top lady names but perhaps Karen was the fresher of the two following her 21-6 win in the semi final.

That certainly was how it appeared, for Mrs Johnstone went into a whirlwind 11-3 lead and it looked as though Lesley might be left hopelessly behind. The holder, however, then decided she would not give up without a fight and the Padgate girl was back in the hunt at 13-15 and 16-18.

But Karen is not at the top of the tree without cause and with the aid of three singles she became Golden Lady for the second time and added £400 to her Yorkshire Bank balance.

Semi final: L Smith (Padgate) 21, S Parfitt (Paddington) 13. K Johnstone (Warrington) 21, M Manchester (Radcliffe) 6.
Final: Johnstone 21, Smith 16.

The Matthew Brown North Ashton Open

at the North Ashton Village Club, Wigan. Finals Day July 27th, 1990.
Prize money: £2,300.

Mike Leach, the former All England Champion, continued on the come back trail after a spell in the wilderness, and though he made a very worth while contribution to play in the closing stages, it was young Gary Wallis of Yorkshire who took the title.

Norman Fletcher, who went out in the 1989 semi finals, fell at the same hurdle this time but with leads of 16-12 and 17-13 he must have been hopeful of getting the better of Wallis. The scores, however, were level at 18-18 and Norman failed to score again.

Leach had more to spare in the second semi final when he defeated David Taberner 21-13 and he fought hard in the final where he was level with Wallis at eights. Gary then leapt to 15-8 before Leach countered with a run of five but Wallis was in a mean mood and the Doncaster bowler kept in front to take the £700 first prize.

Semi final: G Wallis (Doncaster) 21, N Fletcher (Hindley) 18. M Leach (Preston) 21, D Taberner (Garswood) 13.
Final: Wallis 21, Leach 16.

The Manchester Evening News Open Final Stages

at Klondyke Club, Levenshulme, Manchester July 28th, 1990

Prize money: £7,000

Though entries were slightly down on the previous year, this event continues to be one of the best supported on the circuit. The £1,500 first prize is a big attraction.

Mark Britton, who had a splendid season in 1989, confirmed that he is one of the best of the younger school and his win gave him double entry into the Bass Masters.

Brian Duncan, Gary Wallis and Alan Shacklady all made early exits. Duncan, the favourite, fell to Bradford's Chris Mordue.

Jim Collen then beat Mordue and went on to the final via a semi final win over Cheshire's Rob Eaton. Britton had a somewhat easy win over "Dancing Masters" Vernon Lee and after falling behind, 8-13 and 17-19, in the semi final to Barrie Kitson, managed the four shots he needed to reach the final which he won comfortably.

Quarter finals: M Britton (Wigan) 21, V Lee (Blackpool) 12. B Kitson (Oldham) 21, A Briggs (Mirfield) 17. J Collen (Bury) 21, C Mordue (Bradford) 20. R Eaton (Holmes Chapel) 21, W Eccles (Manchester) 12.
Semi finals: Britton 21, Kitson 19. Collen 21, Eaton 18.
Final: Britton 21, Collen 11.

The Tetley/Peoples Open

Finals Day at the Walnut Tree Hotel, Bootle July 29th, 1990

Prize money: £3,000.

The Tetley/Peoples Open has now become one of the most important events in the West Lancs area and seems set to increase its prestige even further. The calibre of the 1990 entry was extremely high and this produced a very attractive last 32 though it was rather surprising that most of the long distance travellers had been knocked out by the semi final stages when four locals were left in to go for the £800 first prize and a place in the Bass Masters.

Of the four it was the lesser known Ian Wright who took the title. 1987 winner, Jimmy Fielding, a prominent member of the Merseyside County side these days, looked a likely winner as the semi finals started but he was 4-9 in arrears before he really got going. A splendid run of nine successful ends was then put together by Fielding as he moved to 19-9 and though Dave Kirk took the next three ends, this delayed the inevitable.

Joe McGee the 1985 winner was in the other semi final and though he led 5-2 and 11-10, Wright took a 14-12 lead and always managed to stay two shots in front to finish 21-17 up.

In the final, the players were level on eight occasions, by the time the game reached 14 all but two singles and a double took Wright to 18-14. Fielding won the jack at the next end but Wright held on to win 21-15.

Quarter finals: I Wright (Liverpool) 21, G Bennett (N Wales) 8. W McGee (Walnut

Tree) 21, E Whitehead (Aughton) 15. J Fielding (Liverpool) 21, C Martlew (Walton Park) 17. D Kirk (Liverpool) 21, E Milligan (Walnut Tree) 11.
Semi finals: Wright 21, McGee 17. Fielding 21, Kirk 12.
Final: Wright 21, Fielding 15.

The Stamford Van and Car Hire Open

at the Ring O'Bells, Northwich. Finals Day August 3rd, 1990.
Prize money: £15,000.

Jim McLarnon continues to be the game's greatest benefactor and the crown bowling world was staggered, but thrilled, when the Stamford Van and Car Hire boss pushed the prize fund up by another £5,000 with the winner again having the use of a new car for a year.

Many of this year's shocks came at sub finals stage when some of the sport's biggest names fell, unexpectedly, by the wayside but there was a strong field for the last eight with Chadderton's David Copeland starting as strong favourite. Liverpool's Roy Lussey struggled against Copeland in the quarter finals but the Chadderton man handled the long marks well and looked to be in with a great chance.

His win of 21-12 was comfortable enough and though there was little in it during the early stages of his semi final with Carl Parker, he recovered from 4-6 to go to 17-7 and 21-10.

Darren Griffiths of Oldham had almost as much to spare in his semi final with Stoke's Phil Owen and was never going to be beaten after dashing to an 11-2 lead.

But Griffiths was always behind in the final, however, though he pulled back Copeland's advantages of 7-2 and 16-9 to remain in with a chance being only two down at 19-17. Copeland, however, had his eye firmly on a brand new white Sierra and with a two at the next end he claimed the £3,500 and the car keys and the crowd dispersed with the news that the prize fund would be even bigger in 1991.

Quarter final: D Copeland (Chadderton) 21, R Lussey (Liverpool) 12. C Parker (Wigan) 21, D Chatwin (Birmingham) 13. D Griffiths (Oldham) 21, W H Smith (Birkenhead) 15. P Owen (Stoke) 21, M Richardson (Wigan) 14.
Semi final: Copeland 21, Parker 10. Griffiths 21, Owen 12.
Final: Copeland 21, Griffiths 17.

The Colwyn Bowling Festival

at Eirias Park, Colwyn Bay, August 5th-10th, 1990

Bernard Marrow, the Wigan and Lancashire county player, took the top prize which goes to the winner of the George Davies tournament. He followed a 21-12, semi final win over Arthur Land of Frodsham with a 21-14 success over Darren Lawton (Failsworth). Lawton also went well in the Capstan Challenge Cup, reaching the semi final stages before going out to Romiley's Joe Bradbury, the eventual winner.

Pat Davies and Jane Jones, the well known Wirral sisters, both reached the semi finals of the Colwyn Rose Bowl. Jane won in 1989, but though she again reached the final she was beaten this time by Lilian Hall in an extremely close game.

The George Davies Tournament Semi finals: B Marrow (Wigan) 21, A Land (Frodsham) 12. D Lawton (Failsworth) 21, E Davies (Old Colwyn) 20.

Final: Marrow 21, Lawton 14.

The Capstan Challenge Cup Semi Finals: J Bradbury (Romiley) 21, D Lawton (Failsworth) 12. A Johnson (Chesterfield) 21, C Beaumont (Leeds) 19.

Final: Bradbury 21, Johnson 10.

The Colwyn Bay Rose Bowl Final: L Hall (Wigan) 21, J Jones (Wirral) 17.

The Bill Hughes Tournament Final: G Little (Hyde) 21, L Lawton (Failsworth) 14.

The Wyre Festival

at the Fleetwood Marine Gardens, July 30th-August 3rd, 1990

Prize money: £5,890.

The Mens Festival Final featured two of the North West's leading players in Mike Leach and Martin Gilpin and it was probably fitting that Leach should crown his come back with success in an event which had seen him go close on a number of occasions.

It was tight all the way in the final between the two with the Preston bowler just moving clear at the finish when a measure helped him to a 21-18 title win, and a cheque for £1,000.

There was, also, a place in the Bass Masters Classic waiting for the Ladies winner and that went to local player Mildred Green who beat Sheila Speed.

At 18 Sheila produced two fine woods but Mildred came through to take the jack and go on to win.

Mens Semi Finals: M Leach (Preston) 21, C Jones (Salford) 19. M Gilpin (Kendal) 21, A Lancaster (Rochdale) 19.

Final: Leach 21, Gilpin 18.

Ladies Semi Finals: M Green (Fleetwood) 21, E Ainsworth (Clayton Le Dale) 14. S Speed (Wigan) 21, S Thompson (Prestwich) 18.

Final: Green 21, Speed 18.

The British Crown Green Junior Merit

at the George and Dragon BC, Hyde, Cheshire, August 19th 1990

Jonathan Lowes, the 1989 champion from Cumbria, was in the field but this event was dominated by youngsters from the host county, Greater Manchester, and two of them met in the final.

David O'Brien, (Stalybridge) gave an outstanding performance throughout and on his way to the final looked the class player. In the other half, Manchester's Marcus Dean escaped defeat in the semi finals when 16-20 to David Bennison from North Lancs and Fylde. But he showed great determination and three singles and a double took him through.

In the final there was little between the two but O'Brien always looked the likely winner and gaining the upper hand in the closing stages, he drew away to win 21-15.

Semi final: D O'Brien (Greater Manchester) 21, S Darling (Warwick and Worcester) 17. M Dean (Greater Manchester) 21, D Bennison (N Lancs and Fylde) 20.
Final: O'Brien 21, Dean 15.

The Henselite British Crown Green Merit

at the Mitchell and Butlers Club, Birmingham, August 11th, 1990

Prize money: £3,000

Phil Owen from the Birches Head Club, Stoke pulled off what, to many, was a surprise win, but the thirty three year old newsagent has been quietly pushing himself to the front over the past few seasons and he went close in the 1989 "All England" before being defeated in the semi finals.

To return, via the Potteries preliminaries, was something of an achievement and to go on and win speaks for itself.

The toughest game must surely have been in the last sixty four when he survived 15-19 and 19-20 scorelines but after that he always seemed to have something in hand as he went through to meet the favourite, Ken Strutt, in the semi finals. Here, whilst the game was often tight, Owen was always in front to win 21-17 and the same could be said of Derbyshire's Pat Heaney. Pat, another model of consistency and appearing in the closing stages for the third year running, was never troubled by Shropshire's Mick Price and he made it to the final by means of a 21-12 card.

But it was always going to be Owen and from a useful 7-1 position he commanded the game at 14-5. A five shot run to Heaney, at this stage, tended merely to paint a better picture, but Owen then allowed his opponent just an occasional look in as he moved on to his greatest triumph by a score of 21-13.

Quarter Finals: P Heaney (Derbyshire) 21, D Walker (G Manchester) 14. M Price (Shropshire) 21, P Garwood (Cheshire) 15. P Owen (Potteries) 21, P Gartside (Merseyside) 19. K Strutt (G Manchester) 21, R Morgan (Wales) 10.
Semi Finals: Heaney 21, Price 12. Owen 21, Strutt 17.
Final: Owen 21, Heaney 13.

The Talbot Trophy

at the Raikes Hall Hotel, Blackpool, Finals Day August 25th, 1990

Prize money: £9,000

After many year absence from the bowling scene, the "Talbot" is again one of top events on the circuit even though the Talbot Hotel itself has disappeared from the scene. The closing stages certainly brought together a classic field and victory went to the clear favourite, popular Stan Frith.

Ken Strutt, as usual, had many supporters and the opening clash between Frith and Strutt was the one which most people would have liked to see as the final.

Stan, however, was always on top and he was rarely troubled as he strolled to a 21-10 win and had almost as easy semi final against Brian Patmore.

In the other half of the draw, Rochdale's Peter Fielding opened with an easy win over David Walker and after leading 12-5 was caught and passed by Wilf Hartley, however, fought back bravely at 14-12. Fielding finally went through 21-18.

Frith started the final with a break of five and moved well clear to 18-11, but a run of six gave Fielding renewed hope. Three singles, however, gave Frith the trophy and a cheque for £1,500.

Quarter Finals: S Frith (Weaverham) 21, K Strutt (Diggle) 10. B Patmore (Burnley) 21, R Ashcroft (Woodplumpton) 15. P Fielding (Rochdale) 21, D Walker (Swinton) 13. W Hartley (Blackpool) 21, I Rigby (Tarleton) 20.
Semi Finals: Frith 21, Patmore 13. Fielding 21, Hartley 18.
Final: Frith 21, Fielding 17.

The Bass Masters

at the Woodland Hotel, Ellesmere Port, Cheshire, August 29th to September 1st, 1990

Prize money: £20,000

The 1990 Bass was just as good as that of the previous year with possibly more thrills, an increase of some £5,500 in prize money and a victory for the mighty Brian Duncan.

From the start of the four day event, the only one to have gone out on television, everyone had the feeling that Duncan was determined to collect the £7,500 first prize and though he made it in the end, his semi final fight back against David Copeland is the tie which will be remembered most. The Preston ace, 14-20 down, looked destined for defeat.

But there were, indeed, many other good games and it was Tommy Johnstone who looked a likely winner when he entered the quarter final stages after near destructive wins over Bob Hitchen (21-6) and Kenny Armitage (21-8). Duncan must have felt that he, too, was faced a quick exit when Johnstone dashed into an 8-0 lead in their quarter final. The Warrington bowler, however, failed to keep the initiative and Duncan, always generously dangerous when behind, surged back to win 21-12.

Tommy Heyes was another who looked good until he met Copeland in the quarter finals, young Kevan Shaw was playing solid stuff and Gary Wallis, after getting the better of last year's winner, Martin Gilpin had battered David Webb 21-8 to go through to a semi final spot.

Shaw, got the better of Wallis by winning an exciting game. In the other semi final Copeland lost his way when six shots ahead of Brian Duncan and requiring just one chalk to make it to the final.

Copeland, no doubt, will re-live that game over and over again. He had several chances to settle Duncan's fate, but failed to prevent a seven-shot winning run.

After that, the final was an anti climax, Duncan played as only Duncan can and with leads of 10-1 and 14-3, crushed the luckless Shaw.

This was Duncan at his best and there was no stopping him as he raced to a second Bass Masters and a 21-4 victory.

Quarter Finals: Brian Duncan 21, Tommy Johnstone 12. David Copeland 21, Tommy Heyes 13. Kevan Shaw 21, Alan Broadhurst 16. Gary Wallis 21, David Webb 8.
Semi Finals: Duncan 21, Copeland 20. Shaw 21, Wallis 19.
Final: Duncan 21, Shaw 4.

The Martell Cognac County Championship Finals
at Bolsover and Bardsley, Oldham, September 2nd 1990

The county championship final might have seemed just a little bit strange with neither Yorkshire nor Lancashire making it through to the last four, and historians might have thought it somewhat unfashionable for Derbyshire to get through. But times have changed and the Midlanders have been on the up and up for some time.

They met Greater Manchester with every chance of success and with the form book showing that they had beaten last year's winners, North Midlands, in the semi finals, their quiet air of confidence in their first final was understandable.

In a match, won and lost in closing stages, there was one single figure winner in the opening 16 jacks and that came at Bolsover where a 21-9 from Robert, Pemberton at the start enabled Derbyshire to hold a 16 shot advantage after eight jacks of their home leg.

Greater Manchester, in their home leg at Bardsley, had to be content with an even share of the first eight cards and an 11 shot advantage looked wafer thin as the match went into its closing stages.

With three winners of four, Derbyshire increased their lead to 31 at home and in the away leg there was a tremendous 21-7 from Dave Ellis who played superbly on short marks against the normally dependable Tommy Heyes. Darren Griffiths tried hard to sort things out for Greater Manchester with a fine, 21-9 but the Mancunians could add just a single shot to the eleven they had in hand and Derbyshire went into the record book with a memorable first win by 19 shots.

Scores at Bardsley Liberal Club: Greater Manchester 209, Derbyshire 197.
Scores at Bolsover Colliery: Derbyshire 226, Greater Manchester 195.

The Mens Waterloo Handicap Final Stages
at the Waterloo Hotel, Blackpool, September 12th, 1990

Prize money: £20,000

Biggest Waterloo news came in the last sixteen. Brian Duncan, the holder and four times winner, was defeated by John Bancroft, one of the best of the younger school.

Duncan, however, was giving most of his opponents a five shot start and when Bancroft opened with a break of five, the writing was on the wall. The "King" did all he could to get back on terms and though he managed to match Bancroft's scoring from that point, he went down 11-21.

Top liners through to the quarter finals included Preston's John Hodgson who shocked Tommy Johnstone with a series of "fires" which took him through to the last four.

Bancroft's 21-18, quarter final defeat of Mike Leach, provided the packed house with the best game of the day and Chris McDonald was also in fine fettle, beating Billy Green and then going to the final via a 21-16 card against Robert Crawshaw.

Bancroft then defeated Hodgson and was always on top in the final against McDonald. He excelled on the medium lengths with McDonald going for the corner when he got the chance.

Quarter finals: J Bancroft (Hyde) 21, M Leach (Preston) 18. J Hodgson (Preston) 21, T Johnstone (Warrington) 18. C McDonald (Wilmslow) 21, W Green (Stockport) 15. R Crawshaw (Wilmslow) 21, S Bennett (Coventry) 19.
Semi finals: Bancroft 21, Hodgson 15. McDonald 21, Crawshaw 16.
Final: Bancroft 21, McDonald 12.

The Ladies Waterloo Handicap Final Stages

at Waterloo Hotel, Blackpool, September 9th, 1990

Prize money: £4,500

Jane Jones of the Wirral became the second member of her family to win the top tournament of the ladies game.

Her victim in the final was her sister, the widely known Pat Davies, the winner in 1987 who was favourite to complete a double.

Pat was in fantastic form in the semi finals following a 21-6 success over Hazel Pashley in her previous game but Jane had to pull all the stops out in her semi to go through.

Fleetwood's Mildred Green reached 20-18 but three successive singles for Jane one a first class draw, made it a family final.

Pat, giving all her opponents three start, fared badly at the beginning to trail 12-3, but then levelled at 16-all and led out with a 9-12 inch wood. Jane's reply was a match winner for she promptly drew inside her sister's wood and went on to win 21-16. Mum Alice Darwood, the senior member of a terrific bowling family, was probably the proudest person on the day and did none too badly by reaching Finals Day herself.

Semi finals: J Jones (Wirral) 21, M Green (Fleetwood) 20. P Davies (Wirral) 21, D Boyd (Midlands) 14.
Final: Jones 21, Davies 16.

Greenalls Champion of Champions

at the Waterloo Hotel, Blackpool, September 22nd, 1990

Prize money: £5,000

The field was extended to 32 with 16 leading competition winners joining the British Crown Green BA's 16 county champions. Ian Rigby, champion of North Lanes and Fylde, played good bowls throughout the day on a green which must be one of his favourites, but he lived dangerously however before taking the title.

In a second round game Bowlers' World Champion Julian Fullerton led him 9-0, but he clawed his way back to win 21-19, and meet the much fancied Ken Strutt in a semi final. This match proved one of the best of the day and after winning it by three shots he disposed of Merseyside's Paul Gartside fairly comfortably.

In the other half of the draw John Bancroft made solid progress wins over the Welsh and North Midlands Merit winners - Glyn Cookson (21-9) and the talented Mark Britton (21-9) won him a place in the final. It gave him a chance to add the title to his Midshire and Waterloo successes but on the day Rigby was too good. Rigby opened up an early gap and kept up the pressure to win 21-11.

Quarter finals: J Bancroft (Midshires) 21, G Cookson (Bass Olympia) 19. M Britton (Manchester E News) 21, K Shaw (Isle of Man) 18. I Rigby (N Lancs and Fylde Merit) 21, K Strutt (Gt Manchester Merit) 18. P Gartside (Merseyside Merit) 21, T Whitehouse (Cumbria Merit) 12.
Semi finals: Bancroft 21, Britton 9. Rigby 21, Gartside 14.
Final: Rigby 21, Bancroft 11.

The Poynton Sports Floodlit Open

Final stages at the Poynton Sports Club, Cheshire
October 6th 1990
Prize money: £3,000

The very popular late season Poynton Floodlit again attracted a splendid entry. The final brought together the pair who have often been described as the big two of Crown Green bowls and Noel Burrows showed that he is back to his best in a thrilling encounter with Brian Duncan.

Semi finals: N. Burrows (Chinley) 21, C. Ball (Shropshire) 15; B. Duncan (Preston) 21, M. Gilpin (Kendall) 12.
Final: Burrows 21, Duncan 17.

The Bass Olympia

Final stages at the GEC Bowls Club, Stafford, October 14th 1990
Prize money: £14,000

The Bass Olympia signalled the closing of the 1990 tournament programme and a huge crowd was treated to a great day's bowling with Ian Bottomley the winner of the £2,800 top prize after an all-Yorkshire final with Gary Wallis. It was the second time in three years Walker had finished runner up.

Semi finals: I. Bottomley (Halifax) 31, A. Murray (Partington) 29; G. Wallis (Doncaster) 31, S. Ainsworth (Solihull) 23.
Final: Bottomley 31, Wallis 30.

PROFILES

Players

Ackland, Janet *Born 19.12.38.* The world Singles gold won by Janet Ackland in New Zealand in December 1988 was not her first championship medal. She won bronze at Worthing in Pairs and Fours when the event was last held in England in 1977.

Janet started bowling at the Guest Keen Steel Works club, Cardiff, where she and her husband Bob were instructed by her father-in-law, the late Jim Ackland. For six years she bowled for most of the time with men, as the club had no ladies' section. In 1965 she joined the Penarth Belle Vue club and still plays there with her husband. Her dedication to the game was evident in 1980 when she gave up her job as an arts and crafts teacher to concentrate on her bowling career. She won her first cap in 1973, and she has gained Welsh national titles in Singles, Triples, and Fours.

Adrain, George *Born 12.4.53.* George comes from one of Scotland's best-known bowling families, with both father (Willie Adrain No. 2) and uncle (Willie Adrain No. 1) prominent double internationals.

In the 1984 World Outdoor Championships, at Aberdeen, George won a gold medal in the Pairs — but not for his native Scotland. He came in from the substitutes pool to partner Skippy Arculli of the United States, and they went on to win the title. He has twice won the Hong Kong Classic Pairs with Willie Wood and once took the Singles title. He teamed up with Grant Knox to win the Pairs gold medal at the Commonwealth Games in Edinburgh in 1986 and won Commonwealth Gold again in New Zealand in 1990. His clubs are Dreghorn (outdoors) and Irvine (indoors).

Allen, Sammy *Born 6.7.38, Bally-mena.* A civil servant, Allen has been

bowling since 1966, and is one of Ireland's most experienced players. A tigerish competitor, he has skipped both indoors and outdoors for his country, represented Northern Ireland at Commonwealth Games level, winning bronze in the Fours in 1986 and silver in 1990 as well as gold in the world Triples 1984 and world Fours in 1988.

Anton, Catherine *Born 5.5.65.* Catherine, a member of the Peterborough & District club, first qualified for the EWBA championships at Leamington in 1982 and has been there almost every year since. Captain of England's junior international team she won the national under-25 Singles in 1987, 1988 and 1990 and claimed the English Two-wood championship in 1989.

Allcock, Tony *Born 11.6.55, Leicester.* Tony Allcock who has an indoor record second to none passed another milestone in his eventful career, winning the outdoor England Singles title for the first time in 1990. He had won his first national outdoor champion success a week earlier in the Triples. World indoor Singles champion twice and a world indoor Pairs titleholder in three of the past four years, England indoor singles winner twice and runner up once in the past four years proclaim his class.

At 17, Tony appeared in his first national championship at Mortlake — partnering Paul Clarke, also 17, and who also went on to win his England badge. Allcock won the EBA Under-25 Singles title three times (1975, 1977, and 1981) and the EIBA Under-31 Singles once, in 1984.

In 1976, aged 20, he was picked for England indoors, and was dramatically promoted to skip during his first series, at Rugby. He has been an indoor regular ever since, and has won the red rose outdoors since 1978. At 24, he partnered Jimmy

Hobday and David Bryant (skip) to the World Triples title at Frankston in 1980, four years later, again with Bryant, he gained a silver medal in the World Pairs at Aberdeen. At the 1988 World Championships in New Zealand, he and Bryant won silver in the Paris. Then he skipped England collegues John Ottaway, Wynne Richards and John Bell to bronze in the Fours. Tony moved from Leicestershire to Gloucestershire to pursue his vocation as a teacher and was principal of a day centre for mentally handicapped adults in Stroud until August 1987, when he resigned to devote more time to bowls. He now plays for Cheltenham (outdoors) and Bentham (indoors).

Baker, Jim *Born 18.2.58, at Belfast.*
As soon as Jim Baker was christened, it was obvious that he was destined to become a bowler . . . his middle name is Green. When he took up bowls at the age of 12 on short mats in a church hall, he was torn between bowls and soccer; in his teens he was a very useful amateur footballer, and in bowls he has won association, national, British Isles, and world trophies.

In 1984, he won the Embassy World Indoor Singles crown, beating England's Nigel Smith in the final. It all started to happen for the double Irish international skip in 1984. He skipped the Irish Triple of Stan Espie and Sammy Allen to the World Triples Championship at Aberdeen.

Baker plays outdoors at Cliftonville, and at the County Antrim indoor club during the winter. He is manager of the Jim Baker Stadium, where this club is located. He is married to Marie and has a daughter. The family home is at Parkgate, a mile from the stadium that bears his name.

He has won five Irish indoor Singles titles as well as the Triples, the British Isles outdoor Singles (1981), and the British Isles indoor Triples (1987). Jim skipped the Great Britain Triple of Brian Middlemass (Scotland) and Mal Hughes (England) to success in the Bicentennial Tournament in Australia (1988), won a Fours gold medal in the World Championships in New Zealand in 1988 and Fours gold again in 1990 when he went back there to play in the Commonwealth Games.

Beare, Garin *Born 26.2.39 at Maputa, Mozambique.* The most successful bowler on the African continent, Garin won the Singles at the African states tournament six times between 1981 and 1990, and has had good results in top class international competition. He finished seventh in the world championship in Scotland in 1984, and at the next world bowls in New Zealand in 1988 took the bronze, behind David Bryant & Willie Wood. In 1982 he was fourth in the Singles at the Commonwealth Games, and though selected for Zimbabwe did not compete in 1986. He was a quarter finalist in the Embassy World Indoor Championship in 1983. At various times since 1973 Garin has won every Zimbabwe national championship; he works as an administration officer in a large timber company. His wife Millie, a keen bowler was born in Scotland and emigrated in 1956.

Bell, Eileen *Age 53.* A part-time hotel receptionist in her home town of Ballynahinch, Eileen, married to a dairy farmer, is a product of the Irish short mat scene. She began bowling over 20 years ago in a local church hall, and then graduated to the outdoor game, scoring her first major success in 1971. The 1980s pushed her to the forefront of ladies' bowls, especially after her success in Canada, when she led for the bubbly Nan Allely to capture the Pairs gold medal at the world championship.

She has been a British Isles title holder on three occasions, but has never managed to achieve the same success indoors, despite having six semi-final appearances and three in the finals. Her Irish indoor record is, however, extremely impressive. She has been out on her own until the emergence of Margaret Johnston. She has won national titles outdoors and indoors in Singles, Triples, and Fours, and made regular international appearances for some years. Her clubs are Belfast BC (outdoors) and Shaws Bridge, Belfast (indoors).

Bell, John N. *Born 14.1.47.* A planning officer in Carlisle, John made his first appearance in the national championships at Mortlake in 1966, when he was only 18. A fine cricketer, he played rubgy for Cumbria, and is a great raconteur.

With Mal Hughes, he won the Newcastle Invitation Pairs in New South Wales in 1978, and has been member of the BBC bowls commentary team. John lost to David Bryant in the final of the first Granada Superbowl, after holding a match-winning position.

He won the national Singles title in 1983, the Triples in 1976, and was also an EBA Top Fours winner in 1983. He has won medals at the last two world outdoor championships — gold in 1984 and bronze in 1988. He has been a regular outdoor international since 1978 and in the English indoor team since 1983. His outdoor club is Wigton, Cumbria, and he plays indoors for the Cumbria Club, Carlisle.

Belliss, Peter James *Born 12.11.51.* Peter, a professional bowler who plays for the Armoho club in Wanganui, won the World Singles crown at Aberdeen in 1984, and made up for his failure to retain it at Auckland in 1988 by skipping Rowan Brassey to the Pairs gold. Like Brassey, Belliss was a top-class Rugby player who took to bowls when a knee injury forced him to hang up his boots. He has twice won the New Zealand Singles title, and has done well abroad, winning the Australian Jack High Masters, the Hong Kong Classic Singles and the Irish Champion of Champions event. He first played for New Zealand in 1978 and has been a regular member of the international teams since 1981. But he was not selected for the 1990 New Zealand Commonwealth Games team, as a result of playing in South Africa a few years ago.

Blair, Angus *Born 13.5.65.* Angus Blair is one of the brightest talents in recent years. He first caught the eye when he reached the semi-finals of the Scottish Indoor Junior Singles Championship in 1982, and two years later won his first outdoor international cap. In 1986, he realized his great potential when he took the Scottish Outdoor Singles Championship with a 21-20 win over Anchor's Brian Sinclair, and he went on to add the British title in 1987 with a final win over Ireland's Ken Hogg. He regained his place in the outdoor international side in 1987. Indoors, he was a beaten finalist in the Dundee Masters in 1986, and won his first indoor cap a year later. Blair comes from a bowls-playing family, with mother, father, and older brother all keen players. His clubs are Haddington (outdoors) and Midlothian (indoors).

Bransky, Cecil *Born 15.5.42.* Born in South Africa, Cecil Bransky reached the South African Singles championship final in 1971. The following year he went one better and captured the title. Later he moved to Israel where he owns a gift and sweet store. He has won 12 national titles since. His international record is impressive and 1985 was special. That year he was runner-up in the Embassy World indoor Singles, runner-up in the Gateway (now Woolwich) Masters and winner of the Irish Jack High Singles. In the last two World championships in 1984 and 1988 he finished fifth and sixth.

Brassey, Rowan James *Born 18.1.56.* Rowan, who played rugby for Auckland before he sustained an injury which forced him to quit the game, is a site supervisor with a building firm. His supporters claim he is the best lead in the world and his display in the World Pairs final in 1988 provided evidence of his skill at drawing to the jack. He won the New Zealand Fours and Pairs 1982, and has collected three silver medals as a Fours lead — World Bowls 1984 and 1988 and Commonwealth Games 1982, as well as a Triples bronze in 1984, Pairs gold with Peter Belliss in 1988 and Commonwealth Games Pairs bronze in 1990. He has also played for New Zealand since 1982 in Test matches, against Australia, England, Scotland and Ireland.

Bryant, David, CBE *Born 27.10.31, at Clevedon.* The achievements of this man on the bowling greens of the world have earned him a niche in the history of sport that will surely never be equalled. Nor is the Bryant saga yet ended.

In 1961 he became champion of the British Isles, and the following year won the first of four Commonwealth Games Singles titles. Twenty-nine years on, he was still excelling in major events, blending the mellow experience of the years and unmistakable skill, style, flair, and showmanship with the enthusiasm of a schoolboy and all the courtesy the bowling public has come to expect of its first gentleman of the green.

He loses with a grace that matches his delight at winning, and there has been plenty of that. Four gold medal Singles victories at Commonwealth Games, in 1962, 1970, 1974, and 1978; Singles wins at the four-yearly world outdoor championships, in 1966, 1980, and 1988; world indoor Singles winner three years running, in 1979, 1980, 1981; world indoor Pairs champion, 1986 and 1987; British Isles Singles winner four times; British Isles Singles champion four times . . . the list seems endless. The twenty-four national titles he has won in Singles, Pairs, Triples and Fours includes six outdoor Singles wins in 1960, 1966, 1971, 1972, 1973, and 1975 and nine indoor Singles titles, in 1964, 1965, 1967, 1969, 1971, 1972, 1977, 1979 and 1983.

In recent years, he won most of the television events at least once, among them the CIS Insurance International Singles (1982, 1983 and 1989) the Kodak Masters (1978, 1979, 1980) the Gateway Masters and the Woolwich Masters (1988), the John Player Classic (1981), the Triples Crown Classic (1982), the UK Singles (1983), the Granada Superbowl (1984), the Liverpool Victoria Superbowl (1987). He also won the Woolwich Masters at Worthing in 1989, which offered a £10,500 top prize. Unfortunately, for the first time in twelve years this event was not televised.

Later that year he won the CIS UK indoor Singles title at Preston Guild Hall and at the Embassy world indoor championships there in March 1990 captured the indoor Pairs title for the fourth time in five years in company with Tony Allcock.

Bryant first played for his country in 1959, and since that time has missed playing in only three outdoor and one indoor international series in those twenty nine years. He has been an inspiration to his club, Clevedon, his county, Somerset, his country, England, and to bowlers everywhere.

Bray, Richard *Born 26.1.64.* A Cornishman who works in the family coal merchant's business at Penwithick and plays for the Stenalees club, Bray won England's national Singles championship at Worthing in August 1988 and he followed this by winning the British Singles title on the same green in July 1989.

Clarke, Paul *Born 7.6.55.* Paul, a banker from Thurmaston in Leicestershire, was one of the most successful bowlers of the 1988 outdoor season, winning championships in the EBA Pairs and Triples, when he and his Belgrave colleague, John Stephenson, emulated David Holt's performance of 1987 by taking two England championships in one season. Paul played for England (Outdoors) in 1980 & 1981.

Corkill, David *Born 15.2.60, Belfast.* From a 10-year-old boy, bedecked in bowling club badges, to one of the most colourful players in the world- that's the success story of David Corkill, who plays indoors at Belfast and outdoors at Knock. He started bowling at an early age in Tullycarnet Park, where he played for Gilnahirk. After learning the basics, he soon moved to the Private Greens with Knock, winning association and national Fours titles in 1977 and 1978, the Irish national Singles in 1980 and 1988, the British Isles Singles in 1981, and the Irish National Pairs in 1983 and 1984.

His indoor honours include the Irish Singles championship (1987 and 1988) and the Irish Fours (1979 and 1981). He represented Northern Ireland in the Commonwealth Games in 1982 and at the world championships in Aberdeen in 1984. In October 1986 he won the Liverpool Victoria Superbowl tournament in Manchester, beating his greatest Irish rival, Jim Baker, in the final of this televised event, and repeated this success in a memorable final with Margaret Johnston in 1988.

Corkill likes fast cars, athletics, and listening to music. But first comes his chosen sport. He is a dedicated fitness fanatic and deep thinker of the game.

Corsie, Richard *Born 27.11.66.*
Another of the young brigade quickly making their mark on the game, Corsie won the Scottish Outdoor Junior Singles Championship in 1983, and the following year made his debut in the outdoor international side, a place he has kept every year since. In 1984, he won the Scottish Indoor Junior Singles title and the Outdoor British Junior title. He played in the Singles at the 1986 Commonwealth Games in his native Edinburgh, where he took the bronze medal. He reached the semi-finals of the UK Indoor Singles in 1985 and climbed the peak of his career in March 1989 when he gave a majestic display against Willie Wood to win the Embassy World Indoor Championship.

Corsie has excelled overseas recently. In November 1987 he and Brian Middlemass won the Pairs at the Hong Kong Classic and two months later he and another young Scot, Angus Blair, won £8,000 at the World Premier Classic event in Australia at Sanctury Cove, Queensland. His 1988 successes included a second Scottish Indoor Junior title and he finished runner-up in the CIS Insurance UK championships. In the 1990 Commonwealth Games he was selected to play in the Singles and ousted David Bryant in a play-off to win a bronze medal.

Cutler, David.J. *Born 1.8.54.*
David won his first England title — the Triples — in 1972, when he was barely 18, and became, at the time, the youngest-ever national champion. Since then, he has collected more national Singles titles than anyone but David Bryant, winning the EBA Under-25 title in 1974, the EBA Singles title in 1979, the EBA Invitation title in 1983 and 1985, and the EBA Champion of Champions in 1984.

His career in the Civil Service took him from his native Cornwall to York, and back to the West Country, where he plays at the Plymouth CS Club, but he took an important step in 1988, when he decided to devote more time to his bowls gear business and became a part-time civil servant.

He played for England (Outdoors): 1975, 77-80, 84-88; (Indoors): 1976-80, 82-88.

Cutts, Roy *Born 14.5.53.* An insurance inspector, Roy has been bowling since he was 17. He was an EBA Triples winner in 1983, and in 1986 won the EIBA Singles and reached the semi-finals of the Embassy World Singles and the CIS UK Singles. The same year, he first represented England outdoors. Indoors, he has been an England international since 1979, always playing second, from which position he exerts a vital morale-boosting influence. He played in that position in England's Commonwealth Games Fours team in New Zealand in January 1990 when he and his colleagues just failed to get into the medals. His outdoor club is Marlborough (Ipswich), his indoor club, Ipswich.

Denison, Danny *Born 27.12.61,*
Torquay. A club championship victory at Newton Abbot in 1984 set Denison on the road to major bowls success the following year. He won the Croxley Script Champion of Champions and a £3,000 first prize, and repeated his success in 1986. This was a great year for him. He also won the Under-31 national indoor Singles final and reached the semi-finals of the Kodak Under 25s. An indoor trial in the 1986-87 season won him his first international cap; he represented his country at Aberdeen in March 1987 and at Hartlepool in 1988. He plays outdoors at Newton Abbot and indoors at the Dawlish club.

Dickison, Ian Anthony *Born 9.3.52.*

Ian is a real estate salesman from Dunedin, who took his chance in 1986 when Peter Belliss was not considered for selection for New Zealand's Commonwealth team, and took the Singles gold medal at Edinburgh. He won the New Zealand Pairs title in 1981, when he was also runner-up in the Singles.. He eventually won the Singles in 1985, and was the runner-up — to David Bryant — in the Gateway Masters in 1986 on his way to Scotland for the Commonwealth Games. At World Bowls in 1988, he won a gold medal in the Triples and a silver in the Fours.

Drummond-Henderson, John Herbert (Jack) *Born 1.12.10.*

Jack Drummond-Henderson won his first ever national championship at Worthing on August 18th 1990, a few months before his 80th birthday.

By the time he won the national Triples with his Cheltenham club colleagues Andrew Wills and Tony Allcock, he had played for Gloucester 205 times, this record including 73 Middleton Cup games, and he has been a prolific tournament winner in Singles, Pairs, Triples and Fours. Jack is still actively engaged in bowls coaching as well as being a keen gardener and working for the Samaritans. His sporting career has embraced football, tennis, athletics (100 yards and 220 yards), and martial arts.

Duff Hugh *Born 22.6.63.*

Fresh faced Hugh Duff, the 1988 World Indoor Champion, began playing bowls when was 18 after being persuaded to try the game by a friend. He adapted instantly, and within two years had reached the last 16 of the Scottish National Indoor Singles. In 1987 he won a Scottish qualifying competition for entry into the World Indoor Championship at Coatbridge, and reached the semi-finals where he pushed David Bryant to a fifth deciding set.

The experience saved him in good stead the following year when he dominated the championship in London's Alexandra Palace, carving through the field of the world's top bowlers for the loss of only two sets. A few months earlier he had gone to the Gretna Green anvil to marry Helen Taylor, herself a bowler. Hugh plays at the Drongan Club outdoors, and indoors at Auchinleck.

Duncan, Brian *Born 24.10.43,*

Wigan Duncan, acknowledged as 'King of the Crown', is the most consistent crown player of the past 20 years. He has now won the Waterloo three times — in 1979, 1986, and 1987 — a feat never before achieved. Other outstanding successes were winning the Bass Masters in 1984 and the Talbot in 1974, the best-known crown green tournament until it disappeared after the 1975 competition but has now been resumed.

A full-time professional, Brian plays outdoors at the Railway Hotel club, Preston, and on the flat at Blackpool/Fylde IBC. His skill at the indoor game is considerable, too. In 1984 he reached the final of the United Kingdom championships at Preston.

Evans, Annette *Born 28.5.44.*

An outdoor international since 1981, Annette Evans lives at Jordanhill, Glasgow, and plays outdoors at Willow Bank and indoors at the West of Scotland club. In 1987 she won the Scottish Women's National Outdoors Singles and followed this by taking the British Isles title in 1988. During the year she was also a National Indoor Singles semi-finalist and was runner-up in the inaugural UK Women's Singles. Annette was in Scotland's gold-winning Fours team at Brisbane in 1984, and also took part in the Women's World Championship in New Zealand in 1988. In 1990 she retired from international competition.

Evans, John C.

John is a popular Devonian, who lost to Tony Allcock in the semi-final of the EIBA Singles in 1987, but entertained television viewers as he fought his way into the following winter's UK Singles quarter-finals, and was runner-up in the EIBA Champion of Champions event in 1988. A former professional footballer with Torquay United, he first qualified for the EBA national championships in the late sixties, and won his first cap in the 1973 series. He won a Pairs silver at the 1974 Commonwealth Games in Christchurch, and a World Fours bronze in Johannesburg in 1976. Played for England (Outdoors): 1973-75, 77-78, 80-82; (Indoors): 1979, 81.

Fitzgerald, Gillian. *Born 23.6.49.* In 1990 Gill Fitzgerald qualified for the Englishwomen's national championships at Leamington for the fouth successive year. On previous occasions she was knocked out in the first round every time. But in 1990 it was different. She won the Two-Wood Singles and the Champion of Champions titles, and just missed a treble after she and her Kettering Lodge colleagues were narrowly beaten in the final of the Fours. Along the way her Singles success had included victories over experienced internationals Brenda Atherton and 1990 Commonwealth Games bronze medalist Jayne Roylance (Two Wood Singles) and Mavis Steele (Champion of Champions final). Mrs Fitzgerald's feat has won her the Woolwich/Daily Telegraph Year Book nomination as the woman bowler of 1990 and she was receiving the Henselite Trophy presented by Douglas Kenn Ltd in London on December 1st 1990.

Fong, Peter *Born 23.5.41.* A marketing manager, Peter plays at the Rewa club, Fiji. He won a gold medal at the 1985 Pacific Championship, was runner-up in the Australian Mazda Jack High tournament in 1986 and was a semi-finalist in the 1987 Gateway (later Woolwich) Masters at Worthing. Peter has appeared in three world bowls championships and five Commonwealth Games. A popular figure on the bowling international scene, he lists poker as his only hobby.

Fuller, Barbara *Born 6.1.33, Tottenham, London.* Barbara Fuller, who skipped England teams in the Triples and

Fours at the Women's World Championship in New Zealand at the end of 1988, first played for her country in 1973 and had been a regular international since 1981. A left-hander, her long list of tournament successes includes many county championship honours with Middlesex, and over the years she has won national Pairs, Triples and Fours. In 1986 she won a Commonwealth Games bronze in the Fours.

Gourlay Family The best known bowls family in Scotland. David Snr (born 24.5.37) was in the Scots side that took the Gold Medal in the overall team event at the World Championships in Aberdeen in 1984. Sarah (born 28.9.37) played lead in the Scots rink that struck gold the following year in the Women's World Championships in Australia. Sarah is a past Scottish and British Singles champion (indoor), while David Snr has won the Scottish and British Indoor Pairs, Triples, and Fours championships. Both are double internationals, having won a host of caps, both indoor and outdoors, and son David (born 22.4.66) continued the family tradition when he played in the Scots side at Aberdeen in the British Isles Indoor Championship in 1987. Both father and son have won the prestigious Tennent's Dundee Masters Championship.

Halmai, Steve E. *Born 26.3.59.* Steve plays for Paddington, indoors and out, and is an all-round player, having been first selected for England at lead (outdoors) in 1983, and three (indoors) in 1984. With his club colleague Gerry Smyth, Steve created a record when he won the EIBA Pairs title two years running in 1987 and 1988. They also won the British indoor Pairs championship in 1988.

Played for England (Outdoors): 1983-85; (Indoors): 1984-85, 87-89.

Holt, David *Born 9.9.66.* From crown green beginnings, Holt's entry on to the flat green scene has been sensational. After only two years of bowling on the flat, he became Singles and Pairs champion of

England. He won both titles at Worthing in 1987, the high spot being his brilliant play in crushing world indoor champion Tony Allcock in the Singles.

An international, he now manages the Blackpool Borough indoor club and plays outdoors at Bolton.

Hughes, Mal *Born 3.8.32, Hartle-pool.*

One of the game's great personalities, Mal Hughes made his outdoor international debut in 1975, becoming one of England's most successful skips. He was England's captain in 1977-78, and is now his country's team manager, bringing to that task the same flair and zest he always shows on the green. Under his leadership England has

He has represented his country at World and Commonwealth Games level, winning a team gold medal in the 1980 World championships. The outgoing Australian crowds responded to his flamboyance on the green by voting him 'Personality of the Games'.

He has played in Test matches in South Africa, represented England three times in the prestigious Australian Mazda Singles, and has won the Australian International Pairs with John Bell and the National Pairs with George Turley. Equally at home on carpet, he skipped at international level from 1975 to 1981, was England's indoor Singles champion in 1975, and British Isles winner the following year. Other successes include the Dundee Masters, and national and British Isles victories in the rinks.

Johnston, Margaret *Born 2.5.43.*

Margaret Johnston's record has put her in the top flight of women bowlers throughout the world, although she did not start bowling outdoors until 1979. Up to that time she had played only in the short-mat game. Living in the small village of Bellaghy, 20 miles from Belfast, she joined in the short-mat circuit, visiting local village and church halls to play in the weekly competitions. Years of practice on the short mats honed her delivery to perfection, and when she hit the outdoor scene in Ireland she made an immediate impact.

In her first year, she reached the final of

the Irish Singles and was a semi-finalist in 1981 and 1982. Her first national title came when she skipped the Fours, and since then she has embarked on a remarkable series of title victories, among them Irish and British Isles Singles and Pairs titles in 1985 and 1986, a Commonwealth Games gold medal in the Pairs at Edinburgh in 1986 and a Singles bronze at the New Zealand Commonwealth Games in 1990. She has been a regular outdoor international since 1981, played for Ireland's indoor team in 1987, and represented her country in the 1985 world championships in Australia. She won the first women's world indoor singles as well as the Bicentennial International Tournament in Brisbane, Australia, in 1988, when representing Great Britain in the Singles, later that year she reached the final of the famous Superbowl Tournament losing in a dramatic finish to David Corkill.

Katunarich, Dennis *Age in 1990: 39.*

A prolific tournament winner, especially since 1984, Dennis has performed well on the international circuit, winning medals regularly at the Pacific Games and other major events. He won the Australian Singles and Fours titles in 1985, and was runner up in the Mazda Jack High in 1987 and 1988. In the Commonwealth Games he was in the Australian Fours team which won bronze.

King, Mervyn *Born 4.1.66, King's Lynn, Norfolk.*

Mervyn, like his father, is a gamekeeper in Wighton, near Wells-next-the-Sea, Norfolk, and plays for the Hunstanton (EBA) club. He came to prominence in March 1988, when he won the EIBA Under-25 championship, and confirmed his potential by reaching the final of the EBA Under-25 Singles in the summer.

He was selected for England in 1990.

Knox, Grant *Born 8.6.60.*

Another of the new young brigade to take the bowls world by storm in recent years, Knox won his first outdoor cap in 1983 and has been ever present since. He teamed up with George Adrain to take the gold medal at the Commonwealth Games in Edinburgh in 1986, but this pair faded at the World Championships in New Zealand in 1988 after winning their first six games. His clubs are Armadale (outdoors) and West Lothian (indoors).

Line, Peter and Wendy A cartographical draughtsman by profession, Peter Line is one of the few top bowlers who can claim to have been around as long as David Bryant, having been first badged by England in 1955 at the age of 24. Since then, he has become one of only seven men to win the England Singles more than once (1961, 1964), and has collected gold medals in the Commonwealth Games (Pairs 1970) and World Bowls (Fours 1972). Between 1955 and 1985, he played for England in 22 outdoor and 13 indoor international series, and in 1986 won the British Isles Triples.

Peter's wife, Wendy, in contrast, did not take up bowls until she was 40, but her achievements now rival those of her husband, for she has won the England Singles, Triples, and Fours, British Isles Triples, and a gold medal in the women's Singles at the 1986 Commonwealth Games in Edinburgh.

Peter and Wendy make a devastating partnership in the new mixed competitions, having won five national mixed titles together in Pairs and Fours.

McCloughlin, John *Born 9.3.58, Lisburn.* A production engineer with a car components manufacturer on the outskirts of Belfast, McCloughlin has been bowling since he was 11. He has represented Ireland both outdoors and indoors. He won a bronze medal in the Irish Commonwealth Games rink skipped by Willie Watson in Brisbane, Australia, and a gold medal in the Jersey Invitation Fours championship. He plays indoors at the Belfast IBC, outdoors at Lisnagarvey, won a gold medal in the Fours in the Irish team in the World Championships in New Zealand and a Fours silver in the 1990 Commonwealth Games in New Zealand.

McCutcheon, Rodney *Born 3.4.62, Bangor.* As a schoolboy, Rodney

first played on the short mats of the North Down area. He soon moved to the outdoor game, joined the Bangor club as a teenager, and has been there ever since. His biggest win came in 1982 when he defeated Tony Allcock in the British Isles Under-25 Singles championship at Ayr. Although his crouch delivery does not suit some coaches, it suits him, having kept him his indoor and outdoor international place.

At the 1990 Commonwealth Games he won a Fours silver medal to add to the Fours gold he won at the World Championships, also in New Zealand.

McIntosh, Alex *Born 24.5.36.* McIntosh took up the game in 1955 and won Newbattle club championship success. He won his first international cap outdoors in 1962, but then did not play again until 1969, keeping his place until 1983. He came back into the side in 1986.

With three national outdoor titles to his credit — the Fours in 1968 and the Pairs in 1973 and 1985 — he has also won four national indoor titles in a remarkable spell between 1968 and 1975. His run began with a win in the Fours, he added two Singles, in 1970 and 1972, and he rounded it off with a Pairs win in 1975. His indoor club is Midlothian.

His first indoor cap came in 1968, and since then he has totalled thirty appearances. He has three Commonwealth Games medals — silver in the Fours in 1970, gold in the Pairs in 1974, and silver in the same event in 1978. He won a World Championship team gold when Scotland took the Leonard Trophy at Worthing in 1972, took the silver in the Fours at the 1980 World Championship, and another silver in the World Triples in 1988. He is now out of the Scottish team.

Moffat, David Morgan *Born 22.1.43, Scotland.* Morgan won a bronze medal in the Fours for his native Scotland when the Commonwealth Games were played at Christchurch in 1974, and liked the country so much he emigrated the following year. He has played for New Zealand since winning medals at World

Championships at Frankston in 1980 (bronze in Triples and Fours), at Aberdeen in 1984 (bronze in Triples, silver in Fours) and at Auckland in 1988 (gold in Triples, silver in Fours). At Commonwealth Games level he has won medals for New Zealand at Edmonton in 1978 (Fours bronze) and at Brisbane in 1982 (Fours silver).

Morris, Trevor Raymond

Born 21.7.56 at Cairns, Australia. A builder from Cairns where the greens are exceedingly fast, Trevor Morris skipped Ian Schuback to the Pairs gold in the Commonwealth Games at Auckland in 1990. He came to prominence in 1985 when he won his State Fours championship, since when he has added the State Pairs and Singles to his impressive list of titles. First selected for Australia in the Pacific Games in 1987, he helped win the Fours gold medal, and went on to win the Fours event in the Bicentennial Games in 1988.

Ottaway, John *Born 2.6.55.*

Ottaway took up bowls at 15. He played the EBF code until 1983, but was selected for England in 1985, and has swiftly become the most respected lead in EBA and EIBA national teams.

Known affectionately as 'The Machine', he won the EBA Invitation '128' Singles and EIBA Lombard Champion of Champions, both in 1986. He was selected as lead for England's Triple and Four for Auckland in 1988, winning bronze medals in each event and he was going back to New Zealand in January 1990 to play in England's Fours Commonwealth Games team. He achieved his best ever individual success at Worthing in August 1989 when he won the Singles title after a memorable semi final victory over Tony Allcock. In 1990 he added the national outdoor Pairs title to his list of successes. He plays both outdoors and indoors for Wymondham Dell, Norfolk.

Parrella, Robert. *Born 9.6.44 in

Italy.* Always a controversial figure, 'Robbie' was born in Italy, where he

trained as a hairdresser, but now owns a taxi in Brisbane. After giving up bocca, he has become one of the best bowlers in the world. His 1990 Singles gold success in the Commonwealth Games at Auckland followed a dramatic come-back after being ignored by the Australian selectors for more than six years.

He won the silver medal - behind Willie Wood - in the Commonwealth Games at Brisbane in 1982, but had to wait until 1989 before he was selected to represent Australia, grasping this opportunity by winning gold medals in Singles and Pairs in the Pacific Games in Suva, then Commonwealth gold at Auckland where he needed to beat David Bryant by at least ten shots in their round robin and won by 25-14 before overcoming Mark McMahon in the final.

His Latin temperament and tendency to fire at the drop of a hat make him one of the most entertaining players to watch, although his strutting antics and aggressive demeanour to not always endear him to his opponents.

Paul, William *Born 9.6.44* Recognized as one of the top Singles players in Scotland, Paul was beaten in the final of the Scottish outdoor Singles in 1982, but bounced back to take the title two years later. He won the Scottish and British Indoor Pairs title in 1978, with Edinburgh clubmate Andrew Binnie, and also won the Scottish Indoor Triples title in 1984. In company with Willie Wood and Alex McIntosh he gained a Triples silver medal at the World Championships in New Zealand in 1988.

He has an uninterrupted run of indoor caps since he came into the side in 1976. He plays at Tanfield outdoors and Edinburgh indoors.

Price, John *Born 14.9.60.* The 1990 world indoor title holder, John is one of Wales's most prolific title winners, having won 11 national championships since 1980. A civil servant with the DSS at Neath, he has been playing bowls since he was 14, and was taught by his father, Harry, with

whom he won the British outdoor Pairs title in 1982 and, with Welsh indoor secretary Ray Hill, the British outdoor Triples in 1983. He was selected as Welsh Singles representative for the 1990 Commonwealth Games in New Zealand.

With his friend and Swansea indoor clubmate Steve Rees, John lost in the final of the Midland Bank World indoor Pairs championship in 1987, having reached the quarter-final of the CIS UK Singles the previous year.

Indoors he has won Welsh titles at Singles (1981, 1987 and 1988), Pairs (1984), Triples (1983) and Fours (1980 and 1984), and he has played for Wales since 1979. Outdoors, he plays for Aberavon and was first capped in 1984.

Price, Mary *Born 27.8.43.* Although bowls is now her only sport, Mary, from Farnham Common (Slough), has played competitive cricket, badminton, squash, and, until recently, hockey. With her national Singles victory at Leamington in 1988, she became the first woman to have won both indoor and outdoor England Singles titles. In 1986 she gained a Triples bronze medal at the Commonwealth Games and was in England's team of five which won the team championship gold medals at the women's World Championships in New Zealand in November 1988. In 1990 she was back in New Zealand for the Commonwealth Games winning bronze with Jayne Roylance in the Women's Pairs. Her outdoor club is Burnham, Bucks, and she plays indoors at the Desborough (Maidenhead) club in Berks.

Rednall, John *Born 26.2.64.* John, who won the British Junior Singles title at Larne in 1988, is a music teacher who lives in Stowmarket in Suffolk, and plays bowls at Marlborough (and indoors at Ipswich) with his England colleague Roy Cutts. He was first selected for England outdoors in 1987, ironically after some impressive performances indoors — reaching the semi-final stages of the 1985 EIBA and CIS

UK Singles — and was finally capped indoors in 1989-1990.

Rees, Stephen *Born 13.2.60.* Stephen Rees, from St Thomas in Swansea, surprised everyone when he beat John Fullarton, Allan McMullan, Tony Allcock, David Corkill and David Bryant on his way to the 1986 CIS UK Singles title, and he has remained a major force in top events ever since with his consistent drawing ability.

A few months after his UK success, he teamed up with his Swansea clubmate John Price and reached the final of the Midland Bank World indoor Pairs at Bournemouth where they lost to Bryant and Allcock. In 1988, he won the Irish indoor Champion of Champions event, and the Welsh outdoor equivalent.

Steve took up bowls in 1978, and was first capped after just six years in the game in 1984. A member of the strong Old Landorians club, he won the British junior title at Paisley in 1986. Indoors he has won the Welsh Pairs (1984), Triples (1985) and Fours (1987).

Rhys Jones, David *Born 28.6.42 at Gorseinon, South Wales.* The experience acquired in playing in 36 outdoor and indoor internationals, success in national and British Isles championships, and teaching experience as director of drama at Gordans School, near Bristol, has admirably equipped David Rhys Jones for his role of the BBC's principal bowls commentator and freelance bowls journalist.

After moving to England to start his teaching work, he joined Clevedon Bowling Club, where he met David Bryant, and they forged a fruitful partnership on the green that has produced six British Isles and 10 English titles in Fours, Triples, and Pairs. Rhys Jones, always content to play a secondary role to Bryant, has complemented him perfectly. Both have a sense of showmanship that should fool no one who meets them on the green.

Richards, Wynne *Born 10.6.50, Merthyr Tydfil.* Welshman Wynne Richards, who began bowling at his father's club at Troedyrhiw when he was 10, is now a Londoner and plays for England.

Since 1905, only seven bowlers have won the English outdoor Singles championship more than once. Richards, with successes in 1984 and 1986, is among that number. He also won the British Isles indoor Singles title in 1985 and the British Isles indoor Fours the following year.

He was in good form again in 1988, winning bronze in Triples and Fours at the outdoor World championships in New Zealand and a few weeks later finishing runner-up to Hugh Duff in the world indoor championship.

Bearded Richards is one of the characters of the game. He turns his slight speech impediment to his own advantage, his sense of humour overriding embarrassment. He has represented England in outdoor internationals since 1982 and indoors since 1986. He lives at Twickenham and plays for Middlesex in indoor county competitions. In summer, he gets his bowls on the other side of the London border, and as a Mid Surrey (Richmond) club member, plays for Surrey.

Roylance, Jayne *Born 8.10.47, Fakenham, Norfolk.* Jayne Roylance comes from an outstanding Norfolk bowling family. Her brother Chris Ward twice won the national Singles title, and another brother, David, is an international.

In 1985 she skipped her North Walsham team to the national Fours title and the following year she was runner-up in the Singles both indoor and outdoor. In 1988 she won the national 2-wood Singles title at Leamington and a silver medal in the Triples at the world championships in New Zealand. Indoors she was a semi-finalist in the National Triples and Singles championships, and gained her first indoor cap during that season. She added the nationals Triples title to her list of honours at Leamington Spa in August 1989 and at the 1990 Commonwealth Games in New

Zealand won a Commonwealth Games bronze medal in the Pairs.

Schuback, Ian *Born 4.9.52.* Ian, a professional tennis coach and bowls player, who plays for the Coolangatta club, Queensland, took up bowls in 1980, having been attracted to it through watching television coverage of the World Bowls championships at Frankston that year.

He made rapid progress to the top, winning the Commonwealth Games silver medal at Edinburgh six years later, and surprised everyone when he skipped Jim Yates to the World indoor Pairs title in 1987. No Australians had ever adapted so successfully to Britain's indoor carpets. This was apparent again in 1990 when he was runner-up to John Price in the final of the world indoor Singles and in company again with Yates also reached the final of the Pairs. He has been a prolific winner of invitation Masters events in Australia, but was surprisingly left out of the Australian team to play at Auckland in the World Championships in 1988. Included in the Australian team for the 1990 Commonwealth Games, however, he won gold in the Pairs with Trevor Morris.

Shaw, Norma, MBE *Born 8.6.37, Nr Wakefield, Yorkshire.* Norma Shaw was the first lady bowler to challenge what many in the bowling world consider the male-dominated closed shop of televised tournaments.

Pride of place is her Singles gold medal at the 1981 World championships in Canada. She won further medals at the subsequent World championships in 1985 and 1988 and the Commonwealth Games. She has won every national championship of the English Women's Bowling Association except the four-wood Singles which continues to elude her. Indoors she is supreme in England, having won the national Singles seven times and innumerable team events. In televised tournaments she has defeated Tony Allcock, Richard Corsie, Willie Wood, Jim Baker, Chris Ward and David Cutler and that is a record few men can claim. Though she can play a heavy wood, her game is founded on the draw shot

Simpson, Cliff *Born 5.7.47.* Cliff

Simpson has been an indoor international since 1982 and played in England's successful outdoor teams in 1989. He has won outdoor national Pairs and Fours, and the British Isles Fours titles, and came within a shot of defeating David Bryant in a dramatic national indoor Singles final in 1983. Cliff, an electrical engineer, plays outdoors at Owton Lodge, and indoors at Hartlepool IBC.

Skoglund, Philip Charles

Born 20.6.37. Phil, has played bowls since he was in his teens. He has won the New Zealand Singles championship five times, the first time in 1958, when he was only 21. He was also Pairs champion in 1972 and 1976, and Fours champion in 1976.

He has been the most prominent New Zealand bowler on the international stage for nearly 30 years, and is universally respected for his good humour as well as his skill. When he skipped his country's Triple to the World title at Auckland in 1988, it was his first gold medal at the top level, an achievement that gained popular acclaim.

Smith, Gary *Born 13.10.58.* An ad-

ministration manager with Barclays Bank, Gary has been playing bowls since he was 15, and is a prolific title winner in Kent, where he now plays for Blackheath and Greenwich and at the Cyphers indoor club at Beckenham.

Although he was runner-up in the EBA Under-25 Singles championship as long ago as 1977, his bowls career has blossomed since he formed a partnership in 1983 with Scottish exile Andy Thomson, with whom Gary has won the EIBA Pairs once (1986) and Fours four times (1983, 84, 88 and 90) and lost to Yates and Schuback in the final of the Midland Bank World indoor Pairs in 1987. Any hint that he was bowling in Thomson's shadow, however,

was emphatically dispelled in 1988, when Gary became the EIBA Singles champion. Later in the year he outbowled the British field to capture CIS Insurance UK Singles title.

Played for England (Outdoors): 1982-84, 87, 88, 89; (Indoors): 1984-87, 88, 89, 90.

Smith, Gary R. *Born 1.4.62,*

Sunderland. Known as 'Gary R.' to distinguish him from England's Gary Smith from Cyphers Club, Beckenham, this Smith has made a favourable impression since making his international debut at Hartlepool in 1988. When Cyphers colleagues Gary Smith and skip Andy Thomson were entrusted with debutants Gary R. Smith and Anglo Scot Ronnis Gass, the move was looked on as something of a gamble. The rink's record of seven wins and two draws justifies the selectors' confidence. Smith led his Sunderland trio to the EIBA Triples title at Melton Mowbray in 1990, defeating Tony Allcock's team in the final

Smyth, Gerry *Born 29.12.60, Kings-*

bury. Gerry has been on the national bowling scene since he was 18, and later became the youngest-ever outdoor international, although he subsequently failed to hold that place despite an outstanding record in the 1980's. He regained his place in 1990 and had a successful series. He won the national indoor Pairs with Steve Halmai in 1987 and 1988, and they have also won the British Isles Pairs title.

Snell, Sydney John *Born 18.9.34,*

Jerilderie, New South Wales. John, a retired investment consultant, lives in Lake Cathie, New South Wales, but crosses the State border to play bowls at the Ivanhoe club, Victoria, whose club Singles title he has won 19 times.

At his peak in the late seventies, he was silver medallist behind David Bryant at the Commonwealth Games at Edmonton in 1978 and at the Fourth World Bowls at Frankston in 1980, but he showed he has lost none of his skill when he reached the quarter-final of the Embassy World indoor championship in 1988.

Souza, George *Born 19.8.42.*A

Hong Kong merchant and former hockey and softball international, George Angelo Souza has played in international events since 1978, winning gold in the Fours at the 1980 world championships and bronze in the Triples at Aberdeen four years later. In 1983 he won the gold medal at the Kodak (now Woolwich) Masters Singles at Worthing, defeated David Bryant in a memorable final finished on a storm-, soaked green. The following year he won the Hong Kong Classic and in the next he obtained a Triples gold medal and silver in the Fours at the Pacific Games.

Steele, Mavis, MBE *Born 9.9.28, Kenton, Middlesex.* Both as a bowler and administrator, Mavis Steele has made a mark on women's bowls, and her great service to the game was recognized in 1983 when she was awarded the MBE. Miss Steele has represented her country in international competition for 33 successive years, has won 11 national titles, including the Singles in 1961, 1962, and 1969, and has gained more medals in women's World championships than anyone else, including silver in the Singles and Pairs in New Zealand, a gold in the Fours and a silver in the Triples in Canada in 1983, a bronze in the Fours in Australia in 1985, and a Commonwealth Games bronze medal in the Triples in Australia in 1982.

She is assistant secretary of the English Women's Bowling Association, was 1989-90 President of the English Women's Indoor BA, and has been involved at all levels of club, country, and national administration for most of her bowling career. She now plays at the Sunbury Sports club, Middlesex, and indoors at Egham, Surrey.

Sullivan, Terry *Born 6.11.35.* Terry was 44 when he was first selected for Wales in 1980, and it was another four years before he really made his mark on British

bowls when he won the CIS UK Singles championship at the Preston Guild Hall, following that triumph with a resounding victory in the Embassy World indoor Singles at Coatbridge in 1985.

His style, based on the South African clinic method, may appear stiff and mechanical, but it has helped Sullivan become one of the most consistent players on the circuit.

Twice winner of the Welsh indoor Singles title, Sullivan underlined his ability on grass when he became the first Briton to win the prestigious Mazda Jack High Masters in Australia in 1988. Like Steve Rees, Terry is a member of the Old Landorians club at Swansea.

Sutherland, Robert (Bob)
Born 21.5.42. Bob Sutherland took up bowls in 1968 after being forced to give up his football career with Glasgow Rangers through injury. He did not take long to make his mark either. He reached the final of the Scottish indoor Singles championship in 1974 before losing out to Willie Wilkie from Dundee. But he soon rectified the situation, bouncing back the following year to beat another Dundee man, Harry Mitchell, in the final. And Bob repeated that victory again in 1983 in what turned out to be his best ever season. He went on to win the British Singles and then added the icing to the cake with a win in the Embassy World Indoor Championship.

He has a total of 33 indoor caps to his credit since his first cap in 1974, and played in the outdoor side in 1974 and again in 1983. His clubs are Bathgate (outdoors) and West Lothian (indoors).

Tau, Geua Vada *Born 3.5.57 at Port Moresby, Papua New Guinea.* Geua was the sensation of the Commonwealth Games at Auckland, winning the women's Singles gold medal without losing a game. Delighted Papua New Guinean athletes in multi-coloured attire flocked into Pakuranga to watch her defeat Millie Khan in the final. Hers was Papua New Guinea's first-ever gold medal at

Commonwealth Games in any sport, and the first medal of any colour for bowls — though Gladys Doyle won the Singles title at the first women's world championships at Sydney in 1969. Placid and unhurried, she nonchalantly swept aside the challenge of three British favourites, Margaret Johnston, Janet Ackland and Senga McCrone, hardly ever bothering to visit the head. Geua, who admits to weighing 89.8kg, plays for the Boroko club in Port Moresby, and is the wife of Tau Tau, who skipped Papua New Guinea to gold in the Pacific Games in 1987, and to fourth place in the 1988 world championships.

Thomas, William *Born 21.10.54.*

Will Thomas, a steelworker from Pontrhydyfen, who plays indoors at Swansea, has been bowling since he was 17, and has been a member of Welsh sides, indoors and out, since 1985. He won the WBA Triples in 1984, was a member of the Welsh four which struck gold at Edinburgh in 1986, and skipped Robert Weale to bronze medals in the Pairs at World Bowls in Auckland in 1988 and at the Commonwealth Games in 1990.

Thomson, Andy *Born 26.11.55, Methil, Fyfe.*

Andy Thomson holds the unusual distinction of playing at international level for Scotland and England. Taking up the game in 1969, he registered his first bowls success at the age of 16, winning the local Buckhaven club championship, and signalled an imminent arrival among the top flight of the sport with a victory in the 1978 Scottish junior championships.

Indoor international honours followed in 1979, but engagement and subsequent marriage to a Kentish girl, Linda, brought the promising newcomer South of the border later that same year. Joining the outdoor Blackheath and Greenwich and indoor Cyphers clubs, he saw his talents flourish in the hothouse atmosphere of stern competition. In 1981, victory in the Kent county Singles over Gary Smith earned him a place in the EBA national Singles at Worthing when he defeated Alan Windsor by the odd shot.

He made his indoor international debut for England in 1981 and outdoor one year later, and performs equally well under both codes. He won the EIBA Singles title in 1989 and 1990, and the Triples in 1981, the Fours in 1983, 1984, 1988, 1989 and 1990, and the Pairs with Gary Smith in 1986.

He has also won British Isles titles in Pairs & Fours. Thompson became Woolwich/Daily Telegraph Bowler of the Year in 1989.

Ward, Chris *Born 25.12.41, Fakenham.*

Norfolk's Chris Ward is one of only a handful of players who have won the English Singles more than once (1977 and 1982). He was first capped in 1977, but his international career has been spasmodic. He won the British Isles Singles title in 1983 at Sophia Gardens, Cardiff, and partnered by his brother David won a bronze medal in the Commonwealth Games Pairs. He is manager of Pinewood Park IBC, Sheringham.

Ward, David S. *Born 26.10.45.*

David Ward's former job as an industrial civil servant with the Ministry of Defence made it impossible for him to enter national competitions on a regular basis, but his great skill has nevertheless been recognized and rewarded by England's selectors, outdoors since 1982 and indoors since 1983. The product of a bowling family, he won a Pairs bronze medal with brother Chris in the 1986 Commonwealth Games. Outdoors he plays for Cromer and manages the Roundwood indoor bowls club at Taverham, Norwich.

Watson, John *Born 22.11.45.*

John Watson first came to prominence in 1975 when he won the Scottish Indoor Junior Singles title, and three years later he added the National Singles title when he beat holder Jim Blake in the final. In 1979 he won his first indoor cap, and has been present every year since with the exception of 1982.

John was the first Scot to win the Embassy World Indoor Singles Championship, when he beat Belfast's Jim Baker in the 1982 final, but he refused his prize money in order to compete in the Commonwealth Games later that year in Brisbane. His decision was rewarded with a gold medal in the Pairs with David Gourlay. His clubs are Foxley (outdoors) and West Lothian (indoors).

Weale, Robert Arthur *Born 3.4.63, Hereford, England.* Robert is a local government officer in Presteigne, and is a top Welsh singles player. At the World championships at Auckland, he came fifth in the Singles, and, with Will Thomas, gained a bronze medal in the Pairs. They also won a Commonwealth Games Pairs gold medal in 1990. He played for Wales in the previous World Bowls at Aberdeen in 1984, when, at 21, he was the youngest competitor.

A member of a large bowling family, Robert achieved a remarkable feat in 1984 when he skipped two brothers and his father to the Welsh Fours title. He qualifies regularly from Mid-Wales for the WBA championships.

Williams, Ken *Born 23.8.33.* One of Australia's most successful bowlers in recent decades, Kenneth Arthur Williams who lives at South Tweed Heads, New South Wales has been bowling for 25 years. His tournament successes include the Australias Fours, the Mazda Jack High (twice), Adelaide Masters Singles (twice), Victorian Masters Singles, Manuwatu Singles (New Zealand) and the Corowa International Singles. He has represented his country at the 1984 and 1988 World championships, winning a bronze medal in the Pairs at Aberdeen and narrowly missing a place in the Singles final at Auckland. He has represented Australia on various occasions in test matches against New Zealand, in the Pacific Games and in World indoor events in Scotland and England as well as the Woolwich Masters in which he finished third in 1989.

Wood, William *Born 26.4.38, Gifford.* Scotland's best known bowler, Wood has strangely never won a national Single's title. The closest he came to emu-

lating his father, also Willie, who won the Scottish outdoor title in 1967, was three years later when he reached the final but lost out to Dick Bernard of Gorebridge. Willie reached the final of the Scottish indoor Singles in 1986, but again had to settle for second best when he lost out to Auchinleck's Neil McGhee.

Singles gold-medallist at the Commonwealth Games in Brisbane in 1982, he lost out 20-21 to Peter Belliss on a last-end measure in the Singles final of the World Championships at Aberdeen in 1984, and had a similar mortifying experience at Henderson, New Zealand, when David Bryant wrested the title from him with a rather adventurous last bowl. He had already won a Triples silver medal at these 1988 World Championships. He reached the final of the Embassy World Indoor Championships only to be outbowled by Richard Corsie and less than three months later took second place again in a major championship when he finished runner up to David Bryant in the 1989 Woolwich Masters. Back in New Zealand for the 1990 Commonwealth Games, he skipped the Scottish Fours team to a gold medal.

Wood won his first outdoor international cap in 1966 and has played in every series since, winning 63 caps. He also has 15 indoor caps to his credit, as well as a Scottish indoor Triples win in 1984 and a Fours win in 1986. His clubs are Gifford (outdoors) and Edinburgh (indoors).

Yates, Jim *Born 11.10.34, Corowa, New South Wales.* Bank manager James John Yates became one of the first two overseas players to win a world indoor title when, in December 1987, he and his skip Ian Schuback from Queensland won the Midland Bank Pairs title at Bournemouth. This success was all the more remarkable since at Moreland, his indoor club, play is confined to 30-foot carpets and 4-inch bowls. He returned to England for the Embassy world indoor championships in 1990 when he and Schuback finished Pairs runners-up to David Bryant and Tony Allcock.

Administrators

Allison, Pam Pam Allison has been secretary of the English Indoor BA since 1979 and since that time it has grown from 133 affiliated clubs to 243. Before holding that office she was competition secretary from 1975-1977 and assistant secretary 1978-79. An outdoor international in 1979, she was a regular indoor international from 1977-1985, but then declined selection owing to pressure of work. During her career she was an outdoor and indoor national finalist and was a member of the Cherwell (Oxford) team which won the Yetton Trophy in 1977, 1979, and 1981.

Ashford, Margaret *Born 24.3.36.* The only woman to have been elected President of both the English Women's Bowling Association (1989) and the English Women's Indoor Bowling Association (1987-1988), Margaret Elizabeth Ashford has been a familiar and popular figure on the bowling greens of the country. She was a playing member of Beccles IBC team which won the Yetton Trophy, the English women's national indoor club championship in 1987.

Barclay, James *Born 5.4.34.* Jim Barclay, honorary secretary of the Scottish Indoor Bowling Association and assistant secretary of the World Indoor Bowls Council, is recognised throughout bowling circles as a popular and devoted administrator who has made a notable contribution to the game. He is a member of the British Isles Indoor BC, secretary of the WIBC Laws of the Game sub committee, and convenes umpires for all indoor televised events. He has won Singles, Pairs, Triples and Fours championships at his outdoor clubs, and skipped indoors for his indoor club, Ardrossan, in the Scottish Cup League, from which the international team is chosen. Since he has been involved in voluntary administration since 1972 and is a full time employee running the largest voluntary administration since 1972 and is a full time employee running the largest local authority Pest Control company in Britain, he has reluctantly given up competitive bowls and plays only at indoor club level.

Barnes, Jim *Born 12.3.14.* President of the Irish Bowling Association in 1979, and its honorary secretary since 1980, Jim Barnes has been engaged in bowls administration for the past 30 years, and has been a member of the Windsor Park club, Belfast since 1955. As a leading Irish official he has played a full part in the British Isles Bowling Council (of which he was President in 1984), Commonwealth Games organisation, and the International Bowling Board, on which he has served since 1980 and is President until 1992, when the next world bowls championships take place at Worthing.

Birch, John James (Ian) *Born Auckland, New Zealand 23.6.31.* Ian Birch has been President of the New Zealand Bowling Association and New Zealand Promotions Director since 1981. A member of the World Indoor Bowls Council, he has been a New Zealand radio bowls broadcaster since 1974 and a commentator on TV New Zealand since 1979. A real estate licensee/director, he is married with five daughters. His bowling career started in 1966, and he is a member of the Epsom club.

Blake, Tom *Born 16.4.13.* President of the English Bowling Association in 1981, and of the English Indoor Bowling Association (1988), Thomas Howes Blake, who lives at Carisbrooke, Isle of Wight, is the only man to have held both offices. He was in the England outdoor international team in 1983, and twice just failed to win a national title, being a Singles semi finalist in 1961 and a Pairs semi finalist three years later. Other positions he has held in bowls include 25 years as county secretary of the Isle of Wight BA, and three times its President (1961, 1976, and 1988), and Chairman of the English Bowls Council 1985-1986. He was a member of the Southern Sports Council from 1967-1987, and Chairman of the Isle of Wight Sporting Council from 1972 to 1987.

Brimble, Peter *Born 22.6.31.* Peter

Brimble has had a colourful bowling career, both as an indoor and outdoor international and national champion, as manager of the England indoor team (seven championships won out of nine) since 1981, and as an administrator. His record since he started bowling at 13, but was banned from competitions until he was 21, is: outdoors: International 1962, 1963, 1964, 1972 (captain). Winner national Triples 1979. Middleton Cup: 119 appearances for Somerset. Winner of 11 county titles and 12 open tournaments. Indoors: International 1960-65, 1967-77. At 28 the youngest international when selected. National Singles winner 1963, Welsh open Singles winner 1962. Peter is the longest serving member of the English Indoor Bowling Association Executive (since 1972), and is a Life Member. He became EIBA President 1984-85, and was President of the World Indoor Bowls Council 1987-88. He has been a life member of the Bristol Club for the past 20 years and has been Chairman of the club since 1973. A Fellow of the Life Insurance Association, he also finds time from his bowling activities to follow the fortunes of Bristol City FC, and describes himself as their No. 1 fan.

Burrows, William (Ireland)

A well known bowling personality throughout the United Kingdom, Billy Burrows, once an Irish Trialist, is honorary secretary of the Association of Irish Bowls. He was President of the Northern Ireland Bowling Association in 1962, of the Irish BA in 1974, and of the World Indoor Bowls Council in 1986-87. A member of the British Isles Indoor Bowls Council, he is also an Irish indoor and outdoor international selector. He lives at Dunmurry.

Clark, Peter Kerry, OBE

Born 30.6.49. at Cromwell, New Zealand. Kerry Clark manages New Zealand's international teams and is an outstanding bowler himself. He has won 30 club and 14 Centre titles, represented New Zealand in the world bowls championships in 1972 and 1976, and at the Commonwealth Games in 1974 (when he won a gold medal) and 1978. Kerry was also New Zealand Masters champion in 1975 and a New Zealand Fours winner in 1977. President of the International Bowling Board 1988-1990, and Chairman of New Zealand BA (1987), he was awarded the OBE for his services to the game in 1989. He is a regional manager in New Zealand's Justice Department.

Colling, Nancie. Best known as

honorary secretary of the English Women's Bowling Association since 1980, Nancie Colling has held continuous office in bowls at club, county and national level since 1957, and she and Mavis Steele are the only women bowlers to have won the national outdoor Singles championship three times. Nancie won under three different names in 1956, 1958 and 1970 following marriages and becoming a widow. She also won the national Two-Wood Singles in 1985. In 1976 she was elected President of the EWBA. Other positions at present held in bowls: Chairman English Bowls Council; honorary secretary British Isles Women's Bowls Council; Junior Vice President Women's International Bowling Board; Patron, Somerset County WBA. Outside bowls she is a church worker, and now lives at Market Lavington, Wilts.

Crosbie, Eric, MBE *Born*

18.1.27. President of the English Bowling Association in 1977, Eric John Crosbie, who now lives at Enfield, has been actively involved in bowls for more than half a century and has been a member of the Selbourne club, Southgate for 56 years, where he was Singles champion in 1947 and 1955, and President in 1951, 1952 and 1980. A former Chairman of EBA Publications Ltd, his other positions in bowls have included these: Founder/chairman Picketts Lock IBC for 16 years; President Middlesex CBA 1967 and 1988; President London and Southern Counties BA 1959, and its honorary secretary from 1963-1965, and from 1967; honorary secretary English Bowls Council since 1975; past Chairman of Francis Drake Fellowship, and founder Chairman of Drake Charity Trust, he was awarded the MBE in 1977. Activies outside bowls have included 23 years as a JP and two as a Crown Court judge. He has also been a Chairman of Income Tax Commissioners; Chairman of the Board of Pentonville Prison; past Chairman of hospital groups.

Crocker, David *Born 29.1.38.*

Secretary of the English Bowls Players Association for the past four years, David Crocker has had considerable international experience. He represented England outdoors from 1972-74 and 1978-79, was a national Pairs winner in 1971, British Isles Pairs champion the following year, and represented England in the Commonwealth Games in 1974. He has held seven county titles and been in three successful Middleton Cup teams, twice as captain. Indoors, he was in the England team from 1972-80 and again in 1984-85. The year 1972 was a golden year for him; he won both national and British Isles indoor titles as well as achieving indoor successes. He lives at Edenbridge, Kent.

Crudge, Dora. A member of BP

Grangemouth bowling club, Dora Crudge has been involved in the administration of the women's game for many years. She has been honorary treasurer of Scottish Women's BA since 1970, is Vice President of the International Women's Bowling Board, chairman of Scottish bowls improving committee, and a member of Scottish bowls coaching committee. Mrs Crudge managed the Scottish team at the 1982 Commonwealth Games in Brisbane,

was director of women's bowls at the Edinburgh Commonwealth Games in 1986, and is a member of the executive committee of the Commonwealth Games for Scotland.

Davidson, Jimmy. A double England international (outdoors 1971-1973, indoors 1972) and national Singles champion in 1969, Jimmy Davidson has had notable influence on the game, expecially during the last decade. A member of the national executive of the National Association of Local Government Officers from 1967-1973, he retired ten years early from his chief officer negotiating post in local government in 1983, but even before then had been using his experience in his career to the service of bowls.

He was involved in the launching of the English Bowls Coaching Scheme in the late 70s and became its first director after it was formed in 1980. He retired from that position in 1987, but continues his national coaching activities. A former secretary of the British Isles Bowling Council, he has been secretary of the World Indoor Bowls Council since it was inaugurated in 1983. He was also founder secretary of the English Bowls Players Association. A member of the executive of the English Indoor Bowling Association, Jimmy is currently Senior Deputy President and Chairman of its Executive and Selection Committee. His valuable services to the game have been recognised by his colleagues; he is an honorary life member of the British Isles Bowling Council, the English Indoor Bowling Association, and the English Bowls Players Association.

Death, Harry Arthur Charles

Born 25.5.13. President of the English Indoor Bowling Association in 1976 and of the British Isles Indoor Bowls Council two years later, Harry Death was founder Chairman of the English Bowls Coaching Scheme in 1979, and has served in that capacity ever since. A member of the Executive of the English Bowling Association for many years, he was made a Life Member in 1983. He is also a Life

Member of the British Isles Bowling Council. Harry was President of Dennyside BA in 1984, and has been a moving spirit of the indoor and outdoor complex at Ipswich.

Drayton, Leslie D'Arcy *Born 23.3.11.* D'Arcy, as he is known to a wide circle of bowlers, has been a father figure in the affairs of the English Bowling Association for some years, and has played a notable part in the expansion of the game, especially the last decade. He has held office as President of every leading organisation of the English, British, and international game; Surrey (indoor and outdoor county associations), the English Bowling Association, the British Isles Bowling Council, and the International Bowling Board. His involvement as a competitive player began in 1937 when he won his first club pairs competition at Westminster Bank BC. He now lives at Great Bookham, Surrey. During the war he was a major in the Royal Artillery and was mentioned in despatches. His banking experience as assistant regional director of the London region of the NatWest Bank until he retired, has been invaluable to the EBA.

Elms, James, MBE *Born 25.8.19.* General Secretary of the English Bowling Association from 1970 to 1982, James Frank Elms was awarded the MBE in 1987 for his services to sport. He was secretary/treasurer of the International Bowling Board from 1976 to 1982, and though he has now retired from bowls administration, he has held the voluntary office of deputy chairman of the executive of the Central Council of Physical Recreation since May 1987. Before taken up his EBS appointment he had 30 years police service, and was a Superintendent at Bournemouth till he retired. He started bowling in 1948, and though he never achieved any great success at competitive level, he obtained a Hampshire county badge in 1964. He now lives at Worthing.

Getty, Hazel. Between 1967 and 1982, Hazel Getty played 48 times for the Irish indoor international team. President of the Irish Women's IBA in 1972, she became its honorary treasurer from 1982-1985, and has been honorary secretary since 1985. She also represents Ireland in the British Isles Women's Indoor Bowling Council, and the World IBC (ladies section). Her involvement with bowls goes back to 1957 when she formed the Cliftonville ladies outdoor club and was elected secretary — a position she has now held for 33 years. Currently Vice President of the Irish WBA, she has also held office in the Northern Ireland Private Greens League.

Glover-Phillips, Reginald, Alfred *Born 1905.* Despite advancing years, Rex, as he is known throughout British bowling, has a record of activity and service in both outdoor and indoor games, which is surely unequalled. Until recently he was serving on twelve committees, among them the General Purpose, Selection, National Competition, and Laws of the Game committees of the EBA, the London & Southern Counties (indoor and outdoor), and Worthing IBC. He was 1974-75 President of the EIBA was an international selector for the EBA since 1978, and for the EIBA from 1975-1989. The offices he has held at county, regional and national level are too numerous to record here, for reference must also be made to his playing record in the game he has loved since the fifties. He gained his Sussex county badge in 1954, played in the Middleton Cup 22 times, won the national Pairs with George Scadgell in 1966, and was an indoor international Trialist in 1968. Rex has won innumerable tournaments, among them county championships and on the social side, has been most supportive of national Presidents. By the end of the 1989 outdoor season he had played for the EBA 404 times, and for the EIBA on 373 occasions. A former dental surgeon, he has been a keen sportsman since his youth, playing wicket keeper for Bristol University, where he also played rugby. After moving to Worthing in 1928, he took up tennis, badminton and golf

before concentrating on bowls. His love of the game was shared by his late wife Georgie, who was a popular President of the English Women's Indoor BA 1978-79.

Gough, Walter Ernest *Born 3.3.15.* A former President of the English Indoor Bowling Association, Walter Gough now lives at Poole. He has played a significant role in the development and growth of the indoor game on the financial and business side, being a former treasurer and development officer of the EIBA, and of the English Bowls Council and of the British Isles Indoor Bowls Council and of the British Isles Indoor Bowls Council. Walter first took up bowls in 1951 after presiding at meetings at Glenfield, Leicestershire to establish sports clubs and use a public park. He subsequently played at Leicester's Abbey Park and Belgrave clubs, and was a founder member of Leicester IBC in 1973.

Hall, Henry John *Born 22.8.29.* The President of the English Bowling Association in 1990, John Hall is serving as Chairman of World Bowls 1992, the committee organising the world championships at Worthing in August next year, in which 29 countries have been invited to take part. John Hall, who describes himself as "just an average bowler" has been an active supporter of the game since taking it up in 1963. After a spell as President of the Pershore, and then the Bredon club, he subsequently became President of Worcestershire, Three Counties BA, and the Midland Counties BA, before accepting national office with the English Bowling Association.

Harrison, David *Born 2.5.45.* A familiar figure at televised bowls tournaments, David Harrison is tournament director and contracts negotiator for the World Indoor Bowls Council, the British Isles Indoor Bowling Council, Scottish Indoor BA, and the All Ireland Indoor BA. Former chief executive of Derbyshire County Cricket Club, he was at that time a member of the Test and County Cricket

Board. Mr Harrison has been appointed Marketing Director of the Woolwich World Bowls Championships at Worthing in 1992 and is the contact for sponsorship, advertising and marketing for this event. Address Box 2, Bakewell, Derbyshire DE4 1TQ Tel. 062-987 672. FAX 062-987 672.

Hill, Raymond John *Born 1929.* A double Welsh international, Ray Hill is honorary secretary of the Welsh Indoor Bowling Association. He played in the Welsh outdoor team from 1980-1986 and represented Wales in the Commonwealth Games in Edinburgh in 1986. His biggest tournament success was winning the Bournemouth Singles in 1983. Indoors, he was a Welsh international from 1978-1987, and won the Welsh national Triples in 1983 and the Fours the following year.

Humphreys, Gareth *Born 15.11.35.* An outstanding Welsh bowler who won a Triples bronze medal at the world championships at Worthing in 1972, gained 15 national and 16 county titles, and played for Wales 90 times, 78 of those as a skip, Gareth Humphreys has since emerged as a notable administrator. He was President of the Barbarians in 1976, of the Welsh BA in 1979, of the Welsh IBA in 1990-91, and of the British Isles BC in 1987. A Welsh selector since 1981 and appointed team manager from 1988 to 1992, he was awarded the Gold Medal of Honour of the national Sports Council for Wales for outstanding service to Welsh sport.

A university graduate - BA (Hon) — he was head of a school geography department but has now retired.

Jack, Robert *Born 1934.* Bob Jack, honorary treasurer of the English Bowling Association since 1974, lives at Birkdale, Southport, one of the homes of British golf, and he has another sporting connection, for David Jack, the famous Arsenal and England footballer and playing partner of the immortal Alex James, was his uncle. Bob played in the Middlesex team of 1969 which won the Middleton Cup, but moved to Lancashire and has

been in their Middleton Cup team since 1970. His playing record also includes Lancashire county successes, Singles winner of the Northern Counties, and he was an international Trialist 1974/5/6. An honorary Life Member of the EBA (since 1982), of Lancashire CBA, and of Winchmore Hill (Middlesex), he has been a trustee of the EBA Charity Trust since its inception, is a director of EBA Publications Ltd, and is Chairman of the Finance Committee of the World Bowls championships to be held at Worthing in 1992.

John, Joan. A Welsh indoor international 1973-1974, Joan John of Radyr, Cardiff, is honorary secretary and a founder member of the British Isles Women's Indoor Bowls Council and joint honorary secretary and founder member of the World Indoor Bowls Council (Ladies section). Her husband Hugh John, is well known as a television sports commentator.

Johnson, David Wallis *Born 25.5.39.* Secretary of the English Bowling Association for the past four years, David Johnson had been active in the Midlands both as a player and administrator since the mid sixties. His experience as a Warwickshire county player — he was a member of their successful Middleton Cup team in 1970, a county champion, and regional coach for the Midlands for the English Bowls Coaching Scheme — coupled with his work as Warwickshire county secretary from 1980 to 1986, equipped him admirably for his present position, which he took up on January 1st 1987. He has supervised the establishment of the new EBA headquarters at Worthing. A former teacher, he pursued an educational career as a teaching adviser specialising in mathematics, becoming head of a department providing advisory services for teachers.

King, Hilary *Born 15.9.31.* Secretary of the Welsh Ladies Indoor Bowling Association, Hilary King played for the Glamorgan outdoor county team for ten years. She is Chairman of the Welsh Ladies Umpires Association, and past tournament secretary of Welsh Ladies IBC. Outside bowls, she does voluntary work as organiser of her local 'Children in Need' appeal, helps the NSPCC, and is a member of the Hospital League of Friends. She lives at Tynewydd, Treorchy, Mid Glamorgan.

Kivell, Roy Frederick George *Born 16.2.20.* Roy Kivell was an outdoor international from 1947 to 1970 (excluding 1957 and 1967), and also played for England indoors in 1977. He won a Pairs gold medal at the Canadian Centennial Games in 1967, and was a Saga Pairs winner in 1985, but his individual achievements did not match his distinguished international career. The nearest he came to a national title was Singles semi final in 1947, and Pairs semi finalist in 1947 and 1961. He has been an EBA Council member since 1952, an outdoor selector since 1983, and is a life member of Devon CBA. Most of his administrative service is indoors. Roy has been on the Executive and Selection committees, of the English Indoor BA since 1975, was President in 1985-86, and is a Life Member. Currently Junior Vice President of the British Isles Indoor Bowls Council, he is also a member of the World Indoor Bowls Council.

McGill, David. Scottish Singles champion in 1976, British Isles champion 1977, a charismatic performer at the early Kodak (later the Woolwich) Masters tournaments, and a Singles bronze medallist and Triples silver medallist at the 1980 world championships, David McGill seemed destined for a great playing future in outdoor competition in the 80s. This unfortunately did not materialise, though he subsequently played for Scotland's indoor team in 1985, 1986 and 1987. A chartered architect by profession, who lives in Edinburgh, he is secretary of the Scottish Indoor Bowls Players Association and is a BBC commentator in televised bowls programmes.

McKay, Richmond. Richmond McKay was secretary of the British Isles Bowling Council from 1981-1985 and resumed the position after the death of his successor in 1988. For five years he was treasurer of the Irish BA, and is not only a Past President and honorary member of that body, but also of the Northern Ireland Private Greens League. Though engaged heavily in Irish bowling administration, Richmond has also been an active player, being a member of Larne BC, and of the Belfast and Co. Antrim indoor clubs. He was an indoor international for four years.

Montgomery, Robert. The 1990-1991 President of the World Indoor Bowls Council, Dr. Bob Montgomery, has had a distinguished career both inside and outside bowls. He became successively, a Bachelor of Agriculture, a Master of Agriculture, a Doctor of Philosophy, and was in government service until his retirement in 1984, being head of the European Community Division of the Department of Agriculture for Northern Ireland. He has since been agricultural consultant on EEC agricultural marketing and processing projects.

He took up bowls after a sporting career in badminton, hockey and soccer, then in rugby where he played for Trinidad's rugby team, and in Nigeria where he took up squash. Back in Northern Ireland, he switched to bowls after a knee injury forced him out of other games, and after being a member of the Donaghadee and Knock clubs, became a founder member of the Northern Ireland Civil Service BC, of which he has twice been President, the second time in its 25th anniversary year. One of the founder members of the P.T. Watson IBC, Belfast, he has been its chairman since 1980. Offices held in Irish national associations over the years include President of the BIIBC in 1973. He represented Ireland in 18 international matches between 1964 and 1971, and was a beaten finalist in the Irish Indoor Singles in 1970. His son Alan played for the Irish international team in 1990.

Parker, Malinda (Linda). President of the Welsh Women's Bowling Association in 1980, Miss Parker has been its

secretary since that time. She has won her national Singles and Triples titles and is an experience outdoor international player, having gained her first cap in 1970. She has skipped Welsh teams to medals on the international scene, winning Fours gold at the Commonwealth Games in 1986, Fours bronze in New Zealand in 1988, and Triples bronze in Australia in 1985. She is also a qualified umpire and coach. Linda's indoor game is limited to short mat at Llandrindod Wells and Knighton, where she lives, for the nearest indoor stadium at Merthyr is 60 miles away.

Smith, Peter. *Born 20.2.25.* Secretary and treasurer of the Scottish Bowling Association since 1982, Peter Smith describes himself as an average bowler and is equally modest about his other close involvements with the game. He served on the committee of the world bowls championship at Aberdeen in 1984, and is a Scottish BA delegate to the British Isles Bowling Council and the International Bowling Board.

Sutton, Doreen Margaret and Sutton, Tom, MBE. Tom Sutton and his wife Doreen have been prominent in Irish bowls for many years. Secretary of the Irish WBA since 1985, Mrs Sutton was also its President in 1985. From 1967-1970 she was an indoor international lead for Ireland and her playing career has also included representation for the Northern Ireland Women's Private Greens Association, of which she has also been President.

Tom Sutton was awarded the MBE in 1987 for his services to bowls. He is a former outdoor and indoor international, treasurer of the British Isles Bowling Council since 1987, was Irish BA treasurer from 1976-1988, President of the Northern Ireland Private Greens League in 1969, President of the Irish BA in 1975 and President of the British Isles Bowling Council in 1980.

Telfer, Bernard *Born 13.9.22.* Secretary of the English Indoor Bowling Association since 1972, Bernard Telfer has steered the fortunes of the English Indoor Bowling Association after it broke away from the English Bowling Association in 1971, when operating as the Indoor Section. At that time there were only 41 indoor bowling clubs in England. Now the EIBA has 280 affiliated clubs and the number rises annually. A former secretary of London Parks Bowling Association, he served on the executive of that body from 1955-1971, becoming secretary, and was President in 1985. His voluntary work for the association won him the Wills 'Castella' award in 1965. He was made a Life Member of the British Isles Indoor Bowls Council in 1989. Outdoors, Bernard joined the Barking Borough club in 1948 and was awarded his Essex county badge in 1965. He has been a member of Barking IBC since its inception in 1965.

Thomas, John Ronald (Ron), J.P. *Born 29.10.28.* A former Welsh outdoor international, British Isles Fours winner who represented Wales in the first world championships in 1966, Ron Thomas also has a considerable indoor record playing for his county from 1955 to 1969 and from 1973-1977 and also winning the British Fours. He has held a number of Welsh national offices, was President of the World Indoor Bowls Council in the year 1989-1990 and has just become treasurer of that body. He was appointed a JP in 1980.

Thomas, Roy Hanbury William, JP *Born 30.5.1924.* President of the English Bowling Association 1991, Roy Thomas has been active in the game since joining Maidenhead Town Bowls club in 1965 . He was club President from 1969 to 1984 and Berkshire President in 1988. A Justice of the Peace for Berkshire in 1967, he was Mayor of the Borough of Maidenhead from 1966-1968 and bowled the first jack and wood when Desborough Indoor BC was opened in 1967. After wartime RAF service, he started a haulage and crane company which became the nucleus of four companies of which he remains chairman. He serves as a trustee of several charity trusts, as does his wife, who is also a keen bowler.

Thompson, Rita *Born 15.8.19.* Rita Thompson, an indoor international player from 1966 to 1970 was President of the Scottish Indoor Bowling Association in 1967 and has been its secretary since 1972. She also serves on the British Isles Women's Indoor Bowls Council and the World Indoor Bowls Council (Ladies Section). She has had successes as an outdoor player at her outdoor club Rutherglen, and at Ayr where she is also a member. In 1976 she won the Ayrshire championships and two years later gained an outdoor international cap.

Thompson, Sydney James, OBE *Born 28.8.12.* The doyen of Irish bowls, Syd Thompson has a record number of 79 outdoor and 51 indoor caps for his country. He has won the Irish Singles, Pairs and Fours outdoors, and the Irish indoor Pairs. He was Chairman of the British Isles Bowling Council in 1963, Irish BA President the following year, and British Isles Indoor Bowling Council President in 1986 and 1987. His activities outside bowls include the chairmanship of the Northern Ireland Engineering Training Board. From 1964 to 1973 he was a member of the Northern Ireland Training board for nine years, and was awarded the OBE for his services.

Thomson, Norman. A member of the Selwood, Frome club since 1959, in which he has served in all club offices, Norman Thomson has been active in bowls administration throughout his bowling life. He was Somerset county President in 1978 and 1981, and has been active as a national administrator. He is also a Life Member of the English Bowling Association, of which he was an eloquent President in 1986. He serves on the association's General Purpose, Finance and Competitions

committees, is the EBA executive delegate to the International Bowling Board, and is a trustee of the EBA Charity Trust. As vice chairman of the 1922 World Bowls Championships at Worthing, he has a vital role to play in the organisation of this event. Other positions he has held include the Presidency of the Barbarians in 1982, and he is a Life Member of the National Association of Visually Handicapped Bowlers.

Williams, Alan Harding *Born 24.8.25.* Honorary secretary of the Welsh Bowling Association since 1987, Alan has a long record of administrative service to Welsh Bowls at club, county, national and international level. He has held most offices in Bedwellty Park BC, Tredegar, and is a founder member of Merthyr IBC, and former secretary and President of Monmouth BA. Before becoming national secretary he was assistant secretary for two years and had been President in 1981. He has also played a prominent part in the Welsh Bowls Umpires Association. President of the British Isles Bowling Council in 1983, he has been an executive member of the International Bowling Board, and as the current Junior Vice President, will become its Senior Vice President later this year.

Webb, John *Born 7.11.12.* Secretary of the English Bowling Federation since

1977, John Webb has held numerous offices in bowls since 1951 and was Lincolnshire county President 26 years ago — around the time he was winning county team championships. He lives at Boston and was first recipient of the Award for Services to the Community instituted in 1980. Highly respected throughout the Federation, John says he is very proud of his lifelong and still active membership of the Salvation Army for whom he has been visiting licenced houses with 'The War Cry' for more than 50 years.

Wiseman, John *Born 25.10.31.* A double England international (outdoors from 1977-79, indoors 1974-1984), John Wiseman has been Chairman of the English Bowls Players Association since 1984, has been a member of the English Indoor Bowling Association Executive for the past six years and is the current Deputy Junior President. He has also been non playing captain and selector of the England indoor team and has been re-appointed for 1990, 1991, and 1992. A certificated advanced coach since 1985, John's playing record has also included twice winning the national indoor Triples and gaining bronze medal with Tom Armstrong in a World Pairs tournament in Newcastle, Australia in 1978. He lives in Somerset at Ilminster and is Chairman of the Donyatt Bowling Club.

Addresses

United Kingdom Organisations:

English Bowling Association Secretary: David W. Johnson, Lyndhurst Road, Worthing BN11 2AZ. Tel: 0903 820222.

English Indoor Bowling Association Secretary: Bernard Telfer, 290A Barking Road, London E6 3BA. Tel: 081-471 1237.

English Women's Bowling Association Secretary: Mrs. N Colling, 'Daracombe', The Clays, Market Lavington SN10 4AY. Tel: 0380 813774.

English Women's Indoor Bowling Association Secretary: Mrs. P Allison, 8 Oakfield Road, Carterton, Oxford OX8 3RB. Tel: 0993 841334.

Irish Bowling Association Secretary: Jim Barnes, 212 Sicily Park, Belfast BT10 0AQ.

Irish Bowling Association (Indoor Section) Secretary: W. Burrows, Flat 4, Glenburn Court, Glenburn Road, Dunmurray, N. Ireland. Tel: 0232 601025.

Irish Women's Bowling Association Secretary: Mrs. D. Sutton, Flat Two, 102 Downview Court, Downview Park West, Belfast.

Irish Women's Indoor Bowling Association Secretary: Mrs. Hazel Getty, 25 Knutsford Drive, Belfast, N. Ireland. Tel: Belfast 741678.

Scottish Bowling Association Secretary: Peter Smith, 50 Wellington Street, Glasgow G2 6EF. Tel: 041-221 8999.

Scottish Indoor Bowling Association Secretary: J. Barclay, 41 Montfode Court, Ardrossan, Ayrshire KA22 7NJ. Tel: 0294 68372.

Scottish Women's Bowling Association Secretary: Mrs. E. Allen, 55a Esplanade, Greenock PA16 7SD. Tel: 0475 24140.

Scottish Women's Indoor Bowling Association Secretary: Mrs. R. Thompson, 1, Underwood Road, Burnside, Rutherglen, Glasgow G73 3TE. Tel: 041-647 5810.

Welsh Bowling Association Secretary: Alan Williams, 48 Pochin Crescent, Tredegar, NP2 4JS. Tel: 049525 3836.

Welsh Indoor Bowling Association Secretary: Ray Hill, 1 Brynheulog Street, Port Talbot, W. Glam SA13 1AF. Tel: 0639 886409.

Welsh Women's Bowling Association Secretary: Miss Linda Parker, Ffrydd Cottage, 2 Ffrydd Road, Knighton, Powys. Tel: 0547 528331.

Welsh Women's Indoor Bowling Association Secretary: Mrs. Hilary King, Hillcrest Villa, Tynewydd, Treorchy, Rhondda, Mid Glam CS42 5LU. Tel: 0443 77168.

English Bowling Federation Secretary: John Webb, 62 Frampton Place, Boston PE21 8EL. Tel: 0205 66201.

English Women's Bowling Federation Secretary: Mrs. Ivy Younger, Irela, Holburn Crescent, Ryton, Tyne and Wear NE40 3DH. Tel: 091-413360.

British Crown Green Bowling Association Secretary: Ron Holt, 14 Leighton Avenue, Maghull, Liverpool L31 0AH. Tel: 051-5268367.

English Short Mat Bowling Association Secretary: Bob Weafer, 2 Preston Close, Church Hill, North Redditch, Worcestershire B98 8RU. Tel: 0527 60990.

British Bowling Council Secretary: A. Richmond, McKay, 43 Belfast Road, Ballynure, Ballyclare, Co Antrim BT39 9T2. Tel: 09603 52334.

British Isles Indoor Bowls Council Secretary: Martin Conlan, 8/2 Backdean, Ravelston Terrace, Edinburgh EH4 3EF. Tel: 031-343 3632.

British Isles Women's Bowling Council Secretary: Mrs. Nancie Colling, Darracombe, The Clays, Market Lavington, Wiltshire SN10 4AY. Tel: 0380 813774.

British Isles Women's Indoor Bowls Council Secretary: Mrs Joan Johns, 16 Windsor Crescent, Radyr, Cardiff CF4 8AE. Tel: 0222 842391.

English Bowls Player's Association President: David Bryant CBE. Secretary: David Crocker, 5 The Ridgeway, Edenbridge, Kent TN8 6AU. Tel: 0732 863894.

Scottish Bowls Player's Association President Bob Sutherland. Secretary: David McGill, 61 Ladysmith Road, Edinburgh EH9 1AF. Tel: 031-663 6418.

English Bowls Council Secretary: E. J. Crosbie, 15 Datchworth Court, Village Road, Enfield, Middlesex EN1 2DS.

English Bowling Association Charity Trust Chairman: M.D. Engel, 8 Hazelwood Road, Northampton NN1 1LP.

Francis Drake Fellowship (The Bowler's Charity) Hon Sec: A.W.B. Greenleaf, 23 Richmond Close, Kirk Road, Walthamstow E17 8PS. Tel: 01-521 229.

English Bowls Umpires' Association Secretary: Norman Deeprose, 24 Elm Green Close, Worcester WR5 3HD (0905) 350717.

Area Secretaries: Northern:N. D. Williams, 3 Trent Avenue, Thornaby on Tees, Cleveland TS17 8HS (0642) 672054. **Midlands:** J. E. Brooks, 21 Valley Prospect, Newark, Notts NG24 4QH (0636) 702730. **Eastern:** G. Henderson, 50 Manser Road, Rainham, Essex RM13 8NL (04027) 55613. **S. Eastern:** B. Ticehurst, 6 Shakespeare Road, Worthing, West Sussex BN11 4AN (0903) 202162. **S. Central:** R. F. Henery, 117 Marlborough Road, Swindon, Wilts SN3 1NJ (0793) 538666. **S. Western:** A. R. Quick, 10 Wearde Road, Saltash, Cornwall PL12 4NP (0752) 842420.

English Bowls Umpire's Federation (EBF) Secretary: C. A. Kemp, 5 Milton Street, Ipswich, Suffolk IP4 4PP (0473) 725259.

English Bowls Coaching Scheme Chairman: Harry C. De'ath, 40 Clive Avenue, Ipswich, Suffolk IP1 4LU (0473) 257407. National Director of Coaching: Gwyn John, 34 Ocean View Road, Bude, Cornwall EX23 8NN (0288) 352391. National Coaches for the Regions **Northern:** Derek Bell, 101 Station Road, Seaton Carew, Hartlepool, Cleveland TS25 1DX (0429) 67104. **Midland:** Vic Cooper, 534 Kettering Road North, Northampton NN3 1HN (0604) 493193. **Central:** Tony Hodgkinson, 4 Pensfield Park, Charlton Mead Est, Westbury, Bristol BS10 6LD (0272) 503261. **Eastern:** Arthur Meeson, 22 Pleasant Rise, Hatfield, Herts AL8 5DU (07072) 68081. **Southern:** Peter Line, Flat 2, Elm Court, 53 Westwood Road, Southampton SO2 1DX (0703) 553995. **S. Western:** Gwyn John, 34 Ocean View Road, Bude, Cornwall EX23 8NN (0288) 352391. **Crown Green:** Graham Preston, 27 Maple Close, Chasetown, Walsall, Staffs, WS7 8RP (05436) 71529. Video Operative: Kelvin Carr, 37 Bramley Rise, Strood, Kent ME2 3SU (0634) 718488. Video Producer: David Rhys Jones, 9 Victoria Road, Clevedon, Avon BS21 7RY (0272) 877280.

English Civil Service BA A.W. Heathcote, 36a Shefford Road, Meppershall, Shefford, Bedfordshire. Tel: 0462 813788. Hon Competitions Sec: Campbell McColl, 7 Blackberry Field, Prestbury, Cheltenham GL52 5LT. Tel: 0242 233189.

London Parks BA, Hon Sec: G. Humphries, 25 Bevens Road, St. Mary Cray, Kent BR5 4DB. Tel: 0689 31739.

Midland Counties BA, Hon Sec: P. J. Donoher, Eight Pines, Victor Avenue, Derby DE3 1AN. Tel: 0332 385727.

Midland Counties Indoor BA Hon Sec: J. Fulcher, 15 Hall Drive, Lincoln LN6 7SW. Tel: 0522 535208.

Home Counties BA D. J. Gascoyne, 12 Ellwood Gardens, Garston, Watford, Hertfordshire WD2 6DR. Tel: 0923 674752.

Home Counties Indoor BA Hon Sec: F. Haines, 59 Burch Road, Northfleet, Gravesend, Kent DA11 9NE. Tel: 0474 560906.

South Western Counties BA Hon Sec: Graham Briggs, 34 Melcombe Avenue, Weymouth, Dorset DT4 7TF. Tel: 0305 784873.

Northern Counties Consultative Committee (EBA) Hon Sec: Eric Johnston, 57 Millholme Avenue, Carlisle CA2 4DW. Tel: 0228 38049.

Eastern Counties BA Hon Sec: F. G. Pedder, 6 Greenacre Park, Clayhill Road, Kensworth LU6 3RE. Tel: 0582 872675.

Eastern Counties Indoor BA G. E. Copeland, 11 Highbury Road, Bury St Edmunds IP33 3QB. Tel: 0284 755383.

International Organisation — Outdoor International Bowling Board 1990-92 President: Jim Barnes (Ireland) 1992-94 President: Alan H. Williams (Wales) Secretary: David W. Johnson, Lyndhurst Road, Worthing, West Sussex BN11 2AZ (0903) 820222.

International Bowling Board
Full Member Countries

American Lawn BA Secretary: E Quo, 8710 Tern Avenue, Fountain Valley, California 92708 USA.

South African BA Secretary: R. B. Heath, PO Box 47177, Parklands, Johannesburg 2121, South Africa.

Australian Bowls Council Executive Officer: A. Hewett, Box Q293, Queen Victoria Rd, Sydney, NSW 2000, Australia.

Welsh BA Secretary: A. H. Williams, 48 Pochin Crescent, Tredegar, Gwent Wales NP2 4JS.

Canadian Lawn Bowling Council Executive Director: Ms Margot Clayton Jones, 1600 James Naismith Drive, Gloucester, Ontario, K1B 5N4 Canada.

Zimbabwe BA Secretary: I. Waldmeyer, PO Box 1336, Bulawayo, Zimbabwe.

English BA Secretary: D Johnson, Lyndhurst Road, Worthing, West Sussex, England BN11 2AZ.

Irish BA Secretary: J. Barnes, 212 Sicily Park, Belfast, Ireland BT10 0AQ.

New Zealand BA Executive Director: PO Box 17-215, Greenlane, Auckland 5, New Zealand.

Scottish BA Secretary: P. Smith, 50 Wellington Street, Glasgow, Scotland G2 6EF.

Associate Member Countries

Federacion Argentina de Bowls Secretary: E. Cataland, Virrey Del Pino 3456, 1426 Buenos Aires, Argentine.

Jersey BA Secretary: P. Mallet, The Flat, Church House, Church Street, St Helier, Jersey.

Botswana BA Secretary: T. Foster, PO Box 1704, Gabarone, Botswana, South Africa.

Kenya BA Secretary: D. Fowler, PO Box 43259, Nairobi, Kenya.

Fiji BA Secretary: W. Smith, PO Box 71, Pacific Harbour, Deuba, Fiji.

Papua New Guinea Secretary: D Bradney, PO Box 953, Lae, Papua New Guinea.

Guernsey BA Secretary: Simon Masterton, Meadow View, Mount Row, St Peter Port, Guernsey.

Bowling Association of Spain Secretary: J. Young, C/Colinas 44, Urbanisation Valtocado, Ctra De Coin, Mijas 29650, Malaga, Spain.

Hong Kong Lawn BA Secretary: J. S. Armitage, GPO Box 1823, Hong Kong.

Swaziland BA Secretary: Ms A. Hayter, PO Box 366, Malkerns, Swaziland.

Israel BA Secretary: PO Box 1069, Netanya, Israel.

Western Samoa BA Secretary, PO Box 9574, Apia, Western Samoa.

Japan Lawn Bowls Federation President: J. Ueyama, 12-2 1 Chrome Hinoguchi-Cho, Nishinomiya, Hyogo-Ken 663, Japan.

Zambia BA Secretary: I. T. R. Fleming, PO Box 11793, Chingola, Zambia.

Affiliate Member Countries

Cook Islands BA Secretary: G. Paniani, PO Box 669, Rarotonga, Cook Islands.

Bowling Federation of India Secretary: R. S. Bentani, Rasoi Limited, 20 R. N. Mukherjee Road, Calcutta 700 001, India.

Bowling Association of Malawi Secretary: D. M. Ross, PO Box 29, Blantyre, Malawi, Central Africa.

Norfolk Island Bowls Council Secretary: B. T. Wilson, PO Box 384, Norfolk Island, South Pacific.

Singapore Convenor: R. Pereira, Lawn Bowls Section, Connaught Drive, Singapore 0617.

Royal Bangkok Sports Club Secretary: P. G. Nystrom, Lawn Bowls Section, 1 Henri Dunant Street, Bangkok 10500, Thailand.

International Women's Bowling Board

President: Pat Weaver (New Zealand) Secretary: Gloria Oliver, 78 Riverbend Road, Napier, New Zealand (070) 436 819.

International Organisation — Indoor

World Indoor Bowls Council Secretary: Jimmy Davidson, 44 Stamford Road, Southbourne, Bournemouth, BH6 5DS (0202) 429755. Tournament Director: David Harrison, PO Box 2, Bakewell, Derby DE4 1TQ (0629) 87634.

Other Officers: President Dr. R. H. Montgomery (Ireland); SVP H. Le Tissier (Guernsey), JVP I. Birch (New Zealand); IPP J. R. Thomas (Wales); Hon. Treasurer W. Gough; Asst. Secretary J. Barclay.

Delegates: England: P. G. Brimble, R. F. G. Kivell, R. H.Secker. Ireland: W. Burrows, I. Cargill. Scotland: J. Barclay, H. Mullin, H. Phillips. Wales: R. Hill, R. J. Turner. Australia: A. Mewett.

World Indoor Bowls Council (Ladies' Section) Secretary: Joan Johns, 16 Windsor Crescent, Radyr, Cardiff CF4 8AE (0222) 842391.

Diary for 1991

Note: These dates were established at the time of going to press, and no responsibility can be accepted for any changes — Ed.

1990
Sat Nov 10-Sun Nov 11 British Isles Short Mat Championships (Sands Centre, Carlisle)
Sat Dec 29-Sun Dec 30 Mackeson Fylde Classic (Blackpool Fylde)

1991
Thur Jan 3 Round 3 Yetton Trophy (Englishwomen's Club Championship)
Sat Jan 5 Round 5 Haven/CU English Club Championship
Wed Jan 9-Fri Jan 11 Bushmills Whiskey Irish Masters final stages (Televised from Provincial Towns IBC, Ballymoney)
Sat Jan 12-Sun Jan 13 Scottish indoor national championship. Semi finals and final (Aberdeen)
Sat Jan 12 Liberty Trophy English County Championship
Sun Jan 13 England International Trial (Bentham)
Thur Jan 17 Zone semi finals Yetton Trophy (Englishwomen's Club Championship)
Sat Jan 19 Round 6 Haven/CU English Club Championship

Sun Jan 20 NatWest Wales v England Under-25 International (Torfaen)
Mon Jan 21 Semi finals CIS Welsh Singles and Under-25 Singles (Llanelli)
Tue Jan 22 Finals CIS Welsh Singles and Under-25 Singles (Llanelli)
Sat Jan 26 Quarter finals Liberty Trophy County Championship
Sat Jan 26 Semi finals CIS Welsh Pairs, Triples, Fours (Torfaen)
Sun Jan 27 Finals CIS Welsh Pairs, Triples, Fours (Torfaen)
Sat Feb 2 Quarter finals Haven/CU English Club Championship
Sat Feb 2 Scottish Women's National Championship finals.
Sat Feb 2-Sun Feb 3 South Wales Electricity Welsh Ladies Singles (Cardiff)
Sun Feb 3 Bushmills Whiskey Irish Inter-Club Championship (continued from 1990) Provincial Towns v Belfast
Sat Feb 9-Sun Feb 10 Bushmills Whiskey Irish Championships final stages (Provincial Towns, Ballymoney)

242

Sat Feb 9-Sun Feb 10
Guernsey v Scotland Test
Match (Guernsey)
Wed Feb 13-Sun Feb 24
Midland Bank World Indoor
Singles/Pairs Championships at
Preston Guild Hall
Wed Feb 13 South Wales
Electricity Welsh Ladies
Championships (Cardiff)
Sat Feb 16 Semi finals Liberty
Trophy County Championship
Sat Feb 16 Semi finals Scottish
Women's CIS League
Sat Feb 23 Senior Fours
Scottish League final (Perth,
12 noon)
Sat Mar 2-Sun Mar 3 Semi
finals and final Haven/CU
English Club Championship
(Lawson Park)
Sat Mar 2 Scottish Women's
CIS League finals (Falkirk,
2-6pm)
Sun Mar 3 Scottish Team
Championship quarter finals
Mon Mar 4-Mon Mar 11
Englishwomen's National
Championships (Lawson Park)
Sat Mar 9-Sun Mar 10 Finals
English National Under-25
Singles (Rugby Thornfield)
Sat Mar 9 Scottish League Cup
final (Aberdeen, 12 noon)
Sun Mar 10 Bushmills Whiskey
Irish Inter-Club Championship
Belfast v County Antrim
Mon Mar 18-22 British Isles
Championships and
Internationals (Aberdeen)

Mon Mar 18 Women's British
Isles Championships
(Prestwick)
Tue Mar 19 Women's British
Isles Internationals (Prestwick)
England v Ireland Wales v
Scotland
Wed Mar 20 Women's British
Isles Internationals (Prestwick)
Scotland v England Wales v
Ireland
Thur Mar 21 Women's British
Isles Internationals (Prestwick)
Scotland v Ireland England v
Wales
Sun Mar 24-Mon Mar 25 Final
stages English Champion of
Champions (Wellingborough)
Sun Mar 24 Scottish team
championship semi finals
Fri Mar 29-Sun Mar 31 Final
stages Mackeson Mixed Pairs
(Scarborough)
Sat Mar 30-Sun Mar 31
Dundee Masters
Sat Apr 6-Sat Apr 13 Finals
English Indoor Championships
including Under-25 Mixed
Double Rinks final (Melton)
Mowbray)
Sat Apr 6-Sun Apr 7 Carling
Black Label Mixed Pairs
(Llanelli)
Sat Apr 6-Sun Apr 7 Welsh
Ladies Challenge Trophy
(Cardiff)
Sunday Apr 14 Final Liberty
Trophy English County
Championship (Melton
Mowbray)

Sun Apr 14 Welsh Ladies Champion of Champions finals (Merthyr)

Friday Apr 19-Sun Apr 21 Final stages Mackeson Mixed Fours (Mote Park, Maidstone)

Sat Apr 13 Scottish Team Championship final (Paisley, 12 noon)

Sat Apr 30 Scottish KO Cup final (Aberdeen, 12 noon)

Sat May 4 NatWest Welsh Club Championship. Section games

Sun May 19 Welsh International Trials

Sun May 26 Welsh County Championship games

Sun Jun 2 English International Trial (Nottingham)

Sun Jun 2 Welsh International Squad Trials

Sat Jun 5 NatWest (English) Middleton Cup County Championship matches

Sat Jun 15 NatWest (English) Middleton Cup matches

Sat Jun 22 NatWest (English) Middleton Cup matches

Sat Jun 22 NatWest Welsh club championships — preliminary round.

Sun Jun 23 Welsh county championship matches

Sat Jun 29 NatWest (English) Middleton Cup matches

Sat Jun 29 NatWest Welsh Club Championship — open draw — Round 1

Mon Jul 1-Tue Jul 2 NatWest British Isles Championships (Wales)

Wed Jul 3-Fri Jul 5 NatWest British Isles International Series (Wales)

Sat Jul 6 NatWest (English) Middleton Cup matches

Sat Jul 20 NatWest Welsh Club Championship quarter finals

Sun Jul 21 Welsh County Championship games

Sat Jul 27 NatWest (English) Middleton Cup quarter finals

Mon Jul 29 Johns Trophy (Englishwomen's County Championship) semi finals and final (Leamington Spa)

Tue Jul 30 Double Rink (Englishwomen's County Championship) semi finals and final (Leamington Spa)

Wed Jul 31-Sat Aug 10 Liverpool Victoria Insurance Englishwomen's National Championships (Leamington Spa)

Sun Aug 4 Junior International Wales v England

Sat Aug 10-Sun Aug 11 Welsh National Under-18 final

Sun Aug 11-Fri Aug 23 Woolwich EBA National Championships (Worthing)

Tue Aug 13-Wed Aug 14 Welsh National Mixed Pairs finals

Sat Aug 17 NatWest Welsh Club Championship semi finals and final.

Sun Aug 18 Welsh County Championship final.
Wed Aug 21-Fri Aug 23 Welsh National Championships
Sat Aug 24 NatWest (English) Middleton Cup County Championship semi finals and final (Worthing)
Sat Aug 31-Sun Sept 1 EBA Champion of Champions finals (venue to be arranged)
Tue Sep 10-Thu Sep 12 Bembridge Bowls & Country Club National 55s & Over finals (Isle of Wight)

Sat Sep 14-Sun Sep 15 NatWest National Club Two Fours (Oxford)

Sun Sep 15 NatWest 18 & Under Singles finals (Oxford)

Tue Sep 17-Wed Sep 18 Liverpool Victoria National Mixed Fours (in aid of Cancer Research Campaign)

Sat Sep 21-Sun Sep 22 McCarthy & Stone National Mixed Pairs finals (venue to be arranged)

World Championships

Men's World Championships

The first outdoor world championships known as 'World Bowls', were launched in 1966 in Australia after the 1966 Commonwealth Games in Jamaica when bowls was not played owing to lack of facilities there. Every four years teams of five have since played under the rules of the International Bowling Board in Singles, Pairs, Triples and Fours, with the W M Leonard Trophy awarded to the teams with the best all round performance.

First World Championships at Kyeemagh BC near Sydney, Australia from October 10th — 23rd, 1966.

Winners: Singles: Gold — D J Bryant (England), Silver — J Henshaw (Scotland), Bronze — R Fulton (Ireland). Pairs: Gold — A Palm, G Kelly (Australia), Silver — J Harvey, N S Walker (South Africa), Bronze — C Smith, D J Bryant (England). Triples: Gold — D Collins, A Johnston, J M Dobbie (Australia), Silver — A Houston, K D Beacom, J Henderson (Canada), Bronze — K Lightfoot, J Prest, L Kessel (South Africa). Fours: Gold — N Lash, R Buchan, G Jolly, W P O'Brien (New Zealand), Silver — W Collins, A Palm, A Johnston, J M Dobbie (Australia), Bronze — W Adrain, W Dyett, R Thompson, H Reston (Scotland). W M Leonard Trophy: Gold — G Kelly, D Collins, A Palm, A Johnston, J M Dobbie, Manager W J Spear (Australia).

Second World Championships at Beach House Park, Worthing from June 5th — 17th, 1972.

Winners: Singles: Gold — M Evans (Wales), Silver — R Bernard (Scotland), Bronze — J Harvey (South Africa). Pairs: Gold — C C Delgado and E J Liddell (Hong Kong), Silver — J F Candelet and R W Folkins (USA), Bronze — J A Harvey and B G Ellwood (South Africa).

Triples: Gold — W M Miller, C Forrester, R Folkins (USA), Silver — E L Davey, J A Marsh, D G Watson (South Africa), Bronze — J R Evans, H Andrews, G Humphreys (Wales). Fours: Gold — N King, C Stroud, E H Hayward, P Line (England), Silver — A R Logan, A McIntosh, J McAttee, H Reston (Scotland), Bronze — C C Delgado, A R Kitchell, R E da Silva, G A Souza (Hong Kong). W M Leonard Trophy: Gold — R Bernard, A R Logan, A McIntosh, J McAttee, H Reston, Manager T Moffatt (Scotland).

Third World Championships at Zoo Lake, Johannesburg, South Africa, from February 18th, 1976.

Winners: Singles: Gold — D Watson (South Africa), Silver — R J Middleton (Australia), Bronze — D J Bryant (England).

Pairs: Gold — W Moseley, D Watson (South Africa), Silver — N McInnes, R W Folkins (USA), Bronze — D A Woolnough, R J Middleton (Australia). Triples: Gold — K Campbell, N Gatti, K Lightfoot (South Africa), Silver — D J Bryant, W C Irish, T W Armstrong (England), Bronze — W Murray, D Hull, J Higgins (Ireland). Fours: Gold — K Campbell, W Moseley, N Gratti, K Lightfoot (South Africa), Silver — D A Woolnough, L Bishop, R Salter, K Poole (Australia), Bronze — J C Evans, W C Irish, T Armstrong, P Line (England). W M Leonard Trophy: Gold — D Watson, K Campbell, W Moseley, N Gatti, K Lightfoot. Manager Leon Kessel (South Africa).

Fourth World Championships at Frankston, Australia from January 16th — February 2nd, 1980.

Winners: Singles: Gold — D J Bryant (England), Silver — J Snell (Australia), Bronze — D McGill (Scotland). Pairs: Gold — A Sandercock, P Rheuben (Australia), Silver

— B Gill, G Jarvis (Canada), Bronze — P Skoglund, K Darling (New Zealand). Triples: Gold — J Hobday, A Allcock, D J Bryant (England), Silver — J Summers, D McGill, W McQueen (Scotland), Bronze — J Malcolm, N Unkovitch, M Moffatt (New Zealand). Fours: Gold — P Chok, G Souza Jnr, E Liddell, O K Dallah (Hong Kong), Silver — J Summers, W Wood, W McQueen, A McIntosh (Scotland), Bronze — J Malcolm, K Darling, M Moffatt, P Skoglund (New Zealand). W M Leonard Trophy: Gold — D J Bryant, J Bell, M Hughes, A Allcock, J Hobday. Manager Bob Stenhouse (England).

Fifth World Championships at Westburn Park, Aberdeen from July 6th 1984.
Winners: Singles: Gold — Peter Belliss (New Zealand), Silver — Willie Wood (Scotland), Bronze — David Bryant (England). Pairs: Gold — Skip Arculli, Jim Candalet (George Adrain Scotland, sub) (USA), Silver — David Bryant, Tony Allcock (England), Bronze — Kenny Williams, Bob Middleton (Australia). Triples: Gold — S Espie, S Allen, J Baker (Ireland), Silver — B Rattray, D Lambert, J Boyle (Scotland), Bronze — R Brassey, J Scott, M Moffatt (New Zealand). Fours: Gold — G Turley, J Haines, J Bell, T Allcock (England), Silver — R Brassey, J Scott, M Moffatt, P Skoglund (New Zealand), Bronze — B Rattray, D Lambert, J Boyle, D Gourlay (Scotland). W M Leonard Trophy: Gold — J Bogle, B Rattray, D Lambert, J Boyle, D Gourlay, W Wood. Manager. Bob Young.

Sixth World Championships at Henderson, Auckland from January 30th — February 4th, 1988.
Winners: Singles: Gold — David Bryant (England), Silver — Willie Wood (Scotland), Bronze — Garin Beare (Zimbabwe). Pairs: Gold — Rowan Brassey, Peter Belliss (New Zealand), Silver — David Bryant, Tony Allcock (England), Bronze — Robert Weale, Will Thomas (Wales). Triples: Gold — Ian Dickison, Morgan Moffatt, Phil Skoglund (New Zealand), Silver — Willie Paul, Willie Wood, Alex McIntosh (Scotland), Bronze — John Ottaway, Wynne Richards, John Bell (England). Fours: Gold — Rodney McCutcheon, John McLoughlin, Sammy Allen, Jim Baker (Ireland), Silver — Rowan Brassey, Ian Dickison, Graham Moffatt, Phil Skoglund (New Zealand), Bronze — John Ottaway, Wynne Richards, John Bell, Tony Allcock. W M Leonard Trophy: David Bryant, Tony Allcock, John Bell, John Ottaway, Wynne Richards. Manager Mal Hughes (England).

Women's World Championships

The first Women's World Championships took place at the Elizabethan Women's BC, Sydney, Australia, and have been held since at four yearly intervals in New Zealand, England, Canada and Australia.

First Women's World Championships at Elizabethan Women's BC., Sydney, Australia, December 1969.
Winners: Singles: G Doyle (Papa New Guinea), Pairs: E Macdonald, M Cridlan (South Africa), Triples: S Sundelowitz, Y Emanuel, C Bidwell (South Africa), Fours: S Sundelowitz, Y Emanuel, C Bidwell, M Cridlan (South Africa).

Second Women's World Championships at Victoria BC Wellington, New Zealand, December 3rd-10th 1973.
Winners: Singles: E Wilkie (New Zealand), Pairs: L Lucas, D Jenkinson (Australia), Triples: New Zealand, Fours: New Zealand.

Third Women's World Championships at Beach House Park, Worthing, England, May 20th-June 4th 1977.
Winners: E Wilkie (New Zealand), Pairs: H Wong, E Chok (Hong Kong), Triples: J Osborne, M Pomeroy, E Morgan (Wales), Fours: L Lucas, C Hicks, M Richardson, D Jenkinson (Australia).

Fourth Women's World Championships at Willowdale Lawn BC, North York, Toronto, Canada, August 1st-5th, 1981.

Winners: Singles: N Shaw (England), Pairs: E Bell, N Allely (Ireland), Triples: L King, R O'Donnell, L Sadick (Hong Kong), Fours: E Fletcher, B Stubbings, G Thomas, M Steele (England).

Fifth Women's World Championships at Reservoir BC Melbourne, Australia, February 13th — March 2nd 1985.

Winners: Singles: Gold — Merle Richardson (Australia), Silver — Maraia Lum On (Fiji), Bronze — Rhoda Ryan (New Zealand), Pairs: Gold — Fay Craig, Merel Richardson (Australia), Silver — Marai Lum On, Willow Fong (Fiji), Bronze — Norma Shaw, Jean Valls (England), Triples: Gold — Dorothy Roche, Norma Massey, Mavis Meadowcroft (Australia), Silver — Sandi Zakoske, Rae O'Donnell, Helen Wong (Hong Kong), Bronze — Rita Jones, Mair Jones, Linda Barker (Wales), Fours: Gold — Sarah Gourlay, Elizabeth Christie, Annette Francenhyte (Scotland), Silver — Dorothy Roche, Fay Craig, Norma Massey, Mavis Meadowcroft (Australia), Bronze — Jean Valls, Brenda Atherton, Betty Stubbings, Mavis Steele (England). Team prize: Jean McKinnon, Fay Craig, Norma Massey, Mavis Meadowcroft, Merle Richardson, Manager D Roche (Australia).

Sixth Women's World Championships at Henderson, Auckland, New Zealand, November 20th — December 2nd, 1988.

Winners: Singles: Gold — Janet Ackland (Wales), Silver — Margaret Johnston (Ireland), Bronze — Millie Khan (New Zealand), Pairs: Gold — Phil Nolan, Margaret Johnston (Ireland), Silver — Heather Roberts, June Fulton, Bronze — Wendy Line, Mary Price (England), Triples: Gold — Marion Stevens, Greta Fahey, Dorothy Roche, Silver — Norma Shaw, Jayne Roylance, Barbara Fuller (England), Bronze — Naty Rozario, Rae O'Donnell, Sandra Zakoske (Hong Kong), Fours: Gold — Marion Stevens, Norma Wainwright, Greta Fahey, Dorothy Roche (Australia), Silver — Norma Shaw, Jayne Roylance, Mary Price, Barbara Fuller (England), Bronze — Pam Griffiths, Mary Hughes, Linda Parker, Margaret Pomeroy (Wales), Sydney Daily Mirror Team Trophy — Wendy Line, Norma Shaw, Mary Price, Jayne Roylance, Barbara Fuller.

Embassy World Indoor Championship

The competition, played at Coatbridge IBC, Scotland from 1979 to 1987 was switched to London's Alexandra Palace in January 1988, and then transferred to Preston Guild Hall in 1989 where it and the World Indoor Pairs have been played since.

Winners: 1979 David Bryant (England), 1980 David Bryant (England), 1981 David Bryant (England), 1982 John Watson (Scotland), 1983 Bob Sutherland (Scotland), 1984 Jim Baker (Ireland), 1985 Terry Sullivan (Wales), 1986 Tony Allcock (England), 1987 Tony Allcock (England), 1988 Hugh Duff (Scotland), 1989 Richard Corsie (Scotland), 1990 John Price (Wales).

World Pairs Indoor Championship

This was played at the Bournemouth International Centre in 1986 and 1987, and at Preston Guild Hall in 1989 and 1990.

Winners: 1986 David Bryant and Tony Allcock (England), 1987 David Bryant and Tony Allcock (England), 1988 Jim Yates and Ian Schuback (Australia) (Played in December 1987), 1989 David Bryant and Tony Allcock (England), 1990 David Bryant and Tony Allcock (England).

International records

Commonwealth Games

The first Empire Games were held in 1911 but the British Empire & Commonwealth Games did not really begin until 1930 when bowls for men was included for Singles, Pairs and Fours. Women's matches were introduced for the first time at Brisbane in 1982 when Triples were played and in 1986 competitions were further extended.

Gold Singles: 1930 Robert G Colquhoun (England), 1934 Robert Sprot (Scotland), 1938 Horace Harvey (South Africa), 1950 James R Pirret (New Zealand), 1954 Ralph F Hodges (S Rhodesia), 1958 Phineas (Pinkie) Danilowitz (South Africa), 1962 David Bryant (England), 1970 David Bryant (England), 1974 David Bryant (England), 1978 David Bryant (England), 1982 Gold — William Wood (Scotland), Silver — Robert Parrella (Australia), Bronze — Peter Belliss (New Zealand), 1986 Gold — Ian Dickinson (New Zealand), Silver — Ian Schuback (Australia), Bronze — Richard Corsie. 1990 Gold — Robert Parrella (Australia), Silver — Mark McMahon (Hong Kong), Bronze — Richard Corsie (Scotland).

Gold Pairs: 1930 T C Hills & G W A Wright (England), 1934 T C Hills & G W A Wright (England), 1938 L L Macey & W Denison (New Zealand), 1950 Robert Henry & Evan P Exelby (New Zealand), 1954 William J Rosbotham & Percy T Watson (Northern Ireland), 1958 John M Morris & Richard E Pilkington (New Zealand), 1962 Robert L McConald & Hugh H J Robson (New Zealand), 1970 Norman King & Peter Line (England), 1974 John Christie & Alex McIntosh (Scotland), 1978 Clementi Cecil Delgada & Eric John Liddell (Hong Kong), 1982 Gold — John Watson, David Gourlay (Scotland), Silver — Lyn Perkins, Spencer Wilshire (Wales), Bronze — Denis Dalton, Peter Rheuben (Australia), 1986 Gold — Grant Knoll, Grant Adran (Scotland), Silver — Ron Jones & Bill Brettger (Canada), Bronze — Chris & David Ward (England). 1990 Gold — Ian Schuback, Trevor Morris (Australia), Silver — George Boxwell, Alfred Wallace (Canada), Bronze — Robert Weale, Will Thomas (Wales).

Fours: 1930 E F Gudgeon, J Edney, P Hough, J Frich (England), 1934 R Slater, P D Thomlinson, E F Gudgeon, F Biggin (England), 1938 W Bremner, W Whittaker, H A Robertson, E Jury (New Zealand), 1950 H Atkinson, H Currer, A Blumberg, N S Walker (South Africa), 1954 George L Wilson, John W H Anderson, Frank N Mitchell, Wilfred A Randall (South Africa), 1958 John H Bettles, Norman King, Walter Phillips, George Scadgell (England), 1962 George Fleming, David Bryant, John Watson, Sidney Drysdale (England), 1970 Clement Delgado, Abdul Kitchell, Roberto E da Silva, George A Souza (Hong Kong), 1974 Kerry Clark, Dave Baldwin, John Somerville, Gordon Jolly (New Zealand), 1978 Kin Fun P Chok, Majid Hassan Jrn, Robert O E Desilva, Omar Kachong Dallah (Hong Kong), 1982 Gold — Robert Dobbins, Bert Sharp, Don Sherman, Keith Poole (Australia), Silver — Rowan Brassey, Danny O'Connor, Jim Scott, Morgan Moffat (New Zealand), Bronze — Sammy Allen, John McCloughlin, Frank Campbell, Willie Watson (Ireland), 1986 Gold — Robert Weale, Will Thomas, Haford Thomas, Jim Morgan (Wales), Silver — Dan Milligan, Dave Brown, Dan Howeby, Dave Duncall (Canada), Bronze — Bill Montgomery, Roy McCure, Ernie Parkinson, Willie Watson (Ireland). 1990 Gold — Denis Love, Ian Bruce, George Adrain, Willie Wood (Scotland), Silver — Rodney McCutcheon, John McCloughlin, Sammy Allen, Jim Baker (Ireland), Bronze — Stewart McConnell, Kevin Darling, Peter Shaw, Phil Skoglund (New Zealand).

Womens Events: Triples: 1982 Gold — Florence Kennedy, Anna Bates, Margaret Mills

(Zimbabwe), Silver — Pearl Dymond, Joyce Osborne, Jennifer Simpson (New Zealand), Bronze — Mavis Steele, Betty Stubbings, Norma Shaw (England).
1986 Singles: Gold — Wendy Line (England), Silver — Senga McCrone (Scotland), Bronze — Bab Anderson (Botswana). Pairs: Freda Elliott, Margaret Johnston (Ireland), Silver — Jenny Nicholle, Maria Smith (Guernsey), Bronze — Jean Valls, Betty Stubbings (England). Fours: Gold — Wales (Linda Evans, Joan Ricketts, Rita Jones, Linda Parker). Silver — Clarice Power, Betty Schenke, Audrey Hefford, Pat Smith (Australia), Bronze — Brenda Atherton, Madge Allan, Mary Price, Barbara Fuller).
1990 Singles: Gold — Gaua Tau (Papua New Guinea), Silver — Millie Khan (New Zealand), Bronze — Margaret Johston (Ireland). Pairs: Gold — Judy Howat, Marie Watson (New Zealand), Silver — Edda Bonutto, Maureen Hobbs (Australia), Bronze — Sarah Gourlay, Frances Whyte (Scotland). Fours: Gold — Dorothy Roche, Audrey Rutherford, Daphne Shaw, Marion Stevens (Australia). Silver — Marlene Castle, Adrienne Lambert, Lynette McLean, Rhoda Ryan (New Zealand). Bronze — Sau Ling Chau, Yee Lai Lee, Natividad Rozario, Jenny Wallis (Hong Kong).

British Isles Outdoor Internationals

The British Isles International Series has been played from 1903-1914 and resumed in 1919. Scotland has won the championships 35 times, England 23, Wales 13 and Ireland 3. The winners and venues are as follows:

1903 England (London), 1904 Scotland (Glasgow), 1905 Ireland (Cardiff), 1906 England (Belfast), 1907 Scotland (Newcastle), 1908 Scotland (Edinburgh), 1909 Scotland (Cardiff), 1910 Scotland (Belfast), 1911 England (London), 1912 Scotland (Glasgow), 1913 Scotland (Cardiff), 1914 Scotland (Belfast), 1919 Scotland (Carlisle), 1920 Wales (Glasgow), 1921 Scotland (Cardiff), 1922 Scotland (Larne), 1923 Scotland (London), 1924 England (Glasgow), 1925 Wales (Llandrindod Wells), 1926 England (Belfast), 1927 England (Southampton), 1928 Scotland (Glasgow), 1929 England (Llandrindod Wells), 1930 Wales (Dublin), 1931 Wales (Westcliff on Sea), 1932 Scotland (Glasgow), 1933 Wales (Cardiff), 1934 Wales (Belfast), 1935 Scotland (Weston-super-Mare), 1936 Scotland (Glasgow), 1937 Wales (Llandrindod Wells), 1938 Wales (Larne), 1939 England (London), 1946 Wales (Glasgow), 1947 England (Newport), 1948 Wales (Bangor), 1949 England (Brighton), 1950 Scotland (Glasgow), 1951 Ireland (Swansea), 1952 Scotland (Dublin), 1953 Scotland (Brighton), 1954 England (Glasgow), 1955 England (Cardiff), 1956 England (Belfast), 1957 Wales (Bournemouth), 1958 England (Glasgow), 1959 England (Cardiff), 1960 England (Belfast), 1961 England (Eastbourne), 1962 England (Glasgow), 1963 Scotland (Cardiff), 1964 England (Belfast), 1965 Scotland (London), 1966 Scotland (Glasgow), 1967 Scotland (Llandarcy), 1968 Scotland (Belfast), 1969 Scotland (London), 1970 Scotland (Glasgow), 1971 Scotland (Aberdare), 1972 Scotland (Bristol), 1973 Scotland (Bournemouth), 1974 Scotland (Edinburgh), 1975 Scotland (Llanelli), 1976 (not played), 1977 Scotland (Worthing), 1978 Wales (Uddingston), 1979 Scotland (Gwent), 1980 Scotland (Nottingham), 1981 Ireland (Worthing), 1982 Wales (Ayr), 1983 England (Cardiff), 1984 England (Larne), 1985 England (Worthing), 1986 England (Paisley), 1987 England (Llanelli), 1988 England (Carne), 1989 England (Worthing), 1990 England (Methilhill).

British Isles Outdoor Championships

The British Isles Championships, currently sponsored by the National Westminster Bank, are held each year in conjunction with the British Isles International Series and are played by the reigning champions from the previous year in Singles, Pairs, Triples and Fours from the four home countries.

The Singles, Pairs and Fours have been played since 1959 and the 1971. Note: The dates given below refer to championships played a year after national titles were won — eg Ottaway listed here as 1989 winner actually won the title in 1990.

Singles: 1959 K Coulson (England), 1960 D J Bryant (England), 1961 E M Johnson (Scotland), 1962 C Mercer (England), 1963 W S Tate (Ireland), 1964 W Gibbs (Scotland), 1965 J Hershaw (Scotland), 1966 L Stanfield (Wales), 1967 R Fulton (Ireland), 1968 J Lamont (Scotland), 1969 R Montroni (Scotland), 1970 P Wright (Wales), 1971, 1972, 1973 D J Bryant MBE (England), 1974 W C Irish (England), 1975 J McLagan (Scotland), 1976 D McGill Jnr (Scotland), 1977 J Russell Evans (Wales), 1978 C Burch (England), 1979 S Allen (Ireland), 1980 D S Corkill (Ireland), 1981 F Muirhead (Scotland), 1982 C C Ward (England), 1983 J N Bell (England), 1984 W Richards (England), 1985 W McLaughlin (Scotland), 1986 A Blair (Scotland), 1987 G Robertson (Scotland), 1988 R Bray (England), 1989 J Ottaway (England).

Pairs: 1959 England, 1960 England, 1961 Scotland, 1962 England, 1963 Scotland, 1964 Ireland, 1965 England, 1966 Ireland, 1967 Ireland, 1968 Scotland, 1969 Scotland, 1970 Wales, 1971 England, 1972 Scotland, 1973 England, 1974 England, 1975 Wales, 1976 Wales, 1977 Ireland, 1978 Wales, 1979 Ireland, 1980 Wales, 1981 Wales, 1982 Wales, 1984 Ireland, 1985 England, 1986 Scotland, 1987 England, 1988 Ireland, 1989 Wales.

Triples: 1971 England, 1971 England, 1973 Scotland, 1974 Scotland, 1975 Ireland, 1976 Scotland, 1977 Ireland, 1978 England, 1979 Ireland, 1980 England, 1981 Ireland, 1982 Wales, 1983 England, 1984 England, 1985 England, 1986 Ireland, 1987 Ireland, 1988 Ireland, 1989 Ireland.

Fours: 1959 Scotland, 1960 Wales, 1961 England, 1962 Ireland, 1963 Wales, 1964 Ireland, 1965 Wales, 1966 Scotland, 1967 Ireland, 1968 Ireland, 1969 England, 1970 Ireland, 1971 England, 1972 Wales, 1973 Ireland, 1974 Ireland, 1975 Scotland, 1976 England, 1977 Ireland, 1978 Scotland, 1979 Scotland, 1980 Wales, 1981 Ireland, 1982 Ireland, 1983 England, 1984 England, 1985 England, 1986 Scotland, 1987 Ireland, 1988 England, 1989 England.

British Isles Indoor Internationals

The indoor internationals were played from 1936-1939 and resumed again in 1949. England have been the winners on 23 occasions, Scotland 17, Wales 3. The series has never been won by Ireland. The winners and venues are as follows:

1936 England (Paddington), 1937 Scotland (Glasgow), 1938 Scotland (Bournemouth), 1939 Scotland (Croydon), 1949 England (Paddington), 1950 Scotland (Paddington), 1951 Scotland (Ayr), 1952 England (Croydon), 1953 England (Boston), 1954 Scotland (Ayr), 1955 England (Croydon), 1956 England (Croydon), 1957 England (Perth), 1958 England (Crystal Palace), 1959 England (Boston), 1960 England (Perth), 1961 Scotland (Crystal Palace), 1962 England (Cardiff), 1963 England (Dundee), 1964 Wales (Crystal Palace), 1965 Wales (Cardiff), 1966 England (Glasgow), 1967 England (Belfast), 1968 Scotland (Desborough), 1969 England (Cardiff), 1970 England (Belfast), 1971 Scotland (Aberdeen), 1972 Scotland (Teeside), 1973 Scotland (Cardiff), 1974 Scotland (Prestwick), 1975 Scotland (Rutherglen), 1976 England (Rugby), 1977 Scotland (Cardiff), 1978 Scotland (Teeside), 1979 Scotland (Aberdeen), 1980 England (Hartlepool), 1981 Wales (Cardiff), 1982 Scotland (Teeside), 1983 England (Ardrossan), 1984 England (Folkestone), 1985 England (Swansea), 1986 England (Swansea), 1987 England (Aberdeen), 1988 Scotland (Hartlepool), 1989 England (Swansea), 1990 England (Prestwick).

Short Mat

The short mat game of bowls continues to flourish throughout the British Isles, offering at a modest price an agreeable form of recreation to people of all ages.

Played increasingly in England, the game takes place on a roll up carpet 45ft long and six feet wide. Carpets are laid down and rolled up after use in places like church halls, sports centres, works canteens and similar premises with an adequate area.

Normal size bowls are used and in most respects the principles, practices and rules of the flat green game are followed.

There are variations stemming from circumstances. A fender is placed at each end to stop bowls running off rink, and out-and-out driving is impossible since a block 15 inches high, three inches wide and three feet long is placed in the centre of the rink. Markings of white tape a foot from each end of the mat indicate the 'ditch' area and others show where the mat and jack are to go and the deadline area of play. In Pairs and Triples play only two woods are used by each player, and as in the flat green Federation code, a player can change positions. Matches usually last an hour.

Various forms of the short mat game are played in the United Kingdom. One type, known as short green (size 60ft by 9ft) took root in Ireland and then in Scotland. Carpet bowls is played in the North East of England, East Anglia and elsewhere. This entails the use of smaller bowls than those of normal size with the use of a 30ft by 6ft carpet and there is also a half mat game (size of carpet 22ft x 6ft).

Laws governing short mat bowling in England were drawn up in 1984 by the English Short Mat Bowling Association which has members all over the country. "We are genuinely nationwide", says the association's secretary Bob Weafer, himself a formidable player, who has succeeded Harry Lockett. "Our chairman is from Cambridgeshire and other committee members come from Somerset, Essex, the West Midlands and Greater Manchester. The largest league in the country is run by the West Midlands Short Mat BA and has 1300 members who play in 90 teams." Mr Weafer's address is 2 Preston Close, Church Hill North, Redditch. Worcester B98 8RU Tel. 0527-60990. There is an associated umpires' body whose secretary Mr Roger Gardiner lives at 44 Stoneyhurst Drive, Curry Rivel, Langport, Somerset TA10 OJH.

The number of people engaged in short mat bowls is difficult to assess, for the game appears to be played somewhere in almost every town and village in the land. In England a number of open tournaments are held each year by the ESMBA and tournaments featuring organised short mat bowls are held at the centres of firms like Warner Holidays, Pontins and Butlins. The game is also spreading elsewhere — on oil rigs off the coast of Scotland, in Japan, France, Spain, Belgium, the Middle East, Australia and parts of Asia and Africa. An important departure in the structure of the game has been in the organisation of British Isles championships. Ireland, where there are 1200 clubs, and England have embraced the short mat game much more readily than the short green version, which has flourished in Wales and Scotland.

In November 1989 the fourth and last British Isles International Championships for mixed indoor short and mat and short green games was held at the Rhondda Leisure Centre. Wales took the team title and Pairs, Scotland won the Singles, and the English trio of Gary Brown and John and David Clayton were winners of the Triples. England's Fours team of Jason Cornes, Trevor Whittaker, John Clarke and Shane Nisbet were runners up to Ireland in the Fours, losing rather unluckily on an extra end — the only time they were behind in the entire game.

In November 1990 all four countries were competing in the first British Isles Short Mat championships — all playing short mat — on Wygreen carpets, at the Sands Centre, Carlisle. During the championships the British Isles Short Mat Council was being formed.

The England team selected for these championships was: Singles: Gary Brown (West Midlands); Pairs: Steve McAlister, Jason Lockett (Cheshire); Triples: Malcolm Follis, John Clayton, David Clayton (West Midlands); Rinks: Gaynor Buchanan, Craig Beechall, Harry Lockett, Carol Beechall (Cheshire).

Team rinks: John Desborough (Cambs), Shane Nisbet (Cambs), John Bellamy (Somerset), Geoff Bellamy (Somerset). Ian Jones (Staffs), Steve Borley (Norfolk), Arne Bishop (Cheshire), Beryl Bishop (Cheshire). Terry Birch (West Midlands), Andy Wesson (W. Midlands), Bill Kinchin (W. Midlands), Des Follis (W. Midlands). Clive Hilton (Merseyside), Geoff McEvoy (Merseyside), John Lax (Merseyside), Stan Shore (Shropshire). Team Manager: Bob Weafer, Captain: Andy McGraw, Vice Captain: Malcolm Follis.

Greenall Singles Championship

at Norbreck Castle Hotel, Blackpool, February 9th-11th 1990

Singles winner Martin Walker of Staffordshire, beat Keith Hanly (West Midlands) in the final. The losing semi finalists were Gary Brown (West Midlands) and Martin Simcock (Staffordshire).

British Isles International Championships for Mixed Short Mat and Short Green.

at Rhondda Leisure Centre, Wales, November 18th-19th 1989

Wales took the team title, Scotland the Singles, Wales the Pairs, and the English trio of Gary Brown, John and David Clayton, the Triples title. Ireland the Fours with the English quartet of Jason Cornes, Trevor Whittaker, John Clarke and Shane Nisbett finishing unlucky runners up after losing out in a sudden death extra end which was the only time they had been behind in the entire game.

All England Short Mat Championships

*at Cocks Moors Wood Leisure Centre, Birmingham,
March 10th-11th 1990*

The championship weekend was an outstanding success for both the West Midlands and Cheshire, who took two titles each, all the runners up, and most of the semi final places. Although this success mirrored the results of previous years, the strength of the other counties is beginning to show, and no doubt championship titles will soon go to other areas.

Singles: Semi finals: Gary Brown (W. Midlands) bt Bernard Stanway (Staffordshire). Steve McAlister (Cheshire) bt Steve Borley (Norfolk).
Final: Brown bt McAlister.
Pairs: Semi finals: Steve McAlister, Jason Lockett (Cheshire) bt Ian Williams, Dave Gregory (Cumbria); Pam & Terry Birch (W. Midlands) bt Malcolm Follis, Bob Weafer (W. Midlands).
Triples: Semi finals: Gary Brown, John and David Clayton (W. Midlands) bt Bob Weafer, Malcolm and Des Follis (W. Midlands). Andy Wesson, Guy Ashforth, Steve Clayton (W. Midlands) bt Bob Lawrensons, Phyllis and Derek Watkinson (Merseyside).
Final: Brown and Claytons bt Wesson, Ashforth, Clayton.
Fours: Semi finals: Gaynor Buchanan, Harry Lockett, Carol and Craig Beechall bt Duggie Simcock, Stan Smith, Ian and Eric Jones (Staffordshire). Bob Weafer, Bill Kinchin, Malcolm and Des Follis (W. Midlands bt Stan Shore, Manny Pereira, Stan Saxon, Audrie Callow (Shropshire).
Final: Buchanan, Lockett, Beechalls bt Weafer, Kinchin and Follises.

Haven Holidays Open Tournament

at Reighton Sands Holiday Village, Filey, April 22nd-28th 1990

Men's Singles: Stuart Airey (Cumbria) bt Billy Ray (Greater Manchester).
Ladies Singles: Kay Leadbetter (W. Midlands) bt Susan Taylor (South Yorkshire).
Singles Plate: Barry Davies (Merseyside) bt Mae Henderson (Greater Manchester).
Pairs: Mike and Richard Sparkes (Sussex) bt Anne and Joe Watson (Cheshire)
Triples: John McConnell, Alma and Billy Vincent (Cheshire) bt Stuart Airey, David and Marion Gregory (Cumbria).
Under-16's: Andrew Pullen (Cheshire) bt Andrea Buchanan (Cheshire)

Pétanque
by Bill Meredith

Pétanque, or boules as it is often called, is played virtually world wide these days. It is generally understood, of course, to be a national sport in France and Belgium, but it is also now the leading pastime in Thailand - as decreed by the country's Princess Mother, Princess Galyani Vadhana. The Princess herself presented the prizes after the "World Ladies" Championship in Bangkok in November.

Boules can be played on practically any surface, apart from grass. Gravel or dust is the best; this prevents the ball from rolling and rewards the accuracy of the throw. To start the game, the jack or "cochonnet", is pitched between six and 10 metres from the throwing circle. The thrower's feet must stay within the circle and in contact with the ground until his boule has landed. After an opposing player has thrown, play continues with the team farthest away endeavouring to get closer to the jack. When both sides have thrown all their boules, the team with one, or more, closest to the jack is awarded a point, or points. The first team to reach 13 points is the winner. The average time for a game of Triples, the most popular form of the game is in the region of 20 to 45 minutes.

The sport is becoming increasingly attractive to women: British national champions were the Scott sisters, Claire and Nicki, and Tracey Cutler.

Britain still trails in the world rankings, but both men and women are improving all the time and players such as Frank Britt, Dave Scarborough and Pip Cledwyn were worthy representatives in the world championships in Monaco. Britt and Scarborough have both represented Britain in the world event for the past two years; Cledwyn played back in the 1970's, when he was at one stage ninth ranked in the world.

The Welsh seem very adept at boules. They have their own league set-up and an outstanding team in Cardiff Pentwyn, whose fine trio of Phil Bradshaw, Dave Turner and Felix Montes were also chosen to represent Britain in Monaco.

Since some 100 teams throughout the country were competing for the honour of making the trip to the world championships, the final representatives had to show that touch of extra class to make the grade.

Garth Freeman, the national administrator of the British Pentanque Association, is convinced that Britain is on the right course. "It is the first time for some years that we have been able to send such experienced players to the world championships, and that is a bonus." Freeman is very optimistic about the future of pentaque in this country. "The whole scene is getting busier, busier and busier," he says. "Every week there are another half-a-dozen or so new terrains, and there is a vast new interest in the sport."

The big advance is that local authorities are taking a much keener interest in a sport which is reasonably cheap to play and cheap to run. In its earlier days, petanque tended to be very much a game attached to pubs. That made it more of a man's sport, associated perhaps with a few pints during the game.

Now the family image is much stronger. A new centre at Foxhills, in Surrey, typifies the exciting fresh approach. Visitors to the centre can play golf, tennis — and, of course, pétanque.

One of the biggest worries of the British Pétanque Association in 1990 was a VAT bill for £10,000. That was considerably reduced in the end, and more good news was that the Sports Council have agreed to support the sport to the tune of £73,000 over the next four years.

This is heartening for a sport which has all the ingredients of sharp competition, friendly rivalry and wonderful warm companionship. Bowls is always recognised as an intimate game, if anything pétanque is even more so. Competitors are always in close contact, playing in a small area and repartee between players is an essential part of the sport.

Morocco beat France in the final of the World Pétanque championships in France on October 8th. The best British team comprising Phil Bradshaw, Felix Montes and Dave Turner finished a highly satisfactory 13th and figured among the trophy winners.

Pétanque Diary 1991 — Fixtures.

March 24:	World Championship Qualifying Series Prel 1.
April 7:	World Championship Qualifying Series Prel 2.
April 12/14:	Pontins Weekend — South Downs.
April 14:	National Juniors Championship. Note: the winners will represent Great Britain at the North Sea Tournament in Eindhoven, Holland (June 28th-30th) and at the World Junior Championship, Malmo, Sweden (August 2nd-4th).
April 20:	Isle of Wight Triples, Warners Holiday Camp.
April 21-27:	The Jersey Open Championship St Helier.
April 28:	National "Come and Try Pétanque" Day.
May 5:	Regional Singles/Doubles/Tripels 1.
May 12:	World Championship Qualifying Series Qual.1
May 19:	World Championship Qualifying Series Qual.2 (Venue to be arranged).
June 1/2:	World Championship Qualifying Series Masters 1 and 2. Regional Singles/Doubles/Triples 2.
June 23:	National Ladies Championship Anchor Hotel Tempsford, Bedfordshire (Ouse Pétanque Club).
June 28/30:	North Sea Tournament (Provisional) Eindhoven, Holland.
July 7:	National Singles Championship.
July 14:	Regional Singles/Doubles/Triples 3.
July 21:	Possible British Open.
July 28:	Possible British Open.
August 2/4:	World Juniors Championship in Malmo, Sweden.
Sept 15:	Champion of Champions Match.
Sept 18/22:	World Seniors Championship in Andorra (prov).
Sept 29:	National Triples Championship at Burleigh College Loughborough.
Oct 6:	Annual BPA versus SPA Match at Racecourse Hotel, Norwich.
Oct 13:	National Doubles Championship.

Regional Presidents

British Pétanque Association National Administrator: Gareth Freeman, PO Box 87, Leatherhead, KT22 8LA, tel 0372-386860. Regional Presidents: **Anglia:** Mrs W Ellison, 112 Homelea Crescent, Lingwood, Norwich, NR13 4BP. Tel 0603 715164. **Chiltern:** Mr G Barton, 41 St Peter's Close, Burnham, Slough, Berks. Tel 0628 605043. **De Cymru:** Mr R Baker, 32, Glan Hafren, The Knap, Barry, South Glamorgan, CF6 8TA. Tel 0446 737999. **Eastern:** Mr P Watts, 72 East Street, Coggeshall, Essex, CO6 1SL. Tel 0376 561776. **East Midlands:** Mr R R Herrick, 5 Somerset Close, Burton-on-the-Wolds, Loughborough, Leics, LE12 5AJ: Tel 0509 881380. **Isle of Wight:** Mr D Sedgewick, St Radegund Quarr Binstead Ryde, PO33 4ER. Tel 0983 883953. **South East:** Mrs J Taylor, 12 Craylands Square, Swanscombe, Kent, DA10 0LW. Tel 0322 844954. **Southern:** Mr M Cheriton, 18 Alum Close, Holbury, Southampton, SO4 1GY. Tel 0703 892891. **West Midlands:** Mr B Perkins, 34 Ulverley Green Road, Olton, Solihull, West Midlands. Tel 021-706 8976.